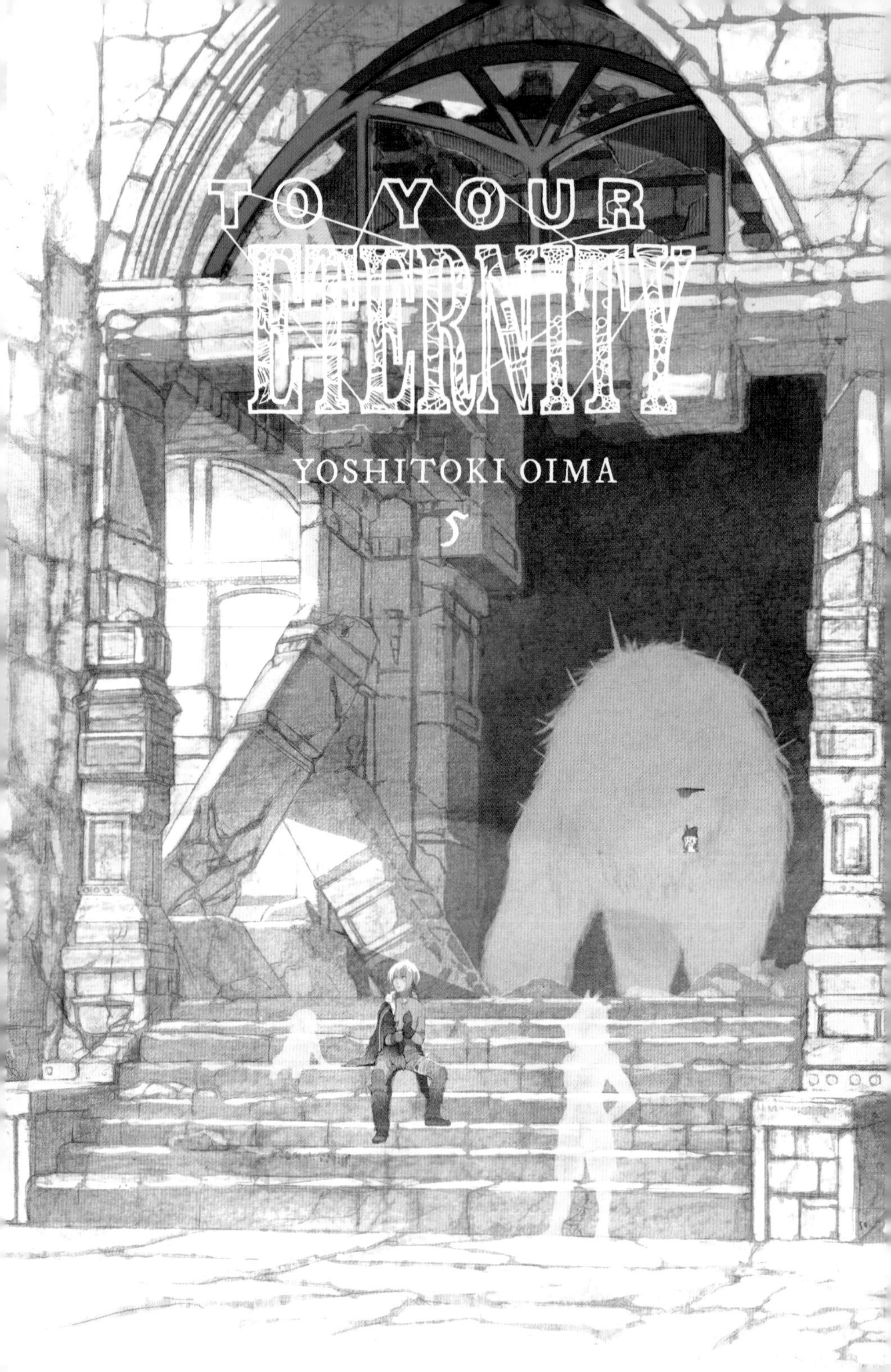
TO YOUR
ETERNITY
YOSHITOKI OIMA
5

CONTENTS

#35 The Spinning Girl

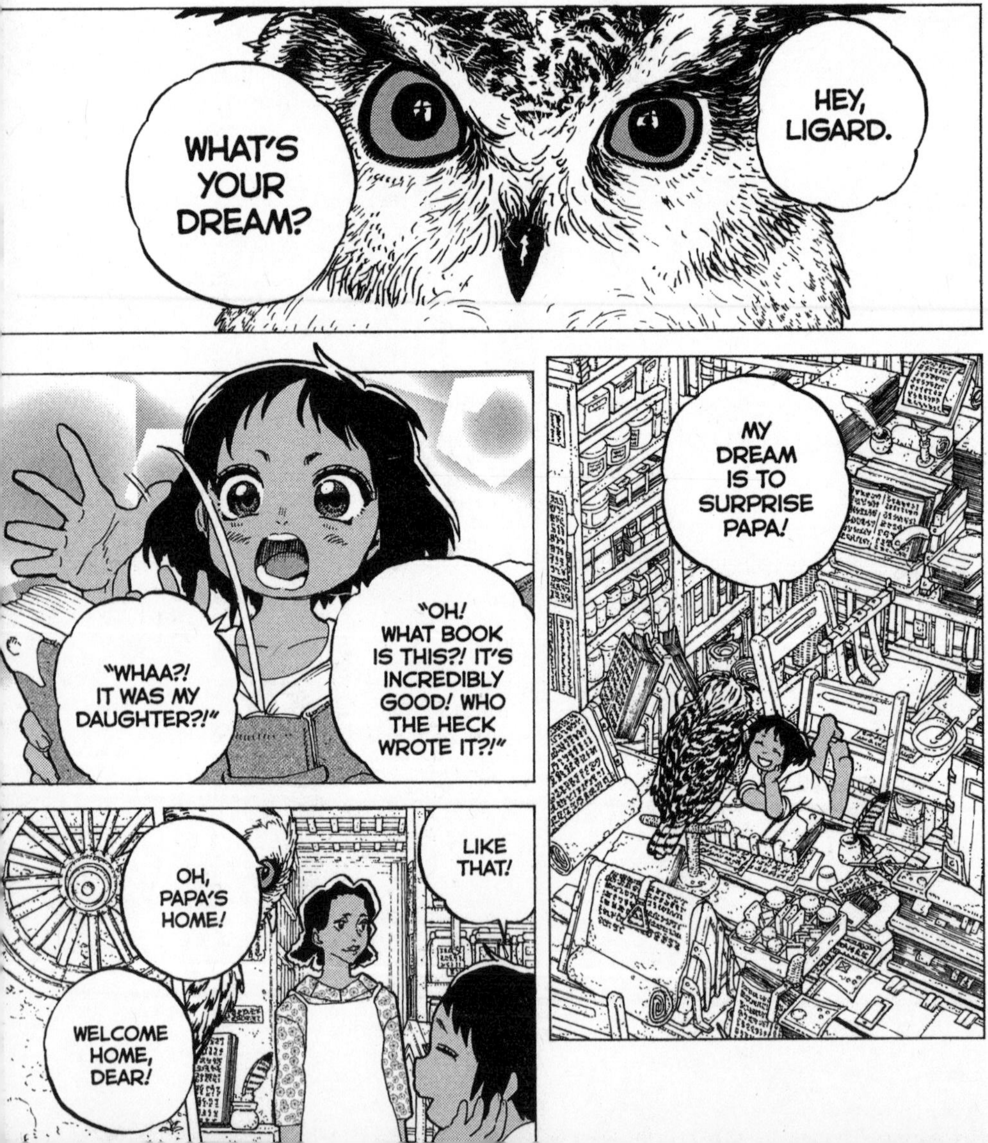
HEY, LIGARD.
WHAT'S YOUR DREAM?
MY DREAM IS TO SURPRISE PAPA!
"OH! WHAT BOOK IS THIS?! IT'S INCREDIBLY GOOD! WHO THE HECK WROTE IT?!"
"WHAA?! IT WAS MY DAUGHTER?!"
LIKE THAT!
OH, PAPA'S HOME!
WELCOME HOME, DEAR!

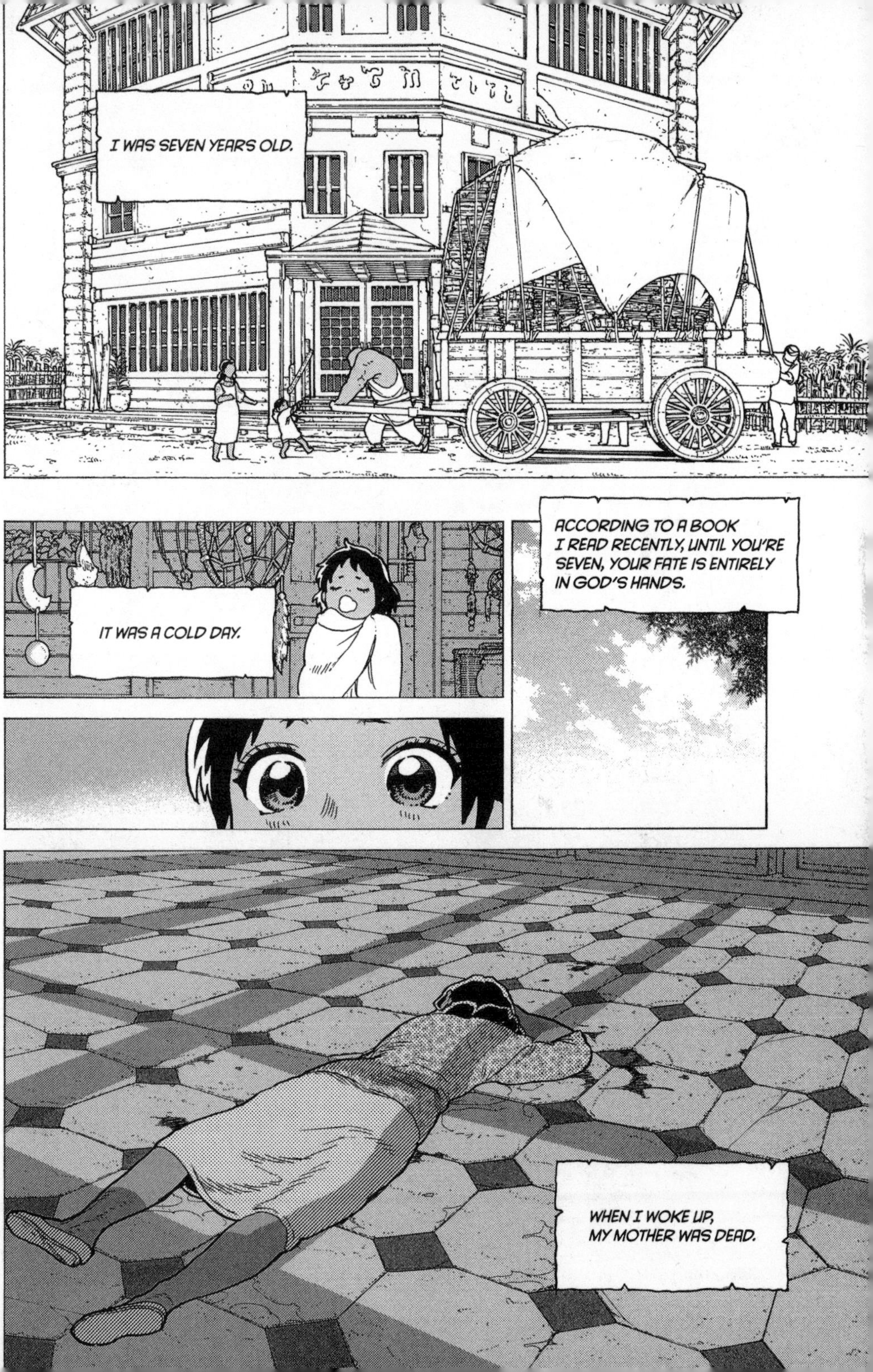
I WAS SEVEN YEARS OLD.
ACCORDING TO A BOOK I READ RECENTLY, UNTIL YOU'RE SEVEN, YOUR FATE IS ENTIRELY IN GOD'S HANDS.
IT WAS A COLD DAY.
WHEN I WOKE UP, MY MOTHER WAS DEAD.

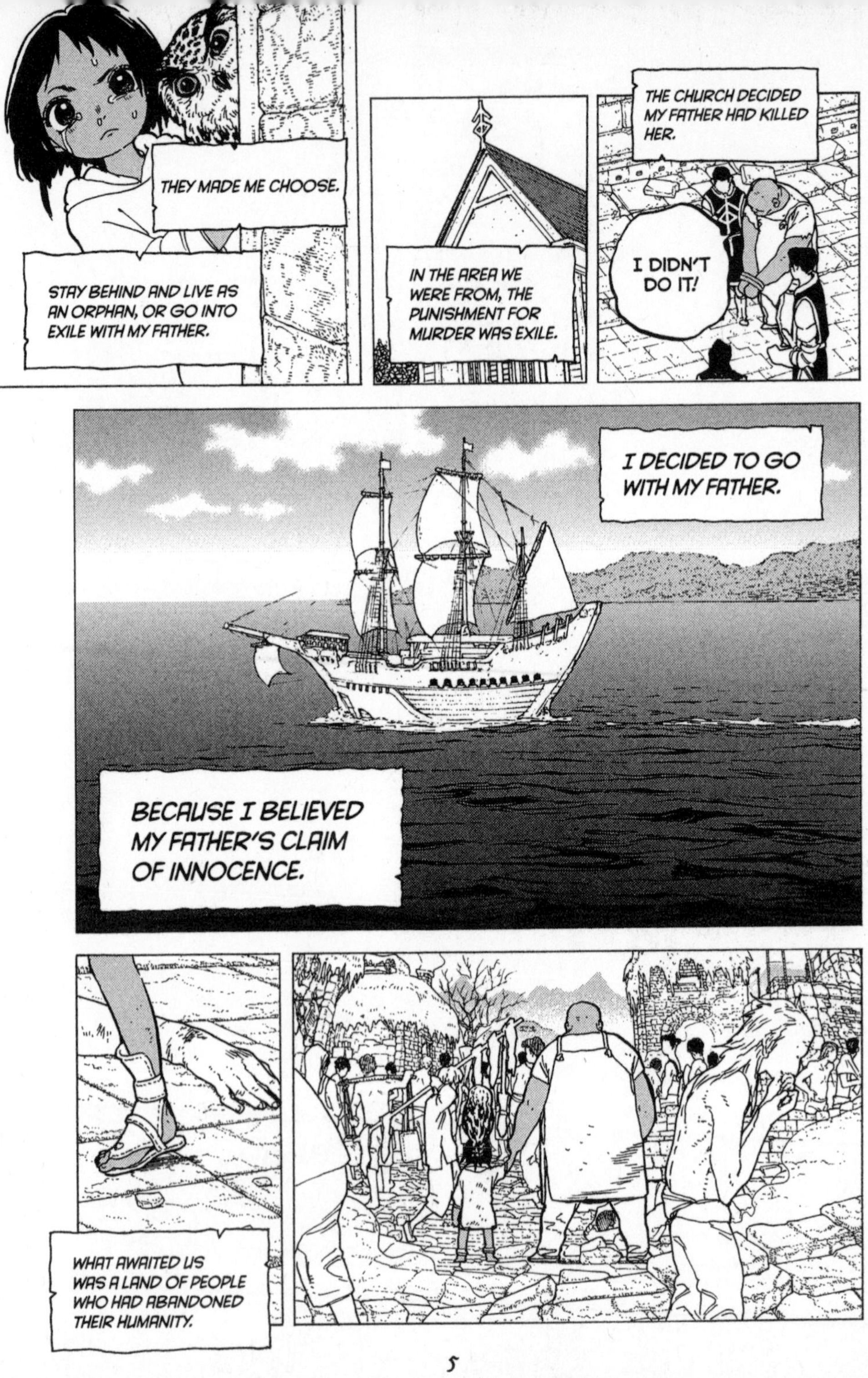
THE CHURCH DECIDED MY FATHER HAD KILLED HER.
I DIDN'T DO IT!
IN THE AREA WE WERE FROM, THE PUNISHMENT FOR MURDER WAS EXILE.
THEY MADE ME CHOOSE.
STAY BEHIND AND LIVE AS AN ORPHAN, OR GO INTO EXILE WITH MY FATHER.
I DECIDED TO GO WITH MY FATHER.
BECAUSE I BELIEVED MY FATHER'S CLAIM OF INNOCENCE.
WHAT AWAITED US WAS A LAND OF PEOPLE WHO HAD ABANDONED THEIR HUMANITY.

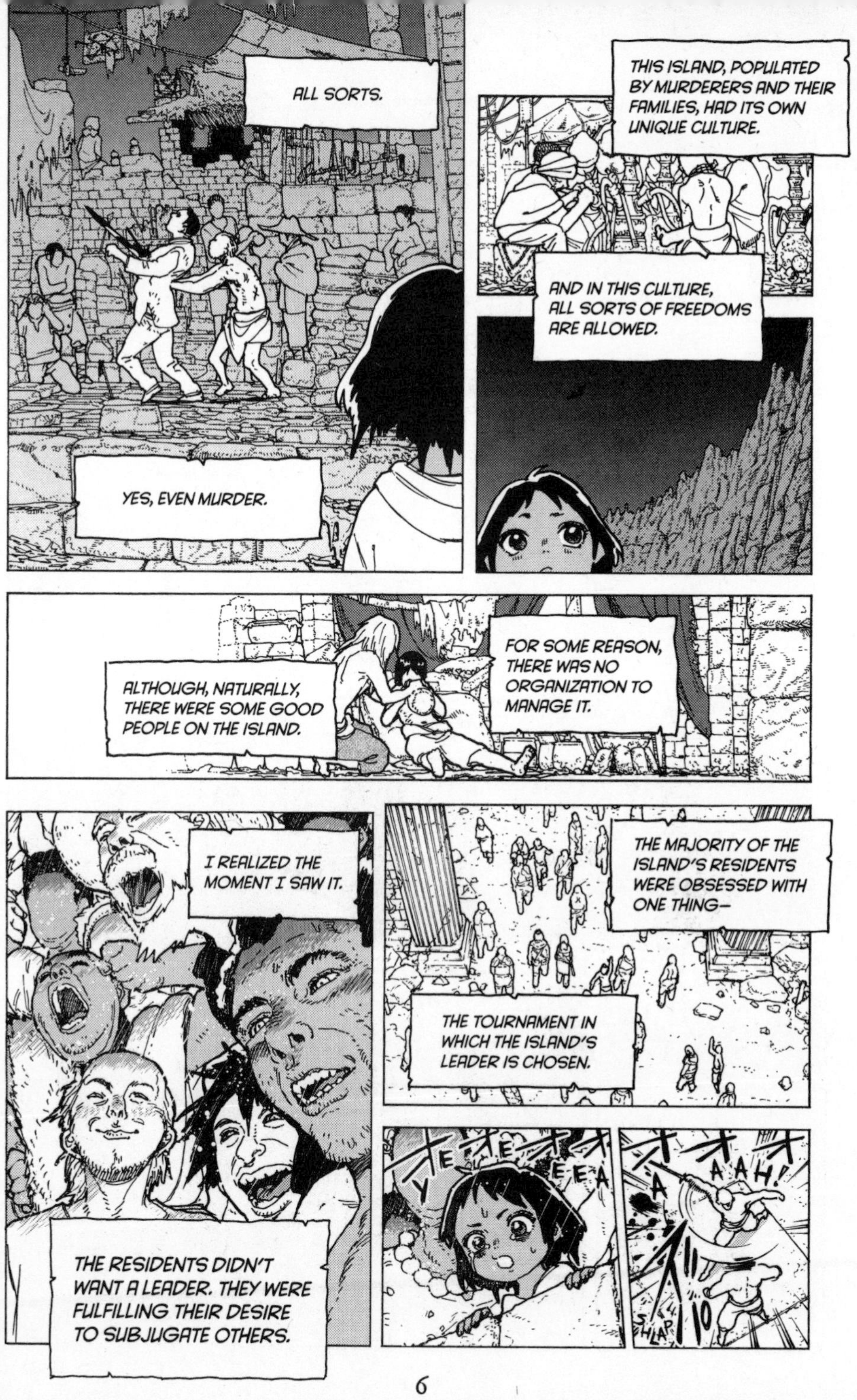
THIS ISLAND, POPULATED BY MURDERERS AND THEIR FAMILIES, HAD ITS OWN UNIQUE CULTURE.
AND IN THIS CULTURE, ALL SORTS OF FREEDOMS ARE ALLOWED.
ALL SORTS.
YES, EVEN MURDER.
FOR SOME REASON, THERE WAS NO ORGANIZATION TO MANAGE IT.
ALTHOUGH, NATURALLY, THERE WERE SOME GOOD PEOPLE ON THE ISLAND.
THE MAJORITY OF THE ISLAND'S RESIDENTS WERE OBSESSED WITH ONE THING—
THE TOURNAMENT IN WHICH THE ISLAND'S LEADER IS CHOSEN.
AAAH!
SHLAP
YEEEEEA
I REALIZED THE MOMENT I SAW IT.
THE RESIDENTS DIDN'T WANT A LEADER. THEY WERE FULFILLING THEIR DESIRE TO SUBJUGATE OTHERS.

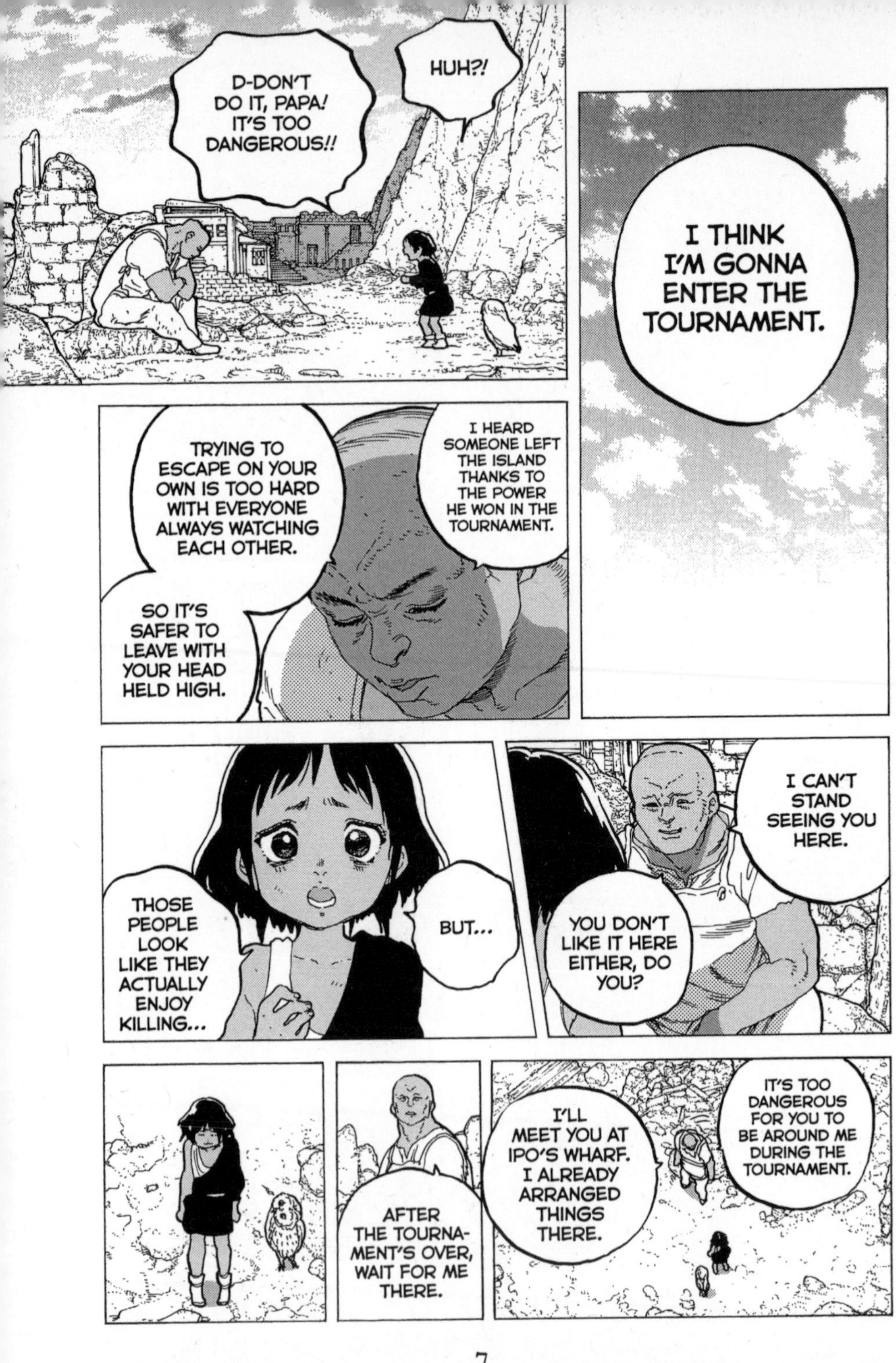
I THINK I'M GONNA ENTER THE TOURNAMENT.
HUH?!
D-DON'T DO IT, PAPA! IT'S TOO DANGEROUS!!
I HEARD SOMEONE LEFT THE ISLAND THANKS TO THE POWER HE WON IN THE TOURNAMENT.
TRYING TO ESCAPE ON YOUR OWN IS TOO HARD WITH EVERYONE ALWAYS WATCHING EACH OTHER.
SO IT'S SAFER TO LEAVE WITH YOUR HEAD HELD HIGH.
I CAN'T STAND SEEING YOU HERE.
YOU DON'T LIKE IT HERE EITHER, DO YOU?
BUT...
THOSE PEOPLE LOOK LIKE THEY ACTUALLY ENJOY KILLING...
IT'S TOO DANGEROUS FOR YOU TO BE AROUND ME DURING THE TOURNAMENT.
I'LL MEET YOU AT IPO'S WHARF. I ALREADY ARRANGED THINGS THERE.
AFTER THE TOURNA-MENT'S OVER, WAIT FOR ME THERE.

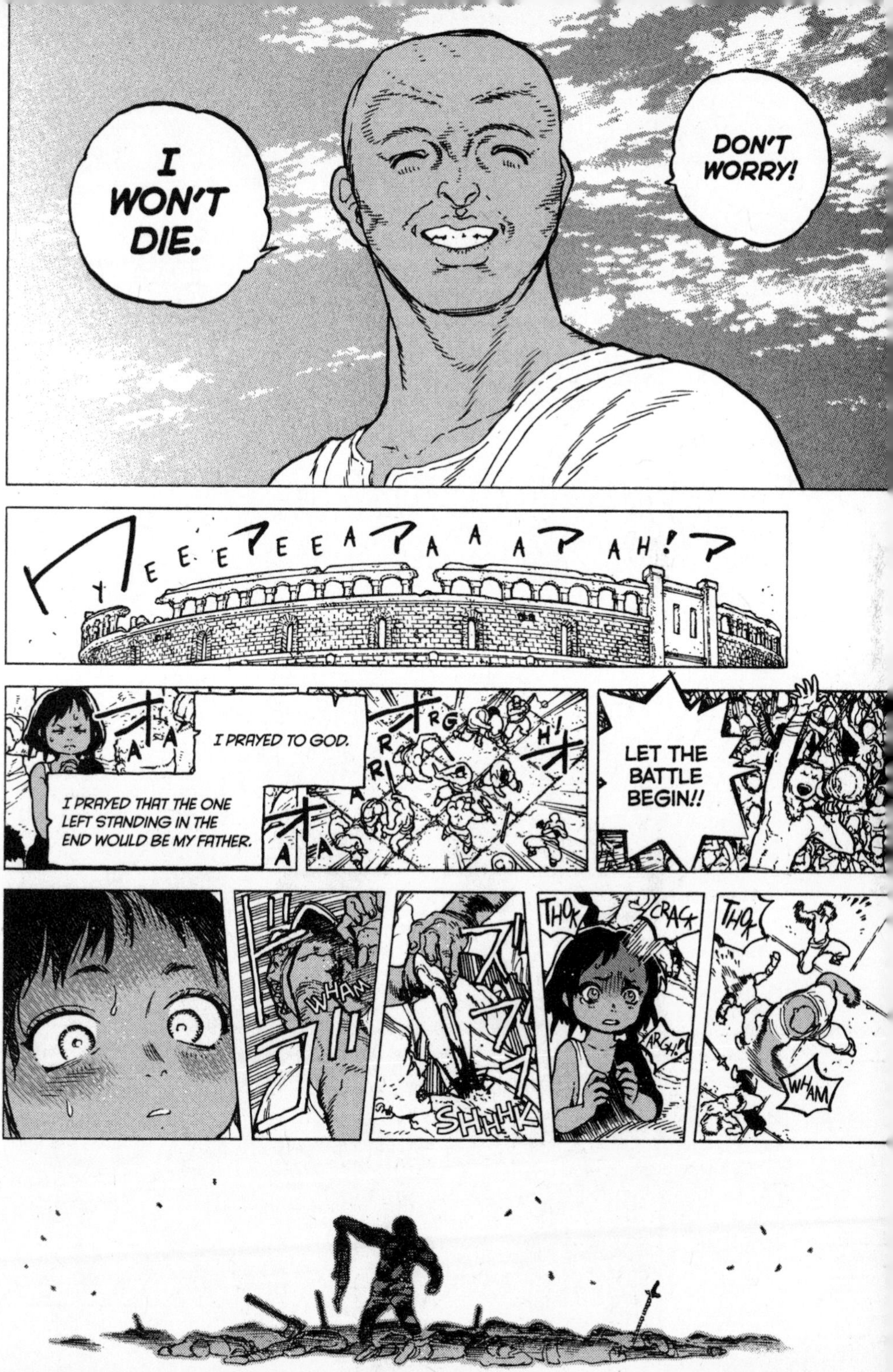
DON'T WORRY!
I WON'T DIE.
YEEEEEAAAAAH!
LET THE BATTLE BEGIN!!
I PRAYED TO GOD.
I PRAYED THAT THE ONE LEFT STANDING IN THE END WOULD BE MY FATHER.
THOK
WHAM
THOK
CRACK
ARGH!
SHHHK
WHAM

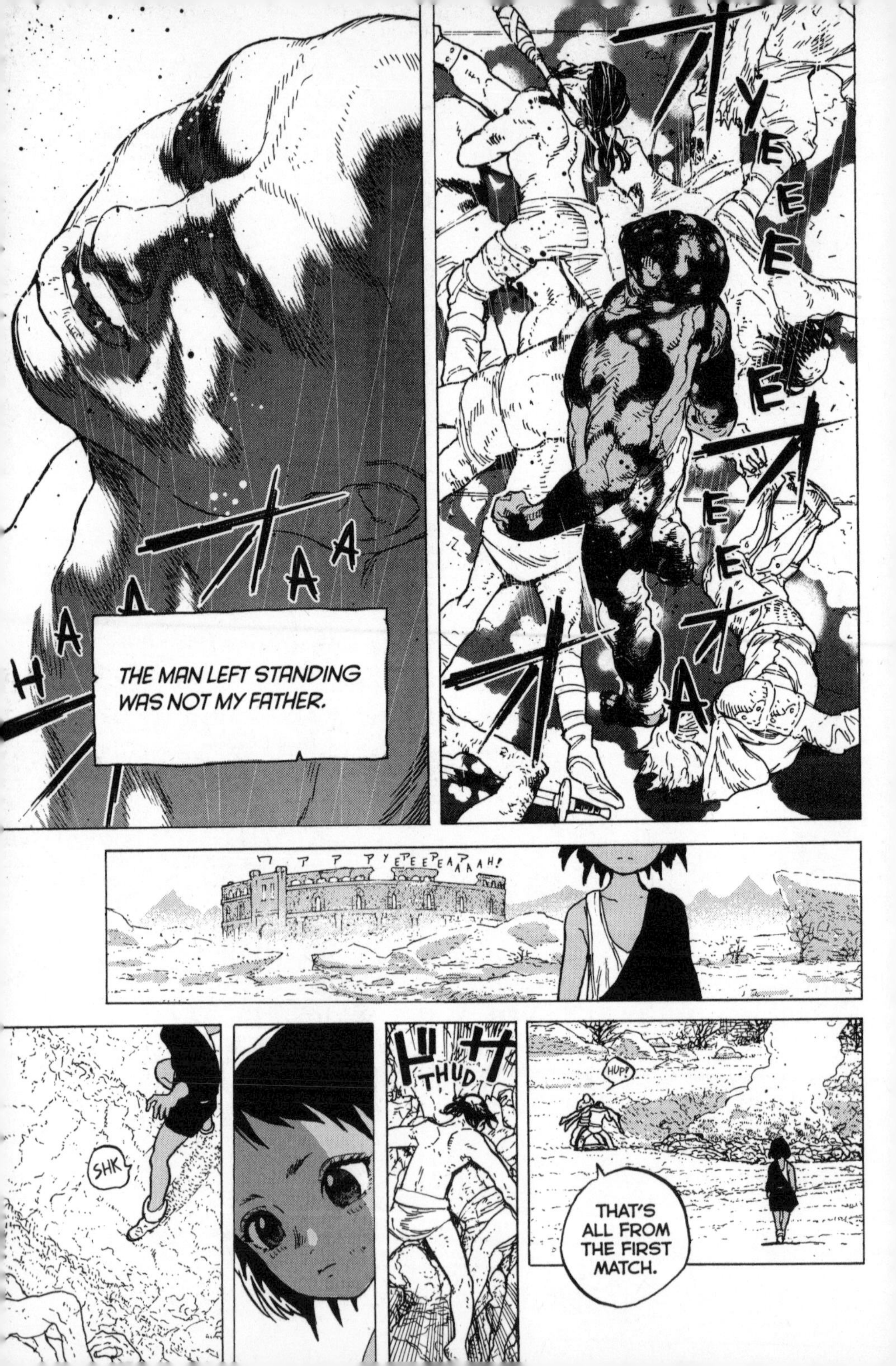
YEEEEEEA
HAAAA
THE MAN LEFT STANDING WAS NOT MY FATHER.
YEEEEAAAAH!
HUP!
THAT'S ALL FROM THE FIRST MATCH.
THUD
SHK

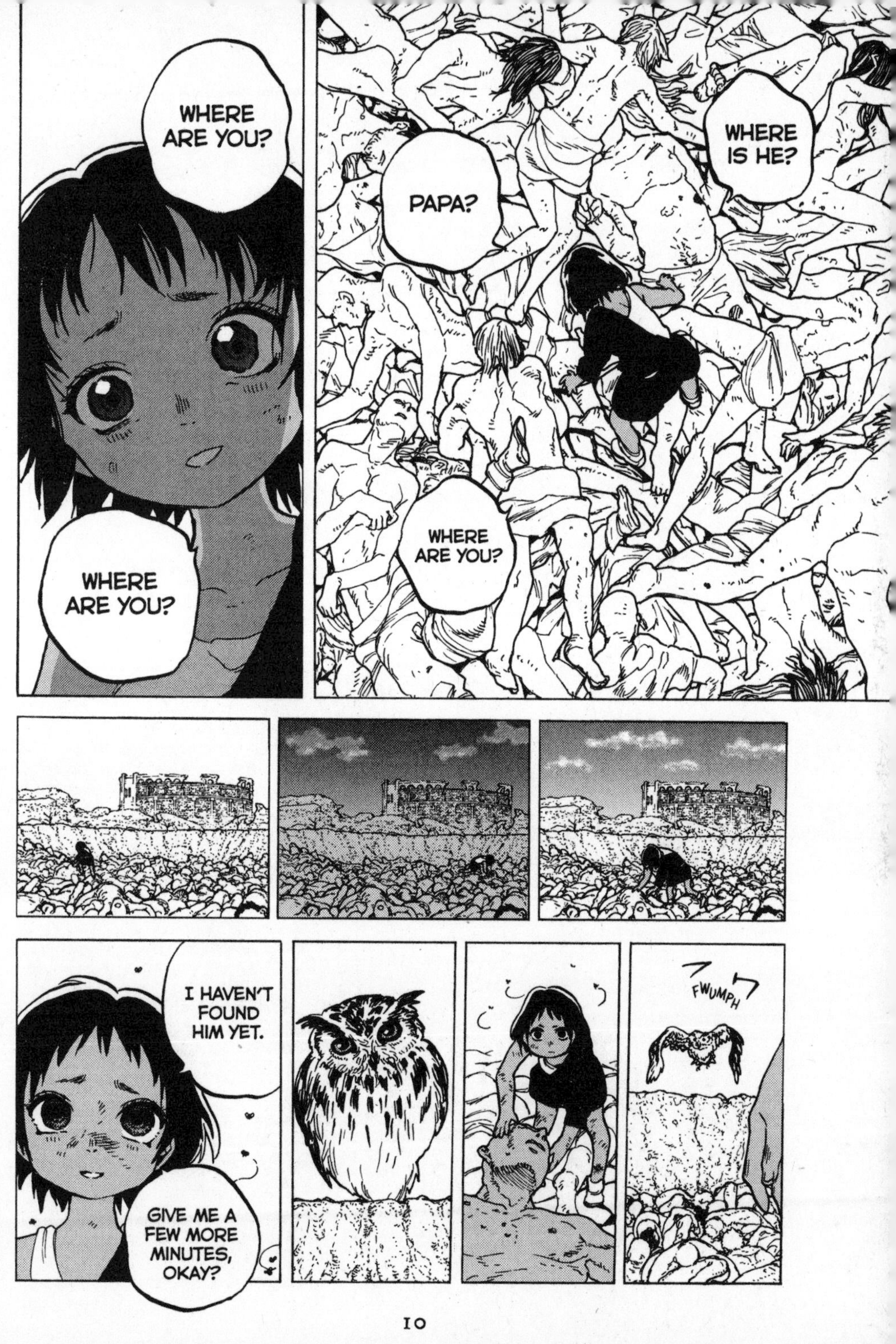
WHERE IS HE?
PAPA?
WHERE ARE YOU?
WHERE ARE YOU?
WHERE ARE YOU?
FWUMPH
I HAVEN'T FOUND HIM YET.
GIVE ME A FEW MORE MINUTES, OKAY?

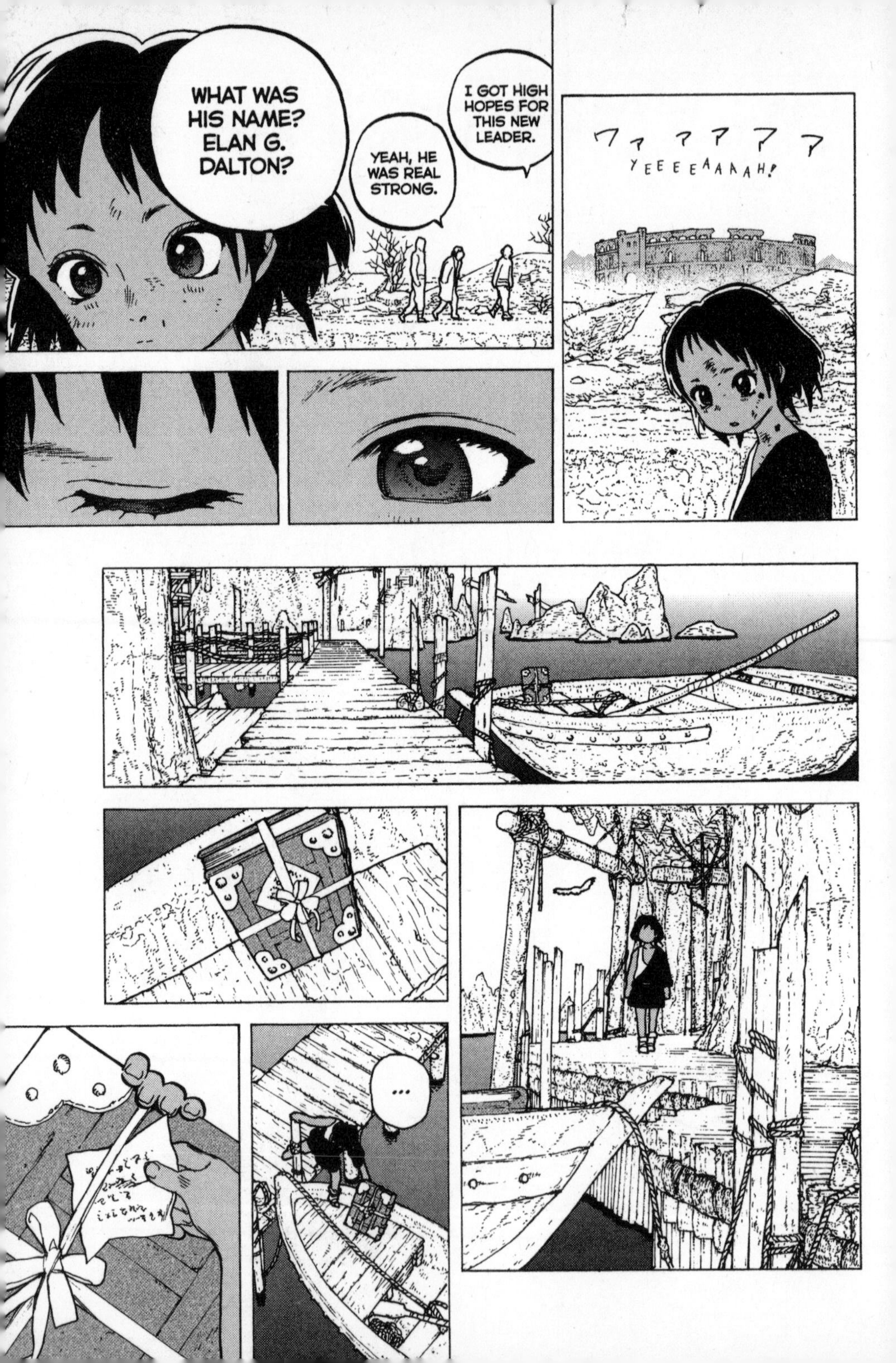
ワァアアアア
YEEEEAAAAH!
I GOT HIGH HOPES FOR THIS NEW LEADER.
YEAH, HE WAS REAL STRONG.
WHAT WAS HIS NAME? ELAN G. DALTON?
...

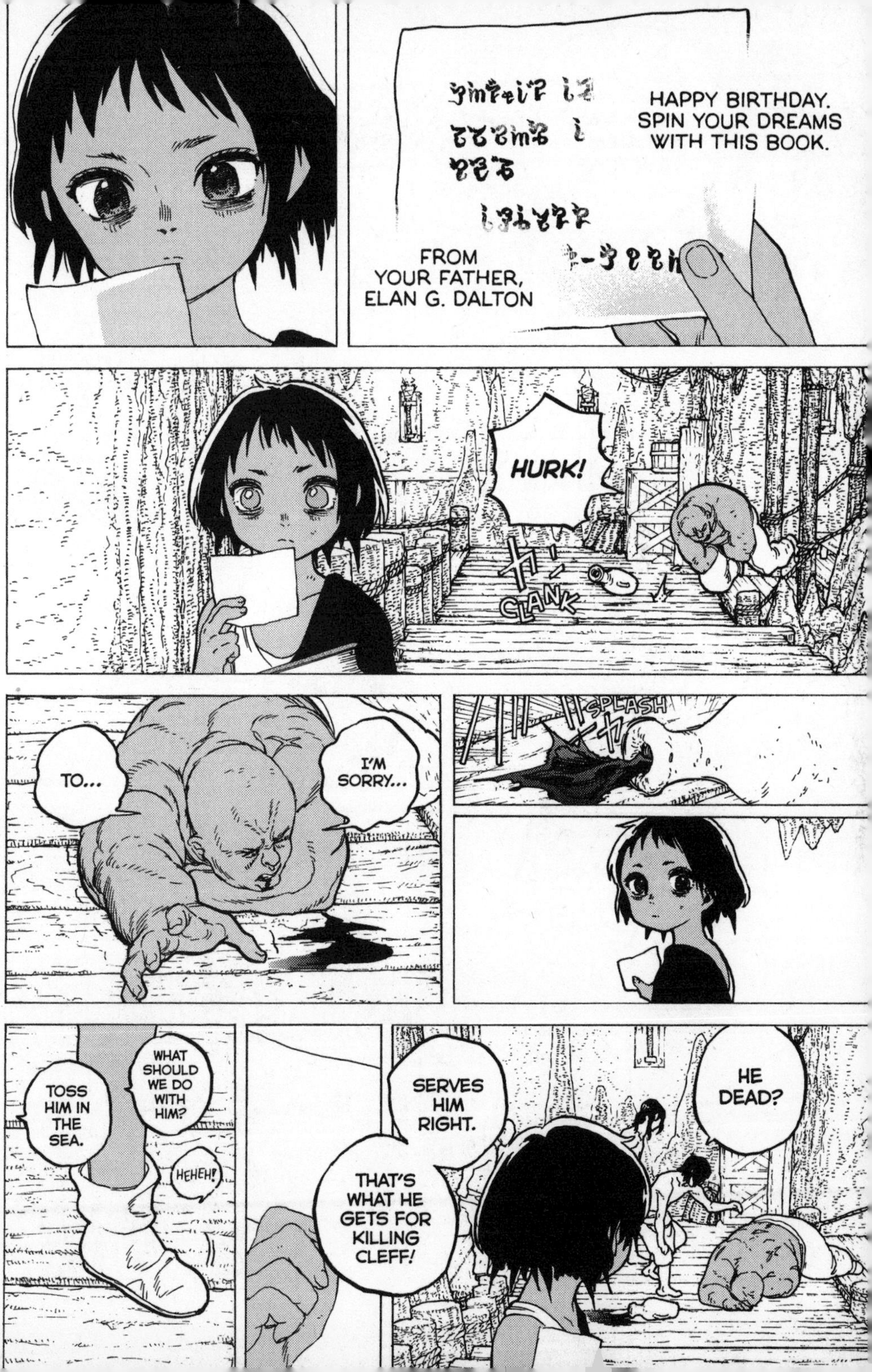
HAPPY BIRTHDAY. SPIN YOUR DREAMS WITH THIS BOOK.
FROM YOUR FATHER, ELAN G. DALTON
HURK!
CLANK
SPLASH
I'M SORRY...
TO...
HE DEAD?
SERVES HIM RIGHT.
THAT'S WHAT HE GETS FOR KILLING CLEFF!
WHAT SHOULD WE DO WITH HIM?
TOSS HIM IN THE SEA.
HEHEH!

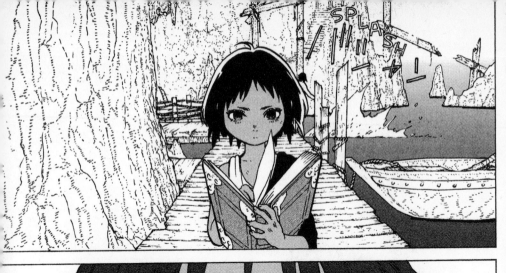

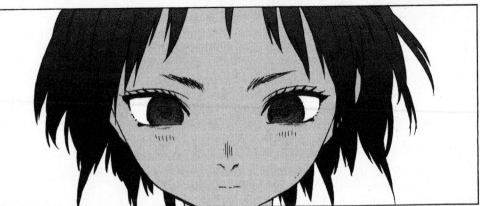

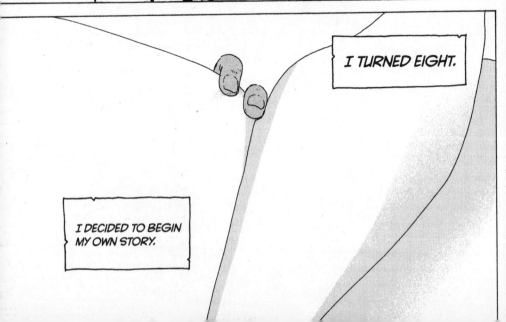

I TURNED EIGHT.

I DECIDED TO BEGIN MY OWN STORY.

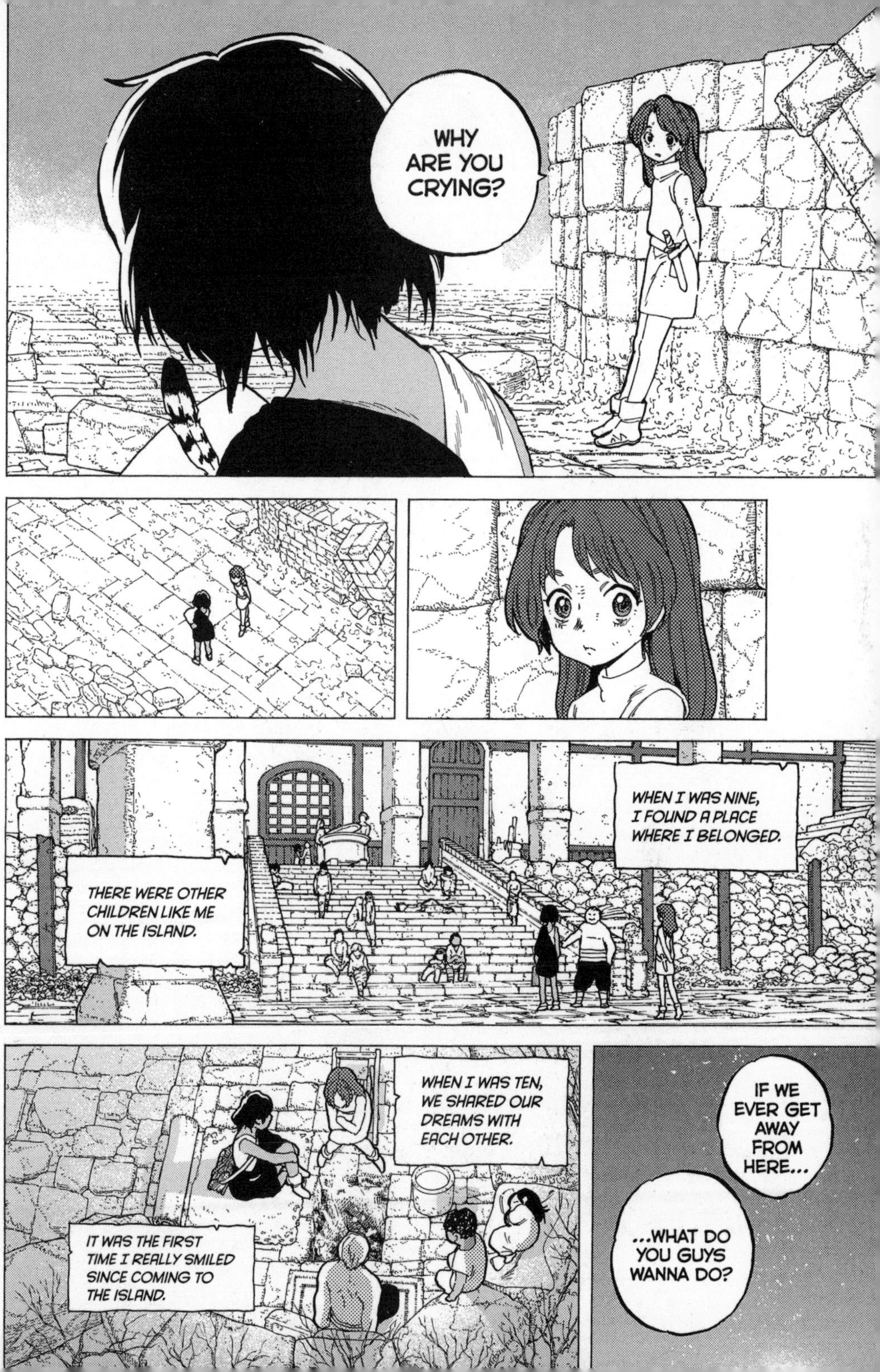
WHY ARE YOU CRYING?
WHEN I WAS NINE, I FOUND A PLACE WHERE I BELONGED.
THERE WERE OTHER CHILDREN LIKE ME ON THE ISLAND.
IF WE EVER GET AWAY FROM HERE...
...WHAT DO YOU GUYS WANNA DO?
WHEN I WAS TEN, WE SHARED OUR DREAMS WITH EACH OTHER.
IT WAS THE FIRST TIME I REALLY SMILED SINCE COMING TO THE ISLAND.

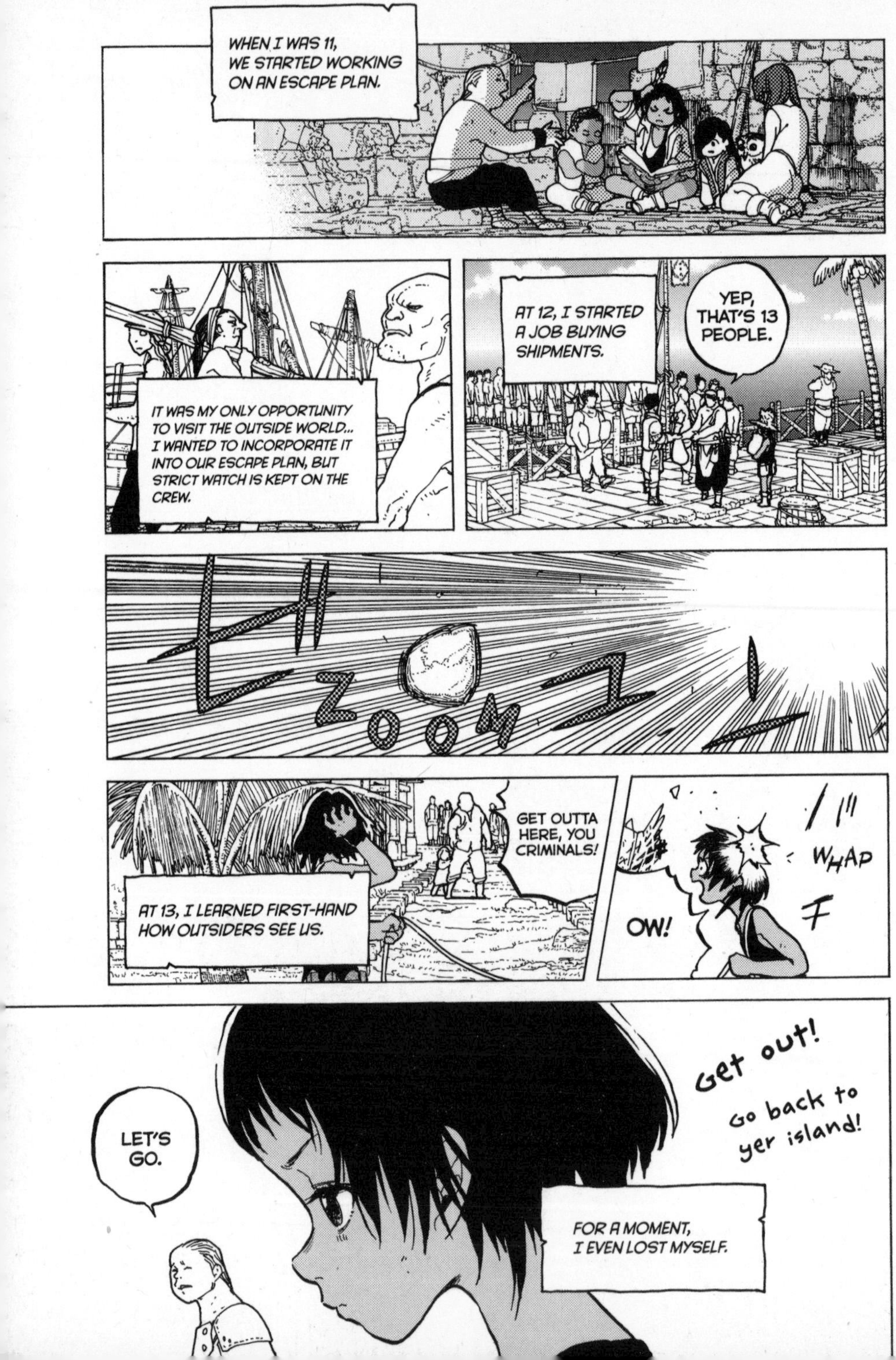
WHEN I WAS 11, WE STARTED WORKING ON AN ESCAPE PLAN.
AT 12, I STARTED A JOB BUYING SHIPMENTS.
YEP, THAT'S 13 PEOPLE.
IT WAS MY ONLY OPPORTUNITY TO VISIT THE OUTSIDE WORLD... I WANTED TO INCORPORATE IT INTO OUR ESCAPE PLAN, BUT STRICT WATCH IS KEPT ON THE CREW.
ZOOM
WHAP
OW!
GET OUTTA HERE, YOU CRIMINALS!
AT 13, I LEARNED FIRST-HAND HOW OUTSIDERS SEE US.
Get out!
Go back to yer island!
LET'S GO.
FOR A MOMENT, I EVEN LOST MYSELF.

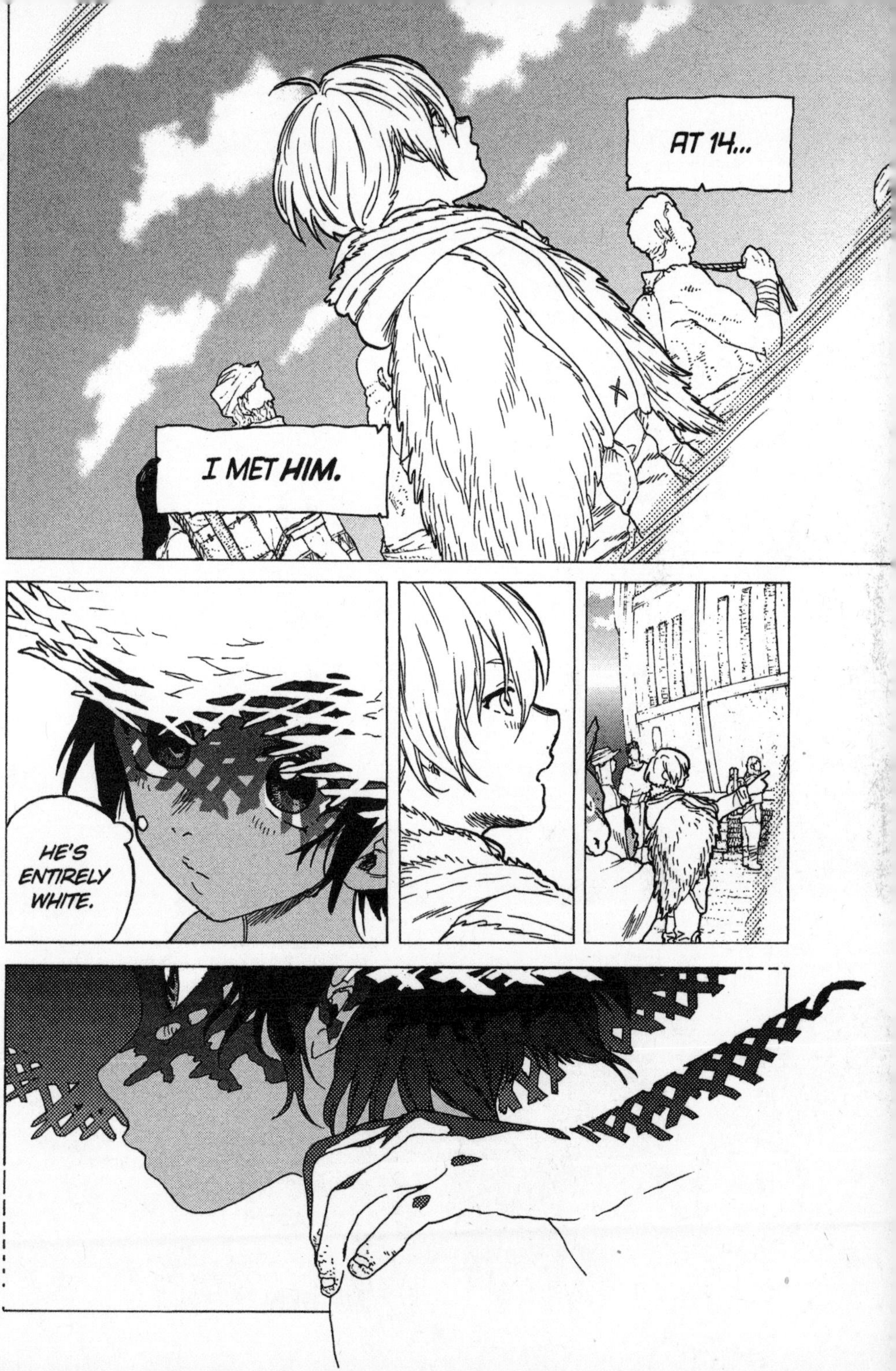
AT 14...
I MET HIM.
HE'S ENTIRELY WHITE.

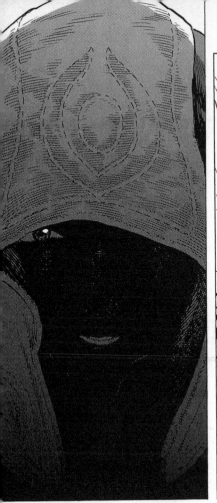

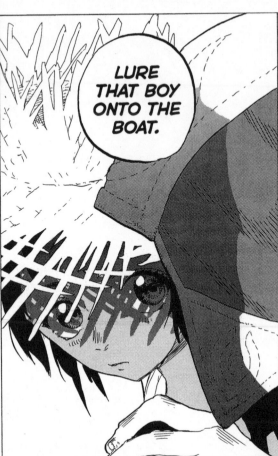

LURE THAT BOY ONTO THE BOAT.

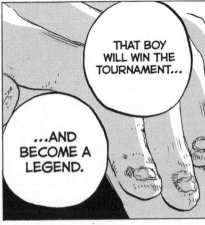

THAT BOY WILL WIN THE TOURNAMENT...

...AND BECOME A LEGEND.

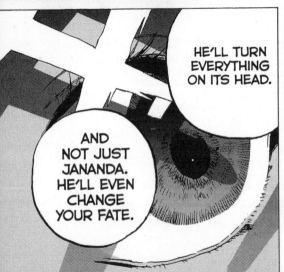

HE'LL TURN EVERYTHING ON ITS HEAD.

AND NOT JUST JANANDA. HE'LL EVEN CHANGE YOUR FATE.

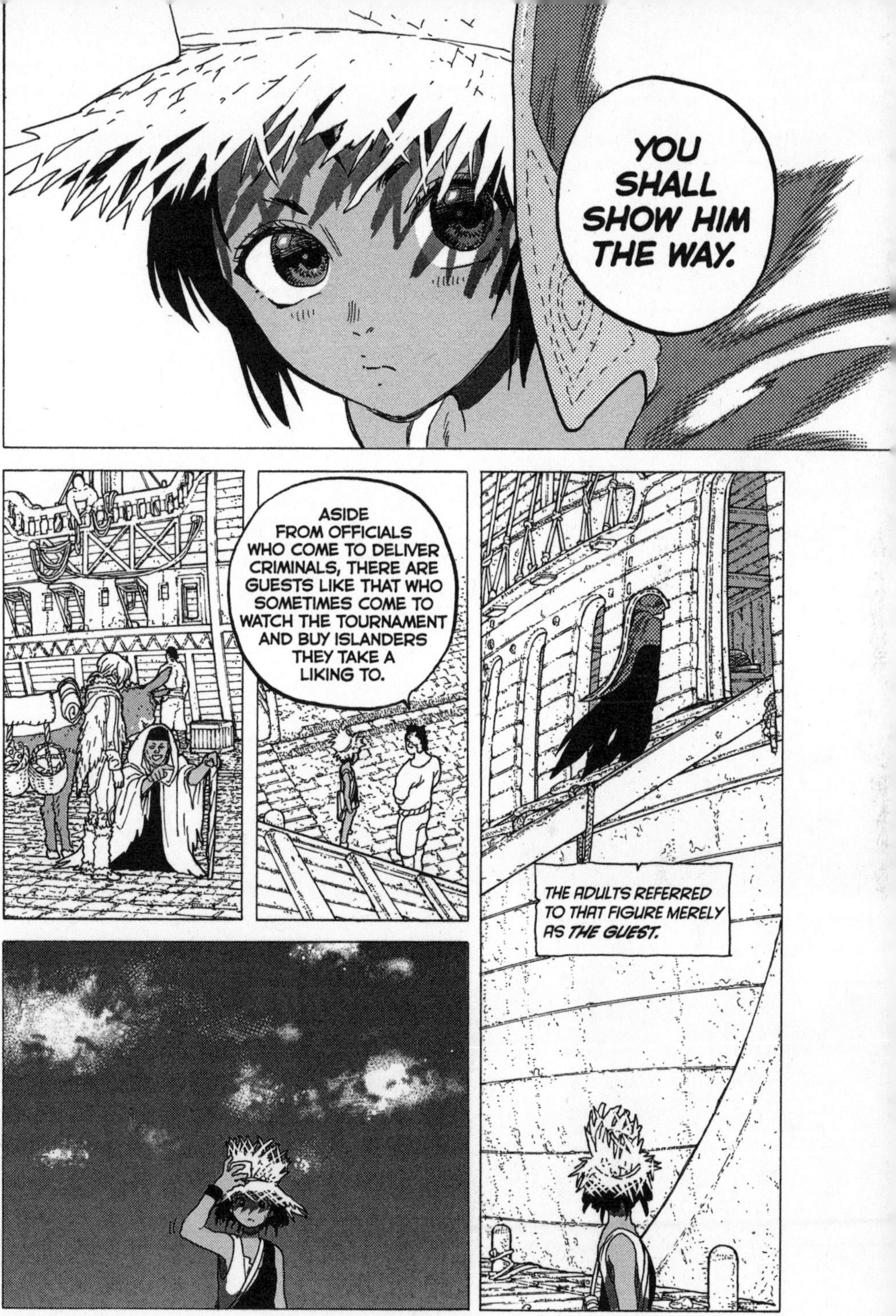
YOU SHALL SHOW HIM THE WAY.
THE ADULTS REFERRED TO THAT FIGURE MERELY AS *THE GUEST.*
ASIDE FROM OFFICIALS WHO COME TO DELIVER CRIMINALS, THERE ARE GUESTS LIKE THAT WHO SOMETIMES COME TO WATCH THE TOURNAMENT AND BUY ISLANDERS THEY TAKE A LIKING TO.

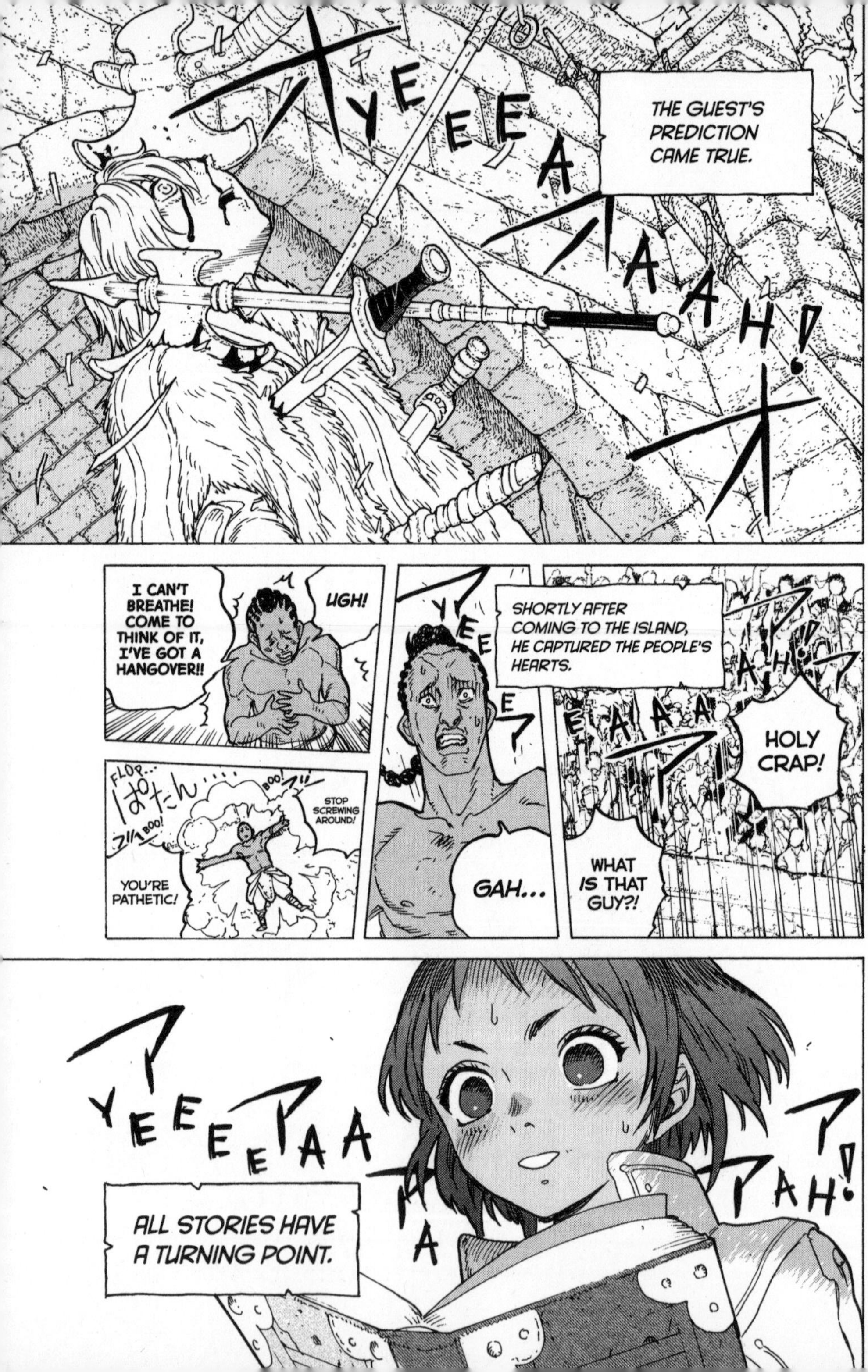
THE GUEST'S PREDICTION CAME TRUE.
YEEEAAAAH!
EAAAAH!
HOLY CRAP!
WHAT IS THAT GUY?!
SHORTLY AFTER COMING TO THE ISLAND, HE CAPTURED THE PEOPLE'S HEARTS.
YEEE
GAH...
UGH!
I CAN'T BREATHE! COME TO THINK OF IT, I'VE GOT A HANGOVER!!
STOP SCREWING AROUND!
BOO!
FLOP...
ぱたん……
BOO!
YOU'RE PATHETIC!
YEEEEAAAAAH!
ALL STORIES HAVE A TURNING POINT.

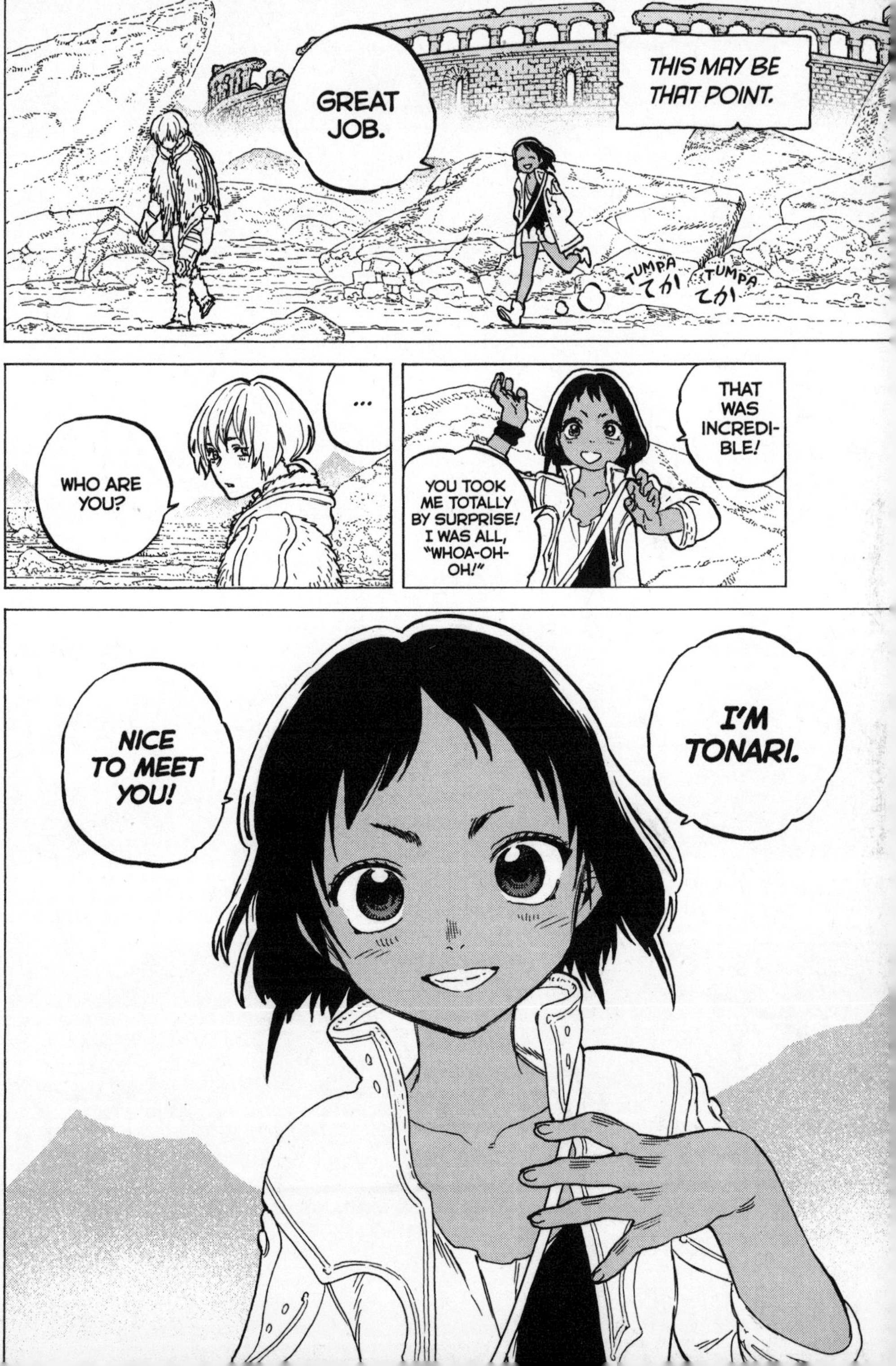
THIS MAY BE THAT POINT.
GREAT JOB.
TUMPA てか
TUMPA てか
THAT WAS INCREDIBLE!
YOU TOOK ME TOTALLY BY SURPRISE! I WAS ALL, "WHOA-OH-OH!"
...
WHO ARE YOU?
I'M TONARI.
NICE TO MEET YOU!

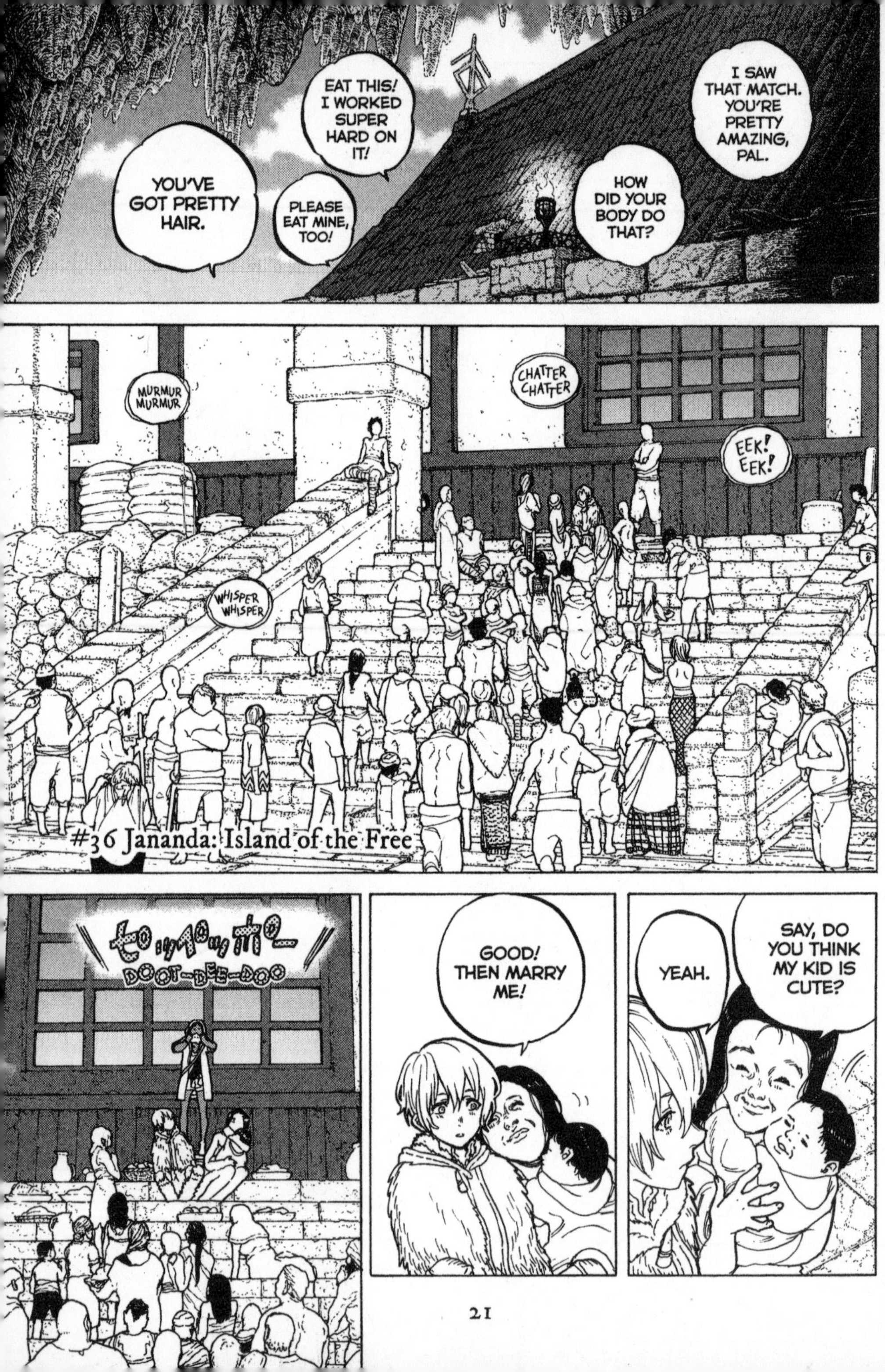
I SAW THAT MATCH. YOU'RE PRETTY AMAZING, PAL.
HOW DID YOUR BODY DO THAT?
EAT THIS! I WORKED SUPER HARD ON IT!
PLEASE EAT MINE, TOO!
YOU'VE GOT PRETTY HAIR.
EEK! EEK!
CHATTER CHATTER
WHISPER WHISPER
MURMUR MURMUR
#36 Jananda: Island of the Free
SAY, DO YOU THINK MY KID IS CUTE?
YEAH.
GOOD! THEN MARRY ME!
DOOT-DEE-DOO

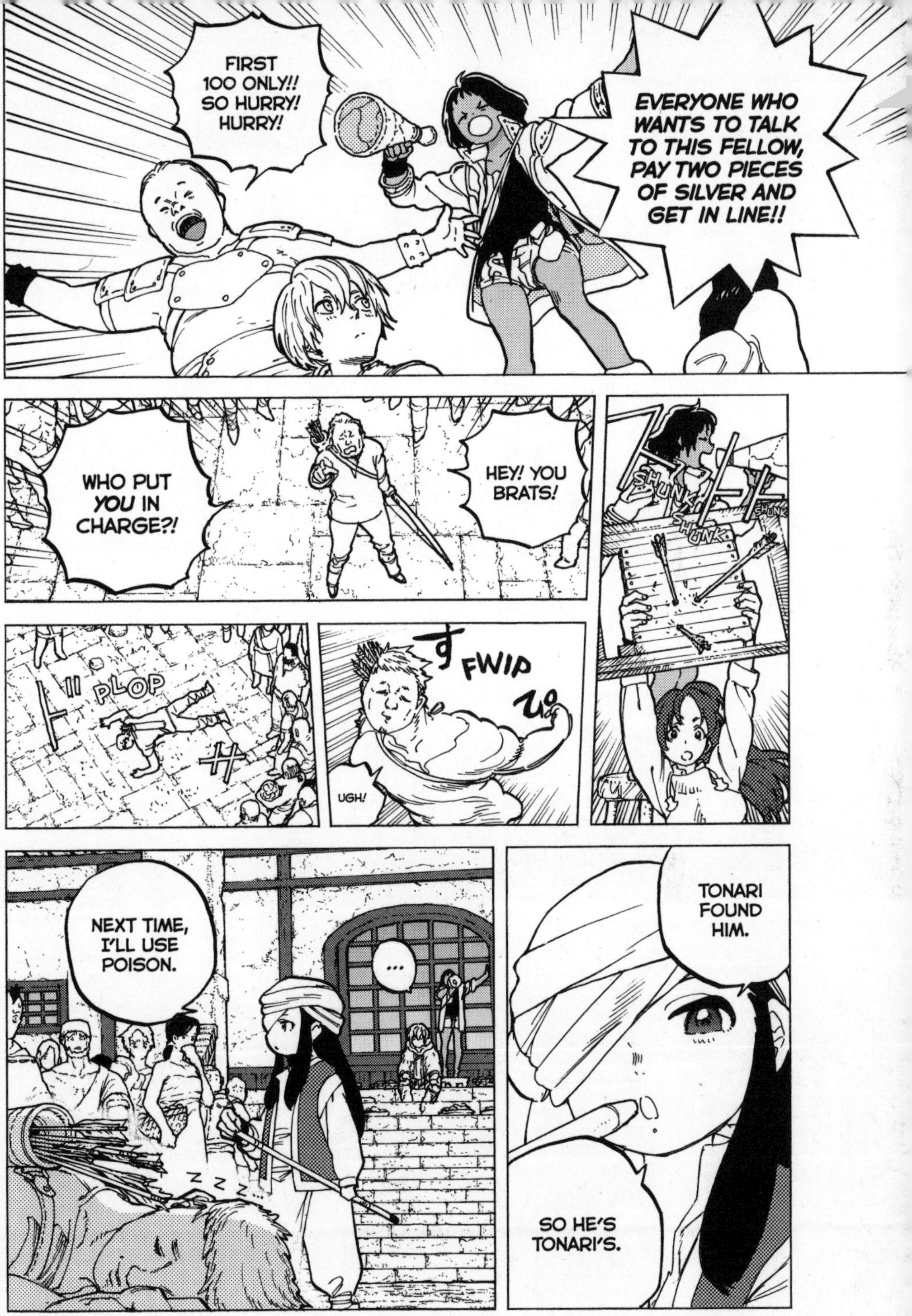
EVERYONE WHO WANTS TO TALK TO THIS FELLOW, PAY TWO PIECES OF SILVER AND GET IN LINE!!
FIRST 100 ONLY!! SO HURRY! HURRY!
SHUNK
SHUNK
SHUNK
HEY! YOU BRATS!
WHO PUT *YOU* IN CHARGE?!
す
FWIP
ひゅ
UGH!
PLOP
TONARI FOUND HIM.
SO HE'S TONARI'S.
...
NEXT TIME, I'LL USE POISON.
Z Z Z...

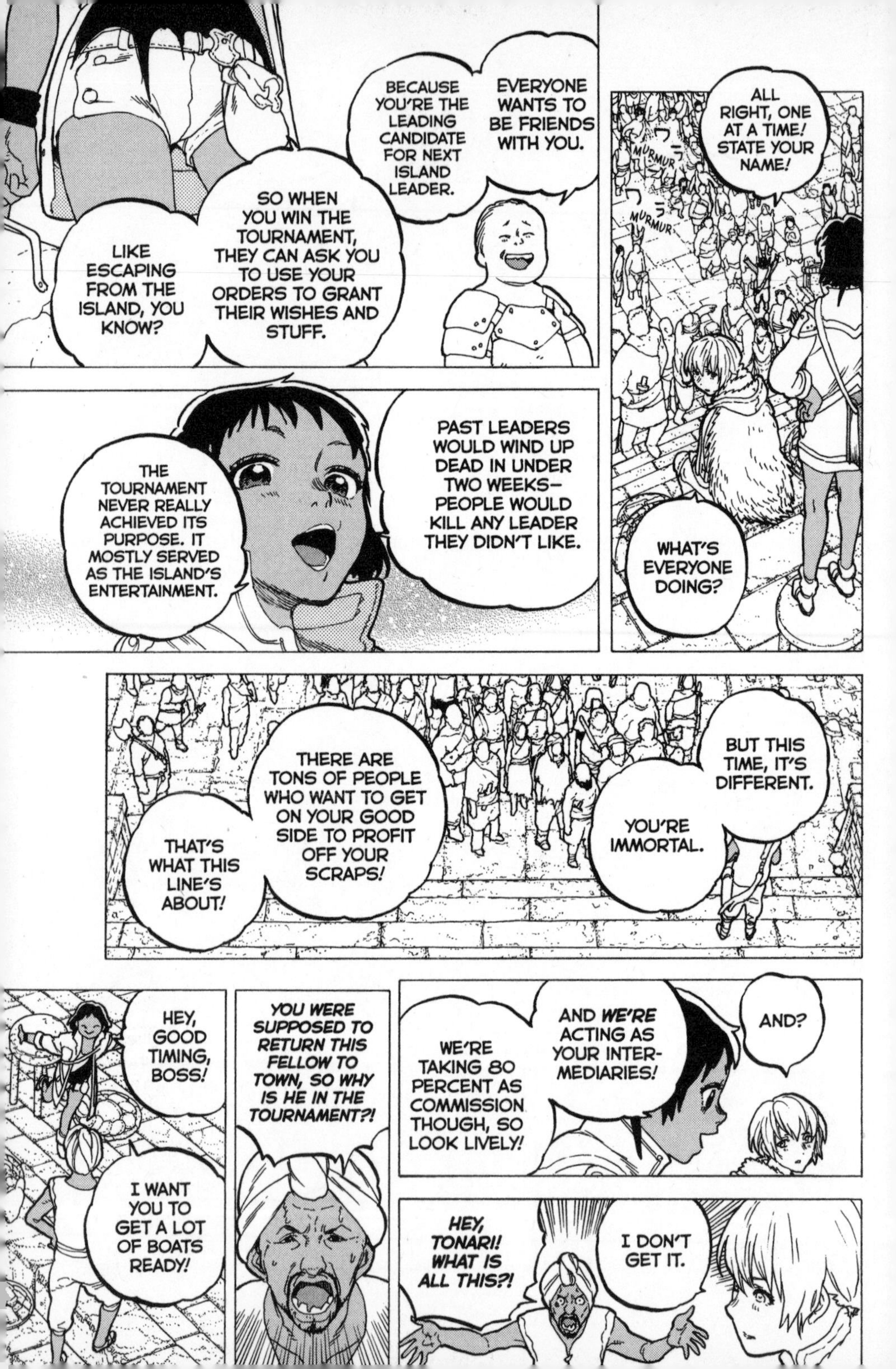

ALL RIGHT, ONE AT A TIME! STATE YOUR NAME!
MURMUR
MURMUR
WHAT'S EVERYONE DOING?
EVERYONE WANTS TO BE FRIENDS WITH YOU.
BECAUSE YOU'RE THE LEADING CANDIDATE FOR NEXT ISLAND LEADER.
SO WHEN YOU WIN THE TOURNAMENT, THEY CAN ASK YOU TO USE YOUR ORDERS TO GRANT THEIR WISHES AND STUFF.
LIKE ESCAPING FROM THE ISLAND, YOU KNOW?
PAST LEADERS WOULD WIND UP DEAD IN UNDER TWO WEEKS— PEOPLE WOULD KILL ANY LEADER THEY DIDN'T LIKE.
THE TOURNAMENT NEVER REALLY ACHIEVED ITS PURPOSE. IT MOSTLY SERVED AS THE ISLAND'S ENTERTAINMENT.
BUT THIS TIME, IT'S DIFFERENT.
YOU'RE IMMORTAL.
THERE ARE TONS OF PEOPLE WHO WANT TO GET ON YOUR GOOD SIDE TO PROFIT OFF YOUR SCRAPS!
THAT'S WHAT THIS LINE'S ABOUT!
AND?
AND WE'RE ACTING AS YOUR INTER-MEDIARIES!
WE'RE TAKING 80 PERCENT AS COMMISSION THOUGH, SO LOOK LIVELY!
I DON'T GET IT.
HEY, TONARI! WHAT IS ALL THIS?!
YOU WERE SUPPOSED TO RETURN THIS FELLOW TO TOWN, SO WHY IS HE IN THE TOURNAMENT?!
HEY, GOOD TIMING, BOSS!
I WANT YOU TO GET A LOT OF BOATS READY!

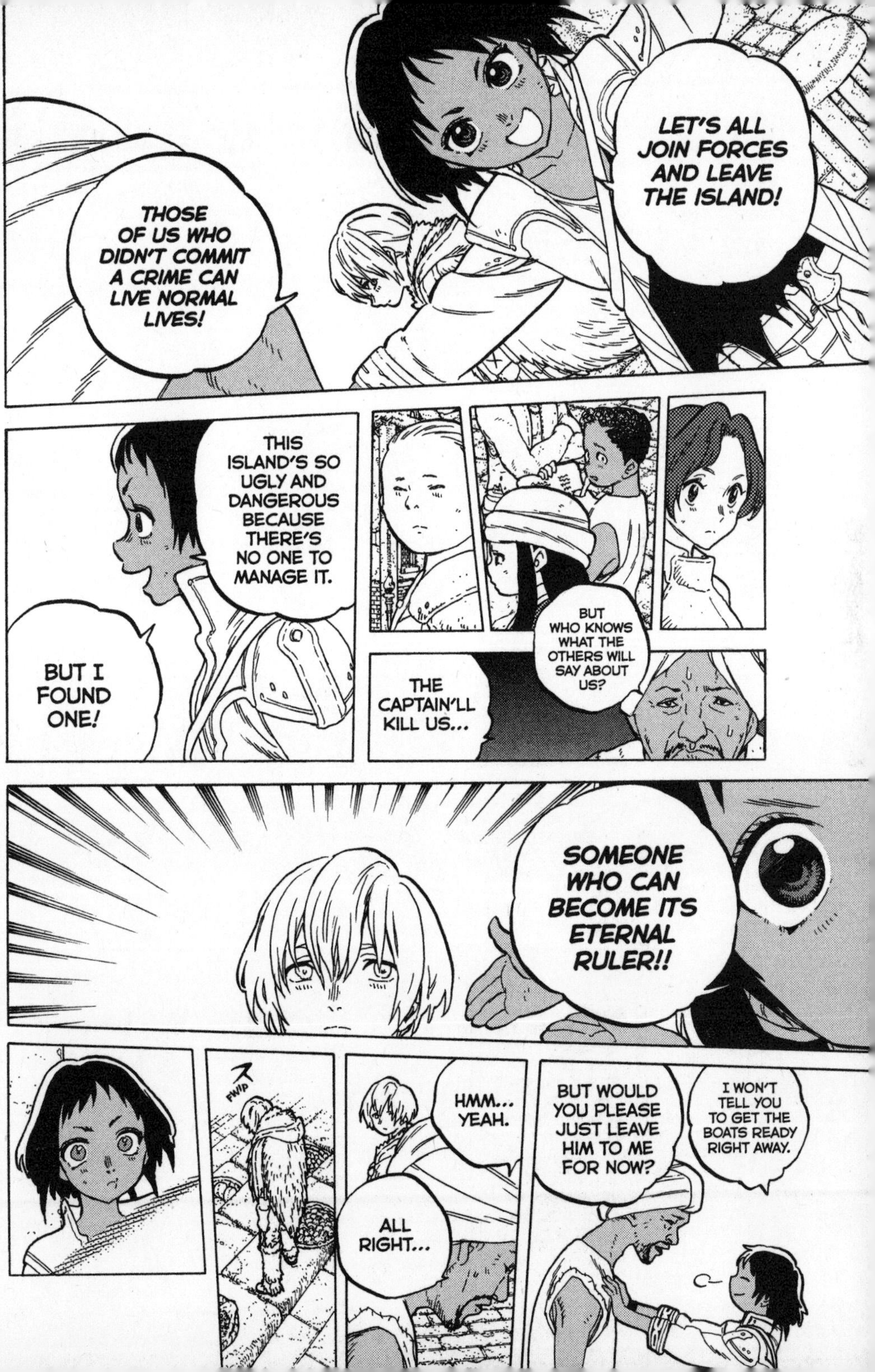
LET'S ALL JOIN FORCES AND LEAVE THE ISLAND!
THOSE OF US WHO DIDN'T COMMIT A CRIME CAN LIVE NORMAL LIVES!
BUT WHO KNOWS WHAT THE OTHERS WILL SAY ABOUT US?
THE CAPTAIN'LL KILL US...
THIS ISLAND'S SO UGLY AND DANGEROUS BECAUSE THERE'S NO ONE TO MANAGE IT.
BUT I FOUND ONE!
SOMEONE WHO CAN BECOME ITS ETERNAL RULER!!
I WON'T TELL YOU TO GET THE BOATS READY RIGHT AWAY.
BUT WOULD YOU PLEASE JUST LEAVE HIM TO ME FOR NOW?
HMM... YEAH.
ALL RIGHT...
FWIP

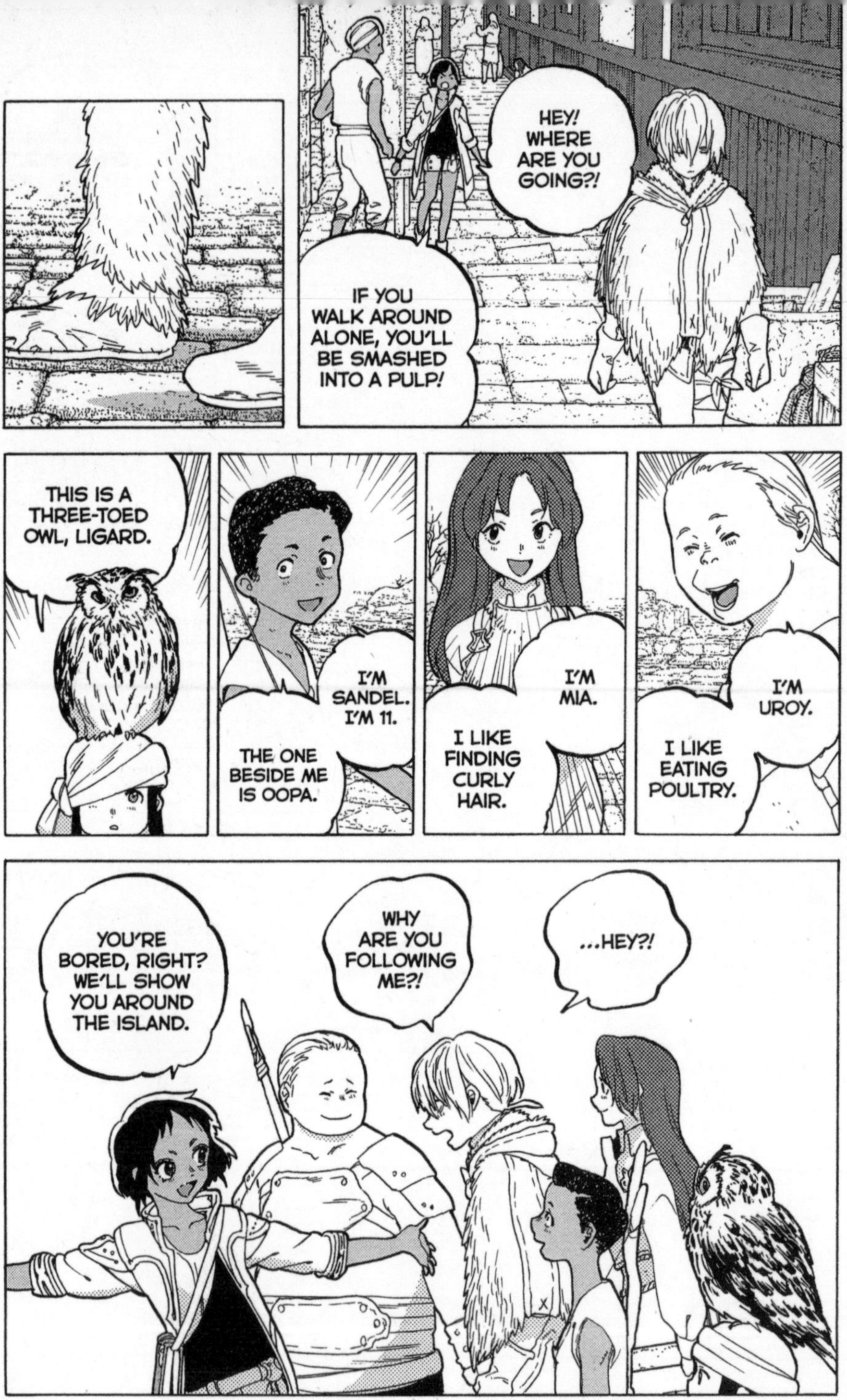
HEY! WHERE ARE YOU GOING?!
IF YOU WALK AROUND ALONE, YOU'LL BE SMASHED INTO A PULP!
I'M UROY.
I LIKE EATING POULTRY.
I'M MIA.
I LIKE FINDING CURLY HAIR.
I'M SANDEL. I'M 11.
THE ONE BESIDE ME IS OOPA.
THIS IS A THREE-TOED OWL, LIGARD.
...HEY?!
WHY ARE YOU FOLLOWING ME?!
YOU'RE BORED, RIGHT? WE'LL SHOW YOU AROUND THE ISLAND.

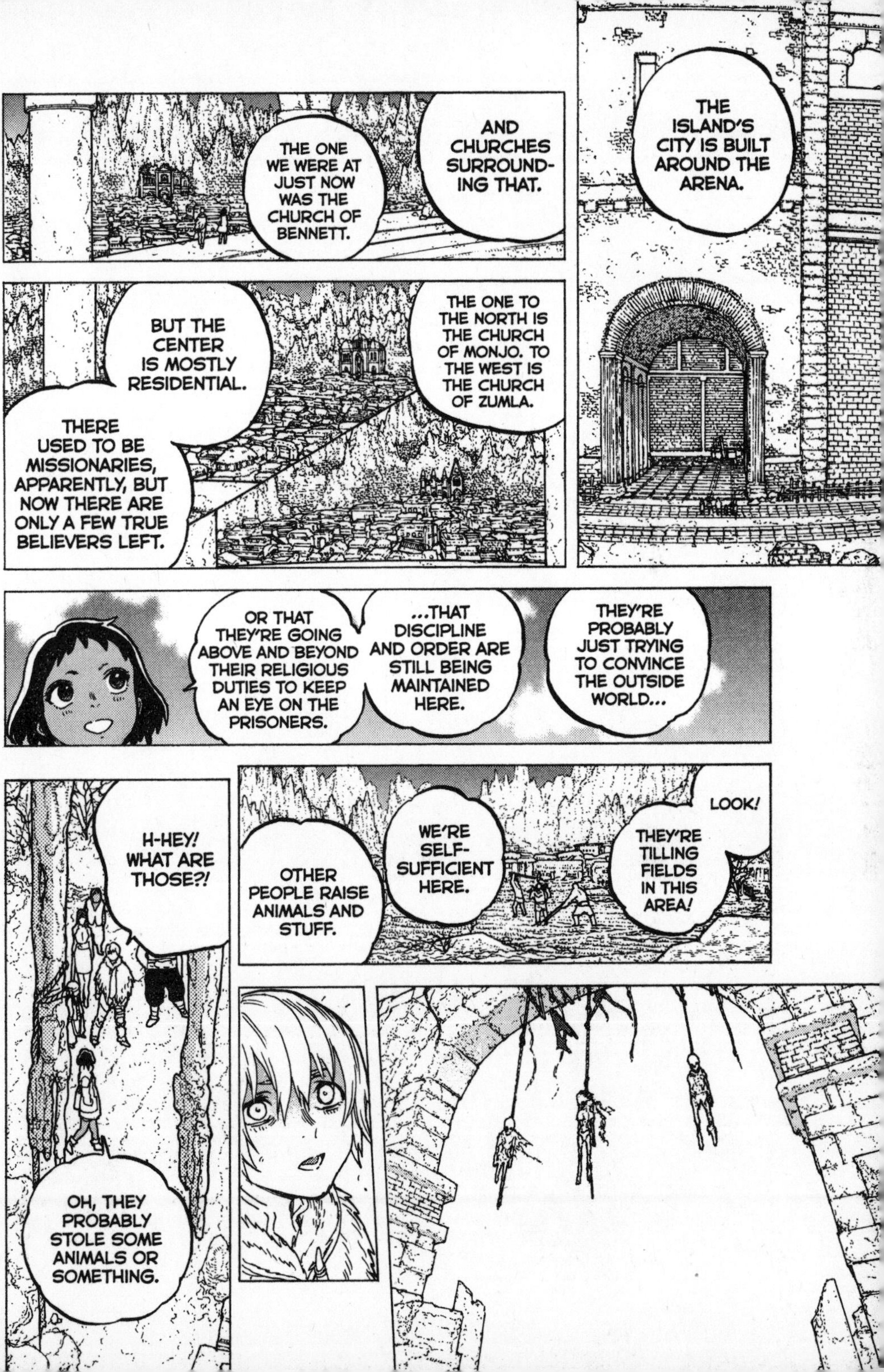
THE ISLAND'S CITY IS BUILT AROUND THE ARENA.
AND CHURCHES SURROUNDING THAT.
THE ONE WE WERE AT JUST NOW WAS THE CHURCH OF BENNETT.
THE ONE TO THE NORTH IS THE CHURCH OF MONJO. TO THE WEST IS THE CHURCH OF ZUMLA.
BUT THE CENTER IS MOSTLY RESIDENTIAL.
THERE USED TO BE MISSIONARIES, APPARENTLY, BUT NOW THERE ARE ONLY A FEW TRUE BELIEVERS LEFT.
THEY'RE PROBABLY JUST TRYING TO CONVINCE THE OUTSIDE WORLD...
...THAT DISCIPLINE AND ORDER ARE STILL BEING MAINTAINED HERE.
OR THAT THEY'RE GOING ABOVE AND BEYOND THEIR RELIGIOUS DUTIES TO KEEP AN EYE ON THE PRISONERS.
LOOK!
THEY'RE TILLING FIELDS IN THIS AREA!
WE'RE SELF-SUFFICIENT HERE.
OTHER PEOPLE RAISE ANIMALS AND STUFF.
H-HEY! WHAT ARE THOSE?!
OH, THEY PROBABLY STOLE SOME ANIMALS OR SOMETHING.

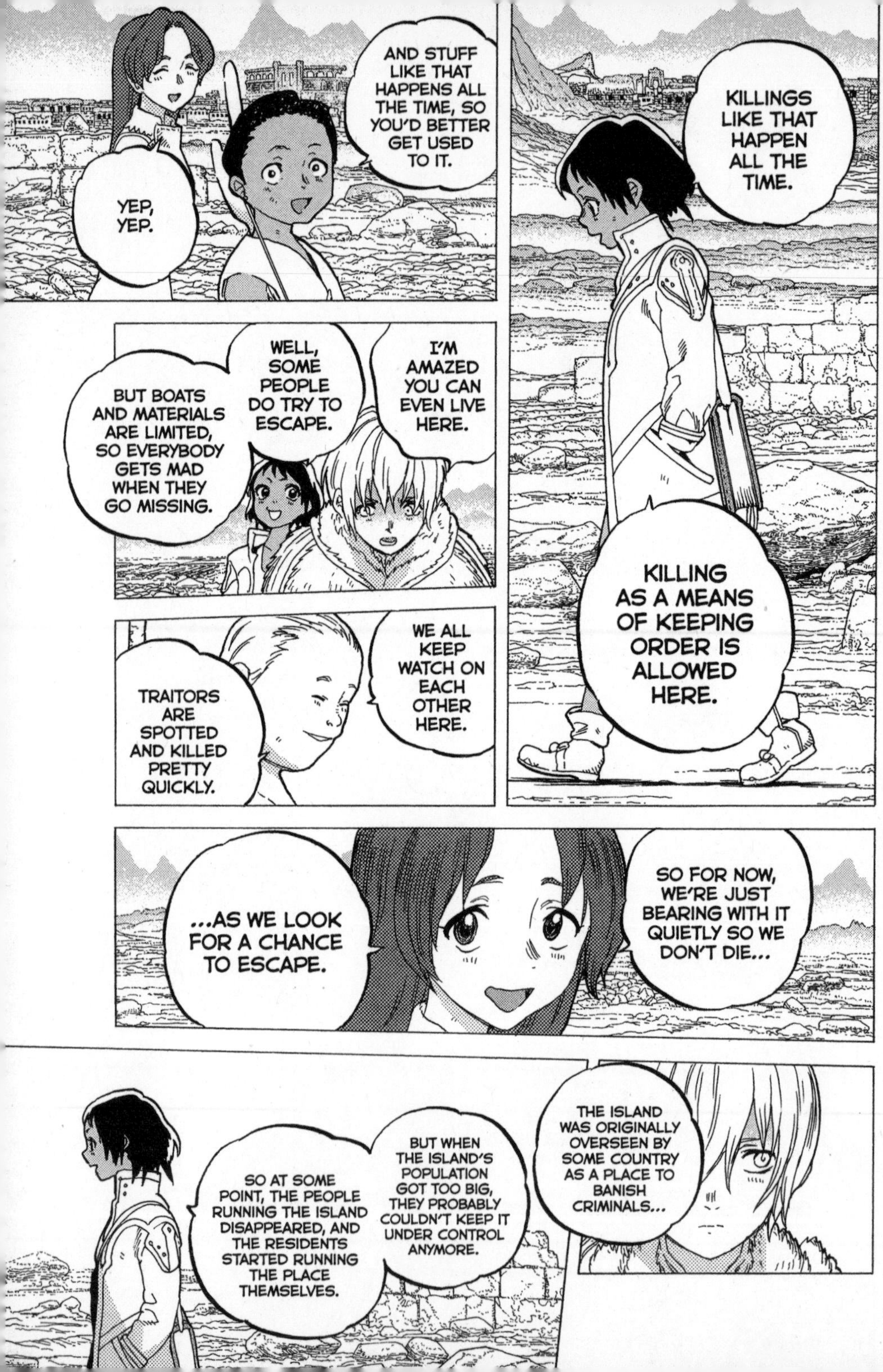
KILLINGS LIKE THAT HAPPEN ALL THE TIME.
KILLING AS A MEANS OF KEEPING ORDER IS ALLOWED HERE.
AND STUFF LIKE THAT HAPPENS ALL THE TIME, SO YOU'D BETTER GET USED TO IT.
YEP, YEP.
I'M AMAZED YOU CAN EVEN LIVE HERE.
WELL, SOME PEOPLE DO TRY TO ESCAPE.
BUT BOATS AND MATERIALS ARE LIMITED, SO EVERYBODY GETS MAD WHEN THEY GO MISSING.
WE ALL KEEP WATCH ON EACH OTHER HERE.
TRAITORS ARE SPOTTED AND KILLED PRETTY QUICKLY.
SO FOR NOW, WE'RE JUST BEARING WITH IT QUIETLY SO WE DON'T DIE...
...AS WE LOOK FOR A CHANCE TO ESCAPE.
THE ISLAND WAS ORIGINALLY OVERSEEN BY SOME COUNTRY AS A PLACE TO BANISH CRIMINALS...
BUT WHEN THE ISLAND'S POPULATION GOT TOO BIG, THEY PROBABLY COULDN'T KEEP IT UNDER CONTROL ANYMORE.
SO AT SOME POINT, THE PEOPLE RUNNING THE ISLAND DISAPPEARED, AND THE RESIDENTS STARTED RUNNING THE PLACE THEMSELVES.

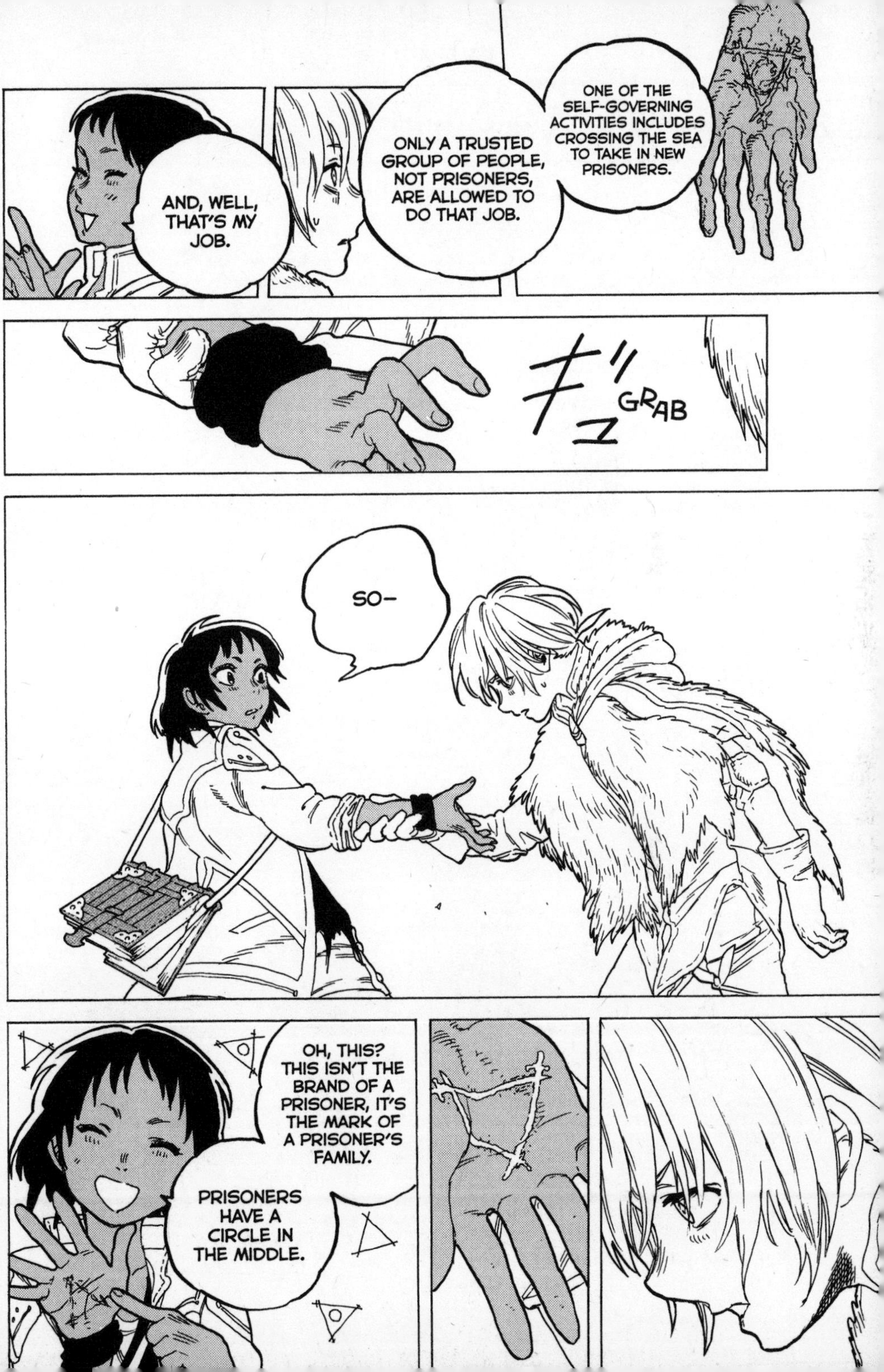
ONE OF THE SELF-GOVERNING ACTIVITIES INCLUDES CROSSING THE SEA TO TAKE IN NEW PRISONERS.
ONLY A TRUSTED GROUP OF PEOPLE, NOT PRISONERS, ARE ALLOWED TO DO THAT JOB.
AND, WELL, THAT'S MY JOB.
GRAB
SO-
OH, THIS? THIS ISN'T THE BRAND OF A PRISONER, IT'S THE MARK OF A PRISONER'S FAMILY.
PRISONERS HAVE A CIRCLE IN THE MIDDLE.

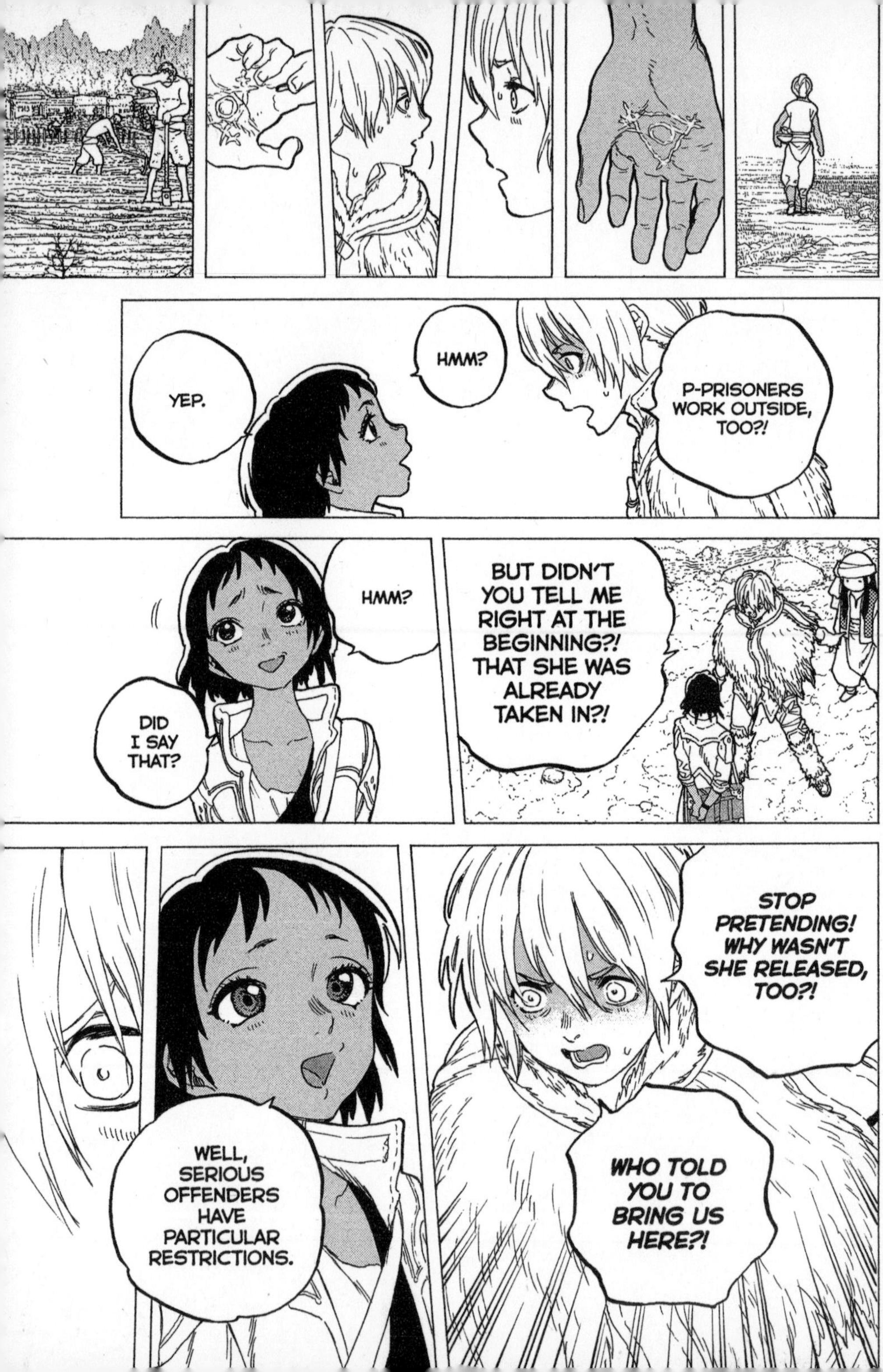
P-PRISONERS WORK OUTSIDE, TOO?!
HMM?
YEP.
BUT DIDN'T YOU TELL ME RIGHT AT THE BEGINNING?! THAT SHE WAS ALREADY TAKEN IN?!
HMM?
DID I SAY THAT?
STOP PRETENDING! WHY WASN'T SHE RELEASED, TOO?!
WHO TOLD YOU TO BRING US HERE?!
WELL, SERIOUS OFFENDERS HAVE PARTICULAR RESTRICTIONS.

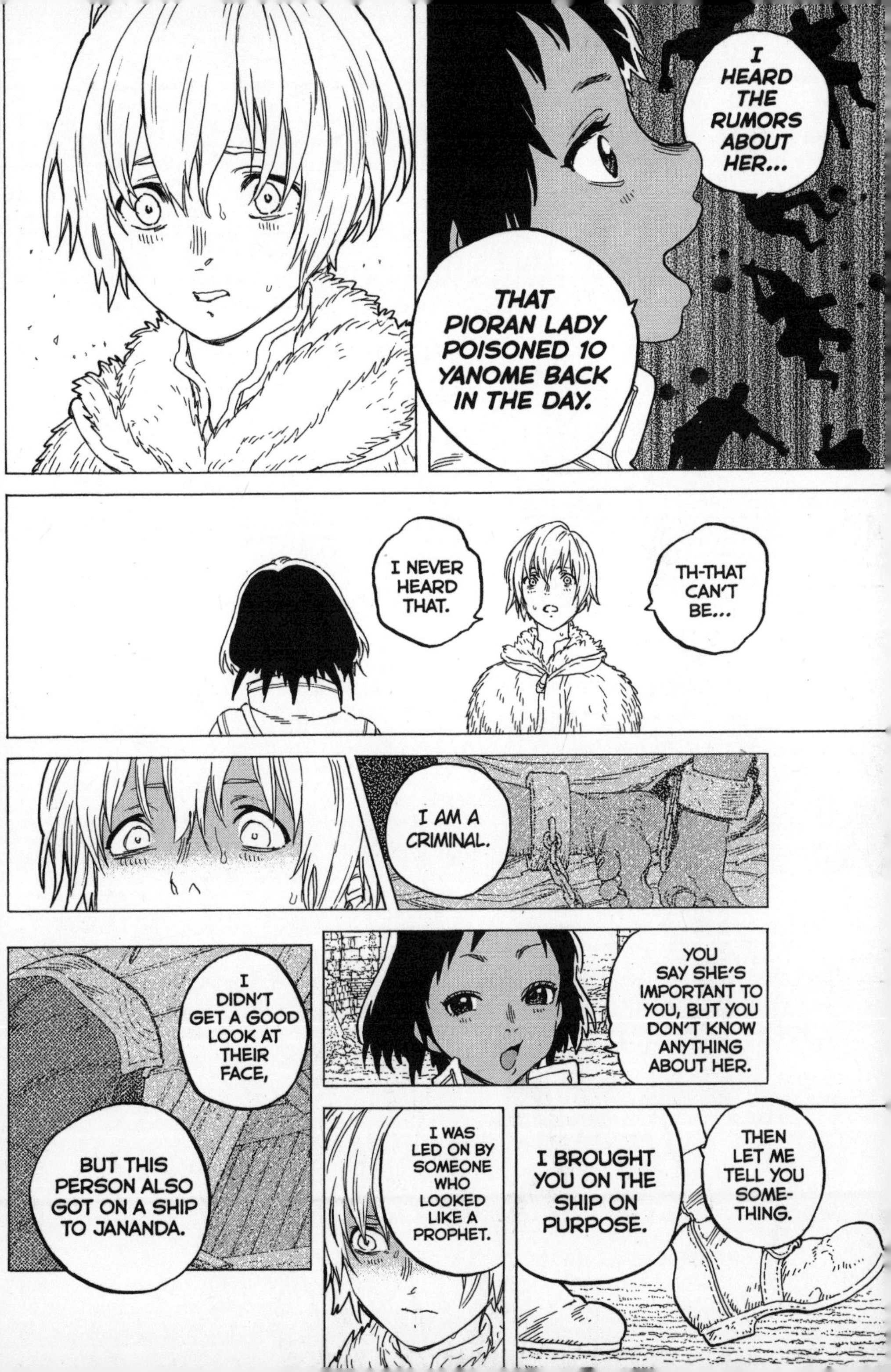
I HEARD THE RUMORS ABOUT HER...
THAT PIORAN LADY POISONED 10 YANOME BACK IN THE DAY.
TH-THAT CAN'T BE...
I NEVER HEARD THAT.
I AM A CRIMINAL.
YOU SAY SHE'S IMPORTANT TO YOU, BUT YOU DON'T KNOW ANYTHING ABOUT HER.
THEN LET ME TELL YOU SOMETHING.
I BROUGHT YOU ON THE SHIP ON PURPOSE.
I WAS LED ON BY SOMEONE WHO LOOKED LIKE A PROPHET.
I DIDN'T GET A GOOD LOOK AT THEIR FACE,
BUT THIS PERSON ALSO GOT ON A SHIP TO JANANDA.

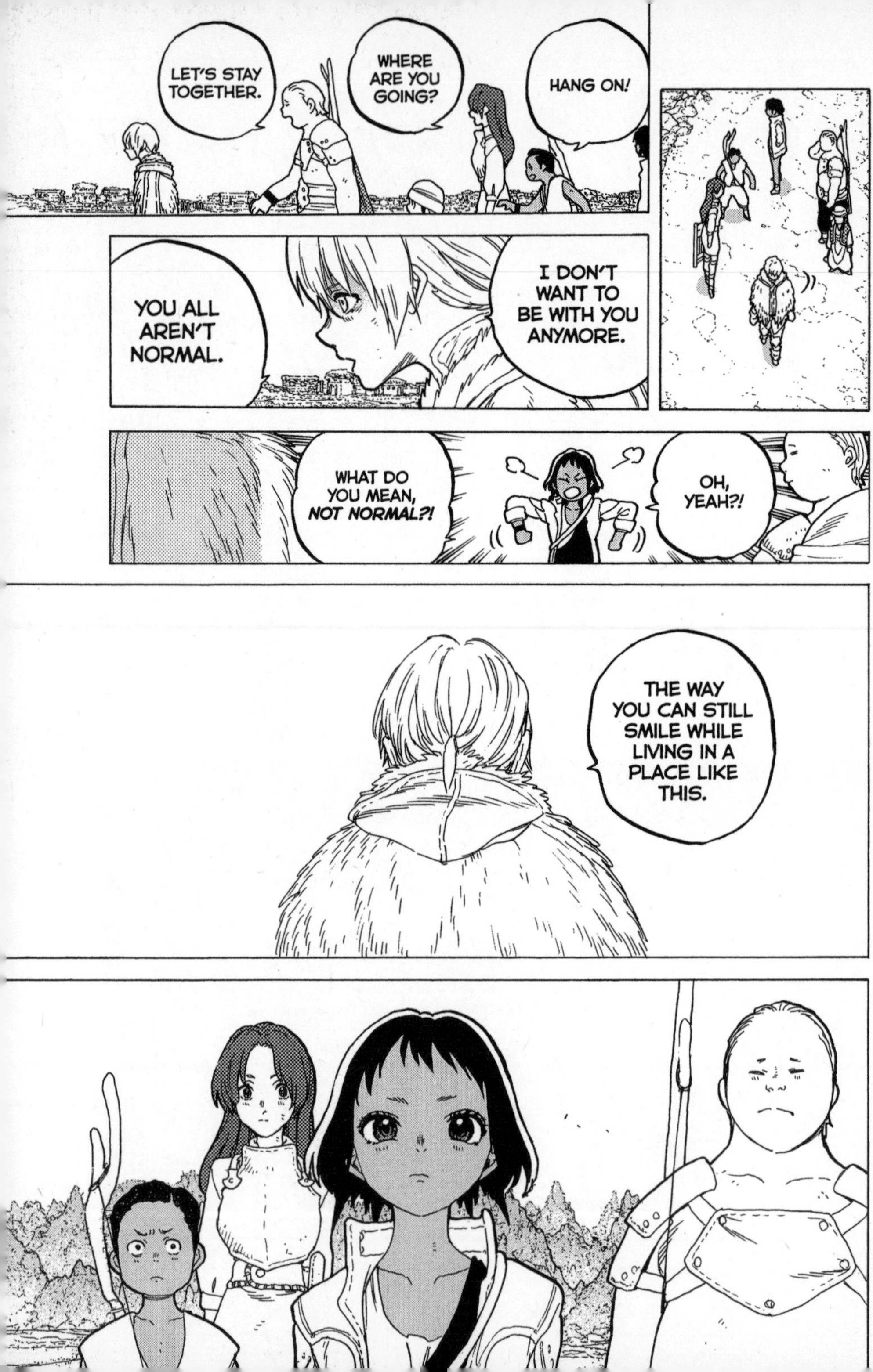
HANG ON!
WHERE ARE YOU GOING?
LET'S STAY TOGETHER.
I DON'T WANT TO BE WITH YOU ANYMORE.
YOU ALL AREN'T NORMAL.
OH, YEAH?!
WHAT DO YOU MEAN, *NOT NORMAL?!*
THE WAY YOU CAN STILL SMILE WHILE LIVING IN A PLACE LIKE THIS.

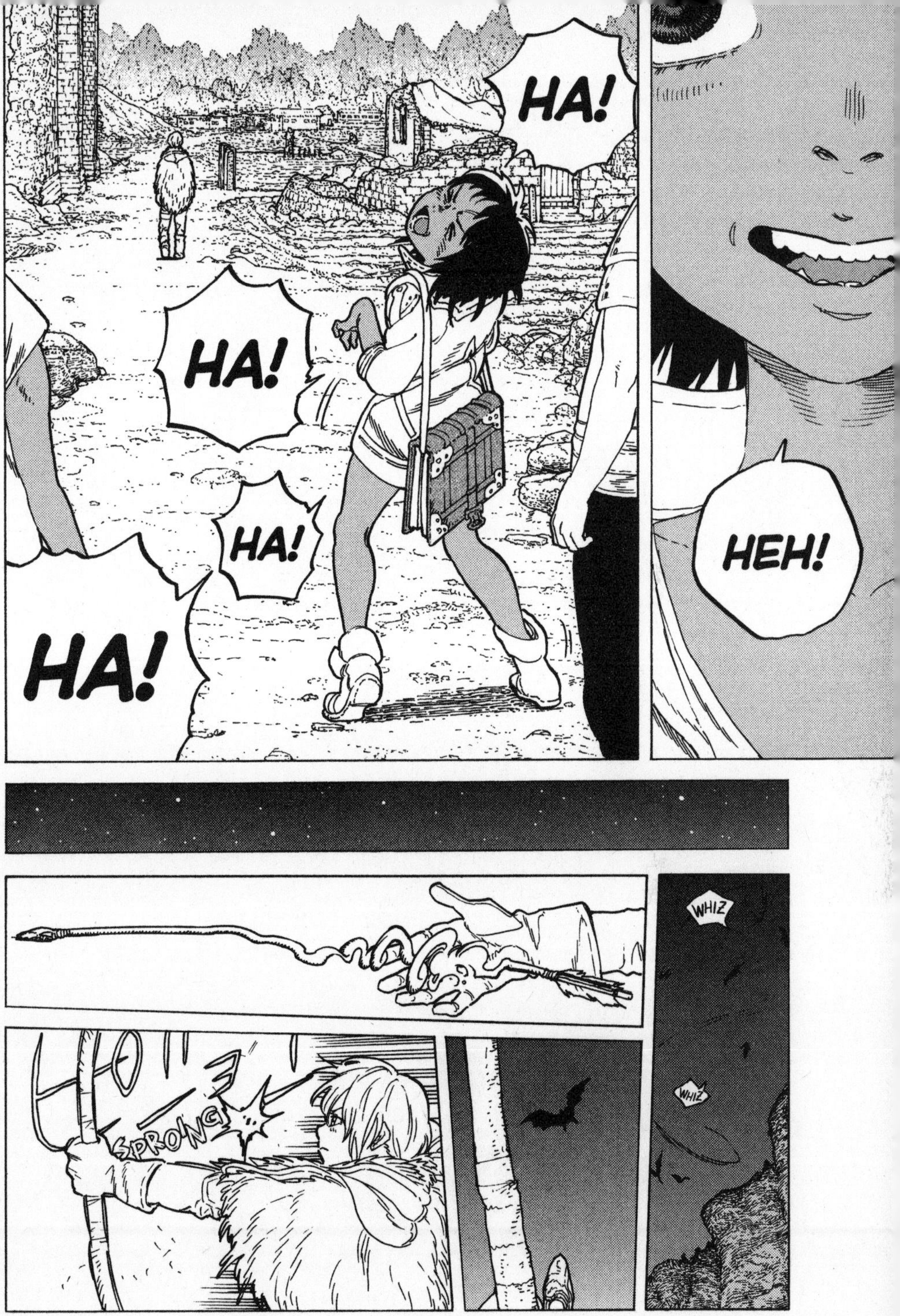
HEH!
HA!
HA!
HA!
HA!
WHIZ
WHIZ
SPRONG

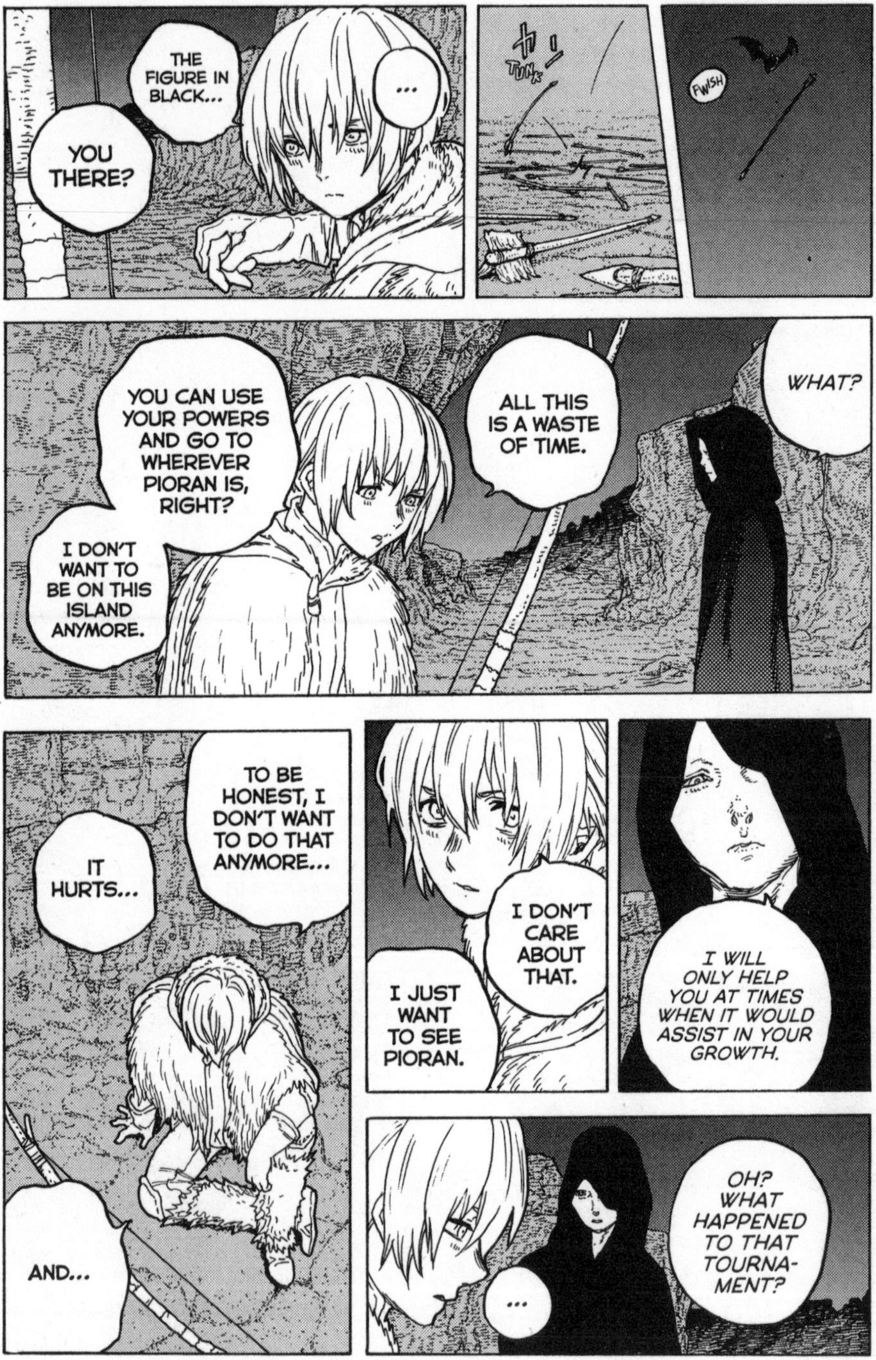
FWISH
TUNK
...
THE FIGURE IN BLACK...
YOU THERE?
WHAT?
ALL THIS IS A WASTE OF TIME.
YOU CAN USE YOUR POWERS AND GO TO WHEREVER PIORAN IS, RIGHT?
I DON'T WANT TO BE ON THIS ISLAND ANYMORE.
I WILL ONLY HELP YOU AT TIMES WHEN IT WOULD ASSIST IN YOUR GROWTH.
I DON'T CARE ABOUT THAT.
I JUST WANT TO SEE PIORAN.
OH? WHAT HAPPENED TO THAT TOURNAMENT?
...
TO BE HONEST, I DON'T WANT TO DO THAT ANYMORE...
IT HURTS...
AND...

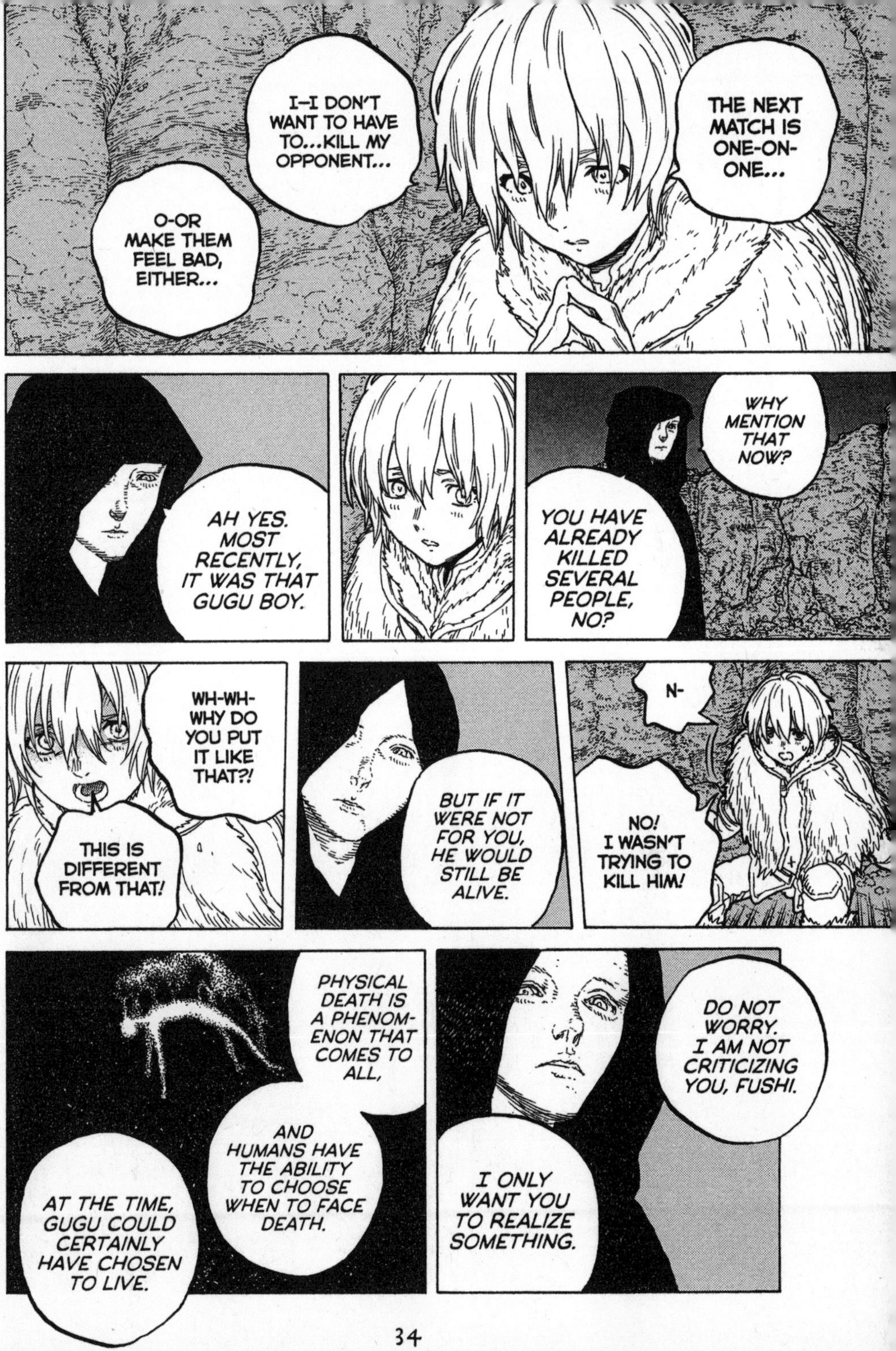
THE NEXT MATCH IS ONE-ON-ONE...
I–I DON'T WANT TO HAVE TO...KILL MY OPPONENT...
O-OR MAKE THEM FEEL BAD, EITHER...
WHY MENTION THAT NOW?
YOU HAVE ALREADY KILLED SEVERAL PEOPLE, NO?
AH YES. MOST RECENTLY, IT WAS THAT GUGU BOY.
N-
NO! I WASN'T TRYING TO KILL HIM!
BUT IF IT WERE NOT FOR YOU, HE WOULD STILL BE ALIVE.
WH-WH-WHY DO YOU PUT IT LIKE THAT?!
THIS IS DIFFERENT FROM THAT!
DO NOT WORRY. I AM NOT CRITICIZING YOU, FUSHI.
I ONLY WANT YOU TO REALIZE SOMETHING.
PHYSICAL DEATH IS A PHENOMENON THAT COMES TO ALL,
AND HUMANS HAVE THE ABILITY TO CHOOSE WHEN TO FACE DEATH.
AT THE TIME, GUGU COULD CERTAINLY HAVE CHOSEN TO LIVE.

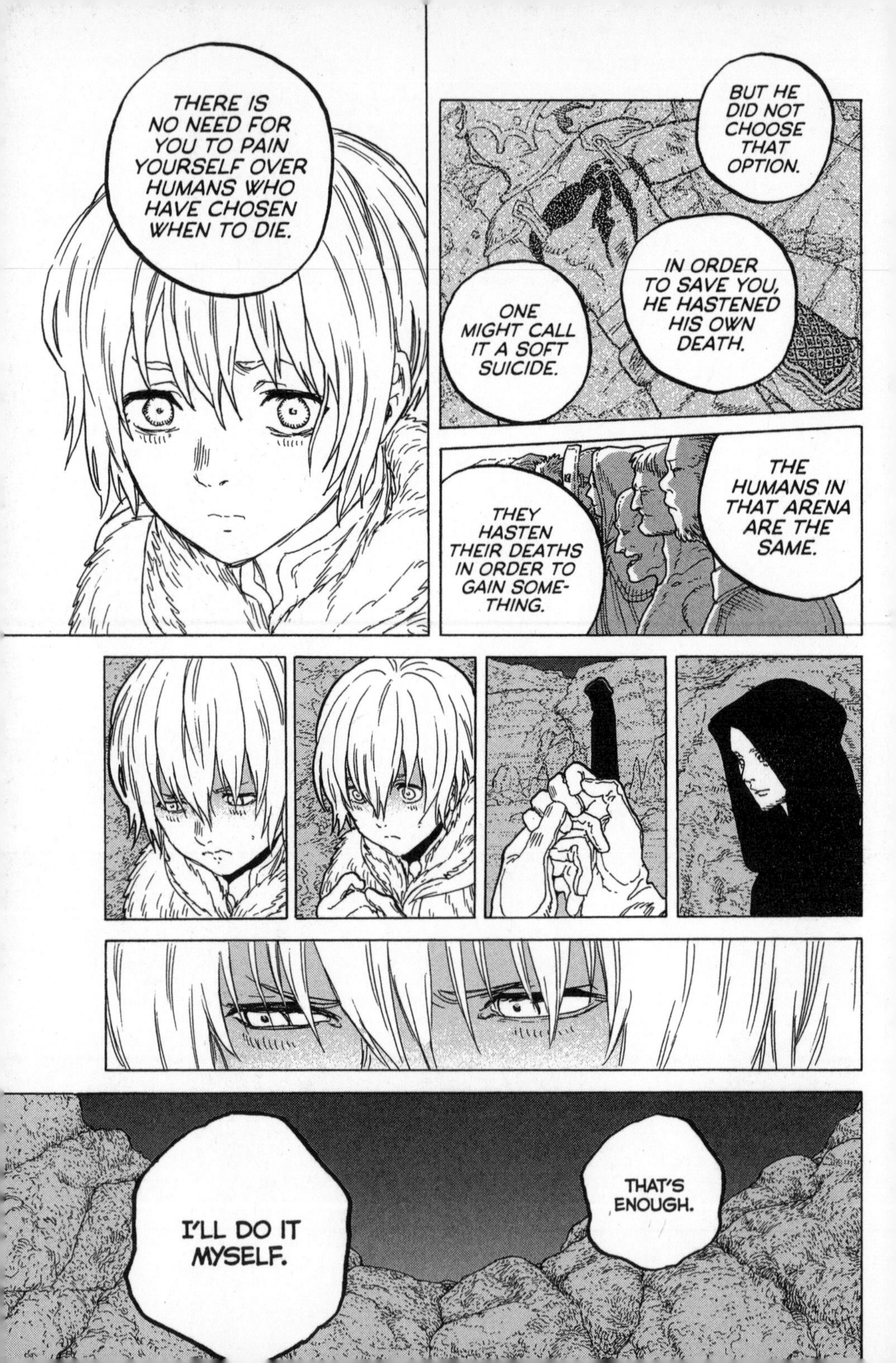
BUT HE DID NOT CHOOSE THAT OPTION.
IN ORDER TO SAVE YOU, HE HASTENED HIS OWN DEATH.
ONE MIGHT CALL IT A SOFT SUICIDE.
THE HUMANS IN THAT ARENA ARE THE SAME.
THEY HASTEN THEIR DEATHS IN ORDER TO GAIN SOME-THING.
THERE IS NO NEED FOR YOU TO PAIN YOURSELF OVER HUMANS WHO HAVE CHOSEN WHEN TO DIE.
THAT'S ENOUGH.
I'LL DO IT MYSELF.

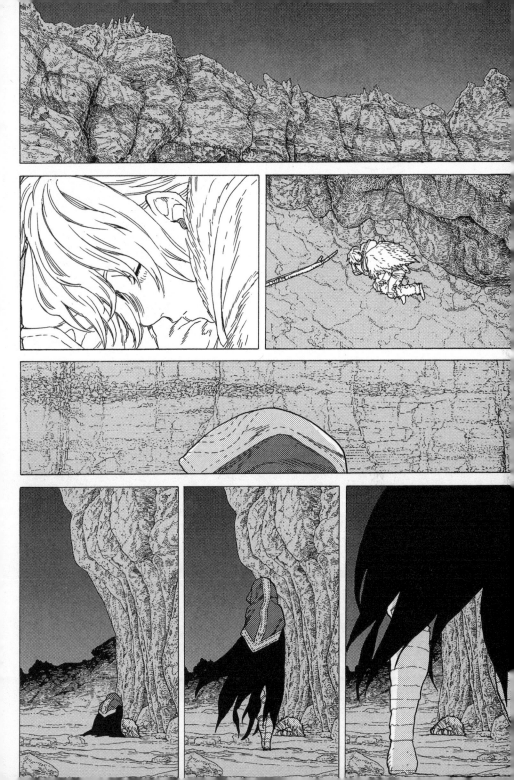

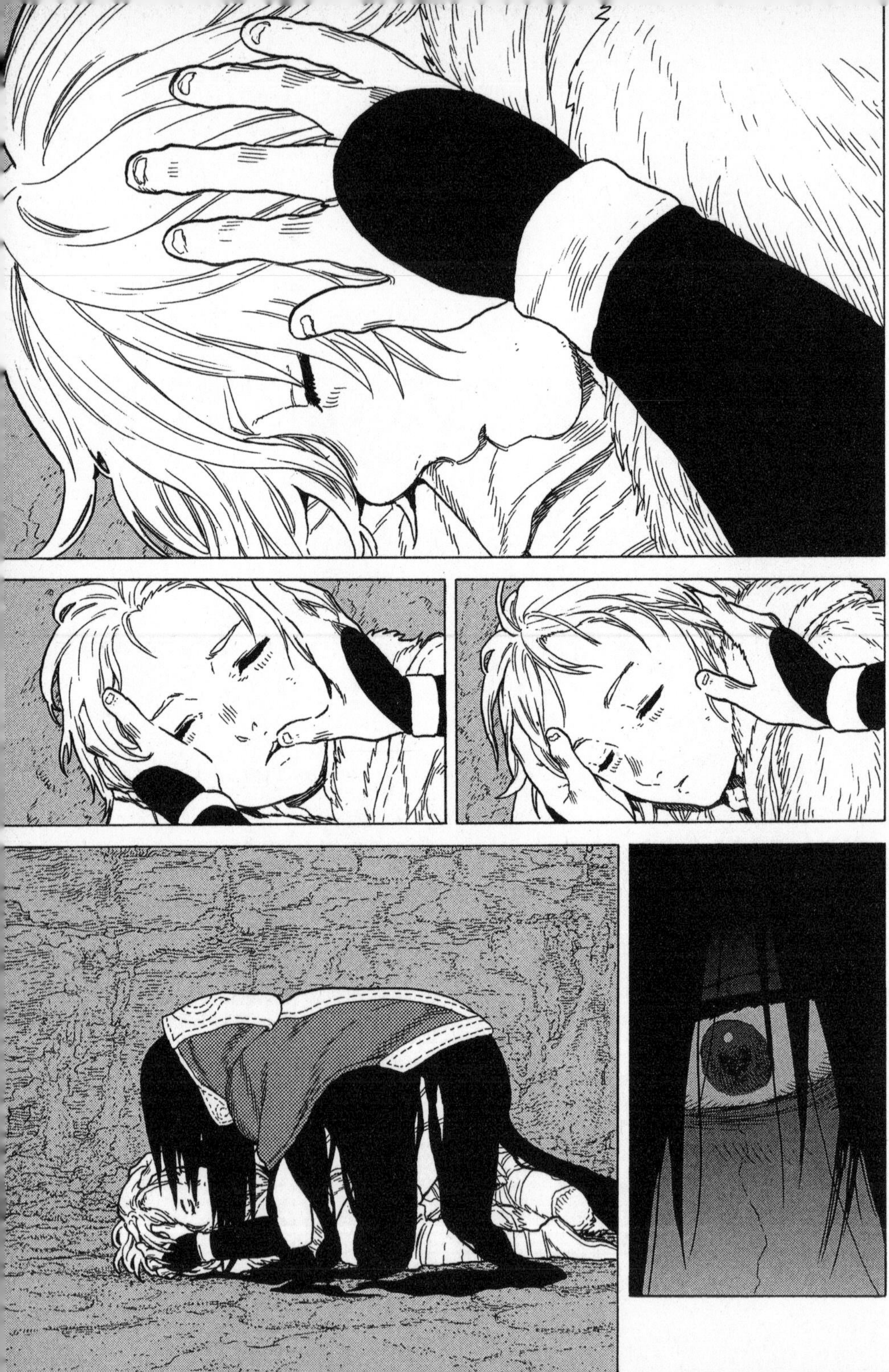

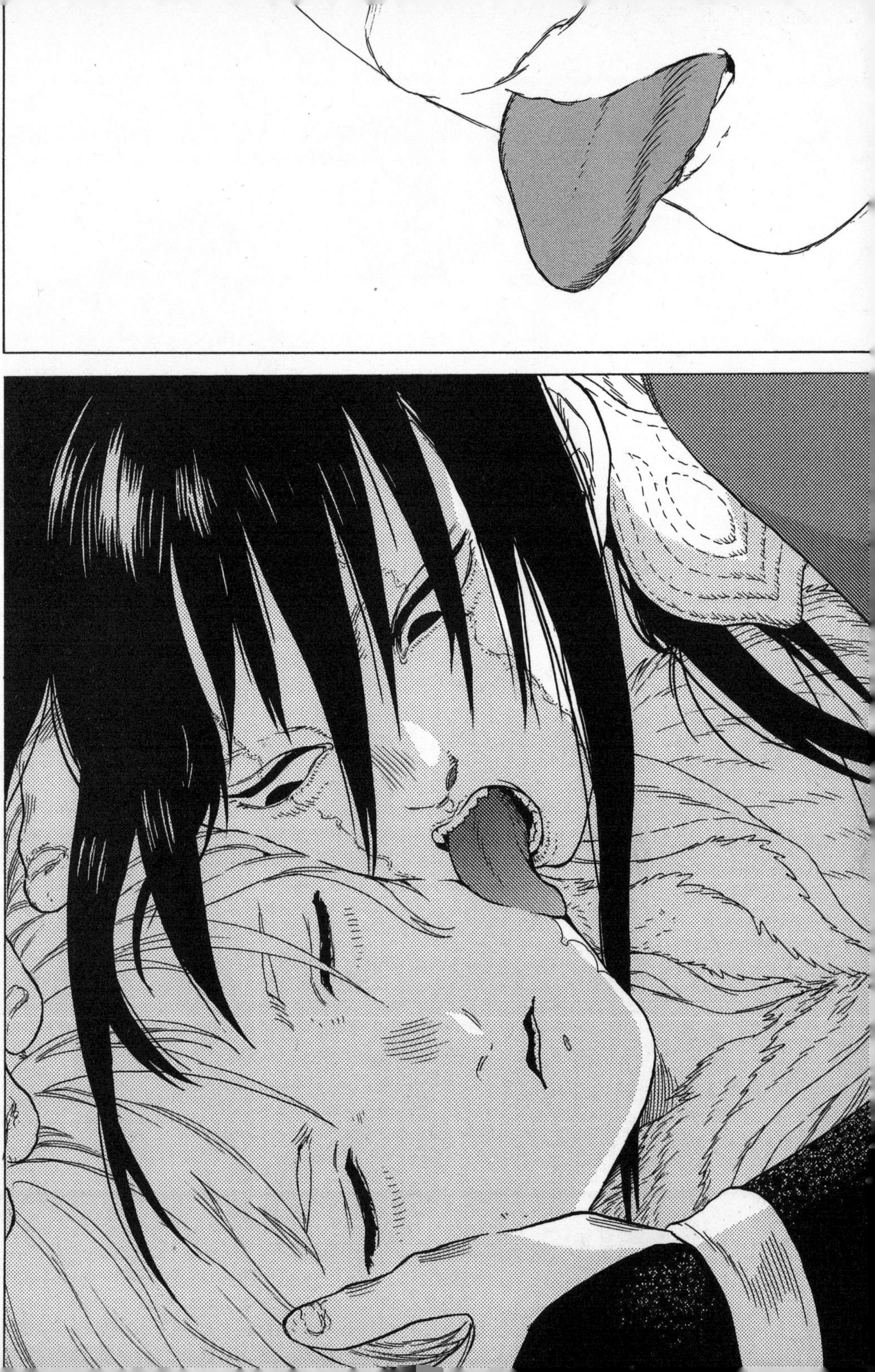

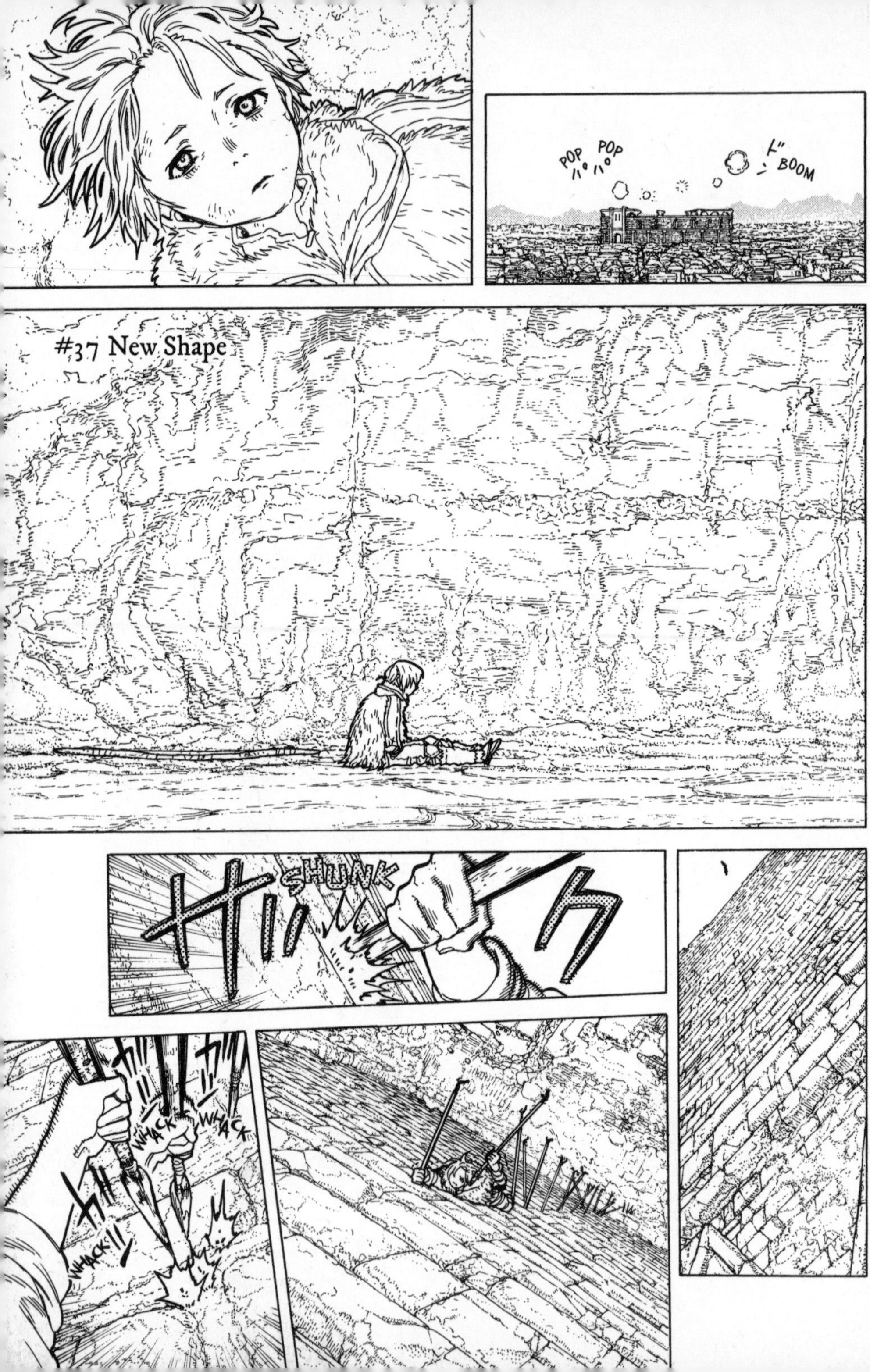
POP POP
BOOM
#37 New Shape
SHUNK
WHACK
WHACK
WHACK

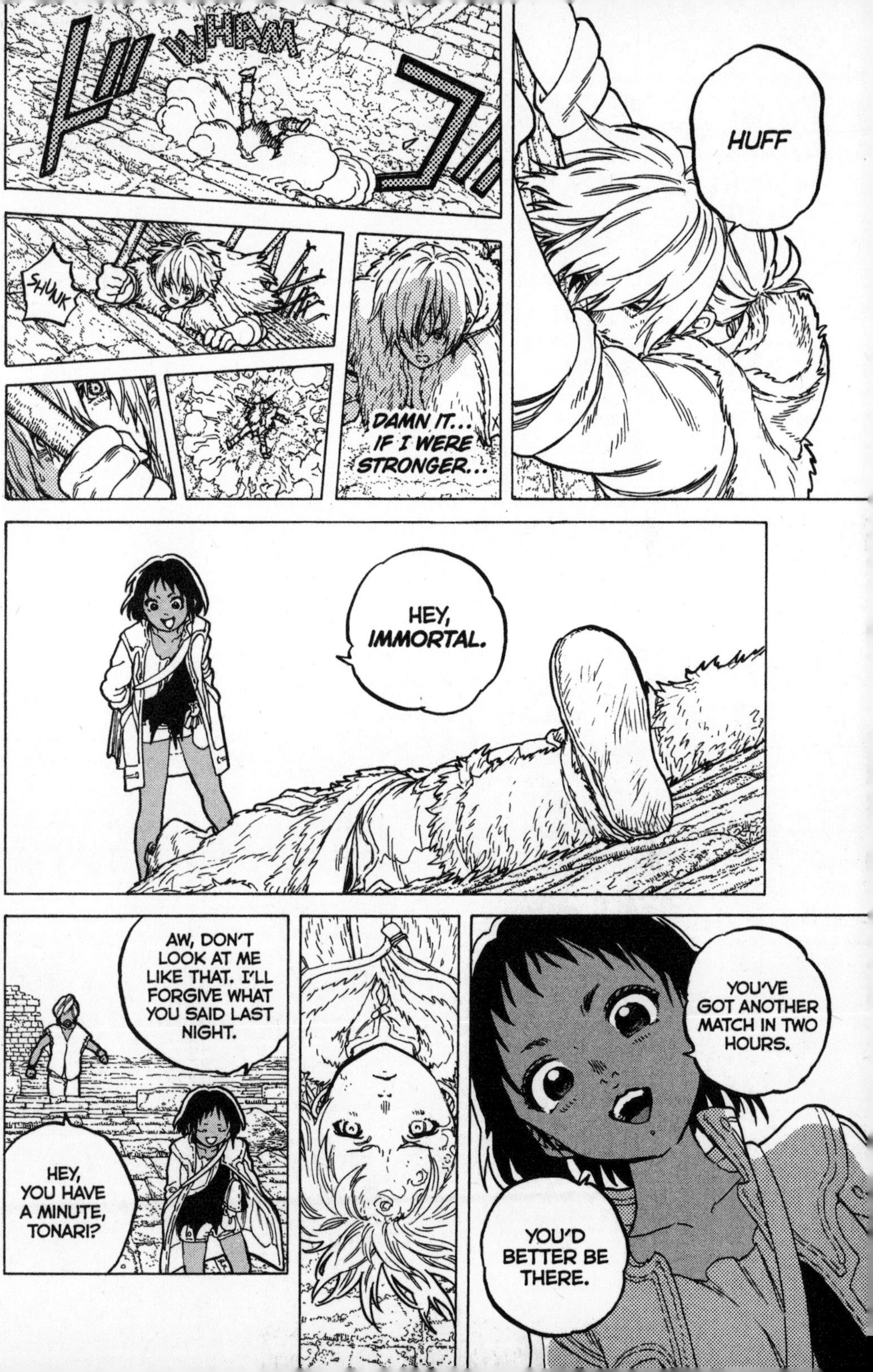
HUFF
WHAM
DAMN IT... IF I WERE STRONGER...
SHUNK
HEY, IMMORTAL.
YOU'VE GOT ANOTHER MATCH IN TWO HOURS.
YOU'D BETTER BE THERE.
AW, DON'T LOOK AT ME LIKE THAT. I'LL FORGIVE WHAT YOU SAID LAST NIGHT.
HEY, YOU HAVE A MINUTE, TONARI?

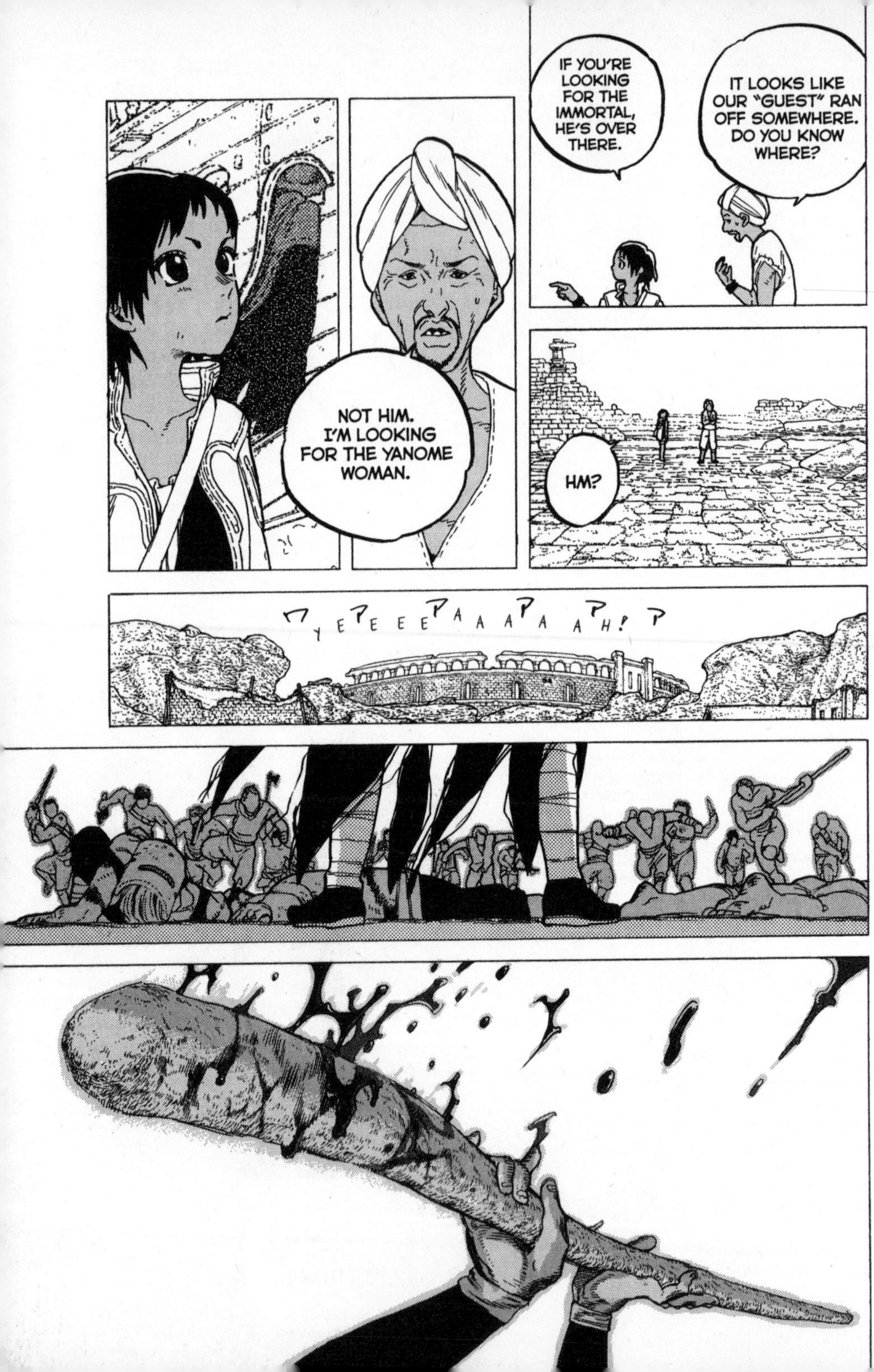
IT LOOKS LIKE OUR "GUEST" RAN OFF SOMEWHERE. DO YOU KNOW WHERE?
IF YOU'RE LOOKING FOR THE IMMORTAL, HE'S OVER THERE.
HM?
NOT HIM. I'M LOOKING FOR THE YANOME WOMAN.
YEEEEAAAAAH!

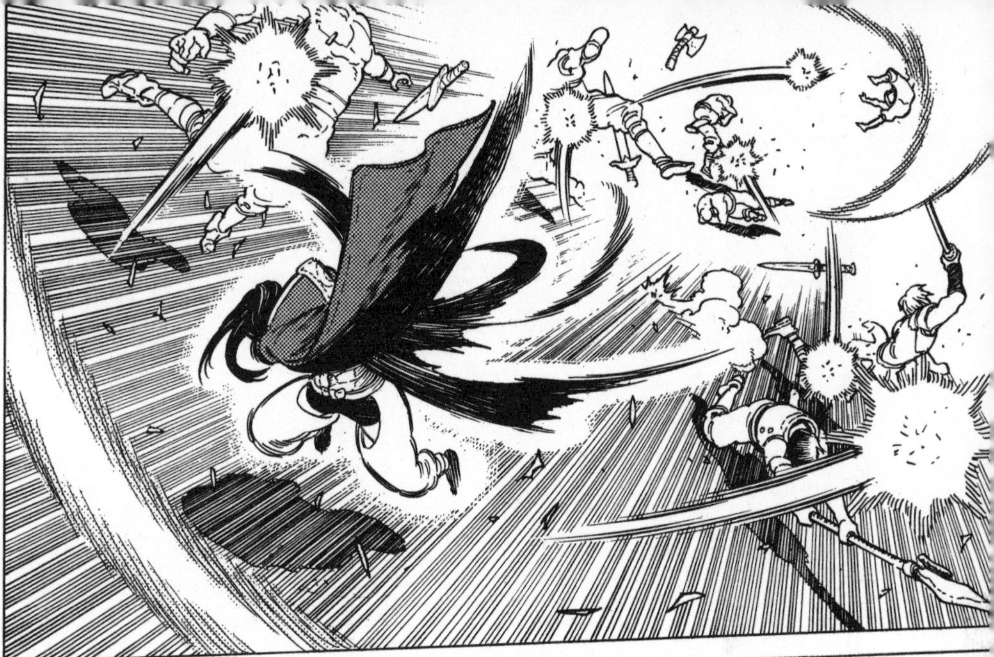
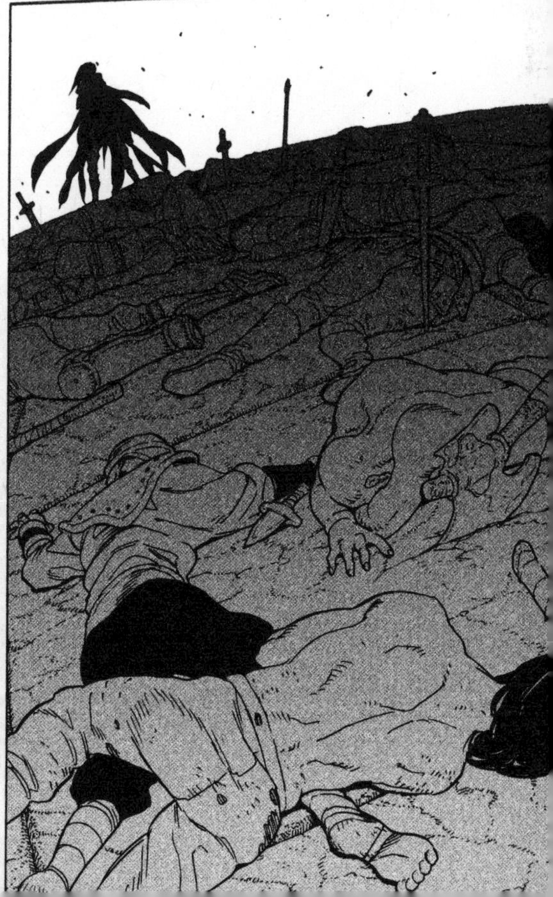
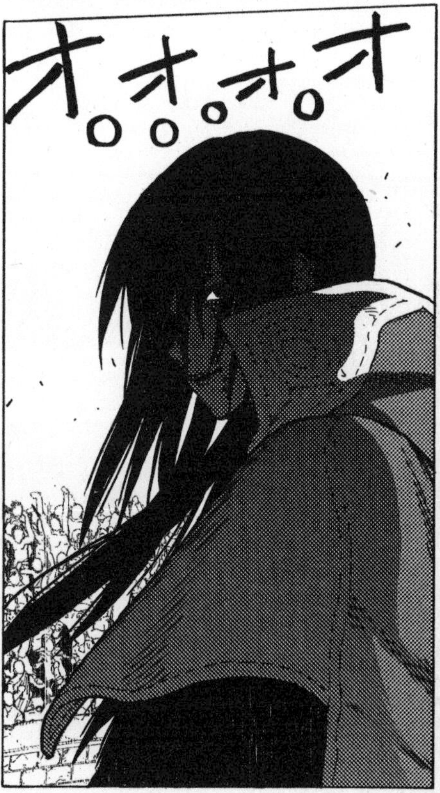
オ。オ。オ。オ

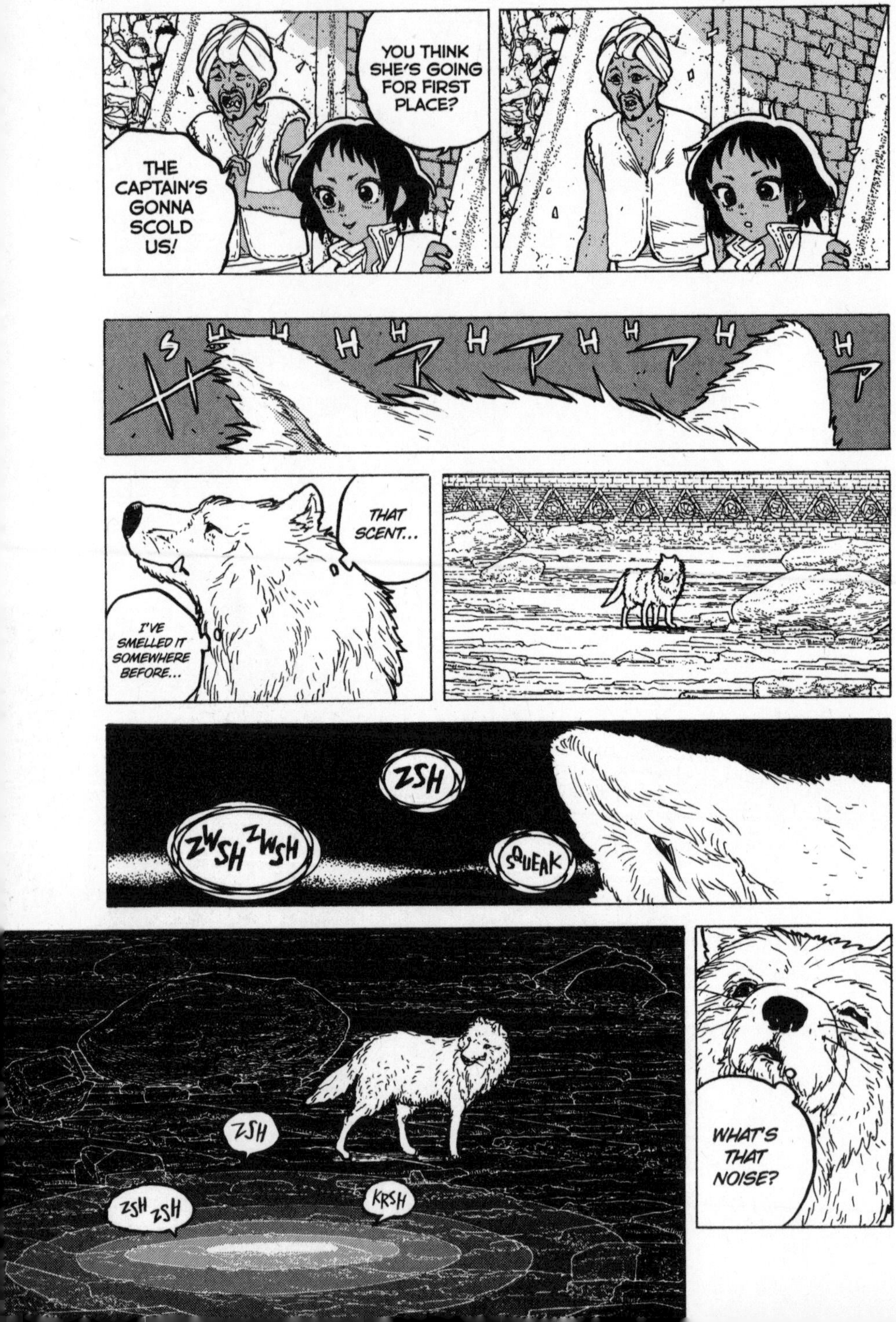
YOU THINK SHE'S GOING FOR FIRST PLACE?
THE CAPTAIN'S GONNA SCOLD US!
SHHHHHHHHH
THAT SCENT...
I'VE SMELLED IT SOMEWHERE BEFORE...
SQUEAK
ZSH
ZWSH ZWSH
WHAT'S THAT NOISE?
KRSH
ZSH
ZSH ZSH

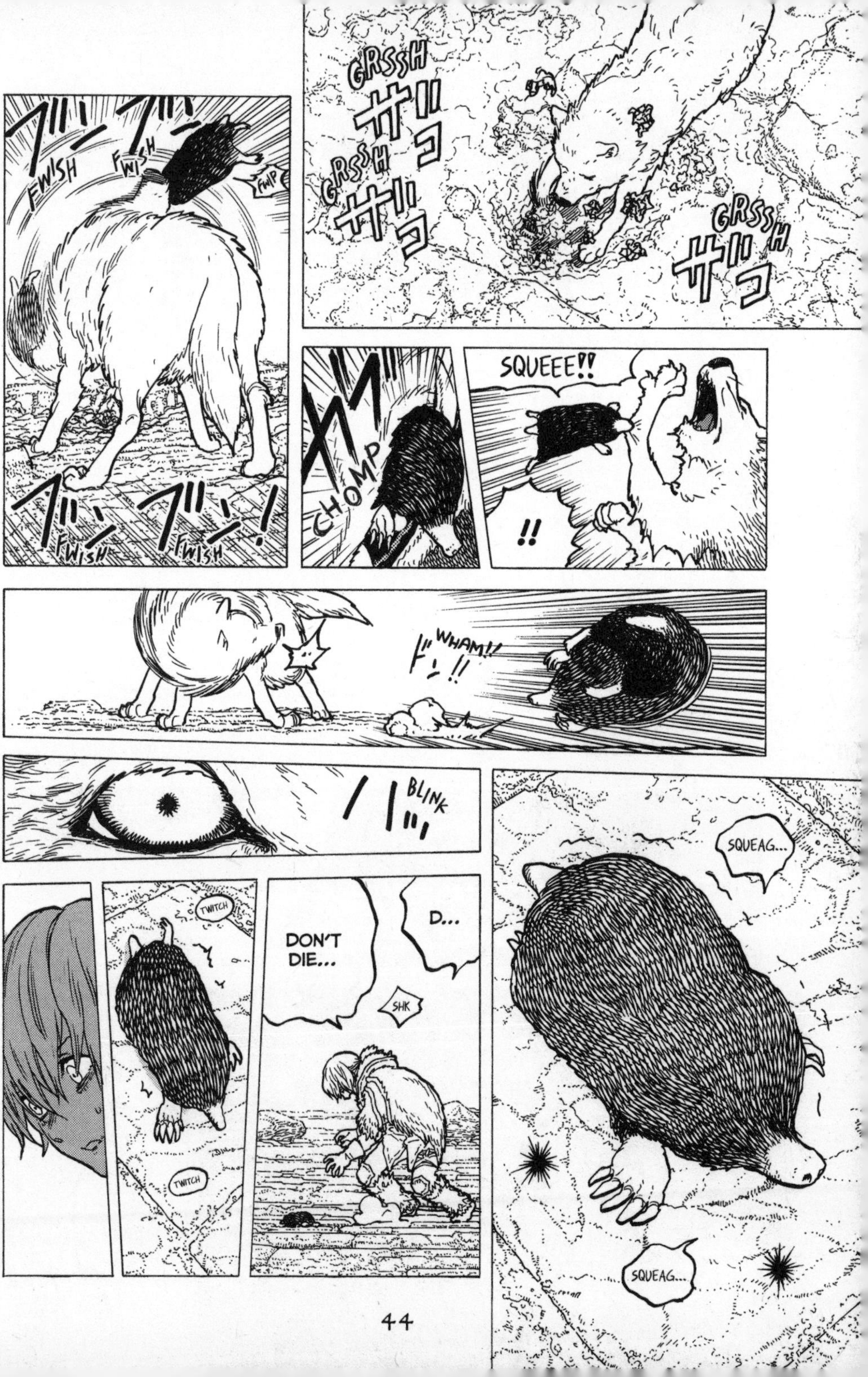

GRSSH
ザッ
GRSSH
ザッ
GRSSH
ザッ
SQUEEE!!
!!
CHOMP
FWISH
FWISH
FWIP
FWISH
FWISH
WHAM!!
ドン!!
SQUEAG...
SQUEAG...
BLINK
D...
DON'T DIE...
SHK
TWITCH
TWITCH

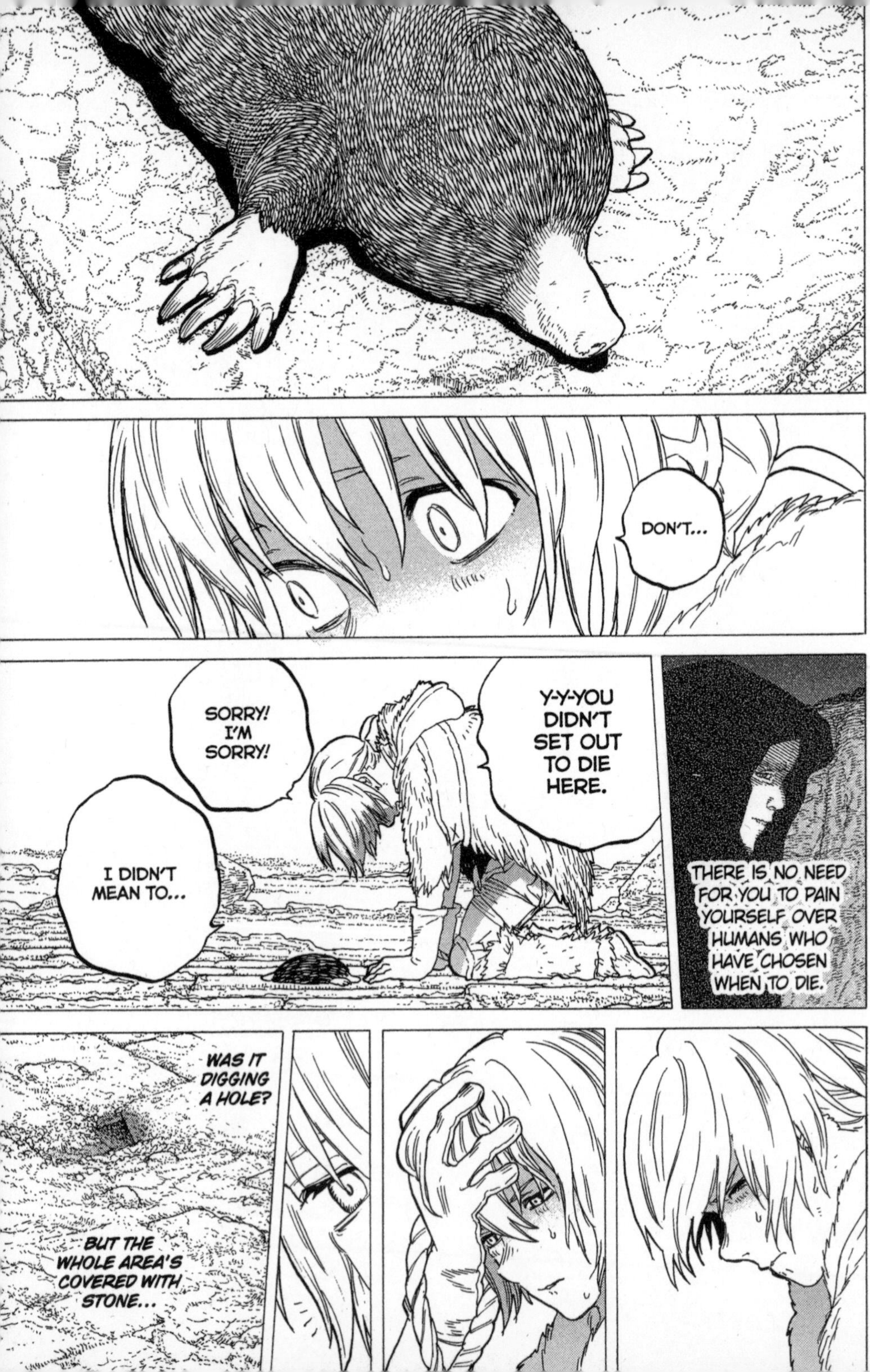
DON'T...
THERE IS NO NEED FOR YOU TO PAIN YOURSELF OVER HUMANS WHO HAVE CHOSEN WHEN TO DIE.
Y-Y-YOU DIDN'T SET OUT TO DIE HERE.
SORRY! I'M SORRY!
I DIDN'T MEAN TO...
WAS IT DIGGING A HOLE?
BUT THE WHOLE AREA'S COVERED WITH STONE...

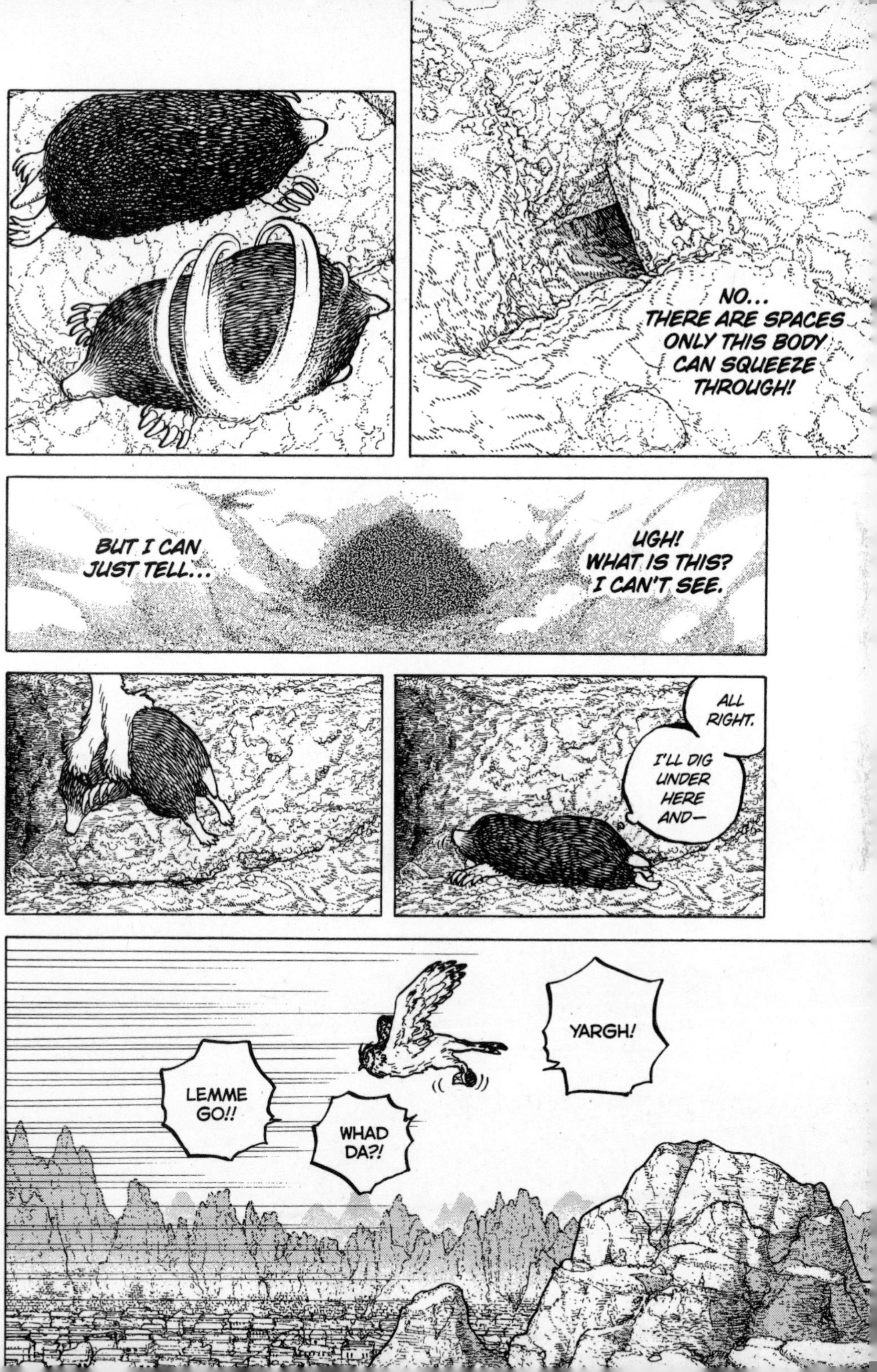
NO... THERE ARE SPACES ONLY THIS BODY CAN SQUEEZE THROUGH!
UGH! WHAT IS THIS? I CAN'T SEE.
BUT I CAN JUST TELL...
ALL RIGHT.
I'LL DIG UNDER HERE AND—
YARGH!
WHAD DA?!
LEMME GO!!

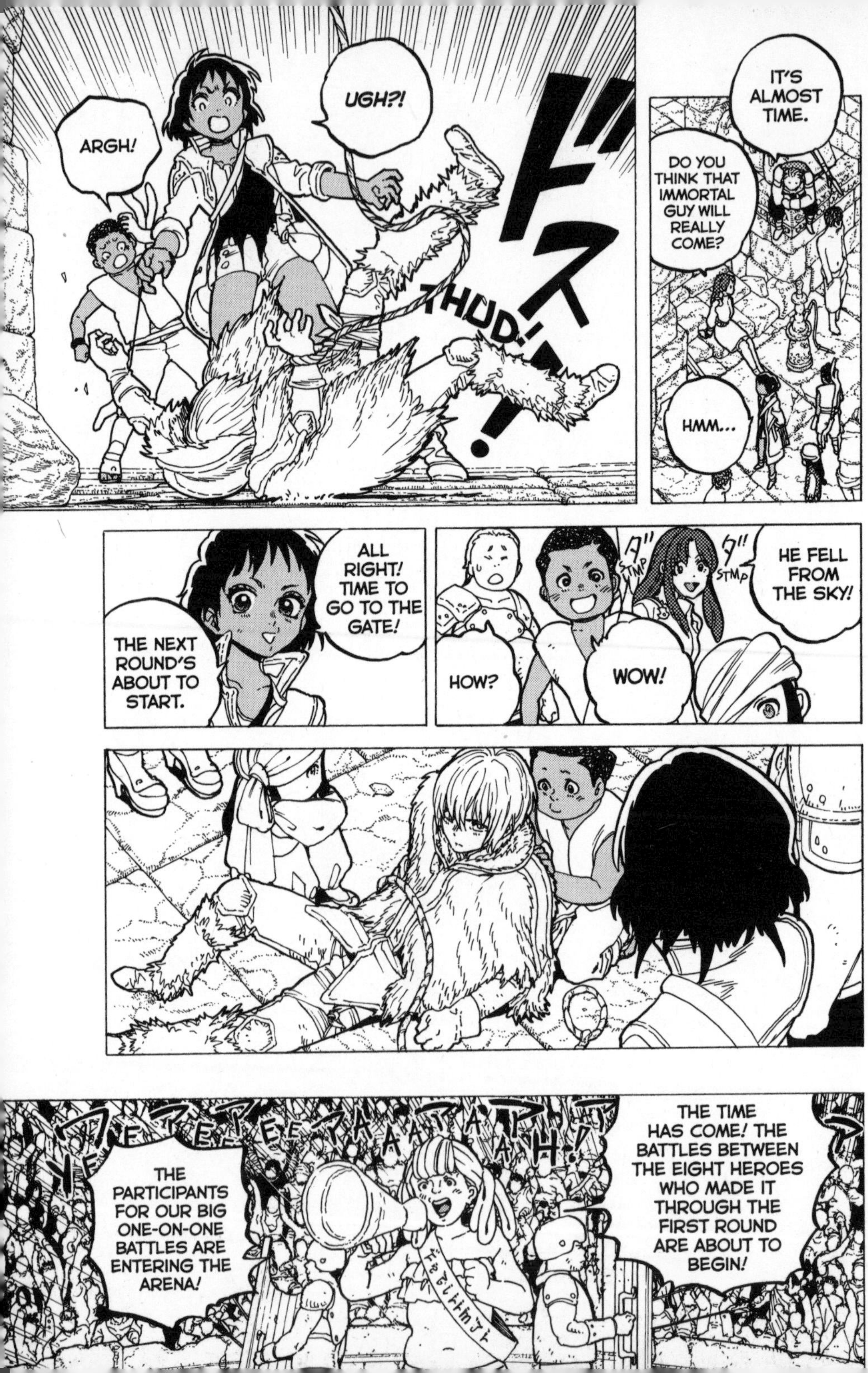

IT'S ALMOST TIME.
DO YOU THINK THAT IMMORTAL GUY WILL REALLY COME?
HMM...
ドス
UGH?!
ARGH!
THUD!
HE FELL FROM THE SKY!
ダ STMP
ダ STMP
WOW!
HOW?
ALL RIGHT! TIME TO GO TO THE GATE!
THE NEXT ROUND'S ABOUT TO START.
THE TIME HAS COME! THE BATTLES BETWEEN THE EIGHT HEROES WHO MADE IT THROUGH THE FIRST ROUND ARE ABOUT TO BEGIN!
THE PARTICIPANTS FOR OUR BIG ONE-ON-ONE BATTLES ARE ENTERING THE ARENA!

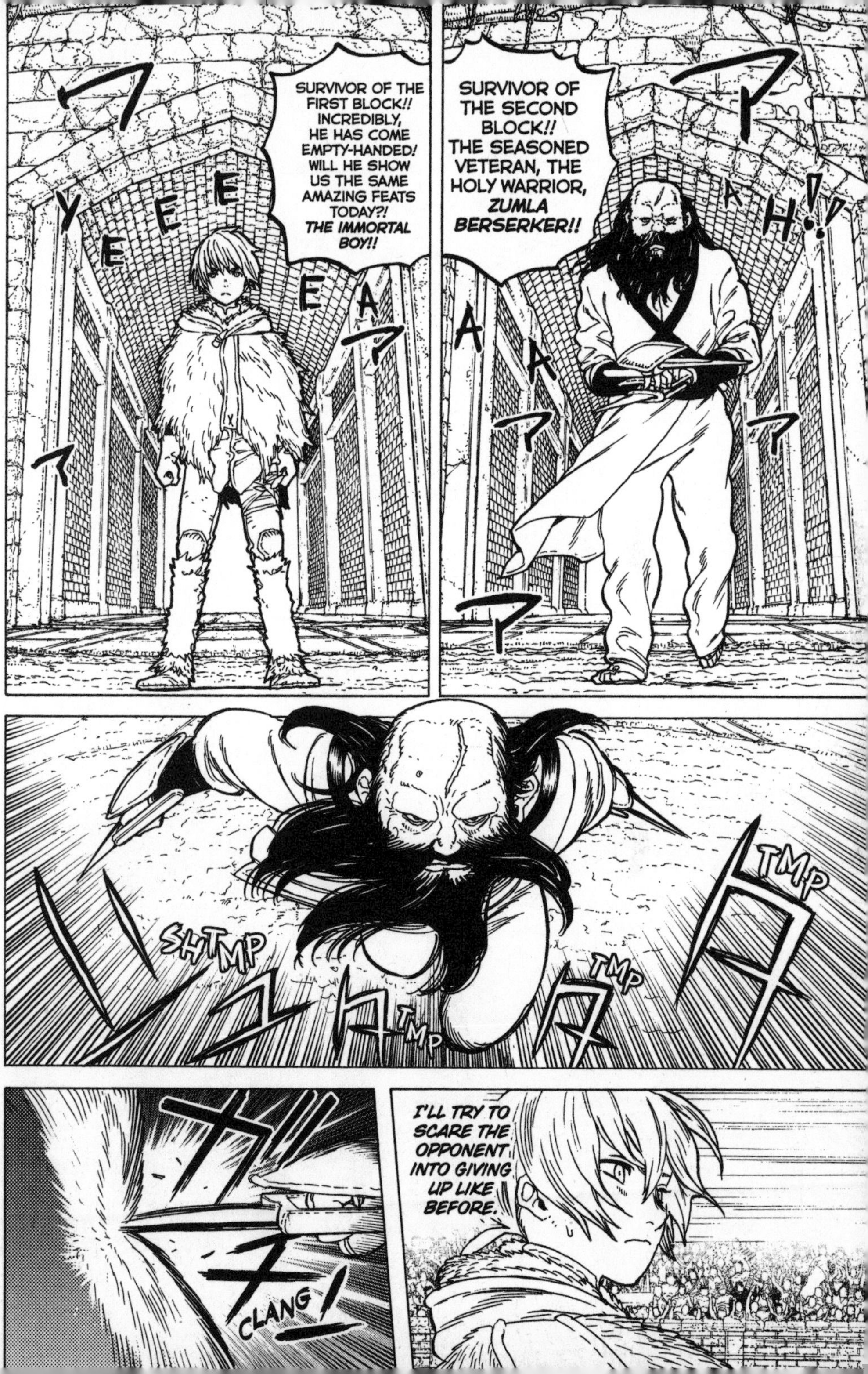
SURVIVOR OF THE SECOND BLOCK!! THE SEASONED VETERAN, THE HOLY WARRIOR, *ZUMLA BERSERKER!!*
AAAH!!
SURVIVOR OF THE FIRST BLOCK!! INCREDIBLY, HE HAS COME EMPTY-HANDED! WILL HE SHOW US THE SAME AMAZING FEATS TODAY?! *THE IMMORTAL BOY!!*
YEEEEA
TMP
TMP
TMP
SHTMP
I'LL TRY TO SCARE THE OPPONENT INTO GIVING UP LIKE BEFORE.
CLANG!

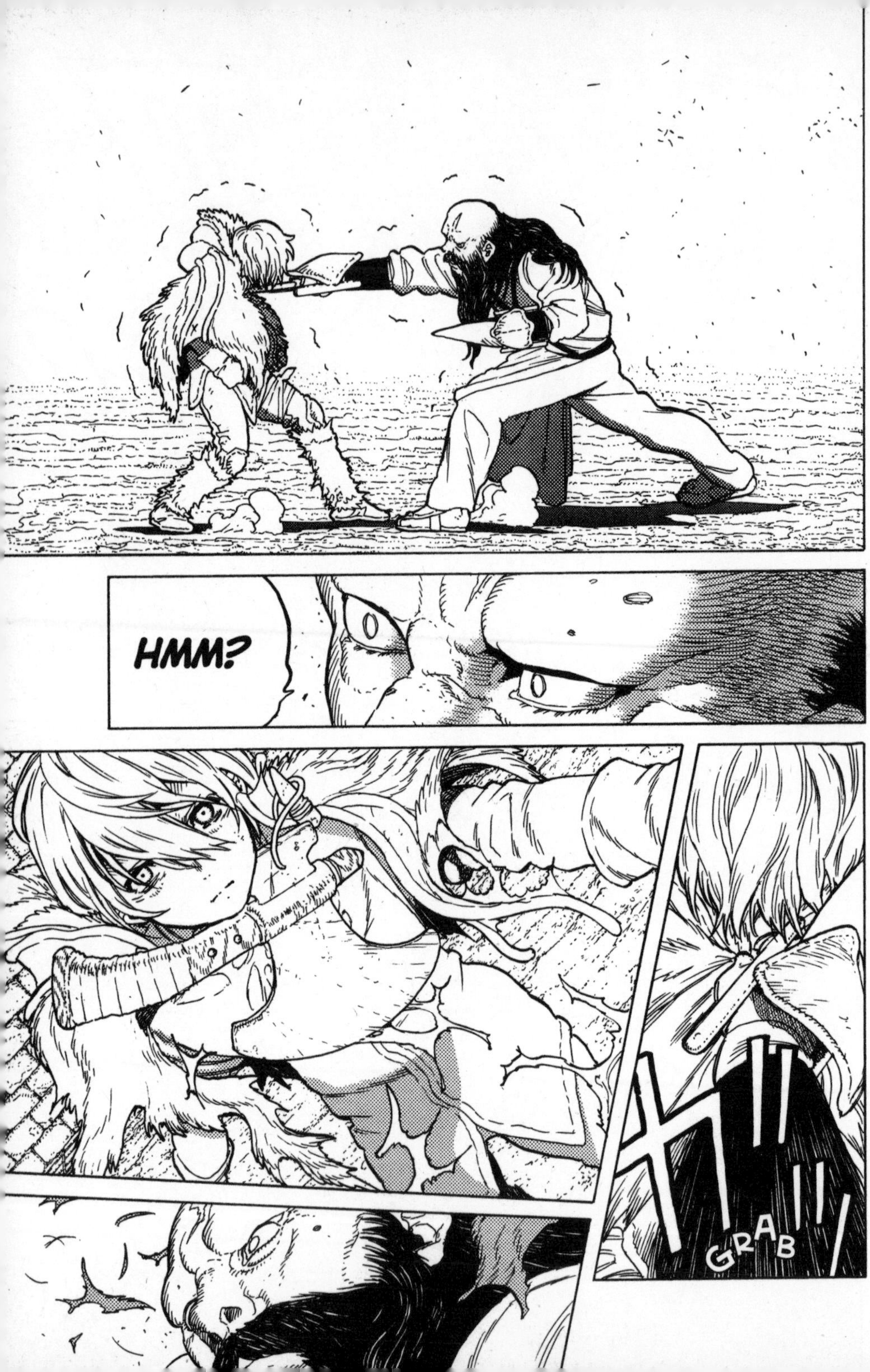
HMM?
GRAB

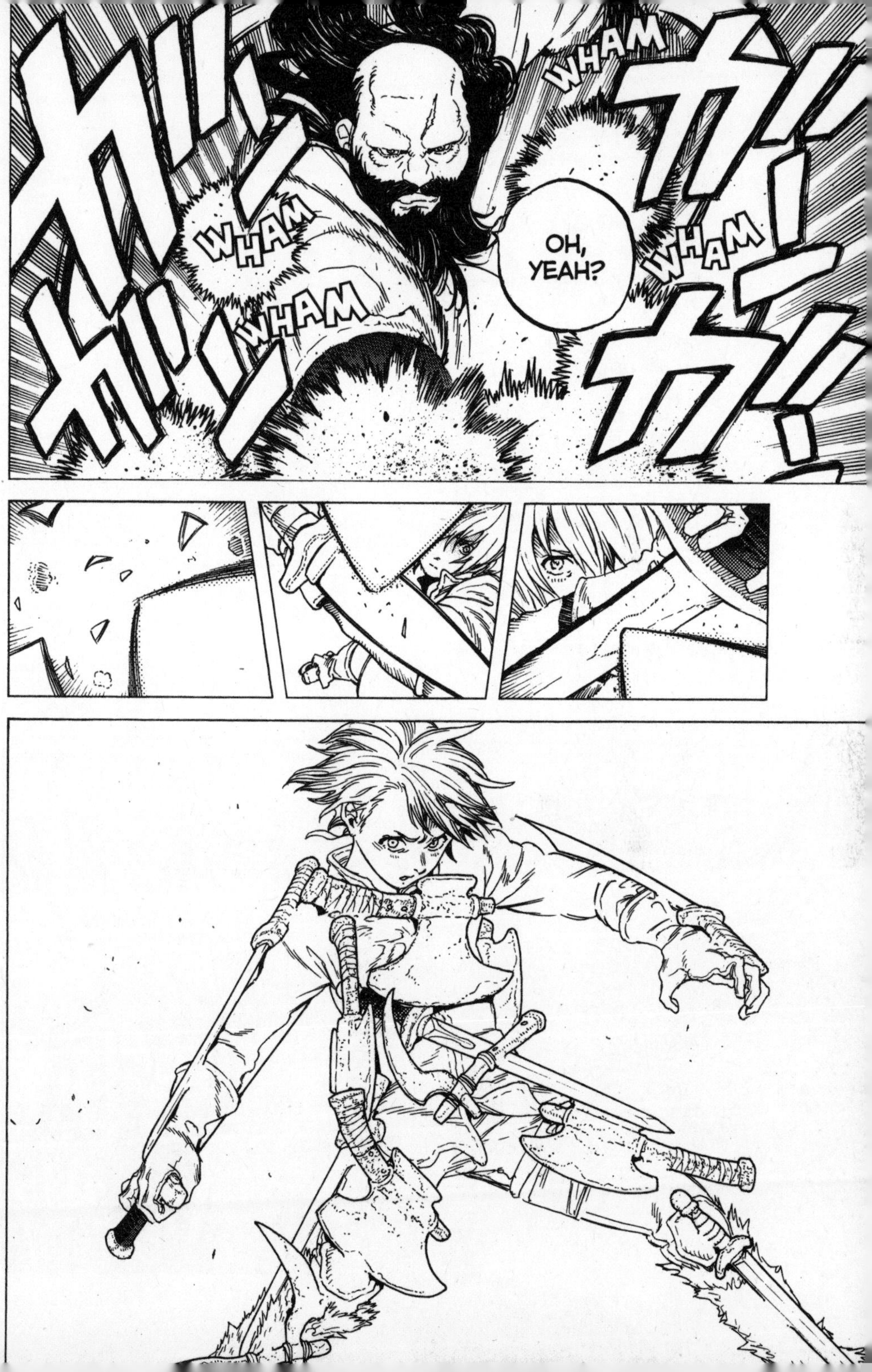
WHAM
WHAM
OH, YEAH?
WHAM
WHAM

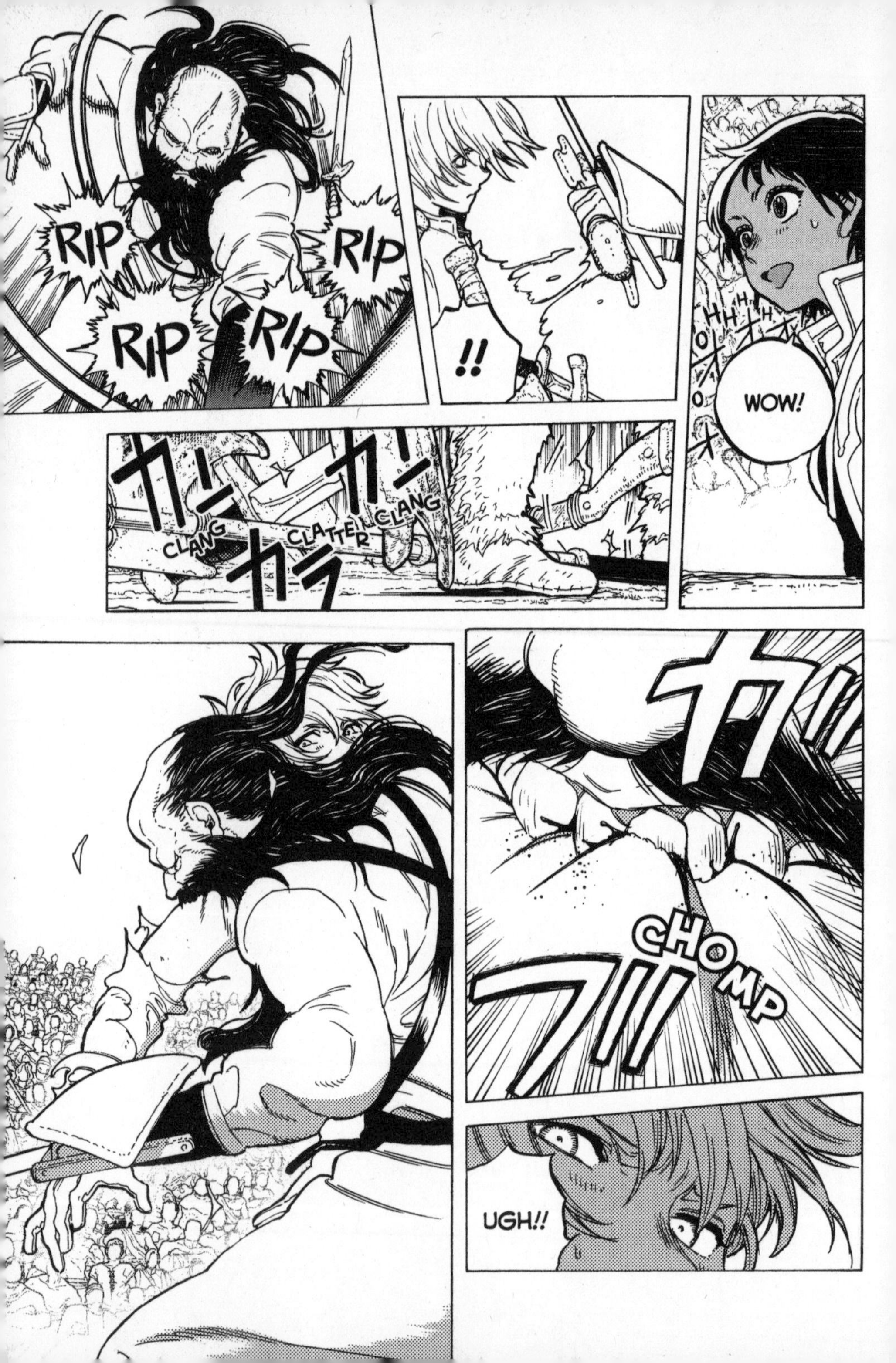
OHHH
WOW!
!!
RIP
RIP
RIP
RIP
CLANG
CLATTER
CLANG
CHOMP
UGH!!

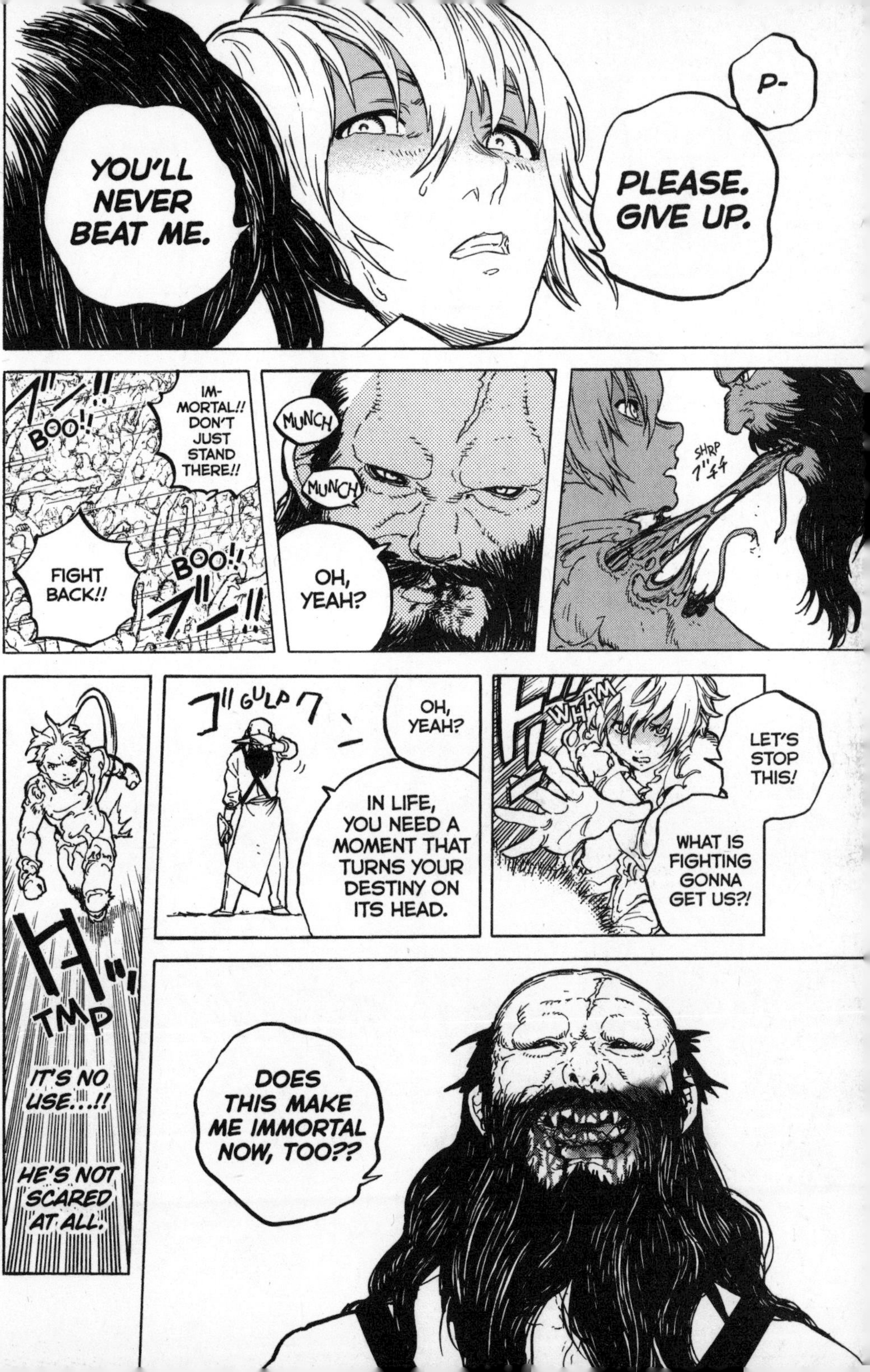
P-
PLEASE. GIVE UP.
YOU'LL NEVER BEAT ME.
SHRP
MUNCH
MUNCH
OH, YEAH?
IM-MORTAL!! DON'T JUST STAND THERE!!
BOO!!
FIGHT BACK!!
BOO!!
WHAM
LET'S STOP THIS!
WHAT IS FIGHTING GONNA GET US?!
GULP
OH, YEAH?
IN LIFE, YOU NEED A MOMENT THAT TURNS YOUR DESTINY ON ITS HEAD.
DOES THIS MAKE ME IMMORTAL NOW, TOO??
TMP
IT'S NO USE...!!
HE'S NOT SCARED AT ALL.

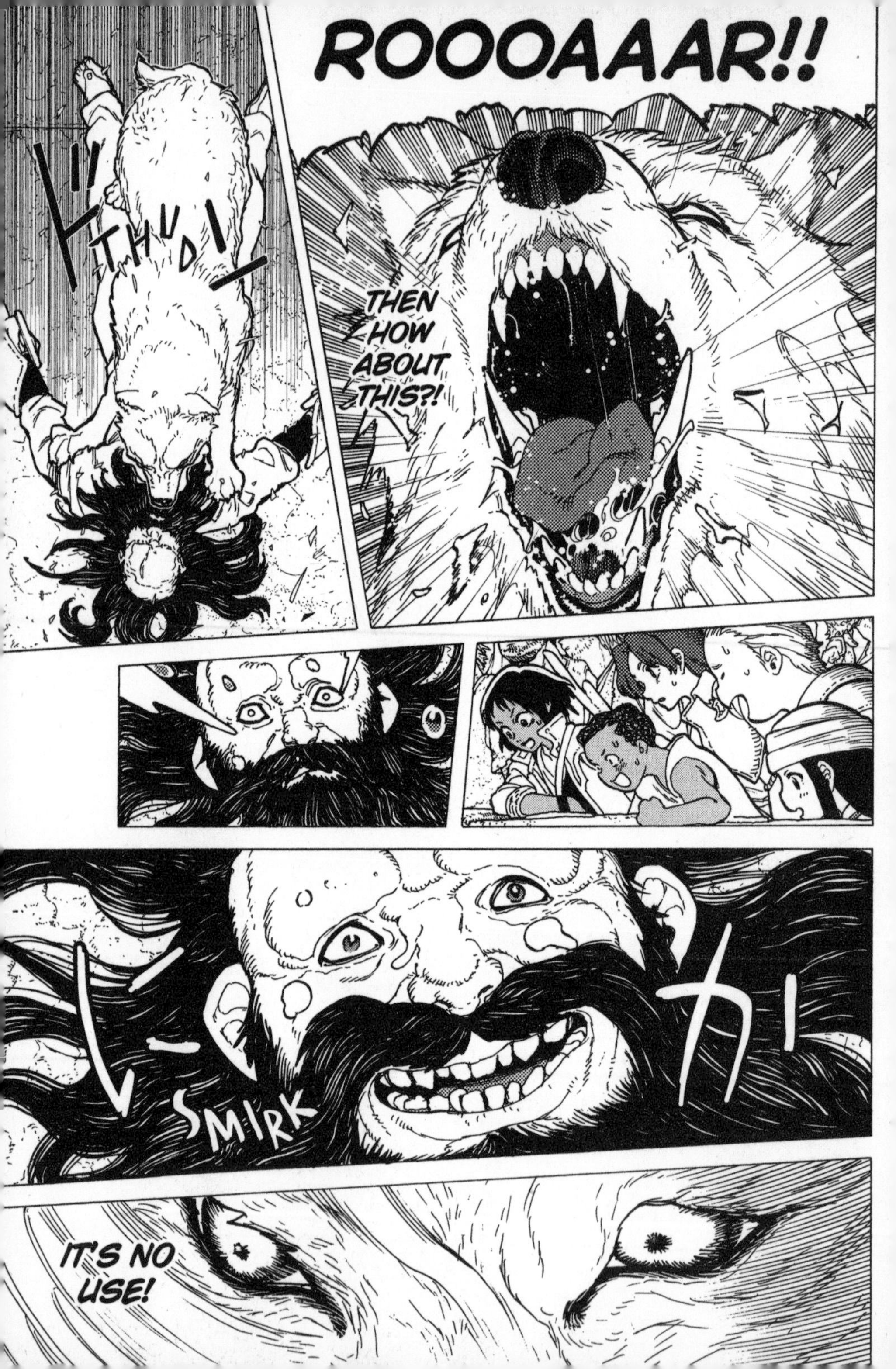
ROOOAAAR!!
THEN HOW ABOUT THIS?!
THUD
SMIRK
IT'S NO USE!

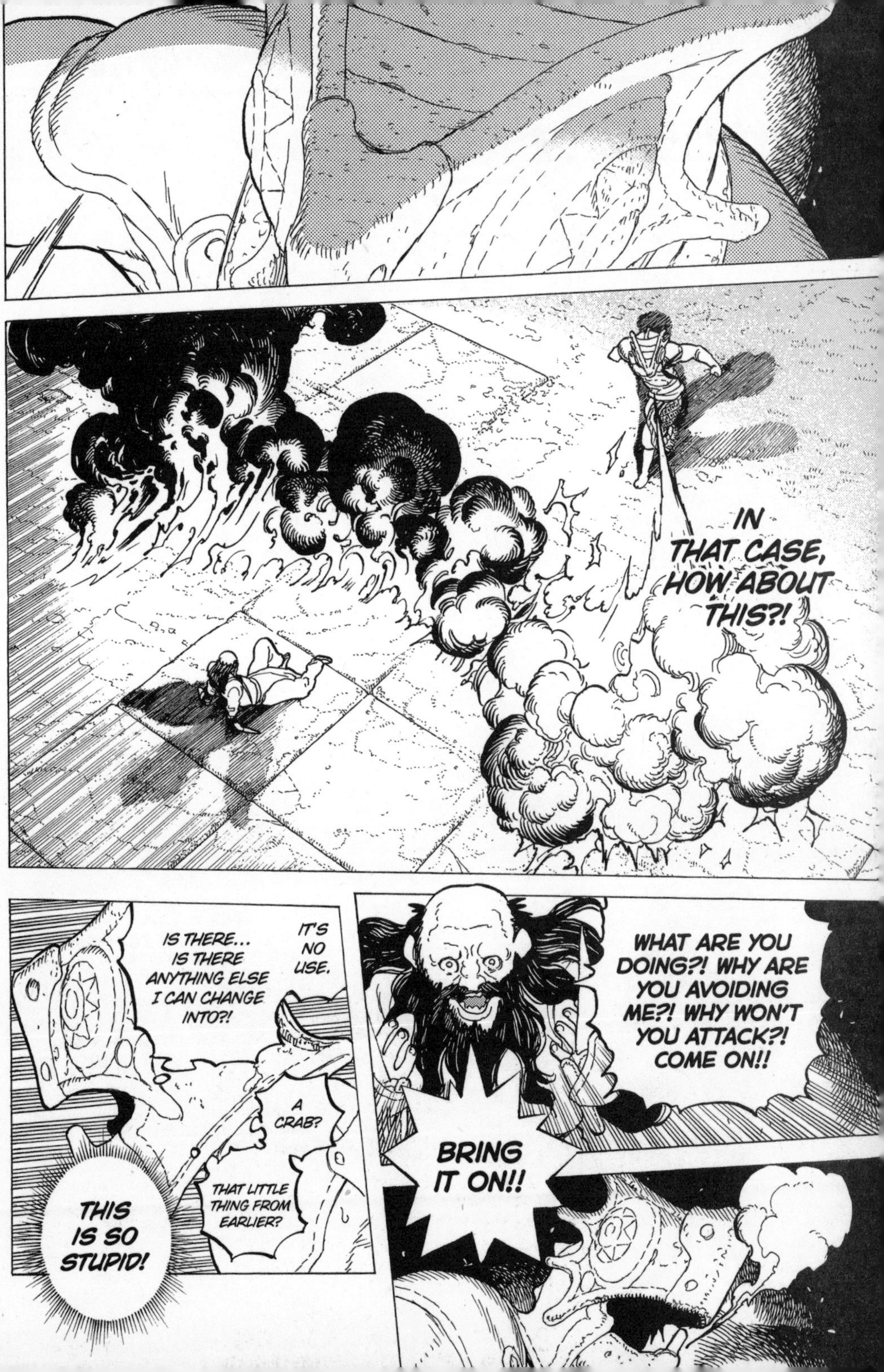
IN THAT CASE, HOW ABOUT THIS?!
WHAT ARE YOU DOING?! WHY ARE YOU AVOIDING ME?! WHY WON'T YOU ATTACK?! COME ON!!
BRING IT ON!!
IT'S NO USE.
IS THERE... IS THERE ANYTHING ELSE I CAN CHANGE INTO?!
A CRAB?
THAT LITTLE THING FROM EARLIER?
THIS IS SO STUPID!

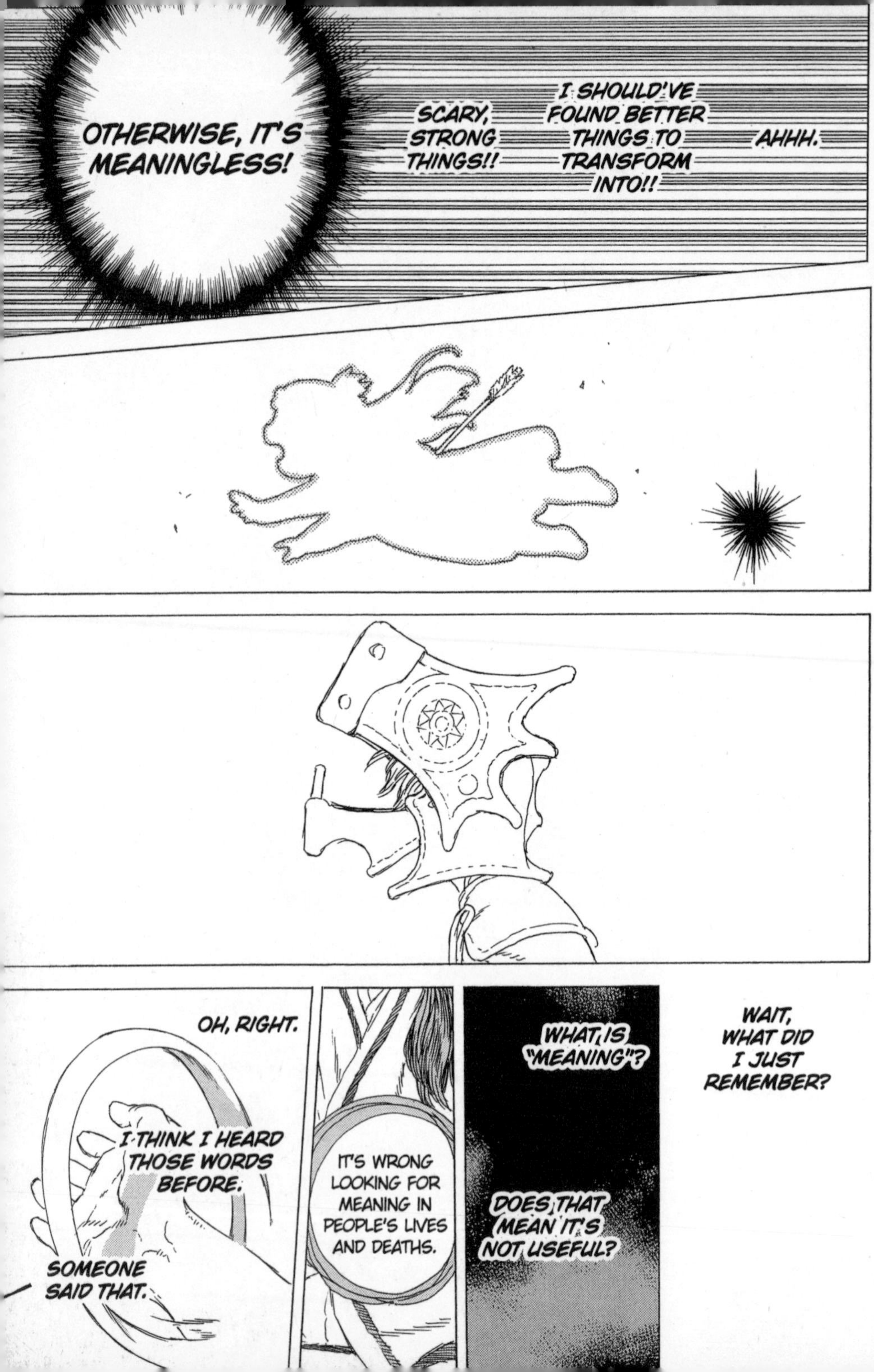
AHHH.
I SHOULD'VE FOUND BETTER THINGS TO TRANSFORM INTO!!
SCARY, STRONG THINGS!!
OTHERWISE, IT'S MEANINGLESS!
WAIT, WHAT DID I JUST REMEMBER?
WHAT IS "MEANING"?
DOES THAT MEAN IT'S NOT USEFUL?
IT'S WRONG LOOKING FOR MEANING IN PEOPLE'S LIVES AND DEATHS.
OH, RIGHT.
I THINK I HEARD THOSE WORDS BEFORE.
SOMEONE SAID THAT.

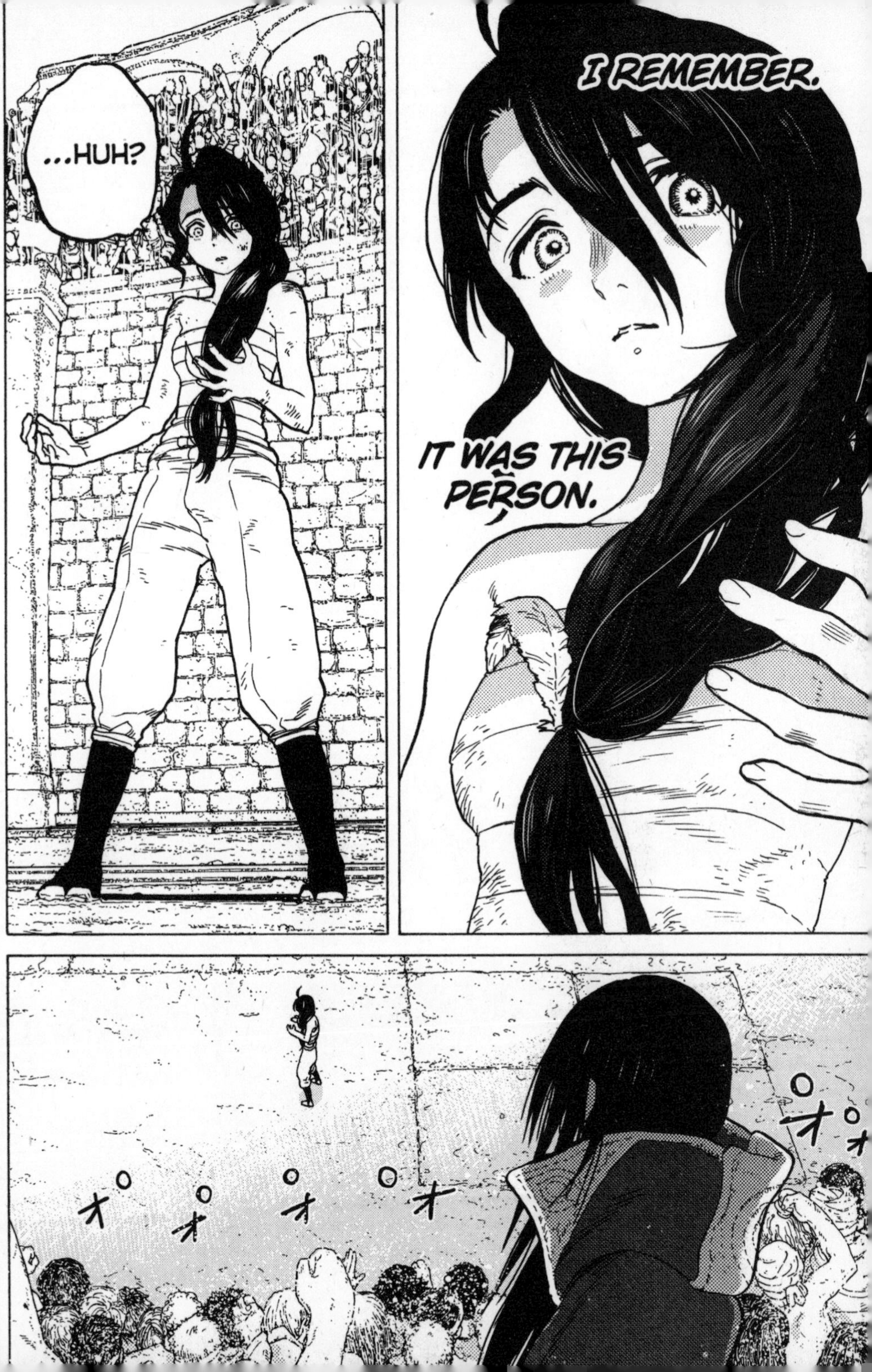
I REMEMBER.
IT WAS THIS PERSON.
...HUH?

#38 Query

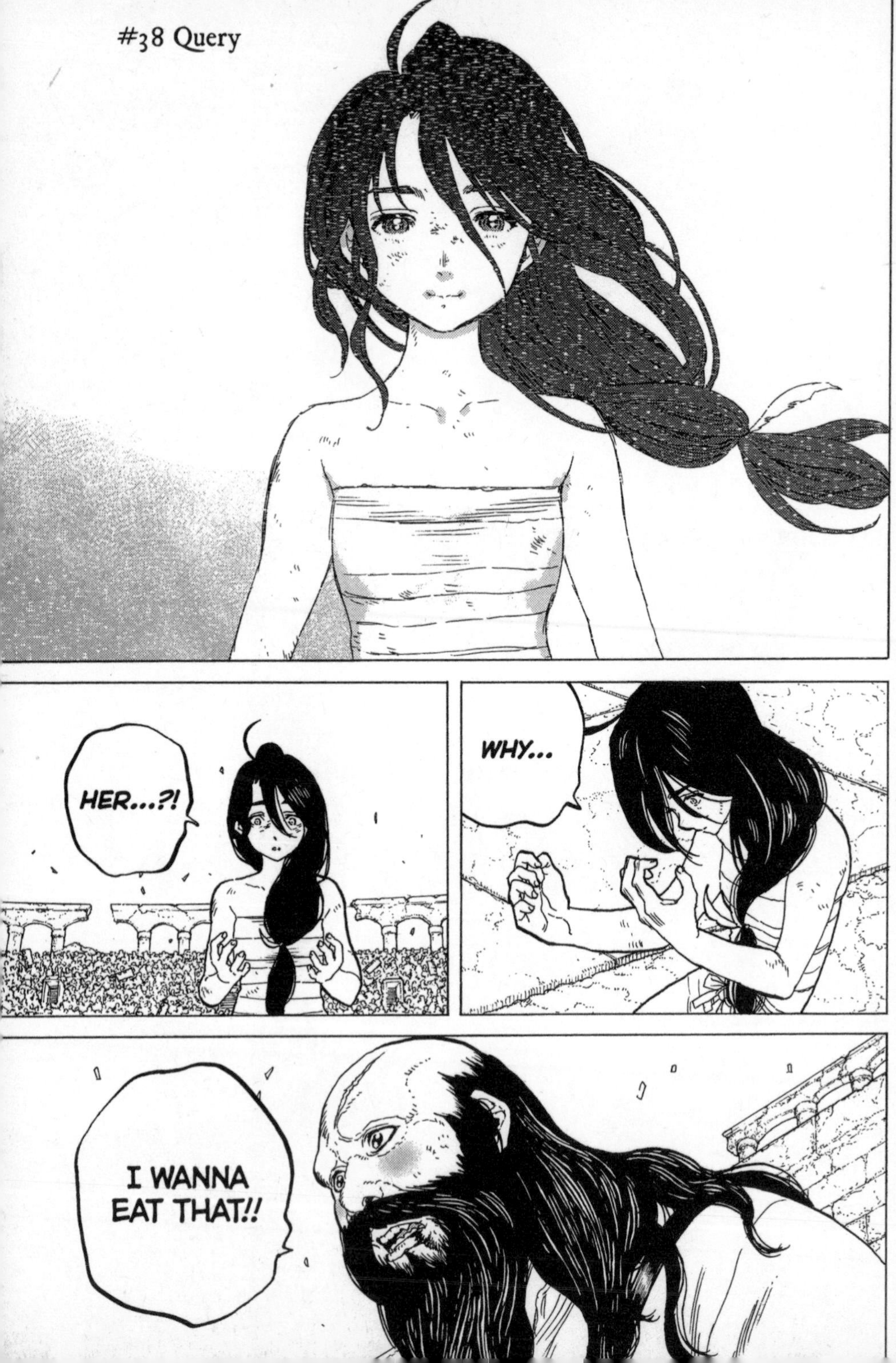
WHY...
HER...?!
I WANNA EAT THAT!!

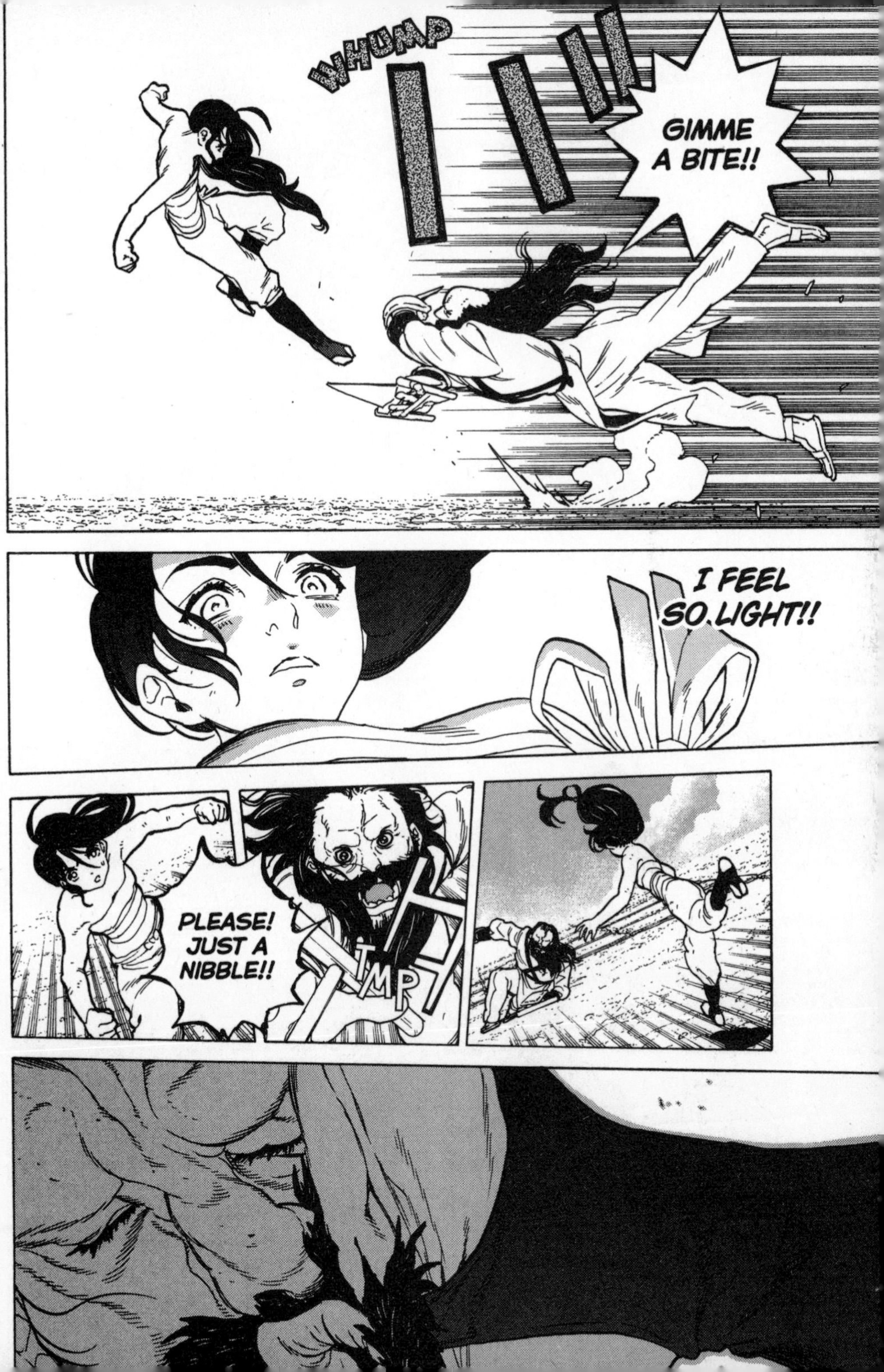
WHUMP
GIMME A BITE!!
I FEEL SO LIGHT!!
PLEASE! JUST A NIBBLE!!
TMP

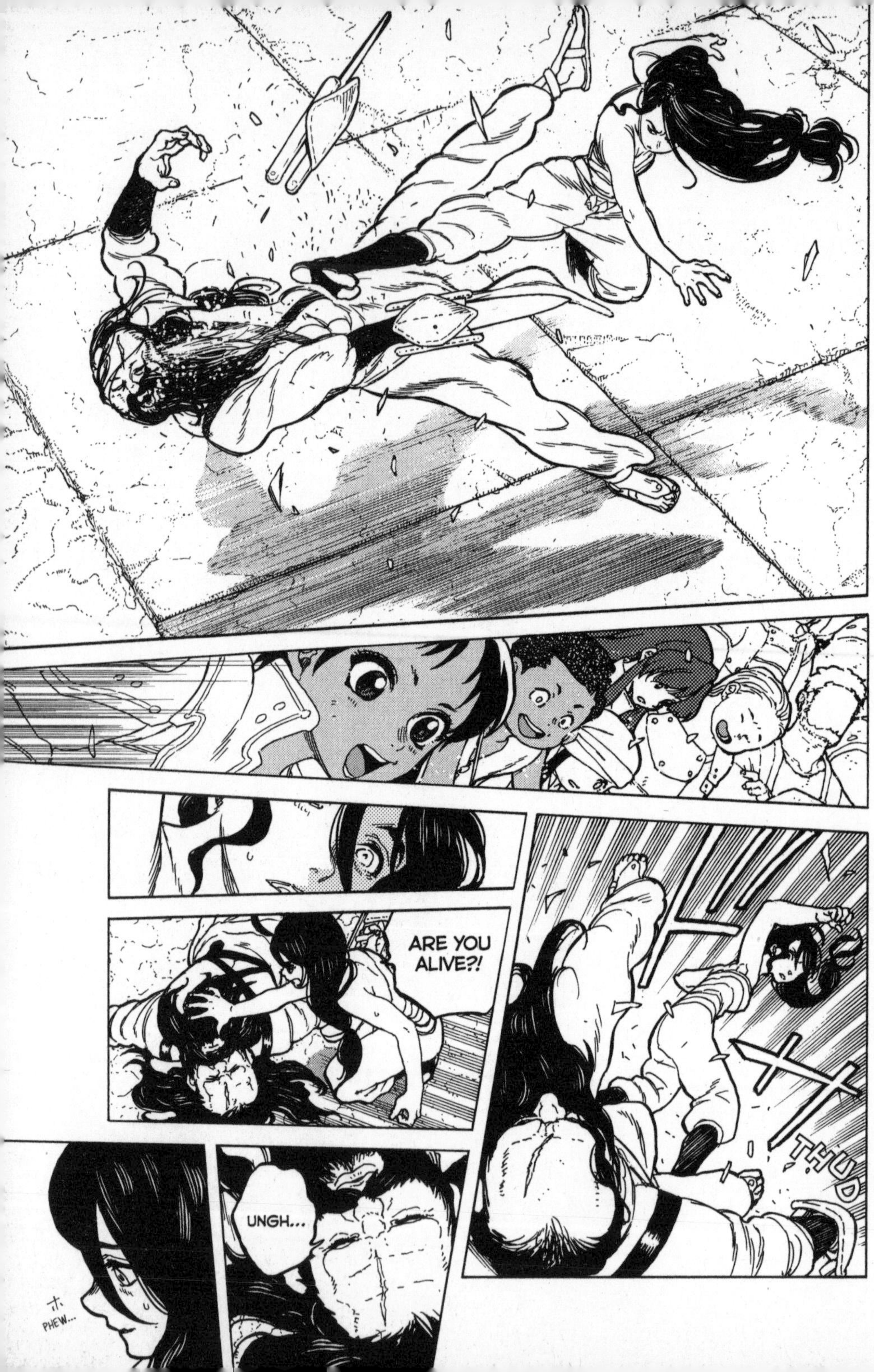
THUD
ARE YOU ALIVE?!
UNGH...
PHEW...

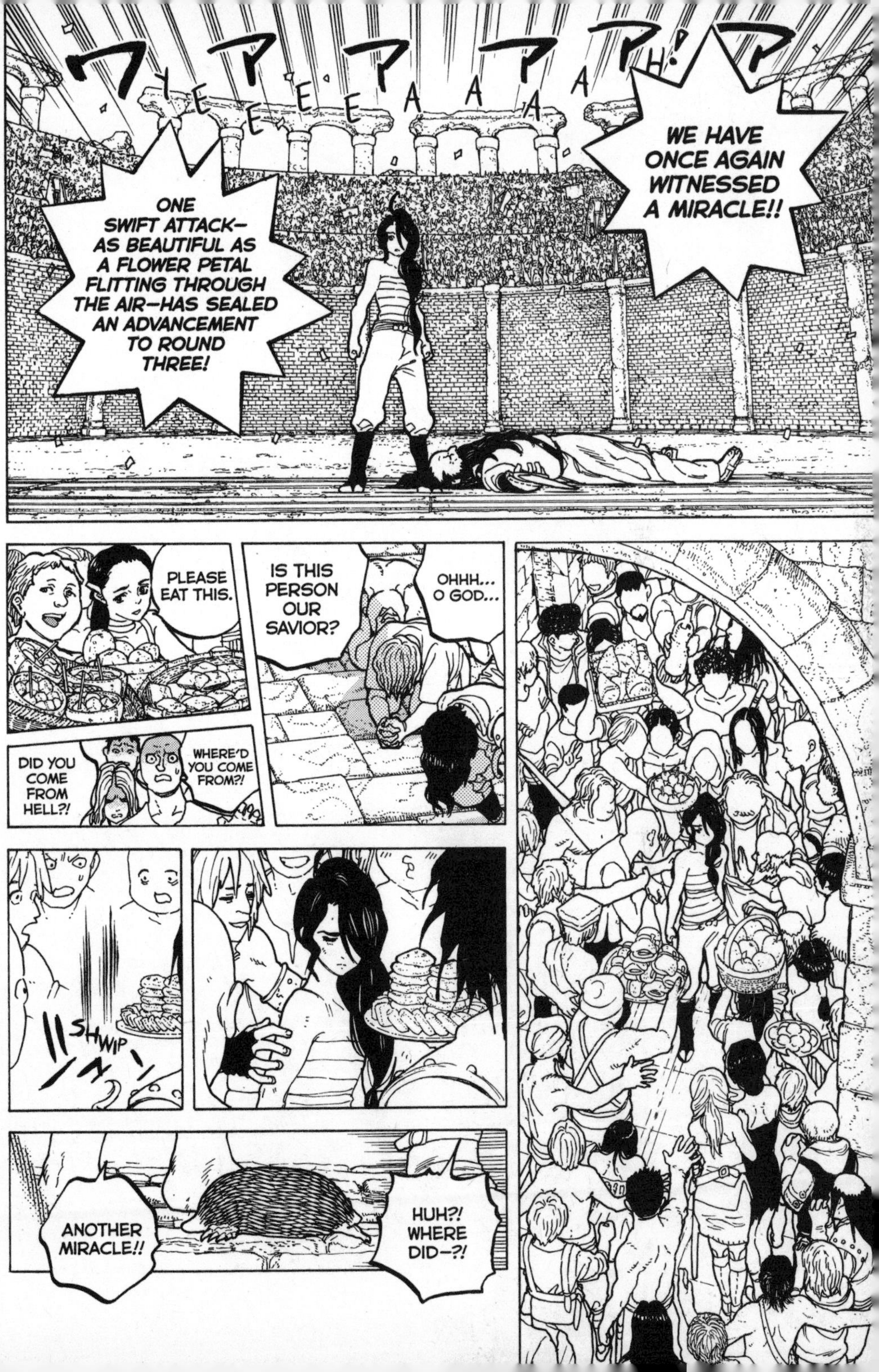
ワアアアア!ア
YEEEAAAAH!
WE HAVE ONCE AGAIN WITNESSED A MIRACLE!!
ONE SWIFT ATTACK—AS BEAUTIFUL AS A FLOWER PETAL FLITTING THROUGH THE AIR—HAS SEALED AN ADVANCEMENT TO ROUND THREE!
OHHH... O GOD...
IS THIS PERSON OUR SAVIOR?
PLEASE EAT THIS.
WHERE'D YOU COME FROM?!
DID YOU COME FROM HELL?!
SHWIP
HUH?! WHERE DID—?!
ANOTHER MIRACLE!!

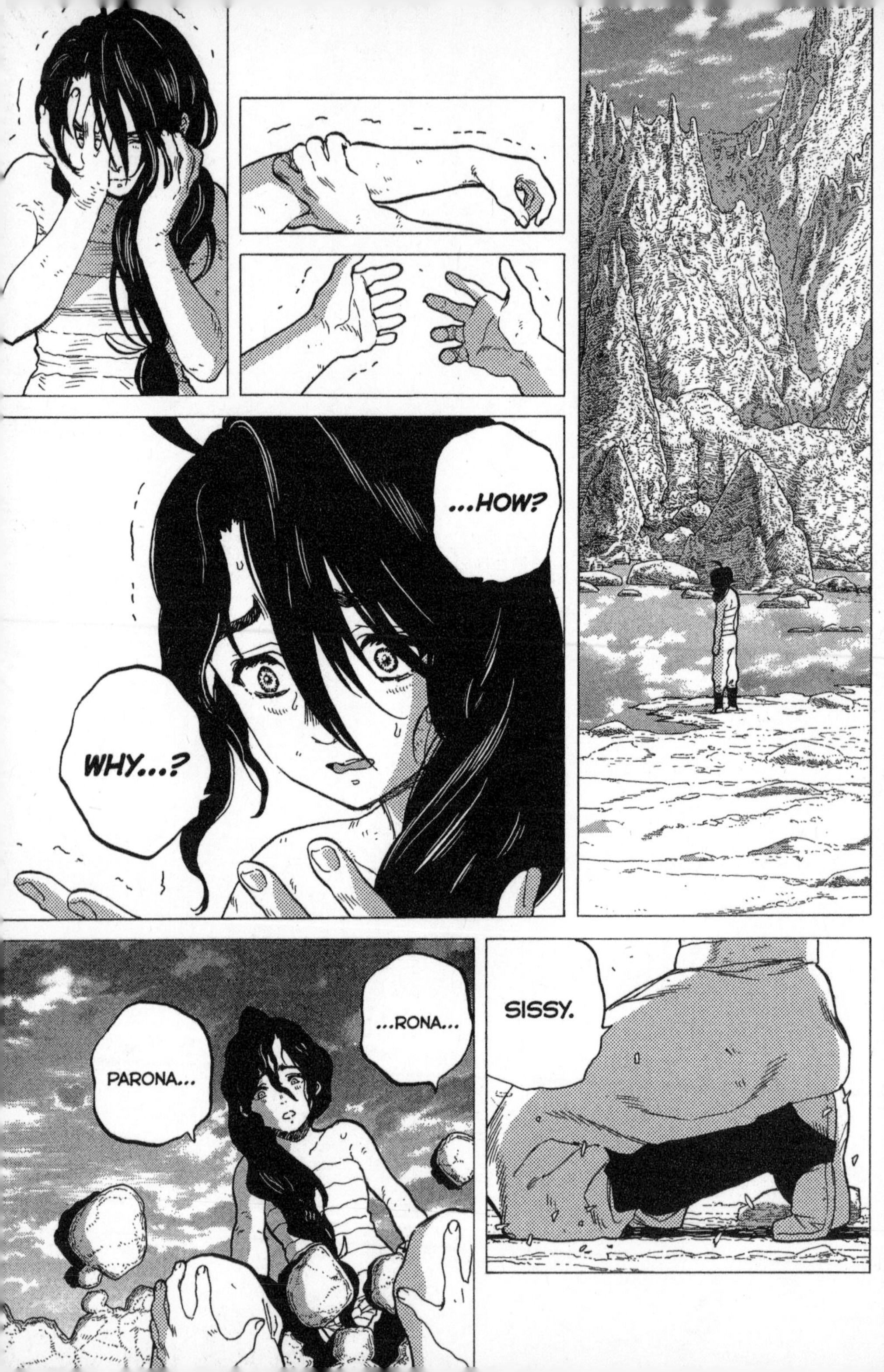
...HOW?
WHY...?
SISSY.
...RONA...
PARONA...

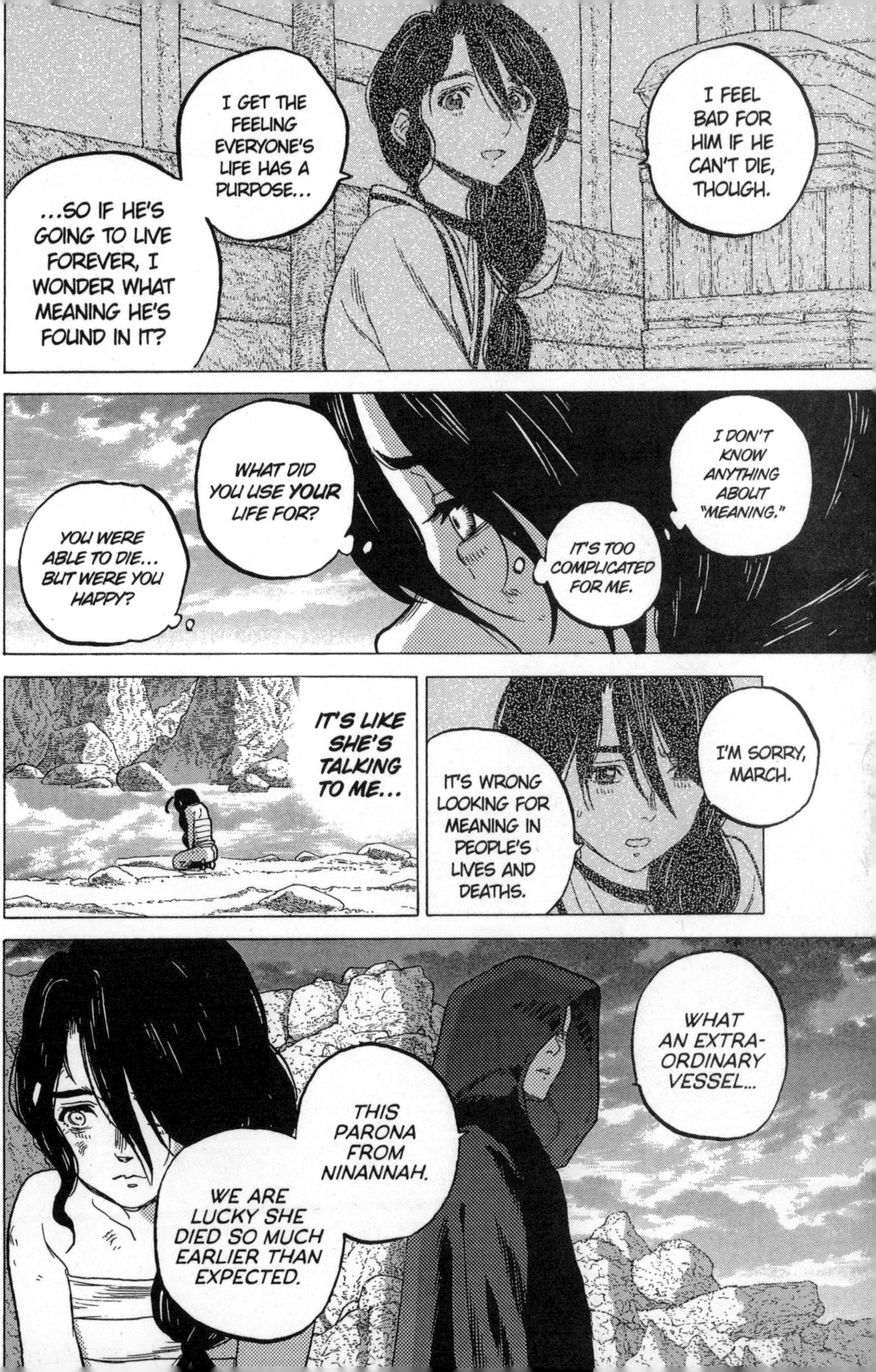
I FEEL BAD FOR HIM IF HE CAN'T DIE, THOUGH.
I GET THE FEELING EVERYONE'S LIFE HAS A PURPOSE...
...SO IF HE'S GOING TO LIVE FOREVER, I WONDER WHAT MEANING HE'S FOUND IN IT?
I DON'T KNOW ANYTHING ABOUT "MEANING."
IT'S TOO COMPLICATED FOR ME.
WHAT DID YOU USE **YOUR** LIFE FOR?
YOU WERE ABLE TO DIE... BUT WERE YOU HAPPY?
I'M SORRY, MARCH.
IT'S WRONG LOOKING FOR MEANING IN PEOPLE'S LIVES AND DEATHS.
IT'S LIKE SHE'S TALKING TO ME...
WHAT AN EXTRA-ORDINARY VESSEL...
THIS PARONA FROM NINANNAH.
WE ARE LUCKY SHE DIED SO MUCH EARLIER THAN EXPECTED.

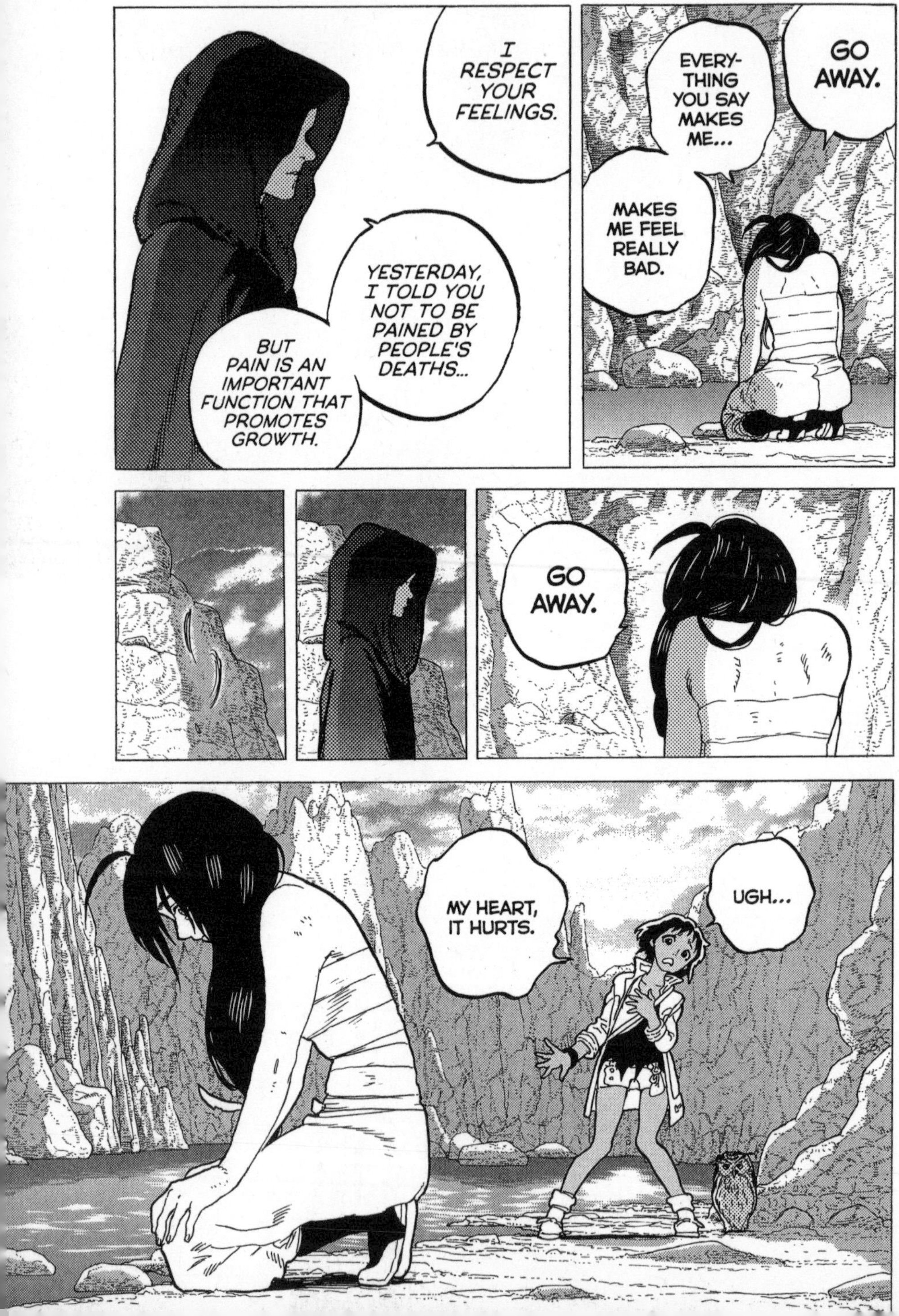
GO AWAY.
EVERY-THING YOU SAY MAKES ME...
MAKES ME FEEL REALLY BAD.
I RESPECT YOUR FEELINGS.
YESTERDAY, I TOLD YOU NOT TO BE PAINED BY PEOPLE'S DEATHS...
BUT PAIN IS AN IMPORTANT FUNCTION THAT PROMOTES GROWTH.
GO AWAY.
UGH...
MY HEART, IT HURTS.

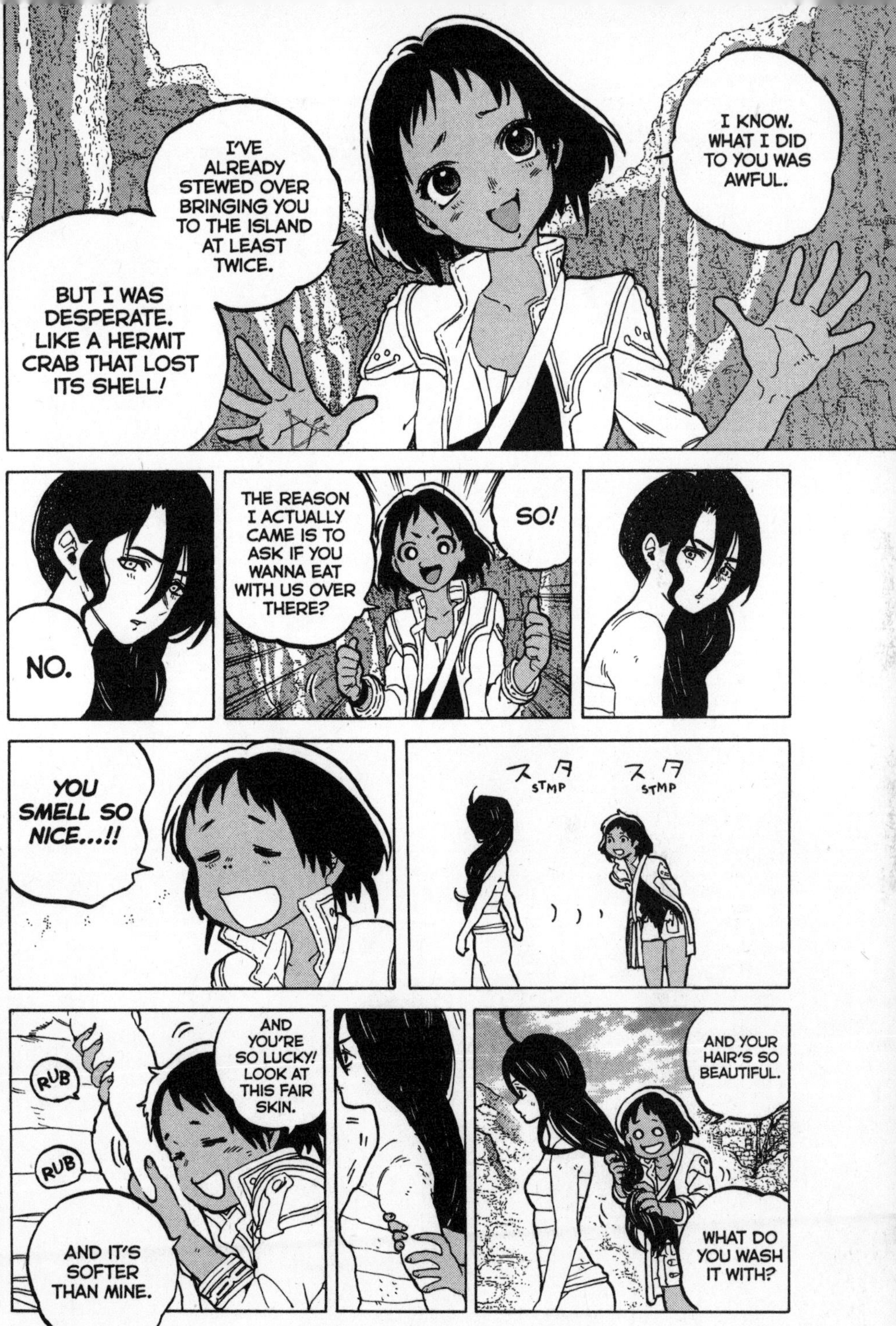
I KNOW. WHAT I DID TO YOU WAS AWFUL.
I'VE ALREADY STEWED OVER BRINGING YOU TO THE ISLAND AT LEAST TWICE.
BUT I WAS DESPERATE. LIKE A HERMIT CRAB THAT LOST ITS SHELL!
SO!
THE REASON I ACTUALLY CAME IS TO ASK IF YOU WANNA EAT WITH US OVER THERE?
NO.
スタ STMP
スタ STMP
YOU SMELL SO NICE...!!
AND YOUR HAIR'S SO BEAUTIFUL.
WHAT DO YOU WASH IT WITH?
AND YOU'RE SO LUCKY! LOOK AT THIS FAIR SKIN.
RUB
RUB
AND IT'S SOFTER THAN MINE.

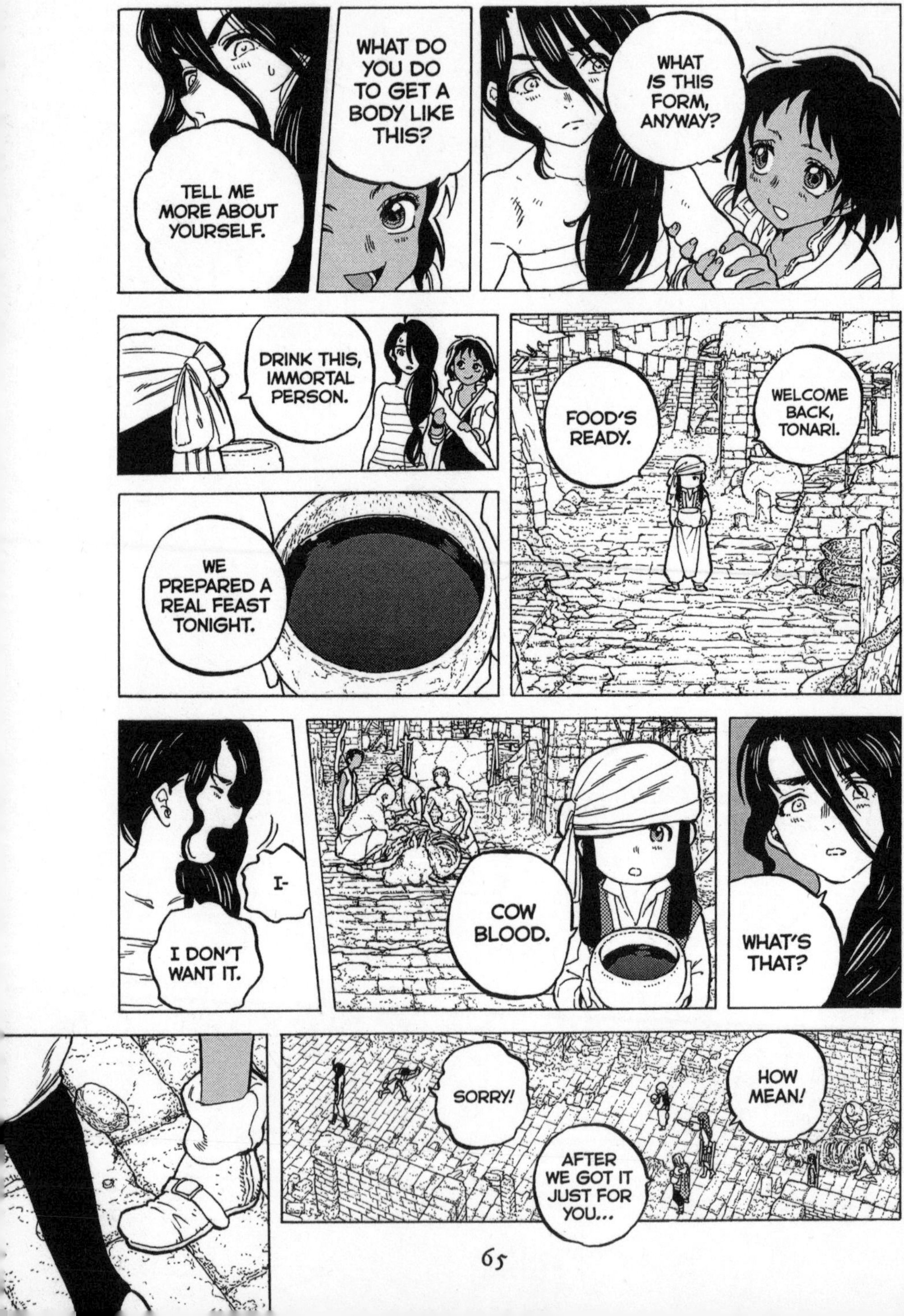
WHAT IS THIS FORM, ANYWAY?
WHAT DO YOU DO TO GET A BODY LIKE THIS?
TELL ME MORE ABOUT YOURSELF.
WELCOME BACK, TONARI.
FOOD'S READY.
DRINK THIS, IMMORTAL PERSON.
WE PREPARED A REAL FEAST TONIGHT.
WHAT'S THAT?
COW BLOOD.
I-
I DON'T WANT IT.
HOW MEAN!
SORRY!
AFTER WE GOT IT JUST FOR YOU...

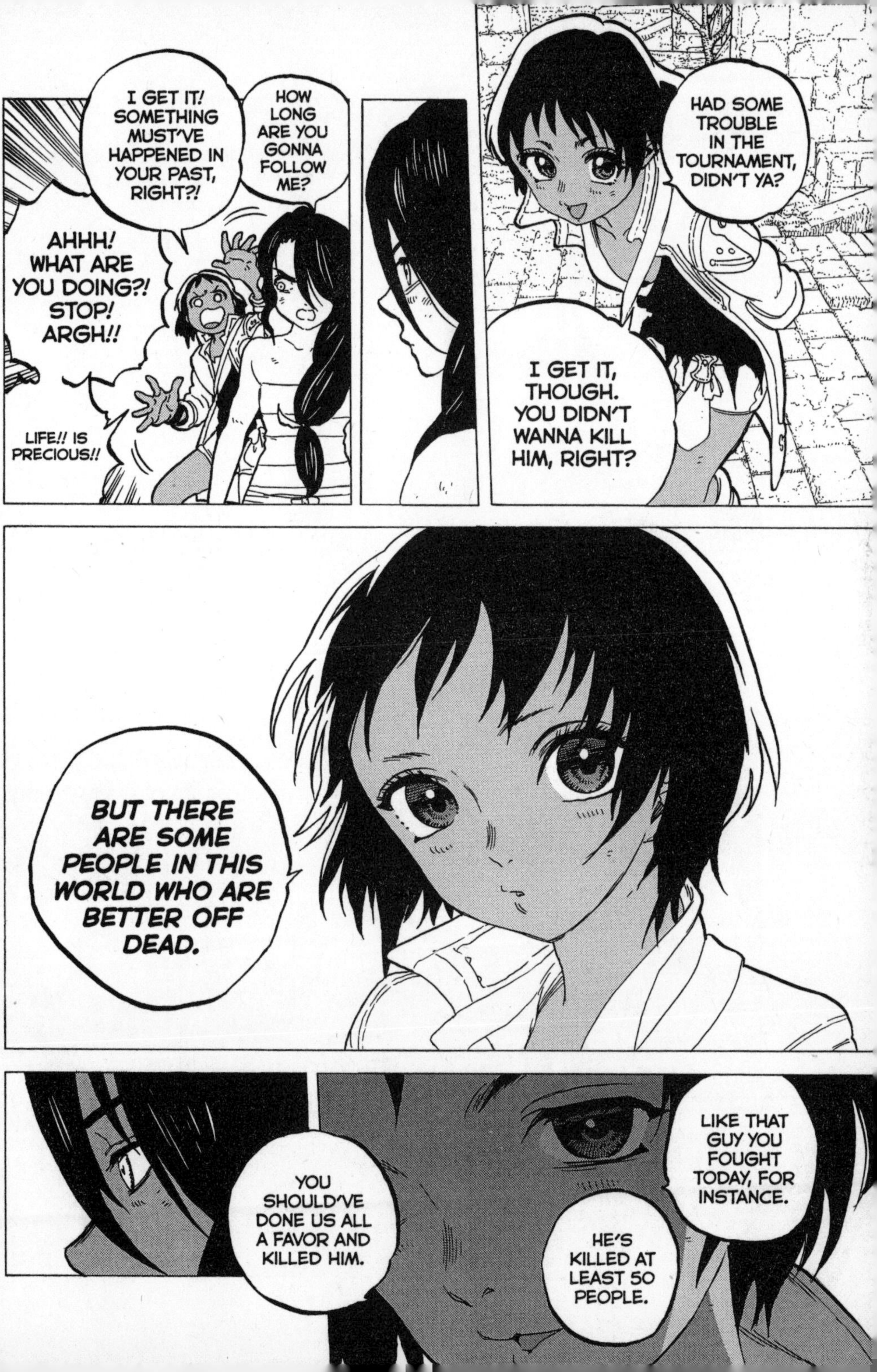
HAD SOME TROUBLE IN THE TOURNAMENT, DIDN'T YA?
I GET IT, THOUGH. YOU DIDN'T WANNA KILL HIM, RIGHT?
HOW LONG ARE YOU GONNA FOLLOW ME?
I GET IT! SOMETHING MUST'VE HAPPENED IN YOUR PAST, RIGHT?!
AHHH! WHAT ARE YOU DOING?! STOP! ARGH!!
LIFE!! IS PRECIOUS!!
BUT THERE ARE SOME PEOPLE IN THIS WORLD WHO ARE BETTER OFF DEAD.
LIKE THAT GUY YOU FOUGHT TODAY, FOR INSTANCE.
HE'S KILLED AT LEAST 50 PEOPLE.
YOU SHOULD'VE DONE US ALL A FAVOR AND KILLED HIM.

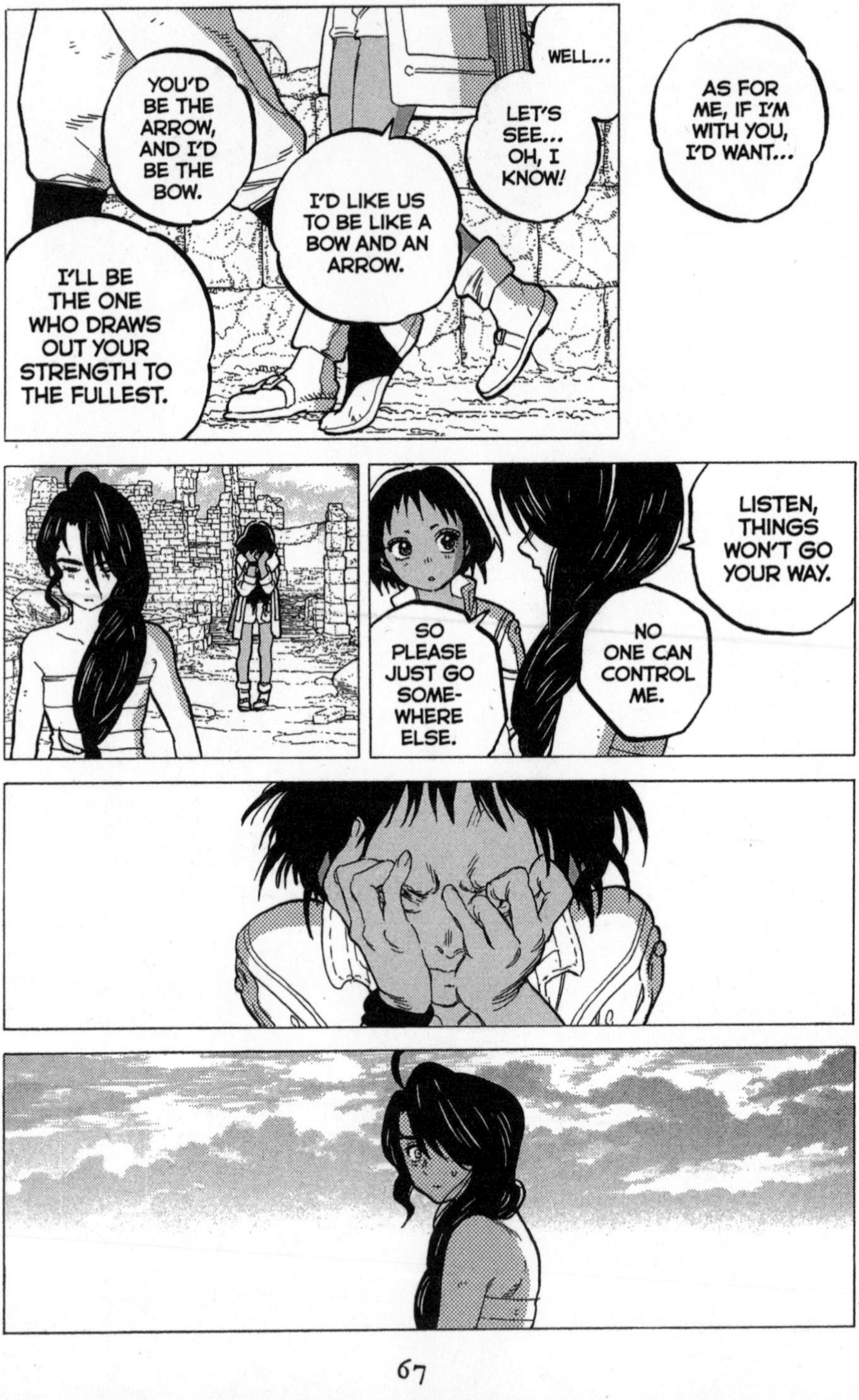
AS FOR ME, IF I'M WITH YOU, I'D WANT...
WELL...
LET'S SEE... OH, I KNOW!
I'D LIKE US TO BE LIKE A BOW AND AN ARROW.
YOU'D BE THE ARROW, AND I'D BE THE BOW.
I'LL BE THE ONE WHO DRAWS OUT YOUR STRENGTH TO THE FULLEST.
LISTEN, THINGS WON'T GO YOUR WAY.
NO ONE CAN CONTROL ME.
SO PLEASE JUST GO SOME-WHERE ELSE.

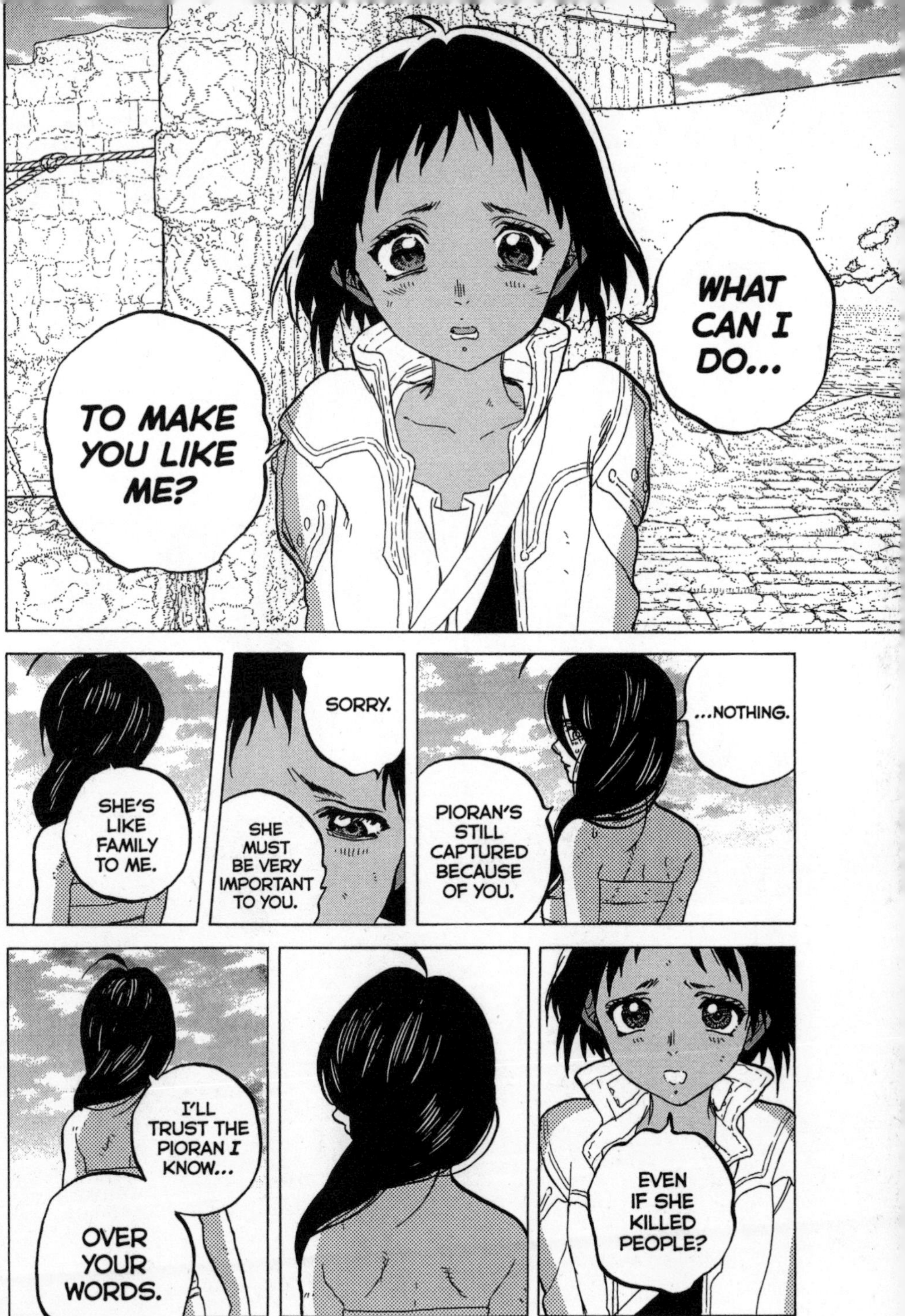
WHAT CAN I DO...
TO MAKE YOU LIKE ME?
...NOTHING.
PIORAN'S STILL CAPTURED BECAUSE OF YOU.
SORRY.
SHE MUST BE VERY IMPORTANT TO YOU.
SHE'S LIKE FAMILY TO ME.
EVEN IF SHE KILLED PEOPLE?
I'LL TRUST THE PIORAN *I* KNOW...
OVER YOUR WORDS.

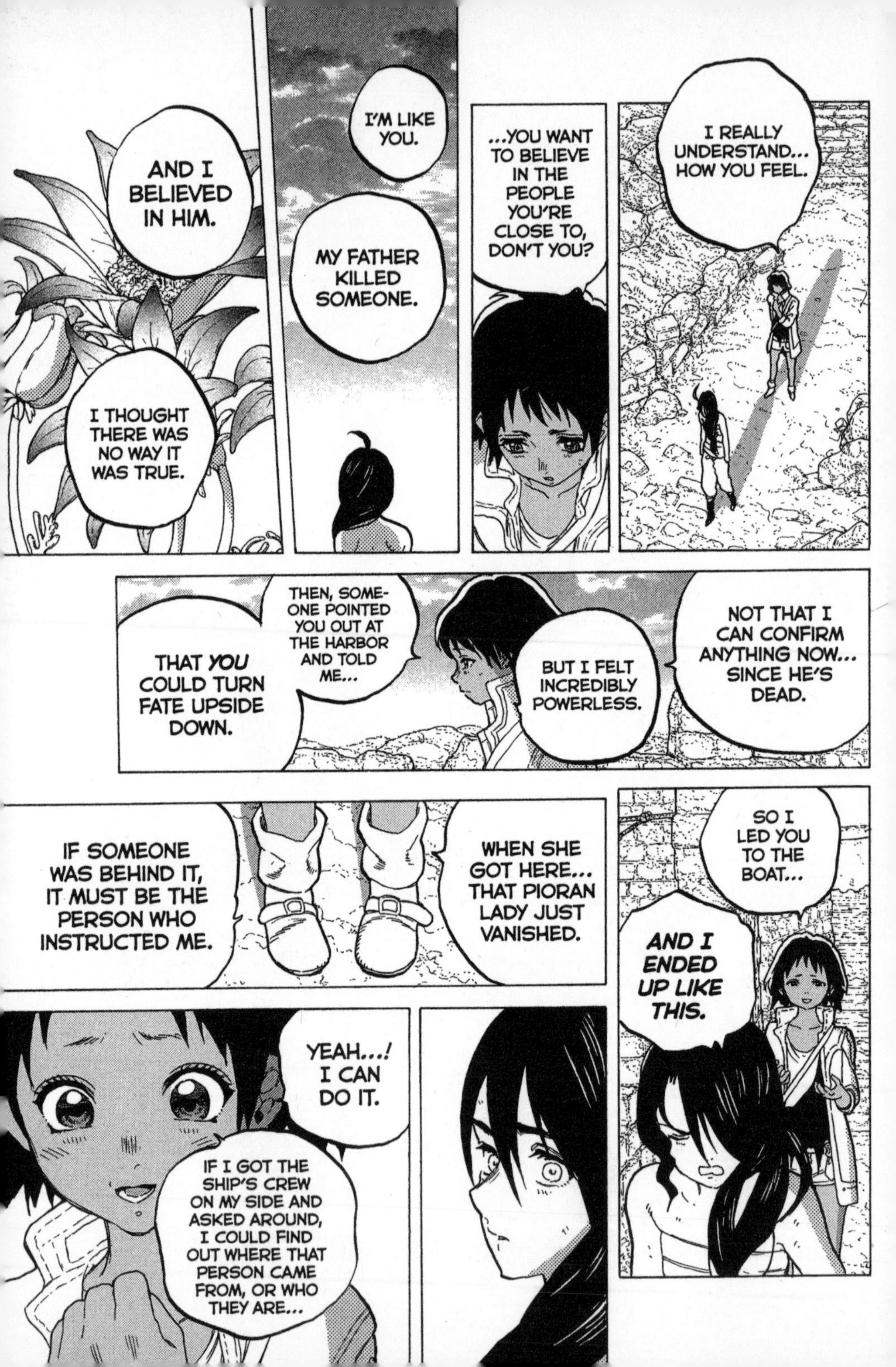
I REALLY UNDERSTAND... HOW YOU FEEL.
...YOU WANT TO BELIEVE IN THE PEOPLE YOU'RE CLOSE TO, DON'T YOU?
I'M LIKE YOU.
MY FATHER KILLED SOMEONE.
AND I BELIEVED IN HIM.
I THOUGHT THERE WAS NO WAY IT WAS TRUE.
NOT THAT I CAN CONFIRM ANYTHING NOW... SINCE HE'S DEAD.
BUT I FELT INCREDIBLY POWERLESS.
THEN, SOME-ONE POINTED YOU OUT AT THE HARBOR AND TOLD ME...
THAT *YOU* COULD TURN FATE UPSIDE DOWN.
SO I LED YOU TO THE BOAT...
AND I ENDED UP LIKE THIS.
WHEN SHE GOT HERE... THAT PIORAN LADY JUST VANISHED.
IF SOMEONE WAS BEHIND IT, IT MUST BE THE PERSON WHO INSTRUCTED ME.
YEAH...! I CAN DO IT.
IF I GOT THE SHIP'S CREW ON MY SIDE AND ASKED AROUND, I COULD FIND OUT WHERE THAT PERSON CAME FROM, OR WHO THEY ARE...

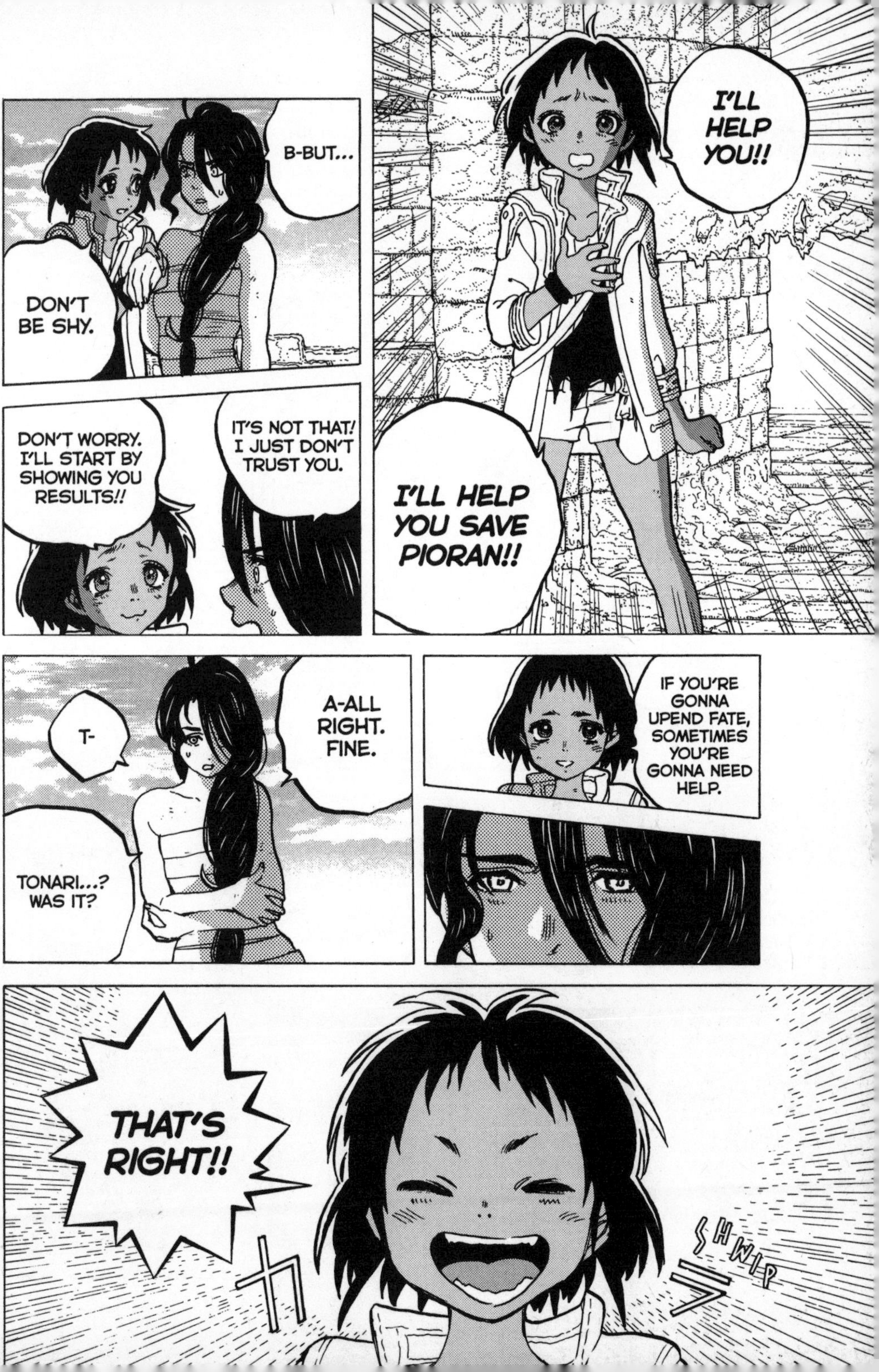
I'LL HELP YOU!!
I'LL HELP YOU SAVE PIORAN!!
B-BUT...
DON'T BE SHY.
IT'S NOT THAT! I JUST DON'T TRUST YOU.
DON'T WORRY. I'LL START BY SHOWING YOU RESULTS!!
IF YOU'RE GONNA UPEND FATE, SOMETIMES YOU'RE GONNA NEED HELP.
A-ALL RIGHT. FINE.
T-
TONARI...? WAS IT?
THAT'S RIGHT!!
SHWIP

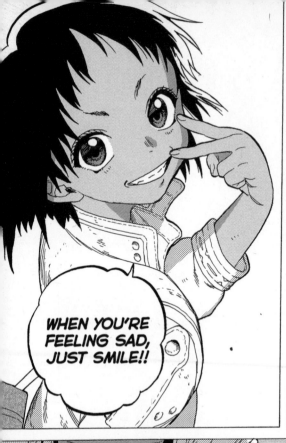

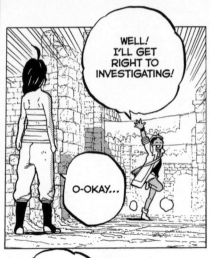

WELL!
I'LL GET
RIGHT TO
INVESTIGATING!

O-OKAY...

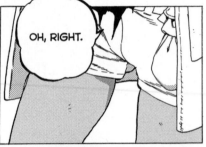

OH, RIGHT.

WHEN YOU'RE
FEELING SAD,
JUST SMILE!!

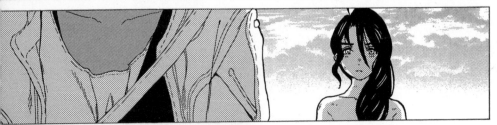

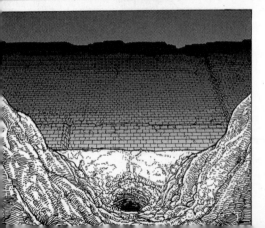

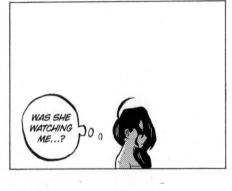

WAS SHE
WATCHING
ME...?

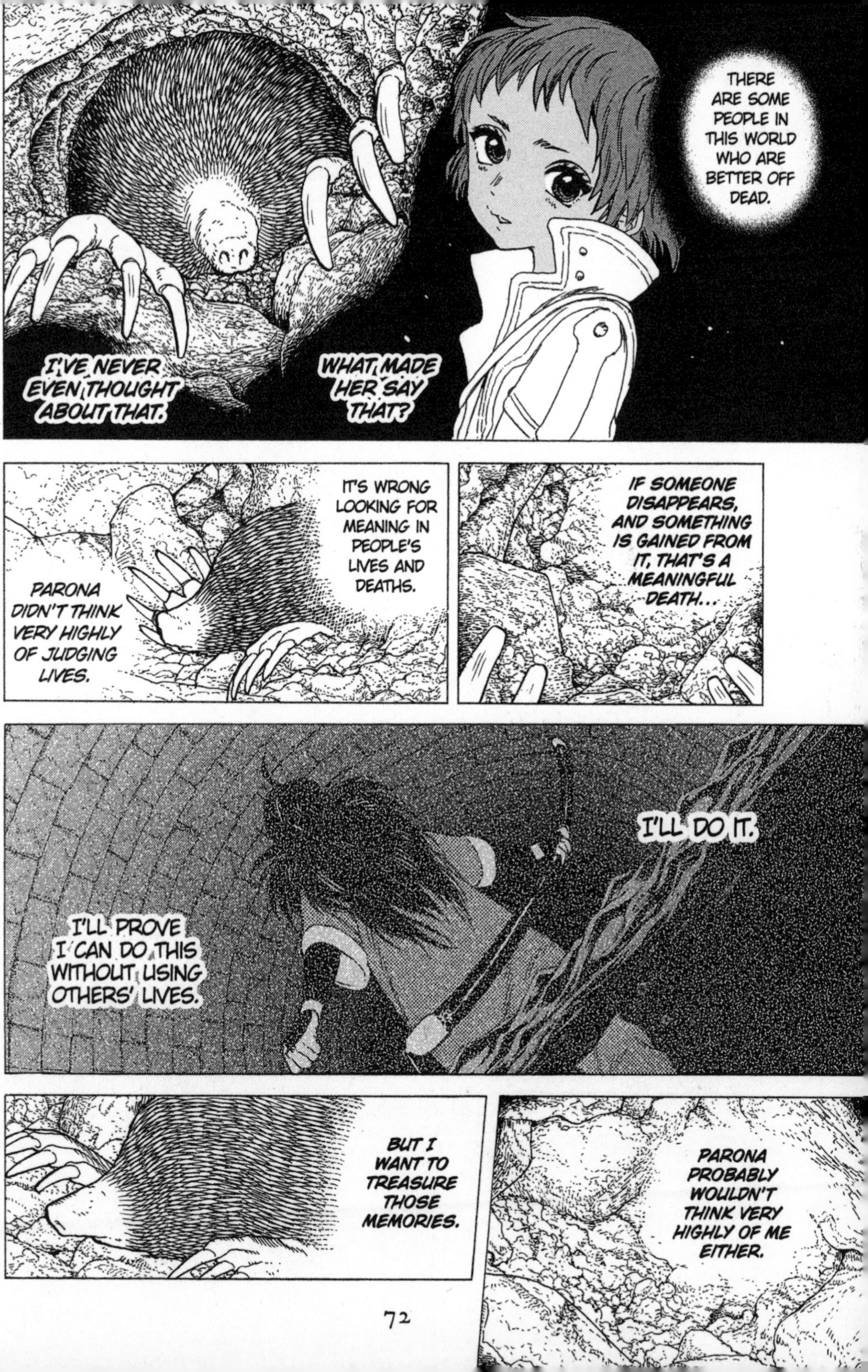
THERE ARE SOME PEOPLE IN THIS WORLD WHO ARE BETTER OFF DEAD.
WHAT MADE HER SAY THAT?
I'VE NEVER EVEN THOUGHT ABOUT THAT.
IF SOMEONE DISAPPEARS, AND SOMETHING IS GAINED FROM IT, THAT'S A MEANINGFUL DEATH...
IT'S WRONG LOOKING FOR MEANING IN PEOPLE'S LIVES AND DEATHS.
PARONA DIDN'T THINK VERY HIGHLY OF JUDGING LIVES.
I'LL DO IT.
I'LL PROVE I CAN DO THIS WITHOUT USING OTHERS' LIVES.
PARONA PROBABLY WOULDN'T THINK VERY HIGHLY OF ME EITHER.
BUT I WANT TO TREASURE THOSE MEMORIES.

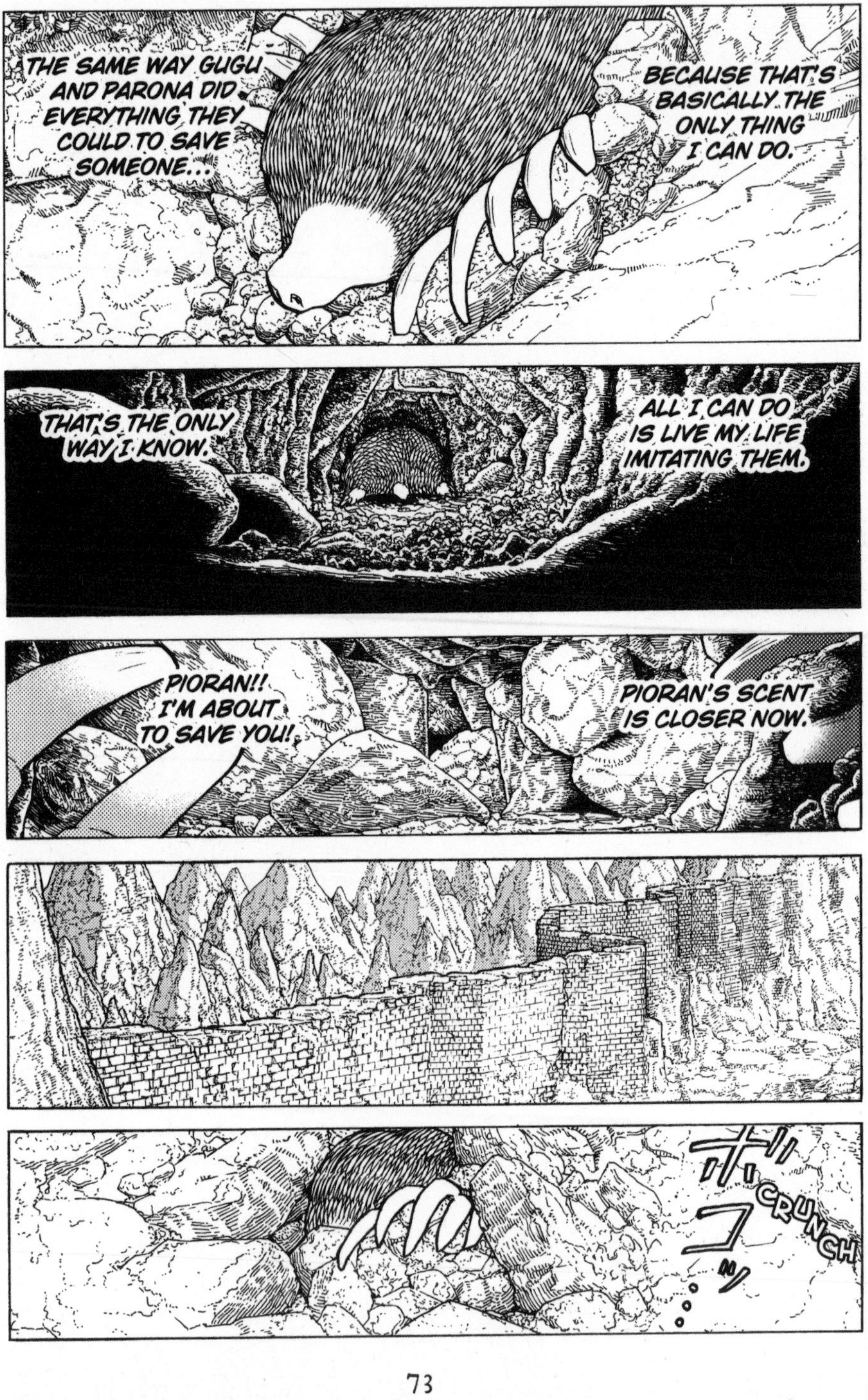
BECAUSE THAT'S BASICALLY THE ONLY THING I CAN DO.
THE SAME WAY GUGU AND PARONA DID EVERYTHING THEY COULD TO SAVE SOMEONE...
ALL I CAN DO IS LIVE MY LIFE IMITATING THEM.
THAT'S THE ONLY WAY I KNOW.
PIORAN'S SCENT IS CLOSER NOW.
PIORAN!! I'M ABOUT TO SAVE YOU!
CRUNCH

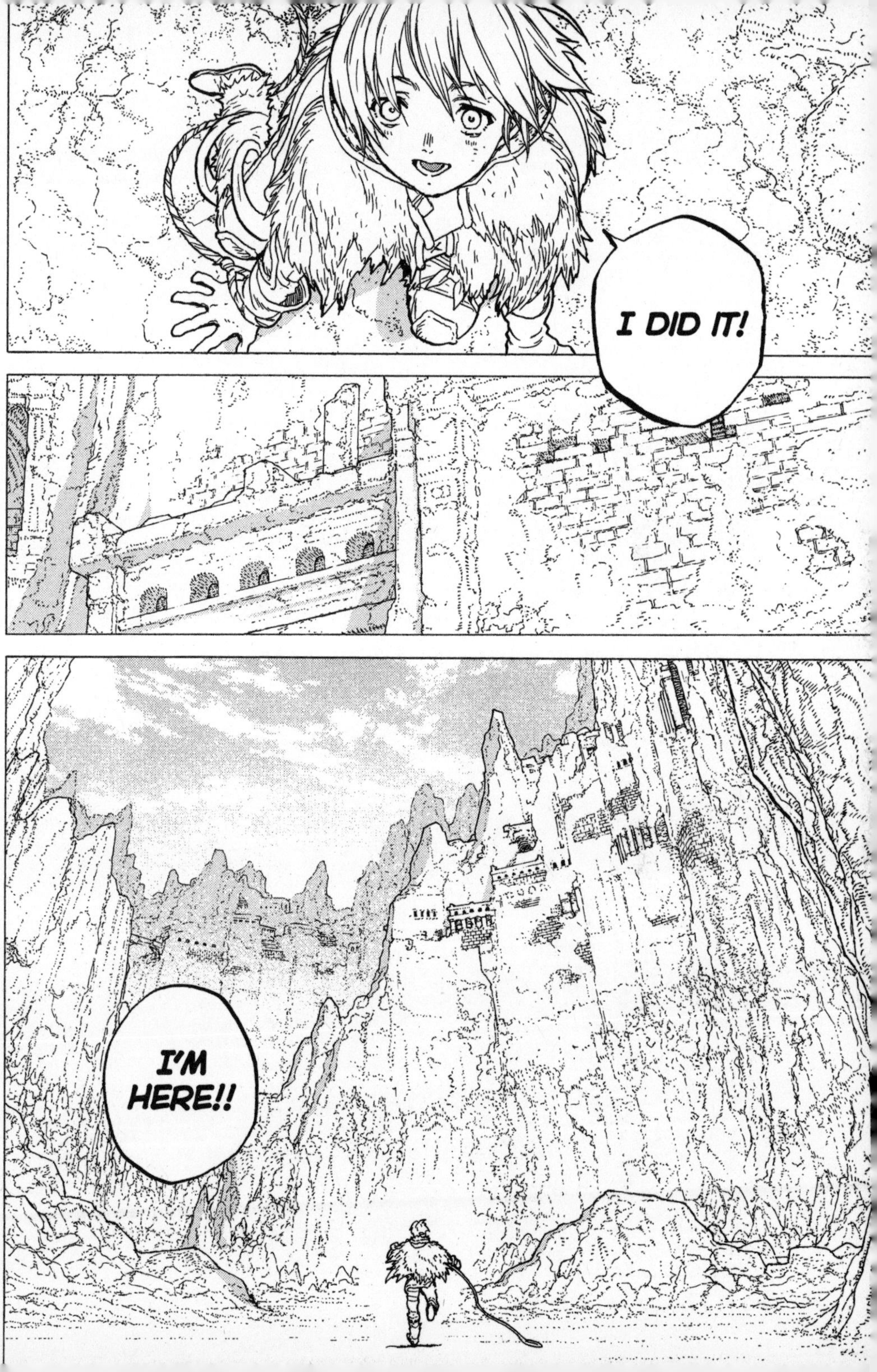
I DID IT!
I'M HERE!!

WHOA!
CLATTER
THUD
HUFF
HUFF
HUFF
HUFF
DAMN IT...
I CAN TELL BY SMELL. PIORAN IS NEAR THERE.
I LOOKED FOR ENTRY AS A DOG, OR THAT SMALL THING, BUT FOUND NONE.
I'LL HAVE TO CLIMB UP AND GO IN THROUGH A WINDOW.
BUT THE STONE WALL IS TOO HARD FOR MY SPEARS.
I TRIED IT WITH ALL MY FORMS, BUT COULDN'T CLIMB WELL WITH ANY OF THEM.

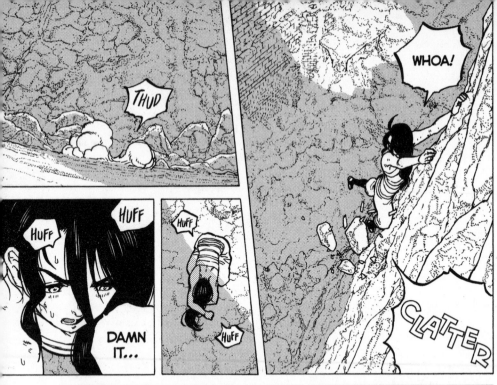

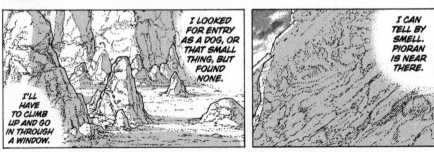

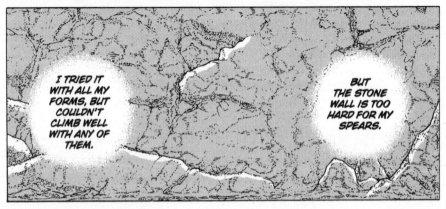

#39 The Proud Warrior

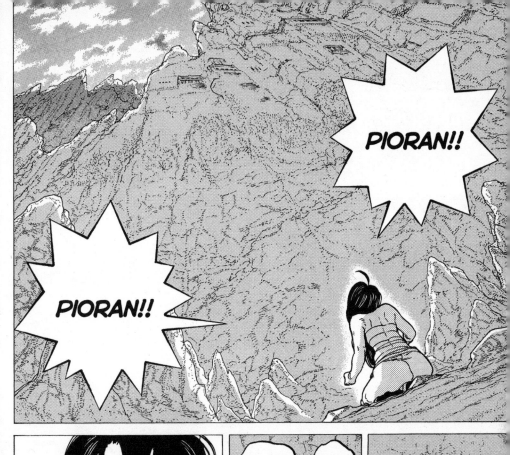

PIORAN!!

PIORAN!!

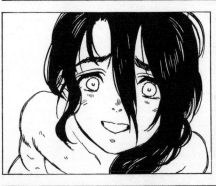

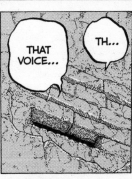

THAT VOICE...

TH...

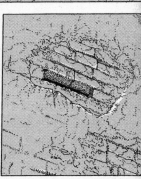

I CAME TO SAVE YOU!!

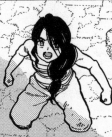

IT'S ME, PIORAN!!

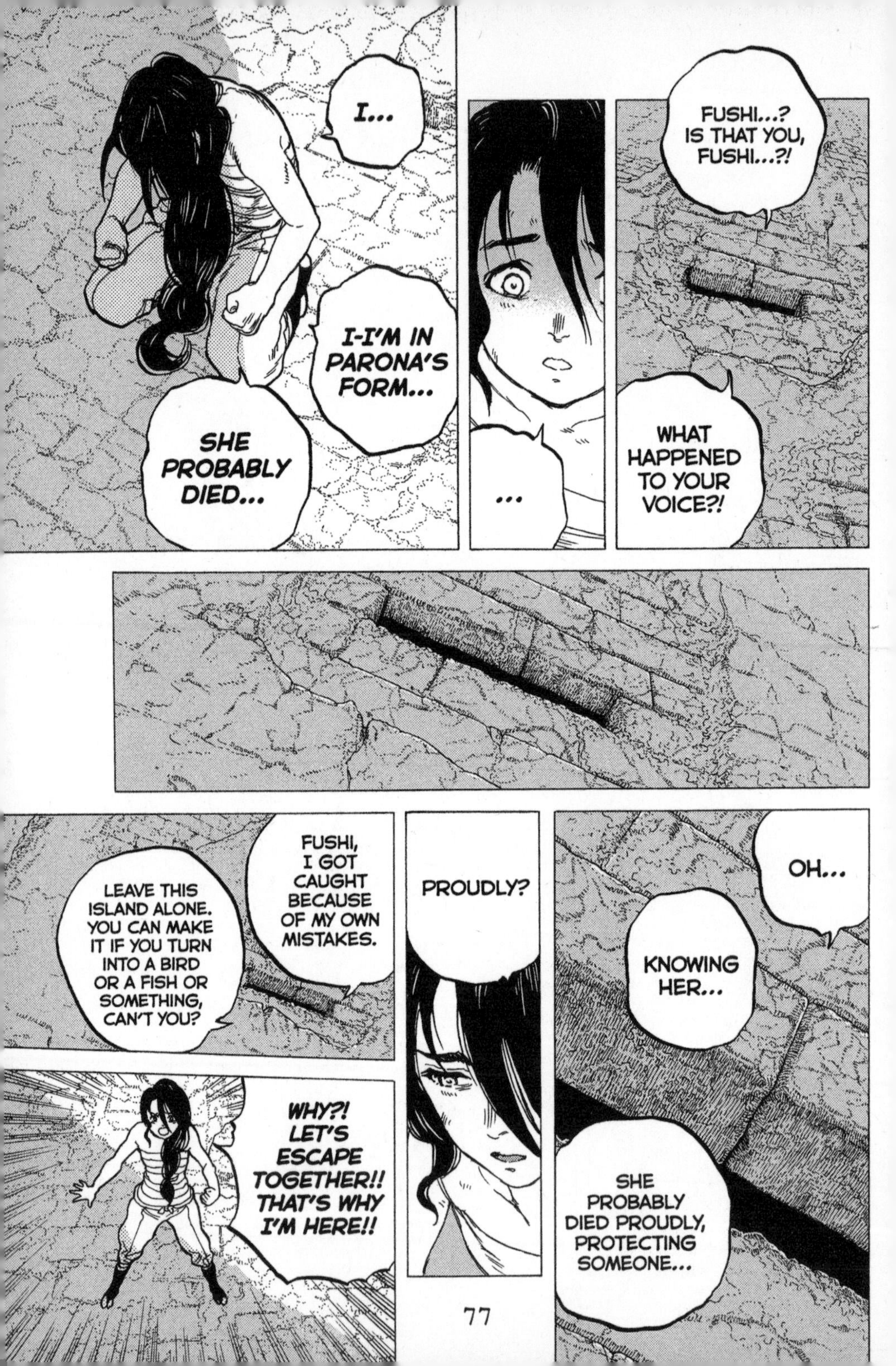
FUSHI...? IS THAT YOU, FUSHI...?!
WHAT HAPPENED TO YOUR VOICE?!
...
I...
I-I'M IN PARONA'S FORM...
SHE PROBABLY DIED...
OH...
KNOWING HER...
SHE PROBABLY DIED PROUDLY, PROTECTING SOMEONE...
PROUDLY?
FUSHI, I GOT CAUGHT BECAUSE OF MY OWN MISTAKES.
LEAVE THIS ISLAND ALONE. YOU CAN MAKE IT IF YOU TURN INTO A BIRD OR A FISH OR SOMETHING, CAN'T YOU?
WHY?! LET'S ESCAPE TOGETHER!! THAT'S WHY I'M HERE!!

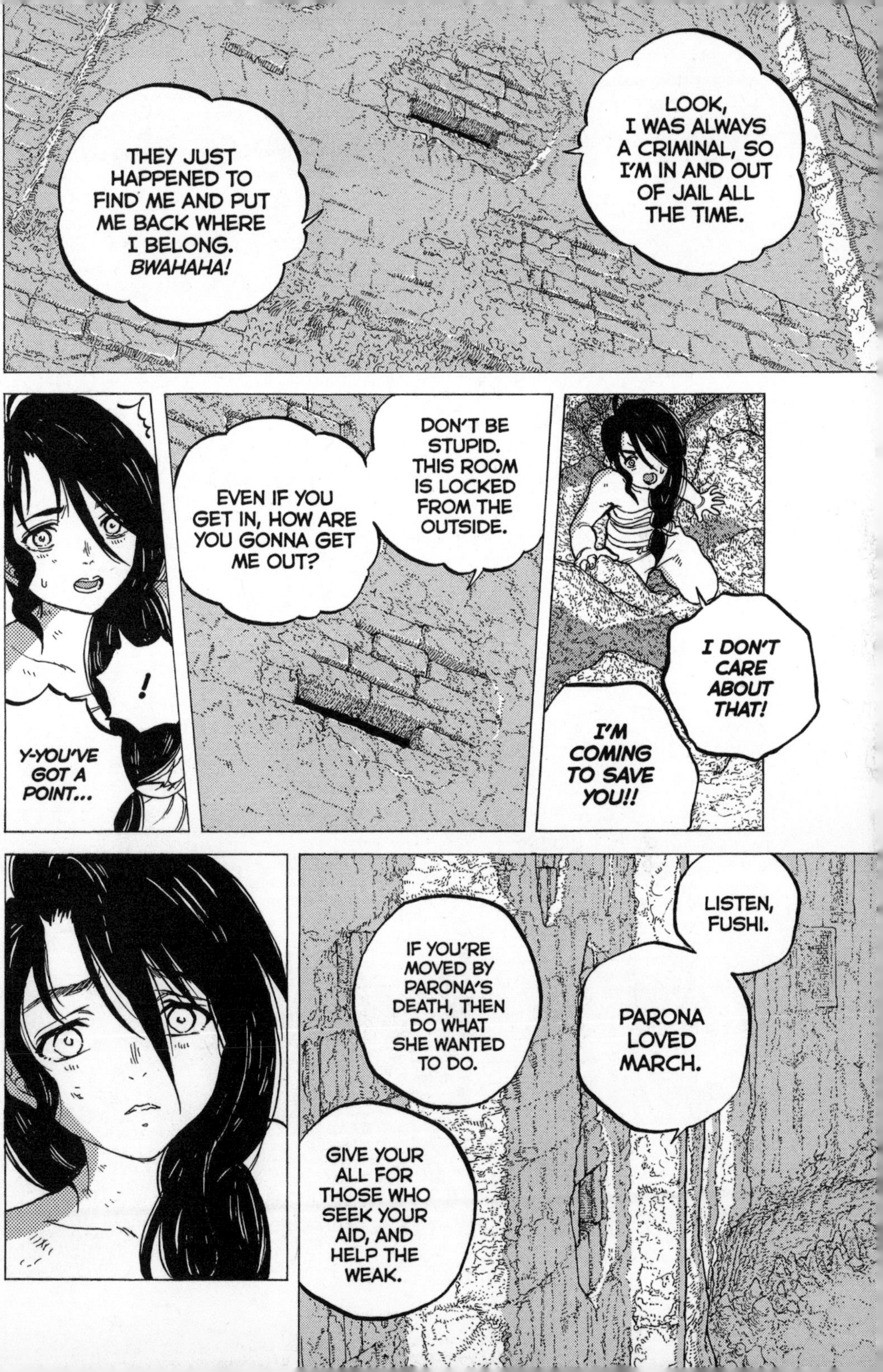

LOOK, I WAS ALWAYS A CRIMINAL, SO I'M IN AND OUT OF JAIL ALL THE TIME.
THEY JUST HAPPENED TO FIND ME AND PUT ME BACK WHERE I BELONG. *BWAHAHA!*
I DON'T CARE ABOUT THAT!
I'M COMING TO SAVE YOU!!
DON'T BE STUPID. THIS ROOM IS LOCKED FROM THE OUTSIDE.
EVEN IF YOU GET IN, HOW ARE YOU GONNA GET ME OUT?
!
Y-YOU'VE GOT A POINT...
LISTEN, FUSHI.
PARONA LOVED MARCH.
IF YOU'RE MOVED BY PARONA'S DEATH, THEN DO WHAT SHE WANTED TO DO.
GIVE YOUR ALL FOR THOSE WHO SEEK YOUR AID, AND HELP THE WEAK.

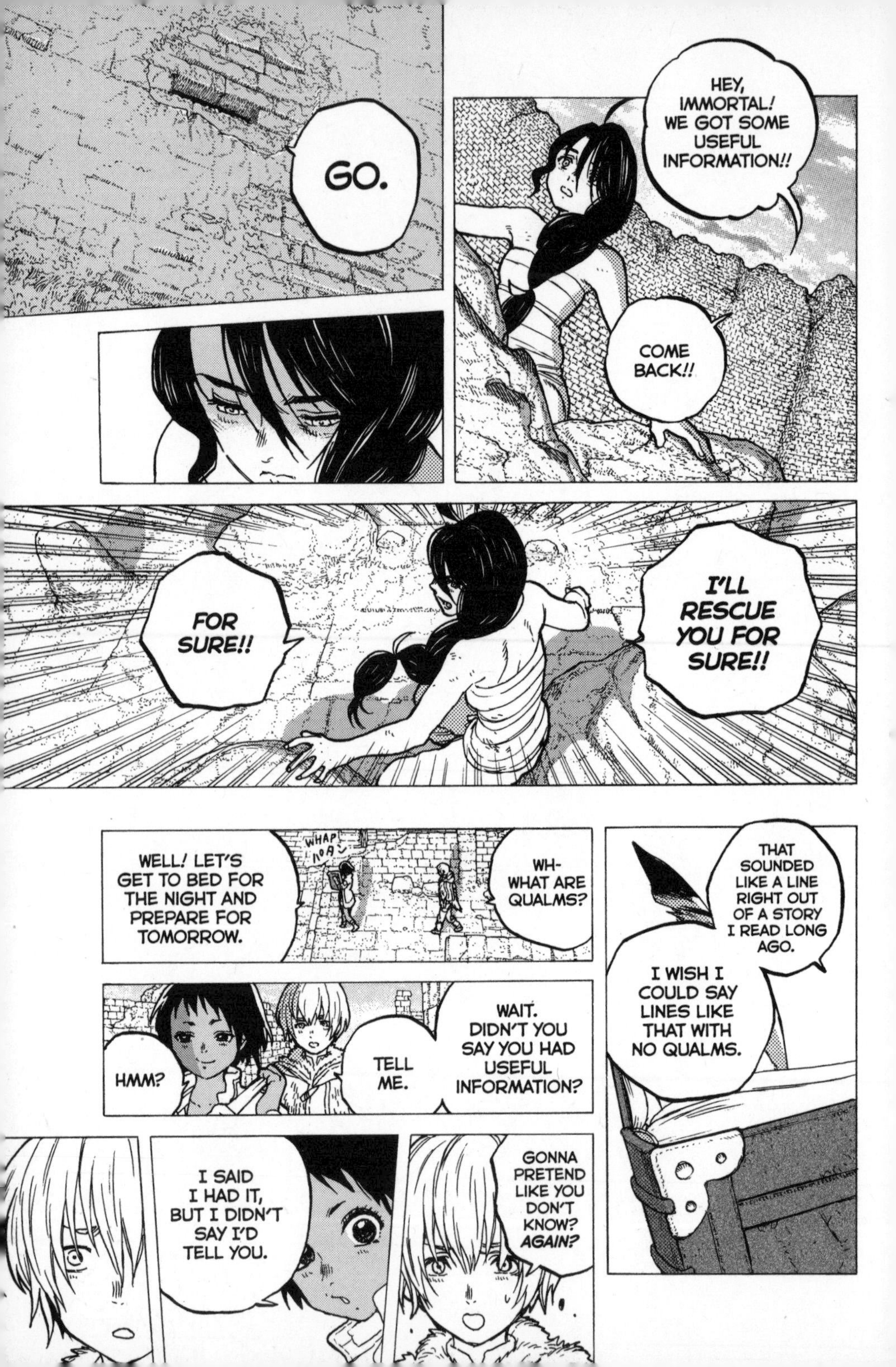
GO.
HEY, IMMORTAL! WE GOT SOME USEFUL INFORMATION!!
COME BACK!!
I'LL RESCUE YOU FOR SURE!!
FOR SURE!!
THAT SOUNDED LIKE A LINE RIGHT OUT OF A STORY I READ LONG AGO.
I WISH I COULD SAY LINES LIKE THAT WITH NO QUALMS.
WH- WHAT ARE QUALMS?
WHAP
WELL! LET'S GET TO BED FOR THE NIGHT AND PREPARE FOR TOMORROW.
WAIT. DIDN'T YOU SAY YOU HAD USEFUL INFORMATION?
TELL ME.
HMM?
GONNA PRETEND LIKE YOU DON'T KNOW? AGAIN?
I SAID I HAD IT, BUT I DIDN'T SAY I'D TELL YOU.

BUT I'LL TELL YOU IF YOU MAKE IT THROUGH THE THIRD ROUND.

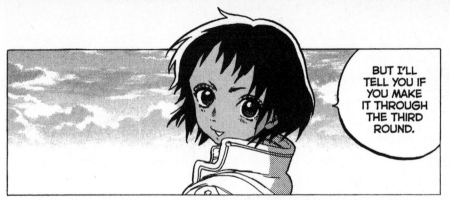

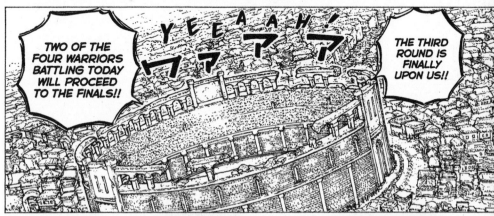

TWO OF THE FOUR WARRIORS BATTLING TODAY WILL PROCEED TO THE FINALS!!

YEEAAH!
ワァァァ

THE THIRD ROUND IS FINALLY UPON US!!

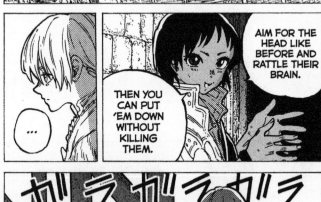

...

AIM FOR THE HEAD LIKE BEFORE AND RATTLE THEIR BRAIN.

THEN YOU CAN PUT 'EM DOWN WITHOUT KILLING THEM.

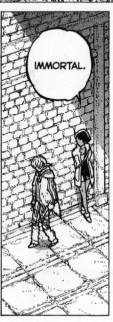

IMMORTAL.

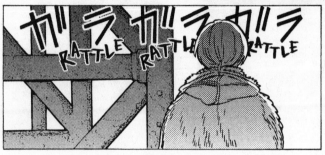

ガラ ガラ ガラ
RATTLE RATTLE RATTLE

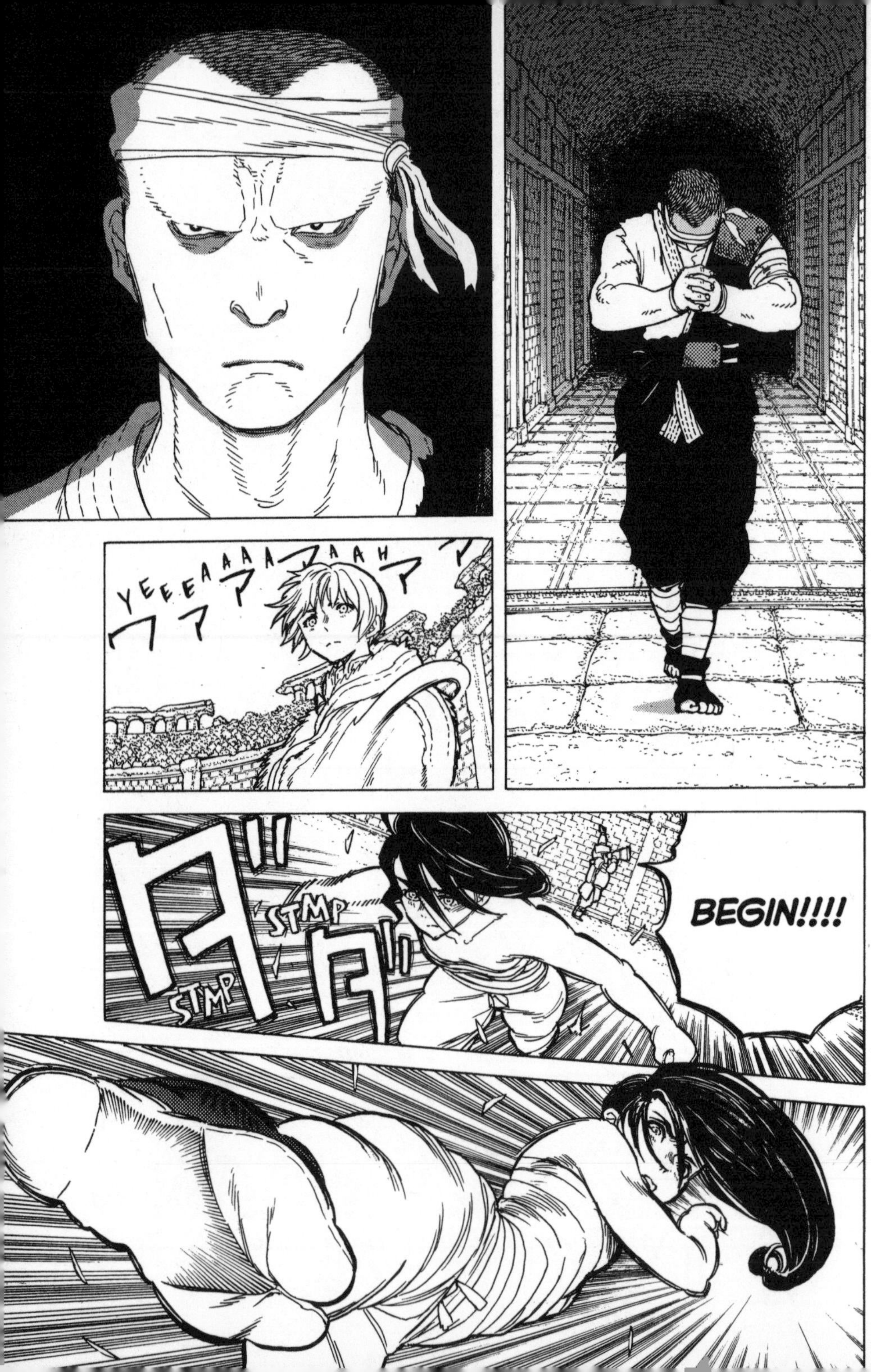
YEEEAAAAAAH
ワァアアアア
BEGIN!!!!
ダダダ
STMP
STMP

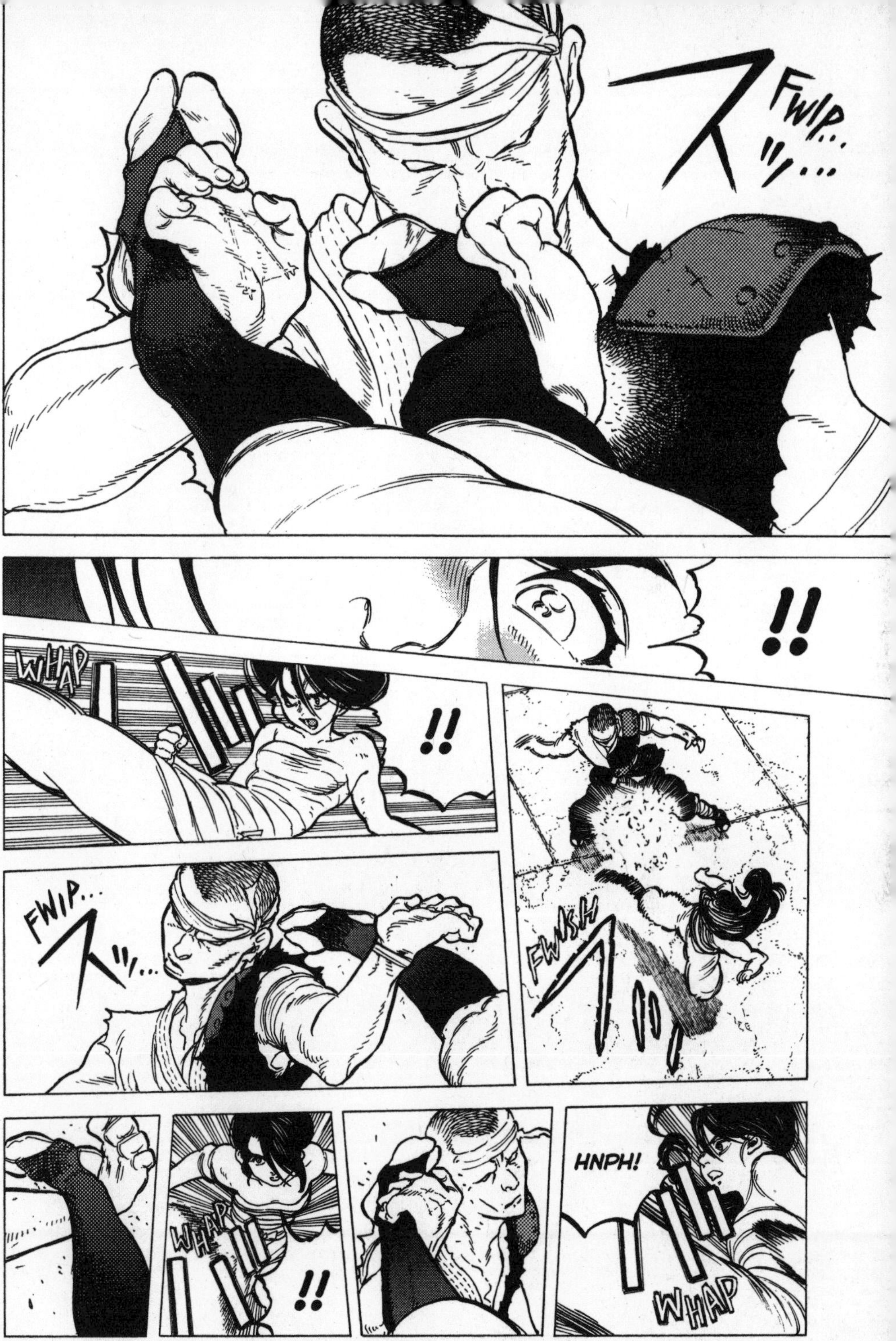
FWIP...
!!
FWSH
WHAP
!!
FWIP...
HNPH!
WHAP
WHAP
!!

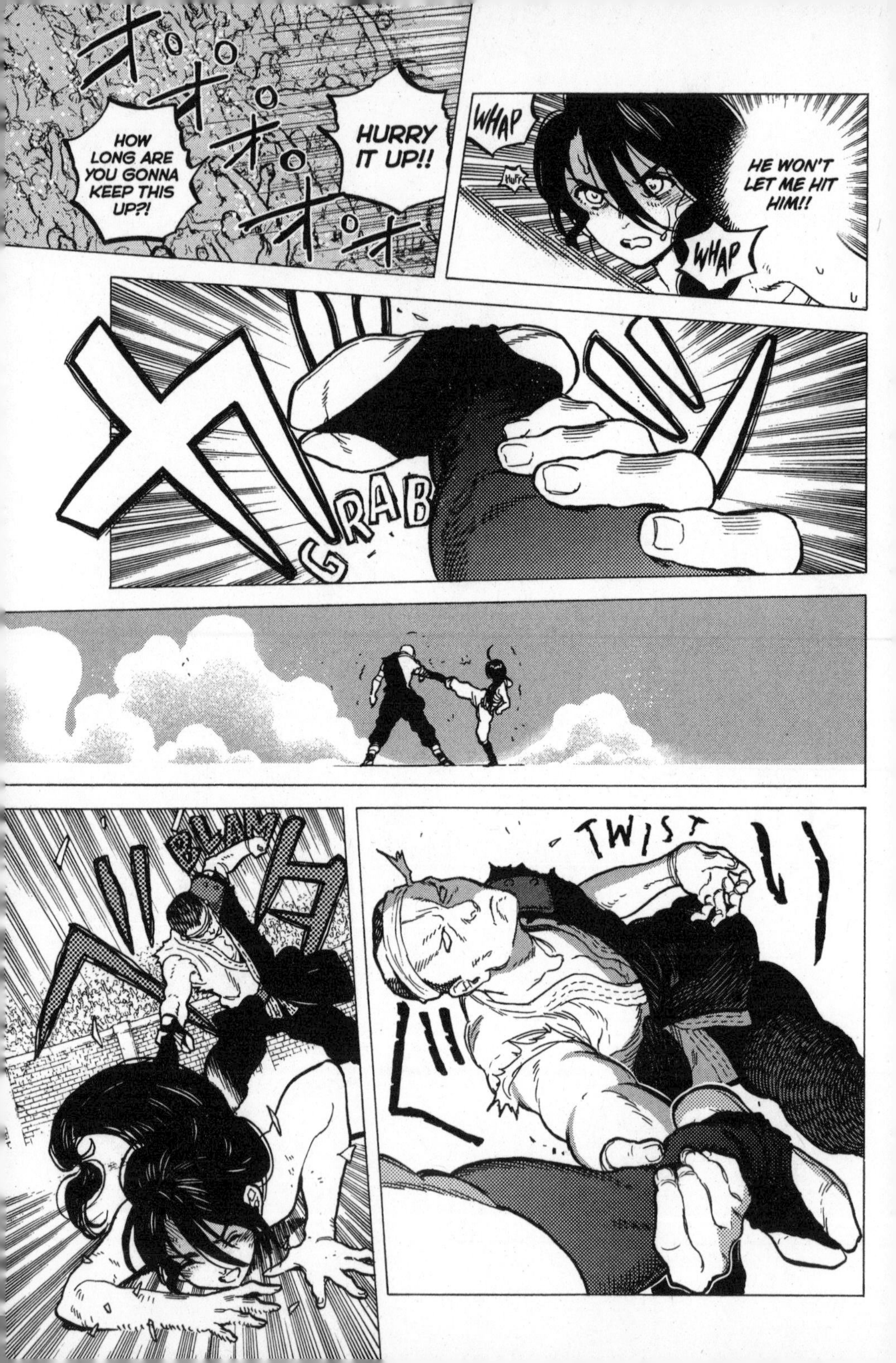
WHAP
HUFF
HE WON'T LET ME HIT HIM!!
WHAP
HURRY IT UP!!
HOW LONG ARE YOU GONNA KEEP THIS UP?!
GRAB
TWIST

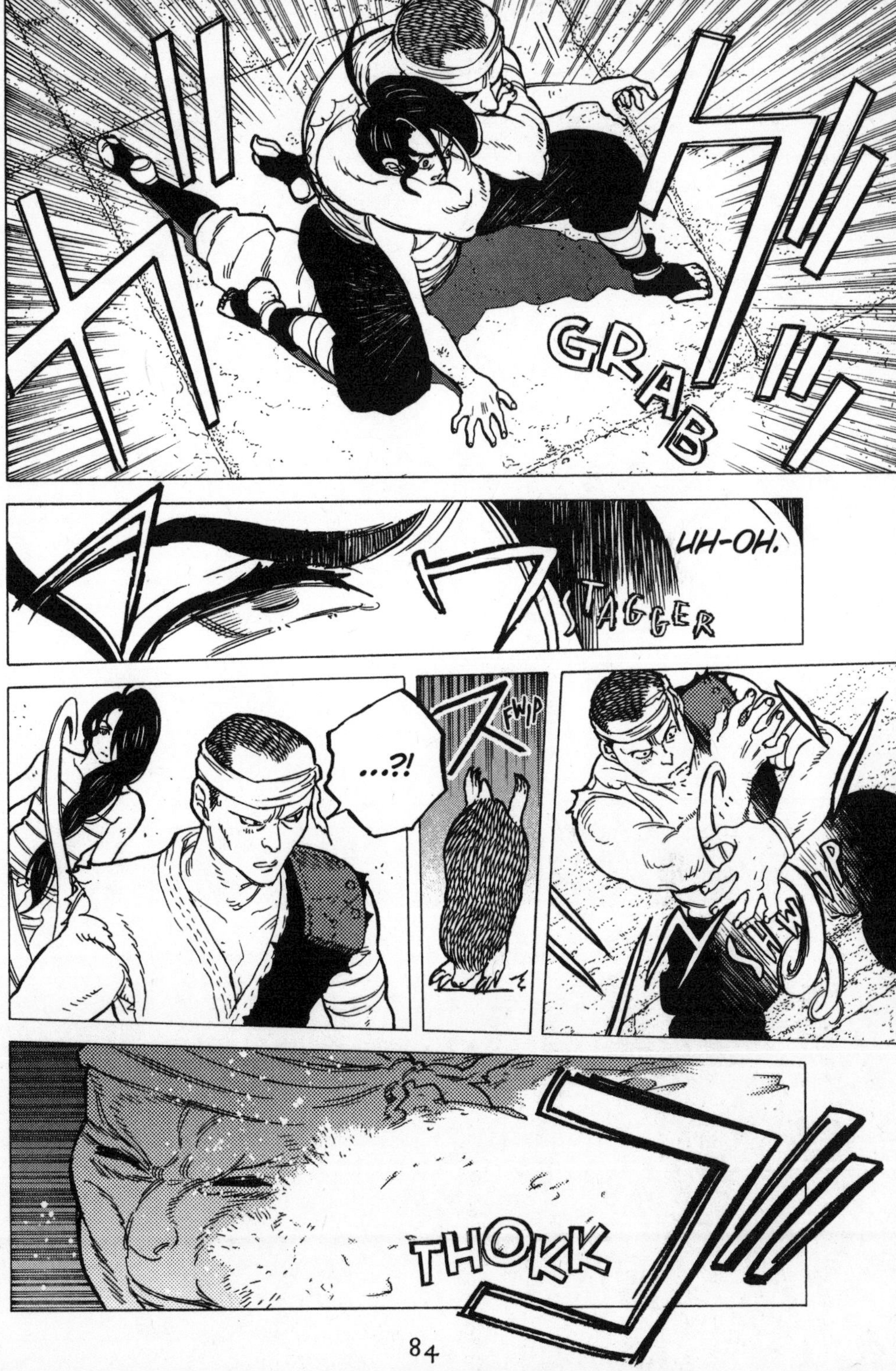
GRAB
UH-OH.
STAGGER
SHWIP
FWIP
...?!
THOKK

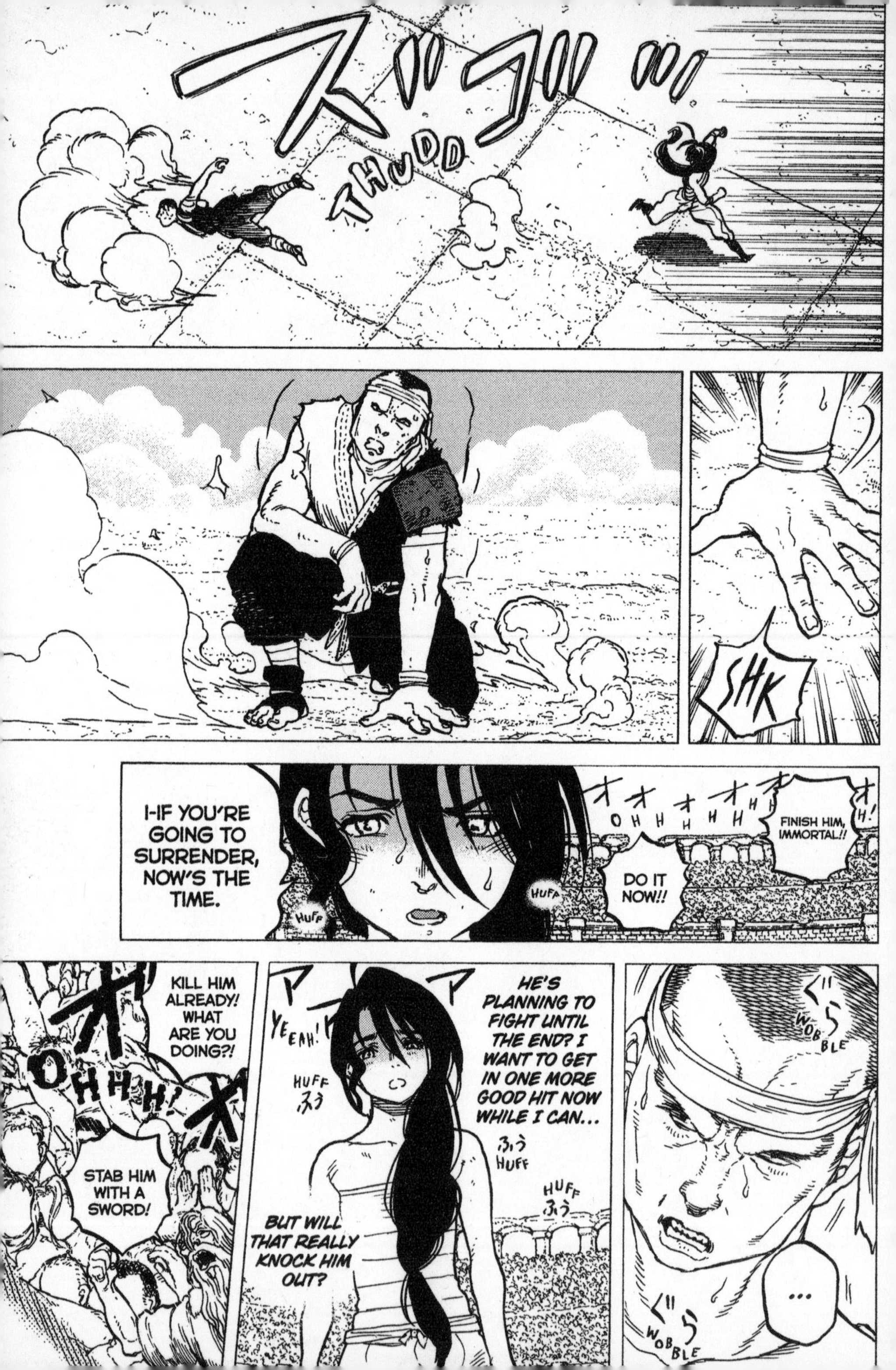
THUDD
SHK
FINISH HIM, IMMORTAL!!
OHHHHHHH!
DO IT NOW!!
HUFF
HUFF
I-IF YOU'RE GOING TO SURRENDER, NOW'S THE TIME.
WOBBLE
...
WOBBLE
YEEAH!
HE'S PLANNING TO FIGHT UNTIL THE END? I WANT TO GET IN ONE MORE GOOD HIT NOW WHILE I CAN...
HUFF
HUFF
HUFF
BUT WILL THAT REALLY KNOCK HIM OUT?
KILL HIM ALREADY! WHAT ARE YOU DOING?!
OHHH!
STAB HIM WITH A SWORD!

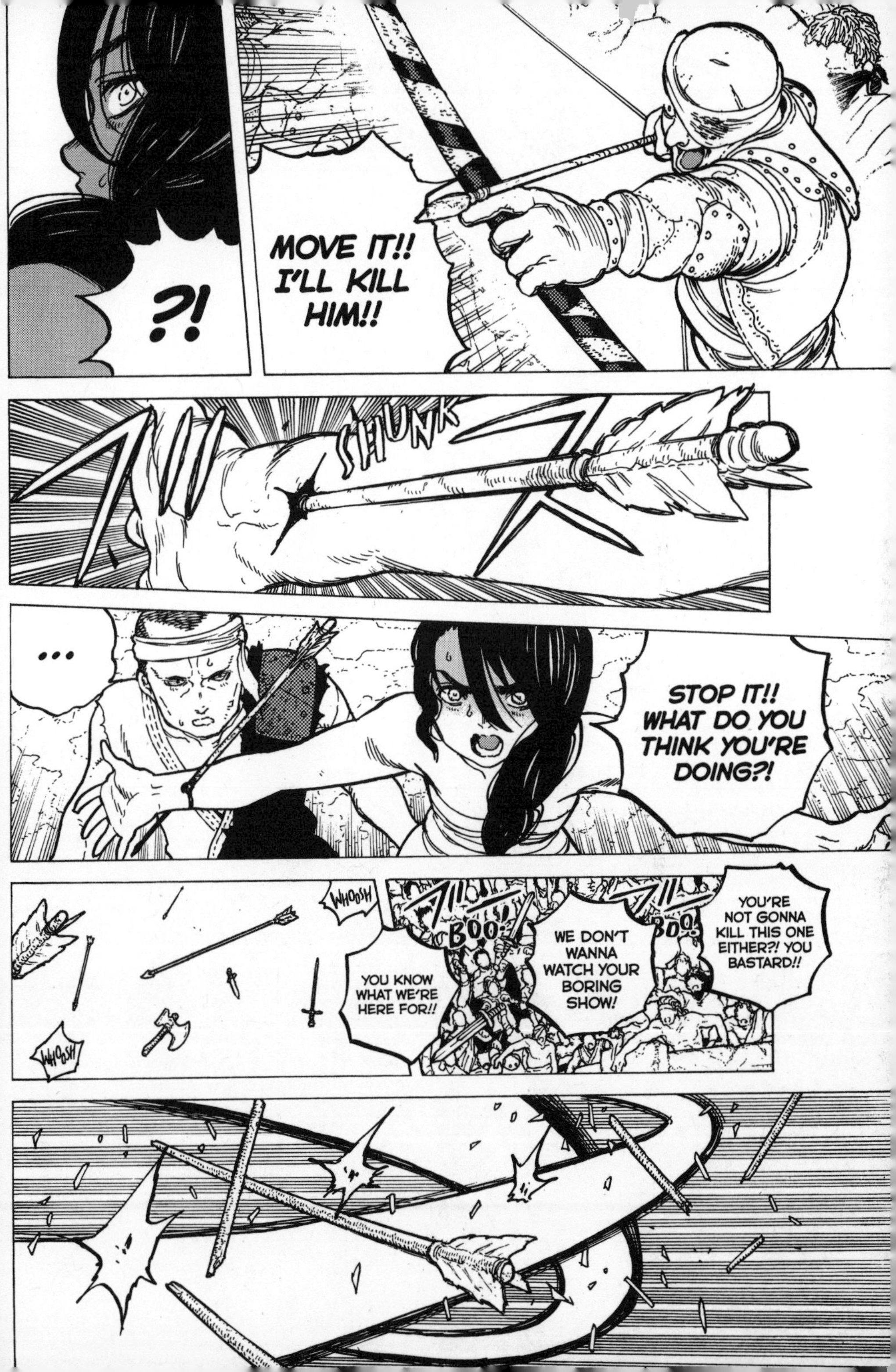
MOVE IT!! I'LL KILL HIM!!
?!
SHUNK
STOP IT!! WHAT DO YOU THINK YOU'RE DOING?!
...
YOU'RE NOT GONNA KILL THIS ONE EITHER?! YOU BASTARD!!
BOO!
WE DON'T WANNA WATCH YOUR BORING SHOW!
BOO!
YOU KNOW WHAT WE'RE HERE FOR!!
WHOOSH
WHOOSH

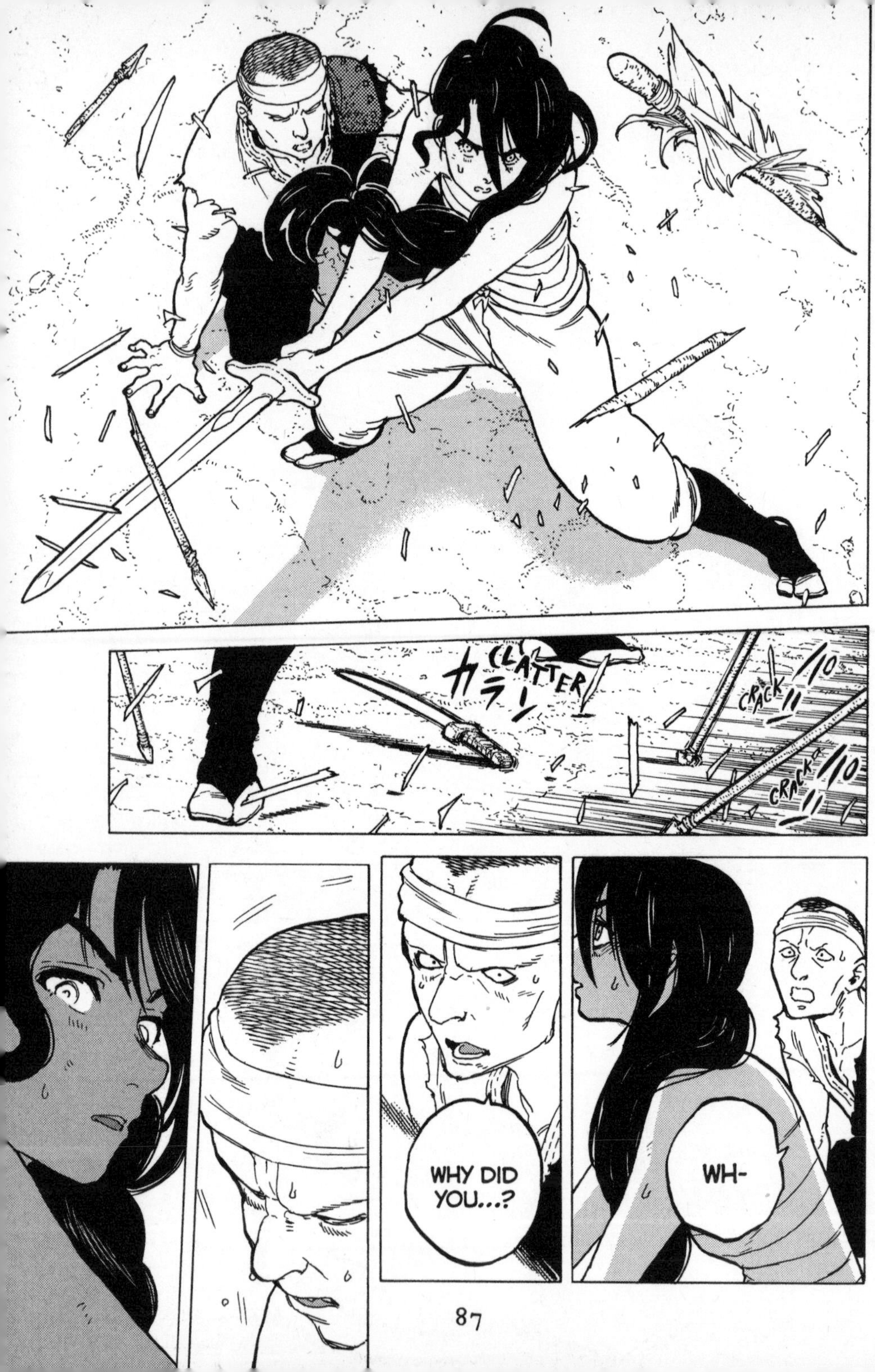
CRACK!!
CRACK!!
CLATTER
カラン
WH-
WHY DID YOU...?

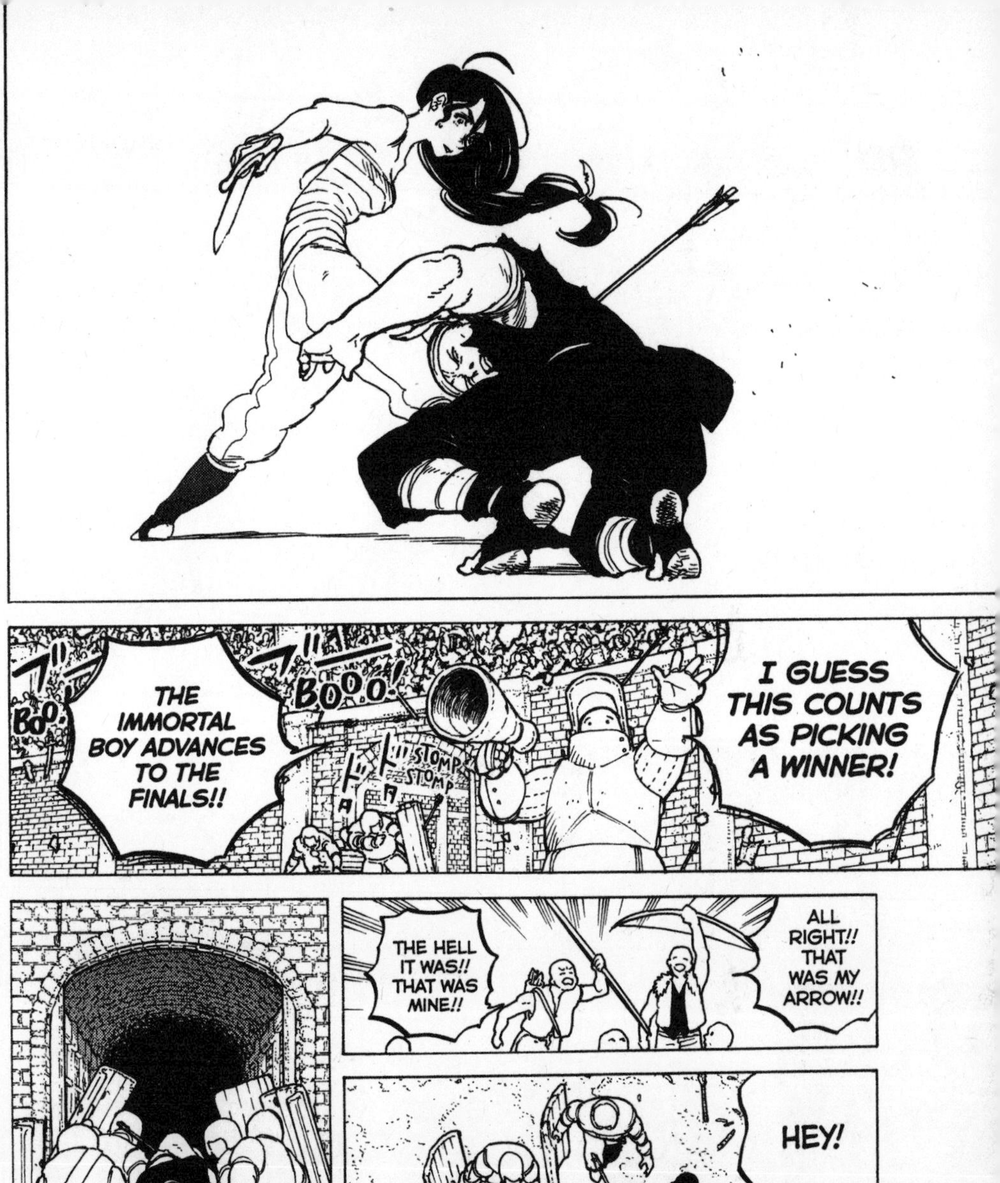
I GUESS THIS COUNTS AS PICKING A WINNER!
BOOO!
THE IMMORTAL BOY ADVANCES TO THE FINALS!!
BOOO
STOMP STOMP
ALL RIGHT!! THAT WAS MY ARROW!!
THE HELL IT WAS!! THAT WAS MINE!!
HEY!
WE'LL GET HIM OUT.

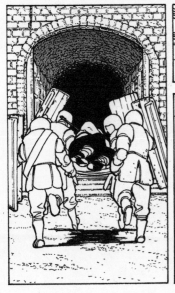

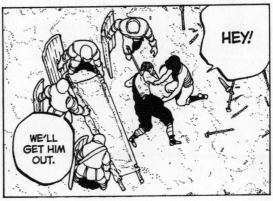

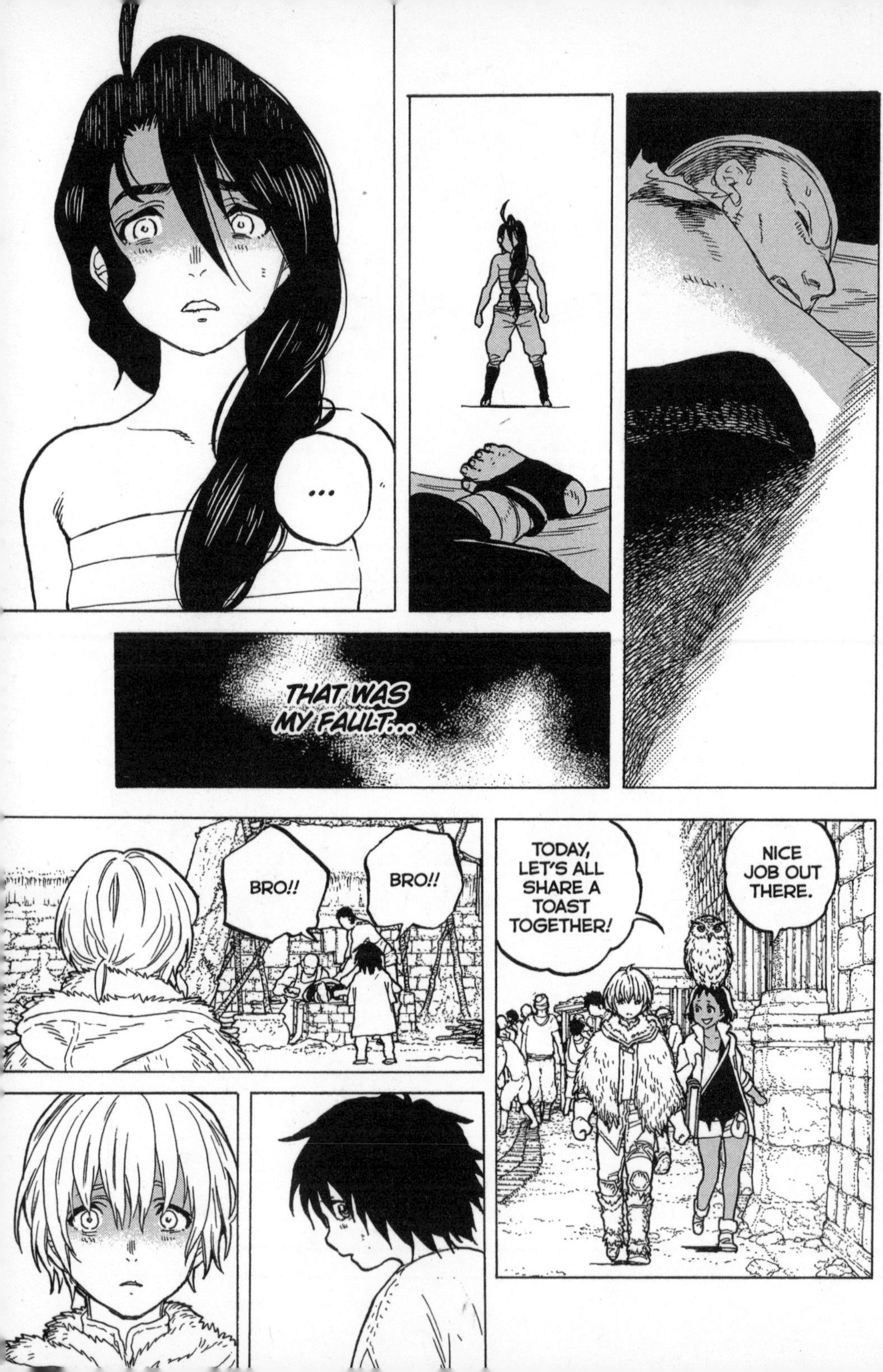
...
THAT WAS MY FAULT...
NICE JOB OUT THERE.
TODAY, LET'S ALL SHARE A TOAST TOGETHER!
BRO!!
BRO!!

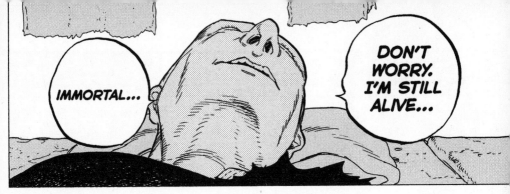

DON'T WORRY. I'M STILL ALIVE...
IMMORTAL...
YOU REALLY TICK OFF PARTICIPANTS LIKE ME, WHO ARE FIGHTING WITH OUR LIVES ON THE LINE.
WHY...
WHY DIDN'T YOU KILL ME?
PROB-ABLY...
BECAUSE THINGS THAT HURT ARE BAD.
SO I DON'T WANT TO DO THEM.
HAHAHA!! WHAT THE HELL?!
YOU'RE A REAL WEIRDO, KID!!
WHAT THE HELL IS A BOY LIKE YOU DOING IN THE TOURNAMENT?
TH-
THERE'S SOMEONE I WANT TO SAVE...

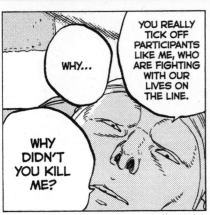

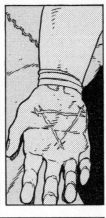

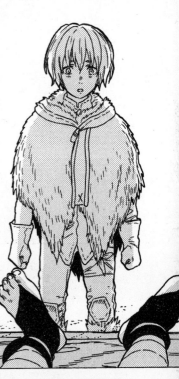

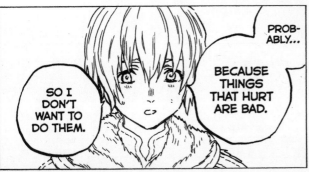

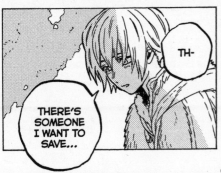

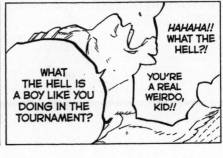

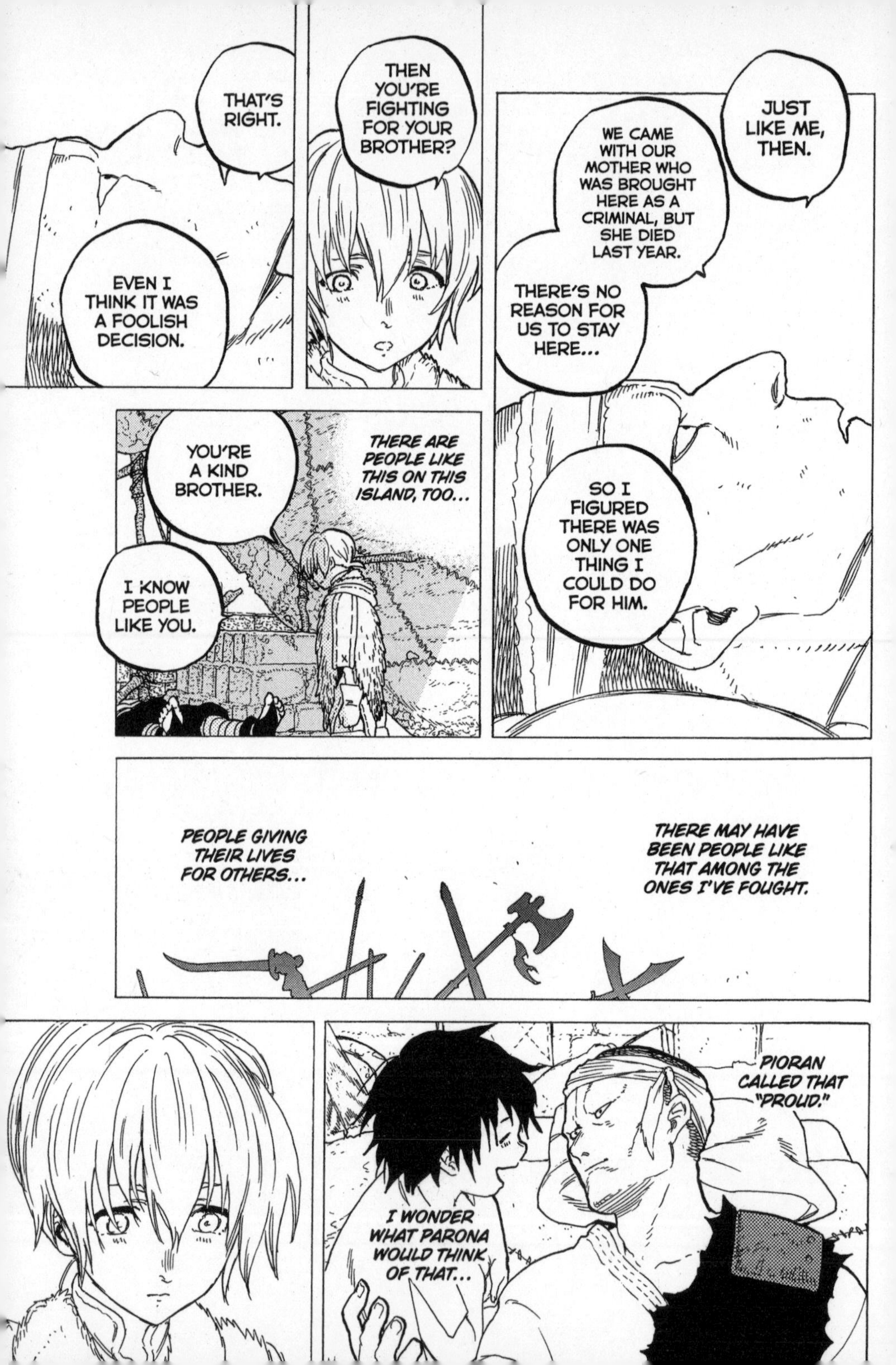
JUST LIKE ME, THEN.
WE CAME WITH OUR MOTHER WHO WAS BROUGHT HERE AS A CRIMINAL, BUT SHE DIED LAST YEAR.
THERE'S NO REASON FOR US TO STAY HERE...
SO I FIGURED THERE WAS ONLY ONE THING I COULD DO FOR HIM.
THEN YOU'RE FIGHTING FOR YOUR BROTHER?
THAT'S RIGHT.
EVEN I THINK IT WAS A FOOLISH DECISION.
THERE ARE PEOPLE LIKE THIS ON THIS ISLAND, TOO...
YOU'RE A KIND BROTHER.
I KNOW PEOPLE LIKE YOU.
THERE MAY HAVE BEEN PEOPLE LIKE THAT AMONG THE ONES I'VE FOUGHT.
PEOPLE GIVING THEIR LIVES FOR OTHERS...
PIORAN CALLED THAT "PROUD."
I WONDER WHAT PARONA WOULD THINK OF THAT...

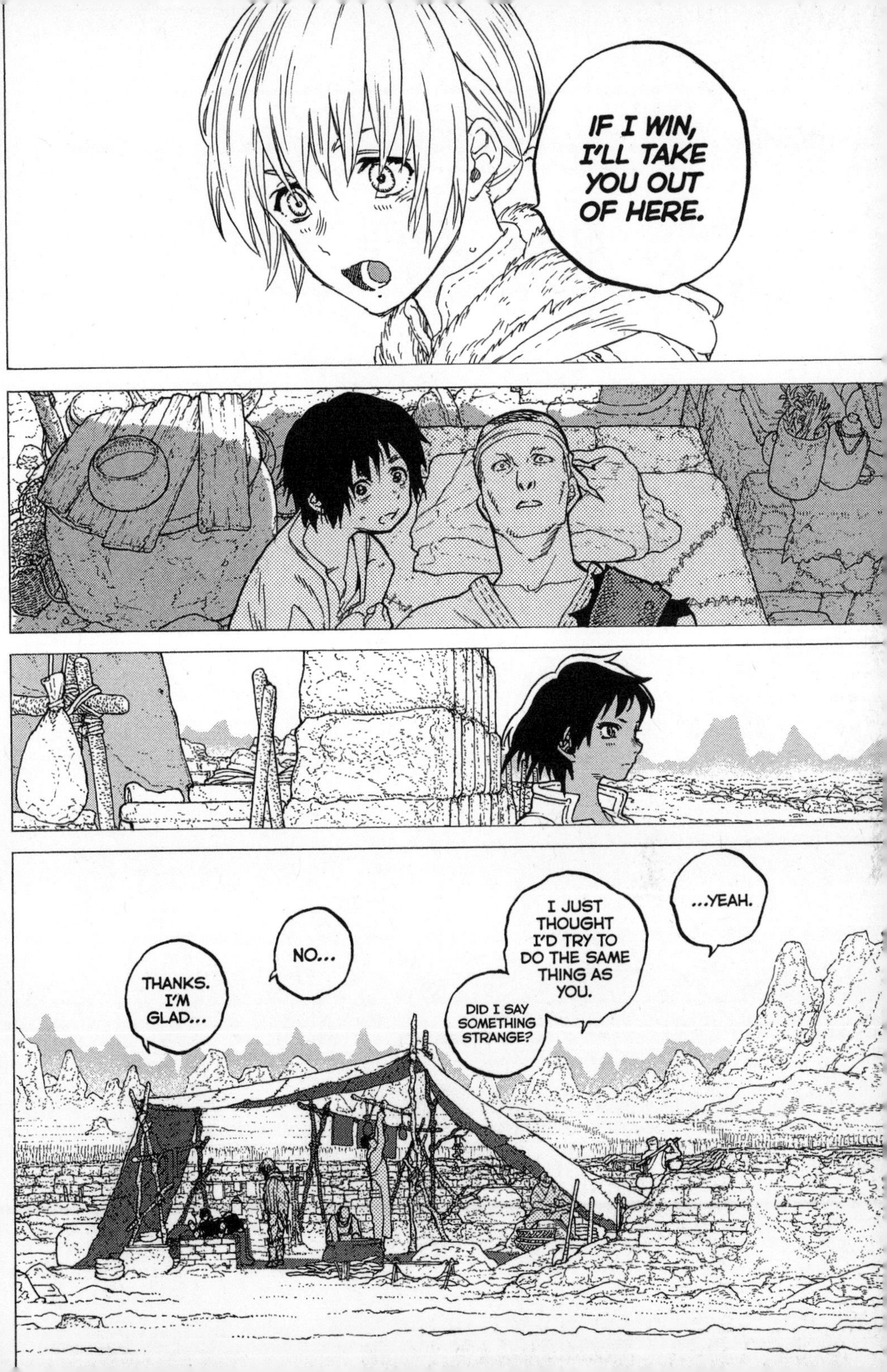
IF I WIN, I'LL TAKE YOU OUT OF HERE.
...YEAH.
I JUST THOUGHT I'D TRY TO DO THE SAME THING AS YOU.
DID I SAY SOMETHING STRANGE?
NO...
THANKS. I'M GLAD...

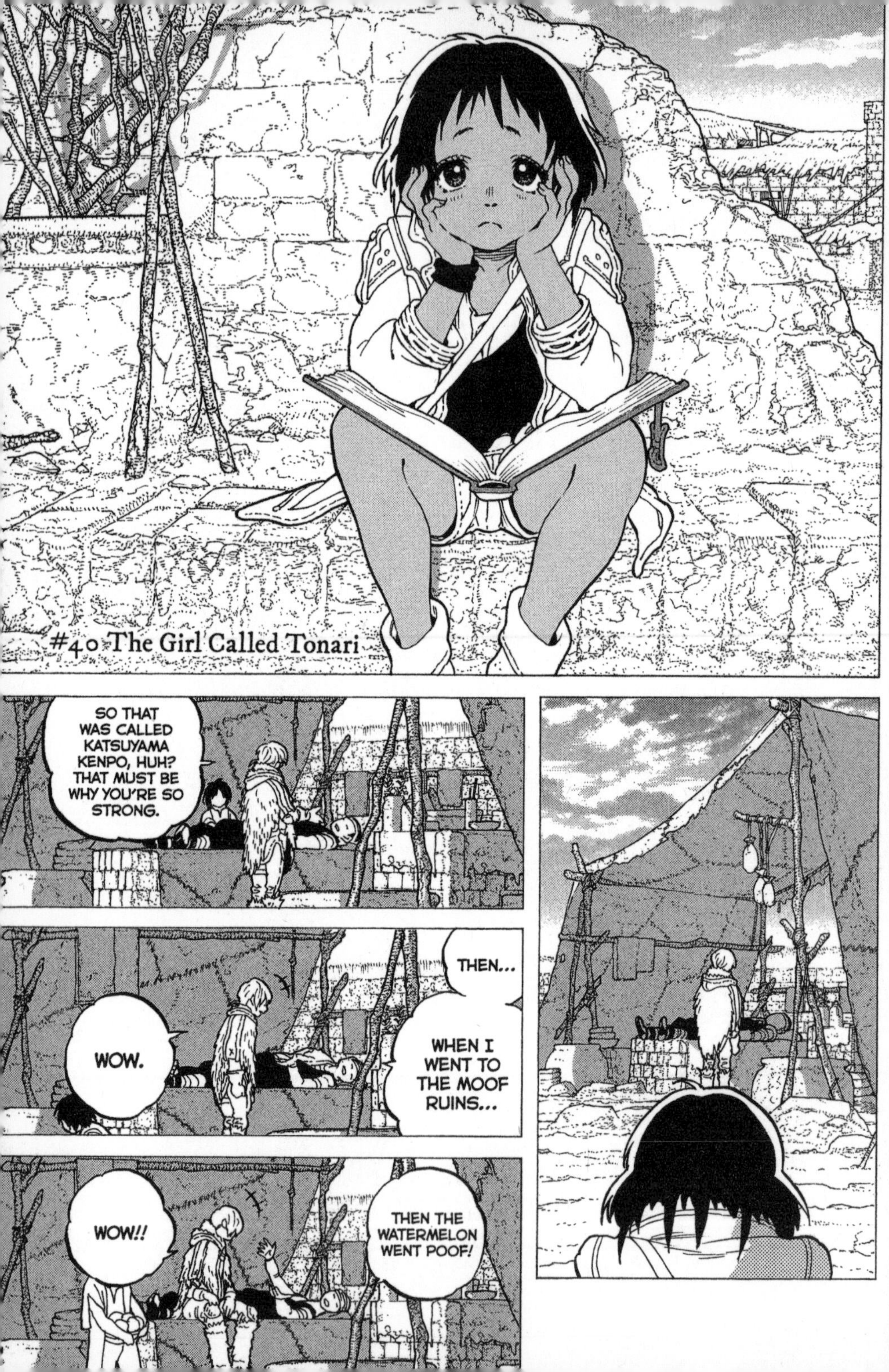
#40 The Girl Called Tonari
SO THAT WAS CALLED KATSUYAMA KENPO, HUH? THAT MUST BE WHY YOU'RE SO STRONG.
THEN...
WHEN I WENT TO THE MOOF RUINS...
WOW.
THEN THE WATERMELON WENT POOF!
WOW!!

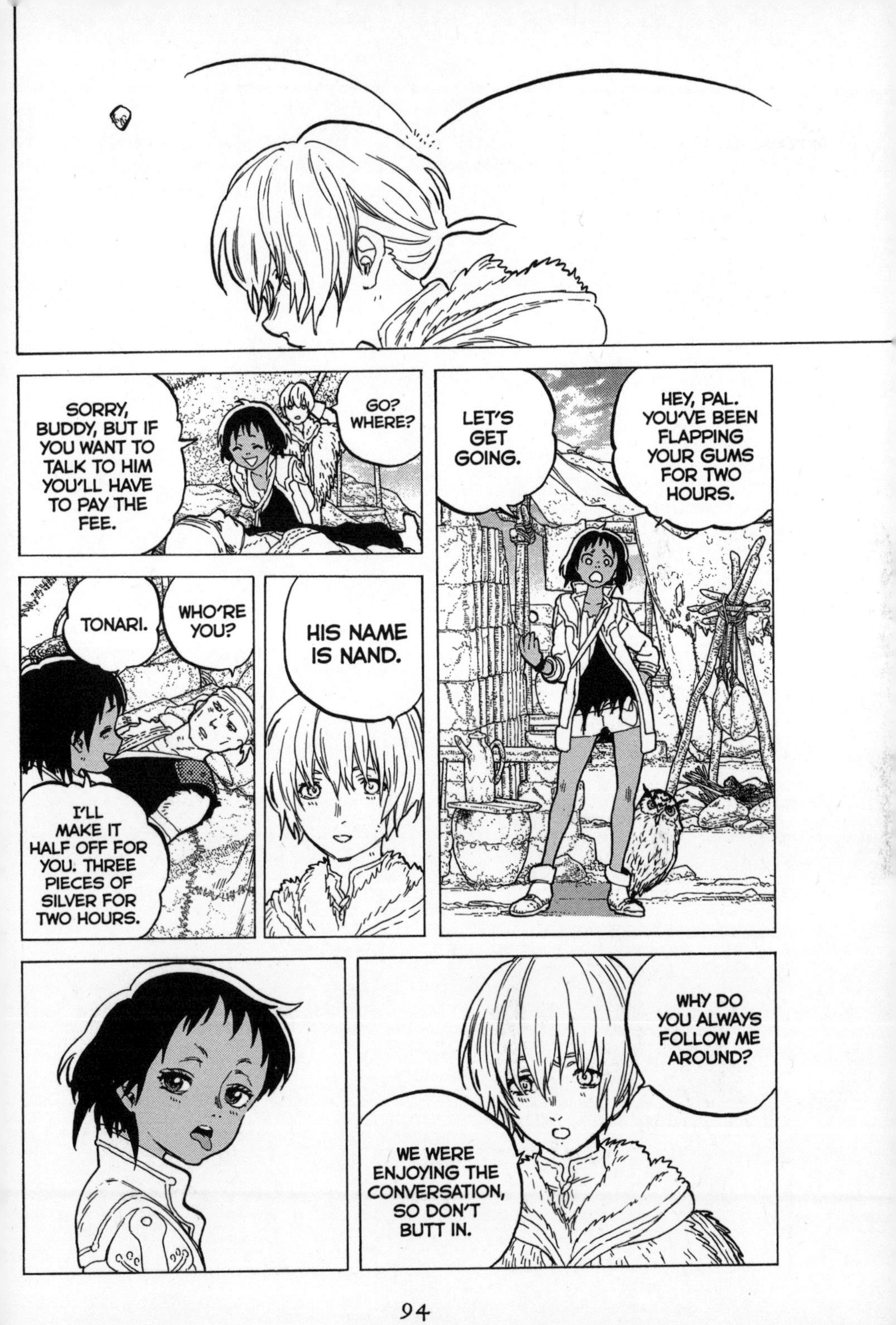
HEY, PAL. YOU'VE BEEN FLAPPING YOUR GUMS FOR TWO HOURS.
LET'S GET GOING.
GO? WHERE?
SORRY, BUDDY, BUT IF YOU WANT TO TALK TO HIM YOU'LL HAVE TO PAY THE FEE.
HIS NAME IS NAND.
WHO'RE YOU?
TONARI.
I'LL MAKE IT HALF OFF FOR YOU. THREE PIECES OF SILVER FOR TWO HOURS.
WHY DO YOU ALWAYS FOLLOW ME AROUND?
WE WERE ENJOYING THE CONVERSATION, SO DON'T BUTT IN.

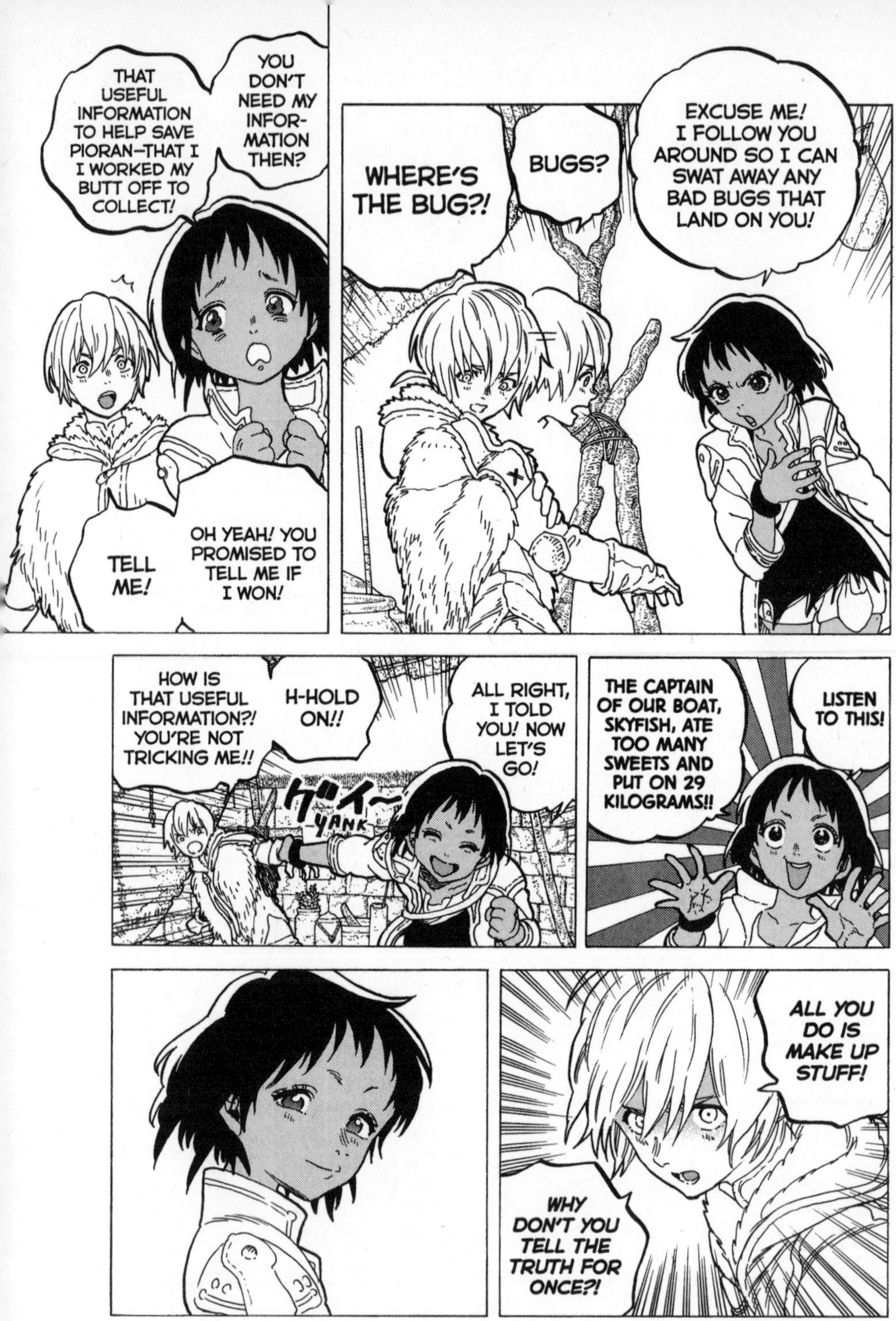
EXCUSE ME! I FOLLOW YOU AROUND SO I CAN SWAT AWAY ANY BAD BUGS THAT LAND ON YOU!
BUGS?
WHERE'S THE BUG?!
YOU DON'T NEED MY INFOR-MATION THEN?
THAT USEFUL INFORMATION TO HELP SAVE PIORAN—THAT I I WORKED MY BUTT OFF TO COLLECT!
OH YEAH! YOU PROMISED TO TELL ME IF I WON!
TELL ME!
LISTEN TO THIS!
THE CAPTAIN OF OUR BOAT, SKYFISH, ATE TOO MANY SWEETS AND PUT ON 29 KILOGRAMS!!
ALL RIGHT, I TOLD YOU! NOW LET'S GO!
グイ～
YANK
H-HOLD ON!!
HOW IS THAT USEFUL INFORMATION?! YOU'RE NOT TRICKING ME!!
ALL YOU DO IS MAKE UP STUFF!
WHY DON'T YOU TELL THE TRUTH FOR ONCE?!

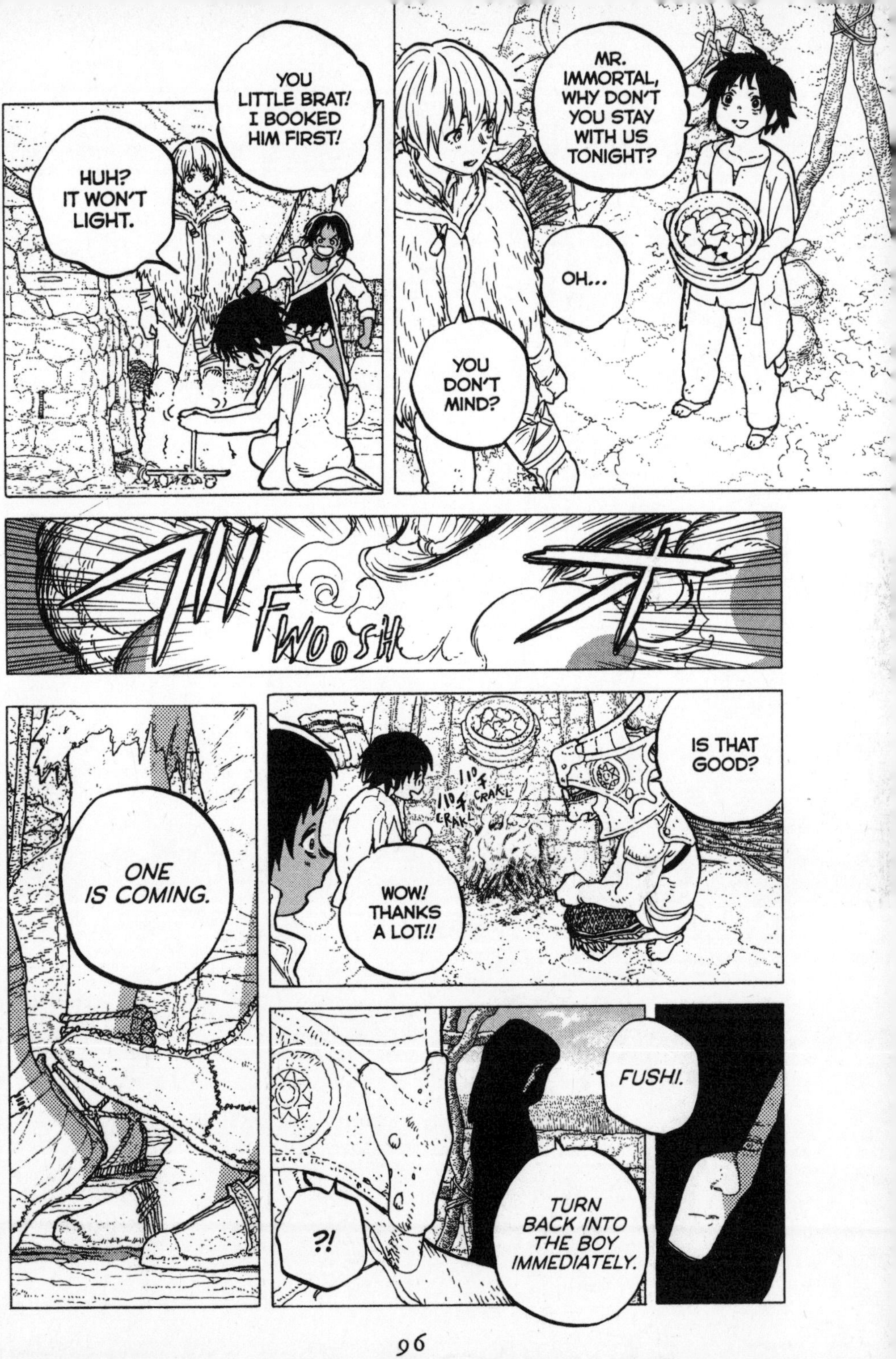
MR. IMMORTAL, WHY DON'T YOU STAY WITH US TONIGHT?
OH...
YOU DON'T MIND?
YOU LITTLE BRAT! I BOOKED HIM FIRST!
HUH? IT WON'T LIGHT.
FWOOSH
IS THAT GOOD?
CRAKL CRAKL
WOW! THANKS A LOT!!
FUSHI.
TURN BACK INTO THE BOY IMMEDIATELY.
?!
ONE IS COMING.

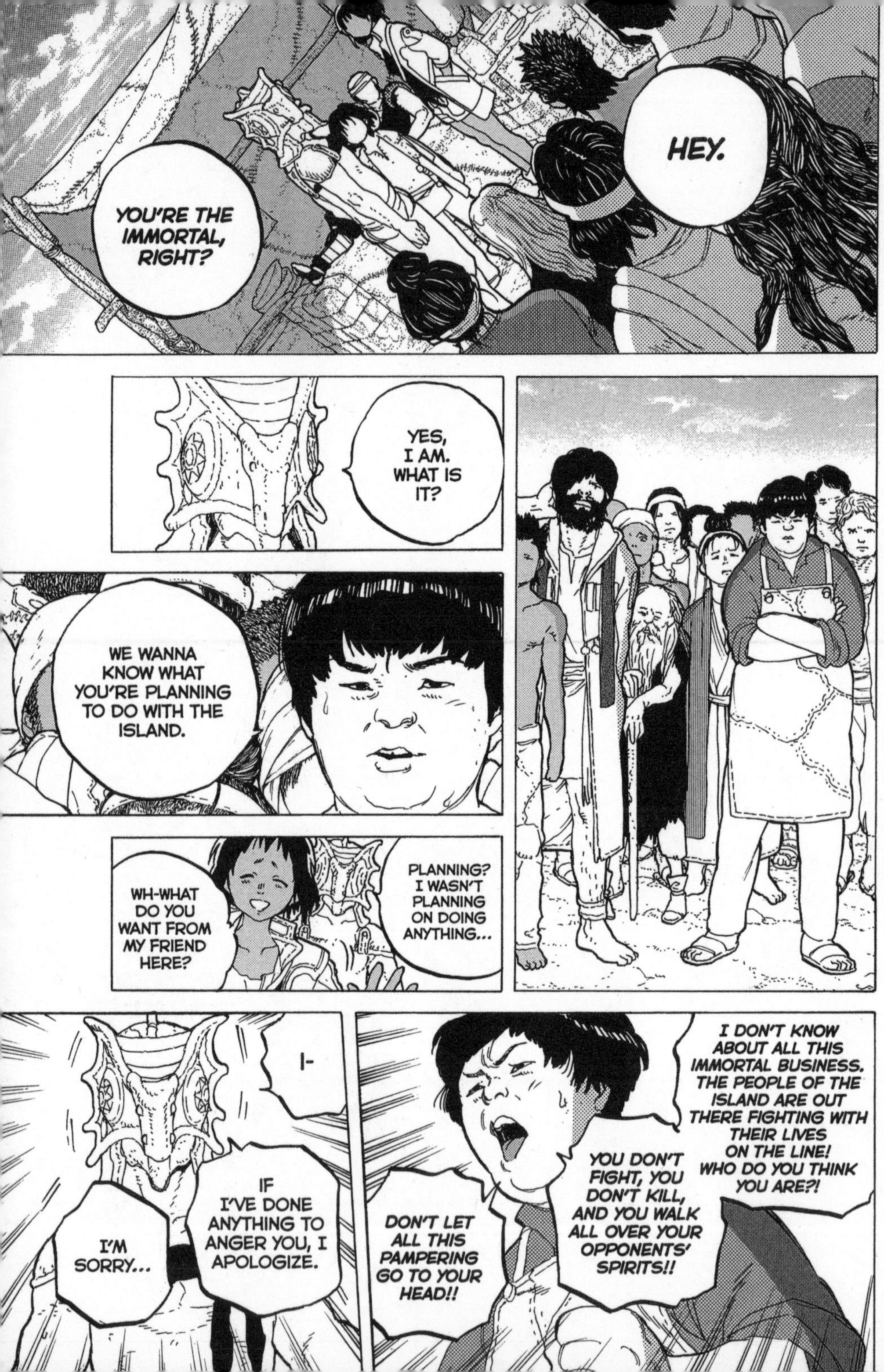
HEY.
YOU'RE THE IMMORTAL, RIGHT?
YES, I AM. WHAT IS IT?
WE WANNA KNOW WHAT YOU'RE PLANNING TO DO WITH THE ISLAND.
PLANNING? I WASN'T PLANNING ON DOING ANYTHING...
WH-WHAT DO YOU WANT FROM MY FRIEND HERE?
I DON'T KNOW ABOUT ALL THIS IMMORTAL BUSINESS. THE PEOPLE OF THE ISLAND ARE OUT THERE FIGHTING WITH THEIR LIVES ON THE LINE! WHO DO YOU THINK YOU ARE?!
YOU DON'T FIGHT, YOU DON'T KILL, AND YOU WALK ALL OVER YOUR OPPONENTS' SPIRITS!!
DON'T LET ALL THIS PAMPERING GO TO YOUR HEAD!!
I-
IF I'VE DONE ANYTHING TO ANGER YOU, I APOLOGIZE.
I'M SORRY...

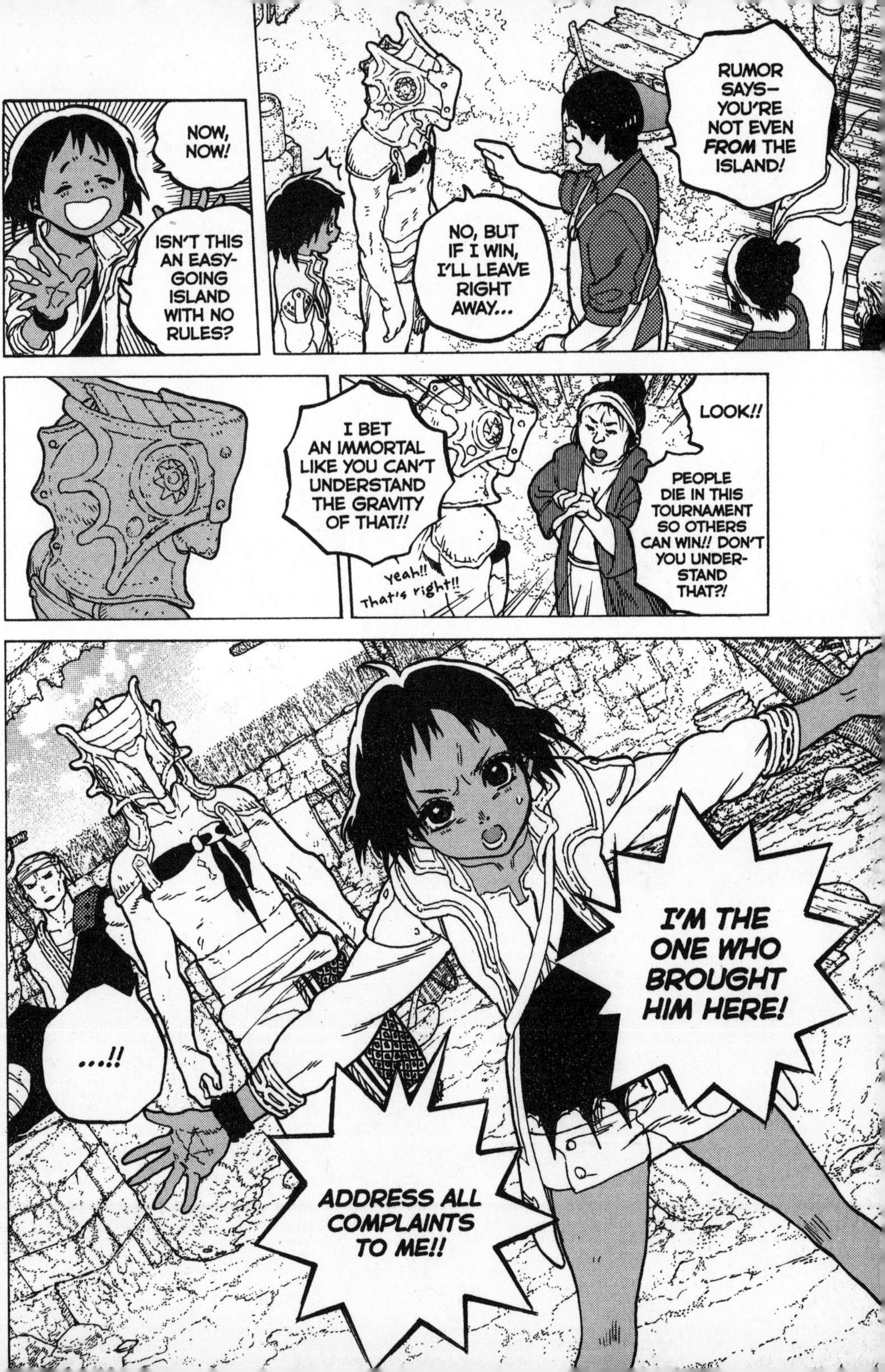
RUMOR SAYS— YOU'RE NOT EVEN *FROM* THE ISLAND!
NO, BUT IF I WIN, I'LL LEAVE RIGHT AWAY...
NOW, NOW!
ISN'T THIS AN EASY-GOING ISLAND WITH NO RULES?
LOOK!!
PEOPLE DIE IN THIS TOURNAMENT SO OTHERS CAN WIN!! DON'T YOU UNDERSTAND THAT?!
I BET AN IMMORTAL LIKE YOU CAN'T UNDERSTAND THE GRAVITY OF THAT!!
Yeah!! That's right!!
I'M THE ONE WHO BROUGHT HIM HERE!
...!!
ADDRESS ALL COMPLAINTS TO ME!!

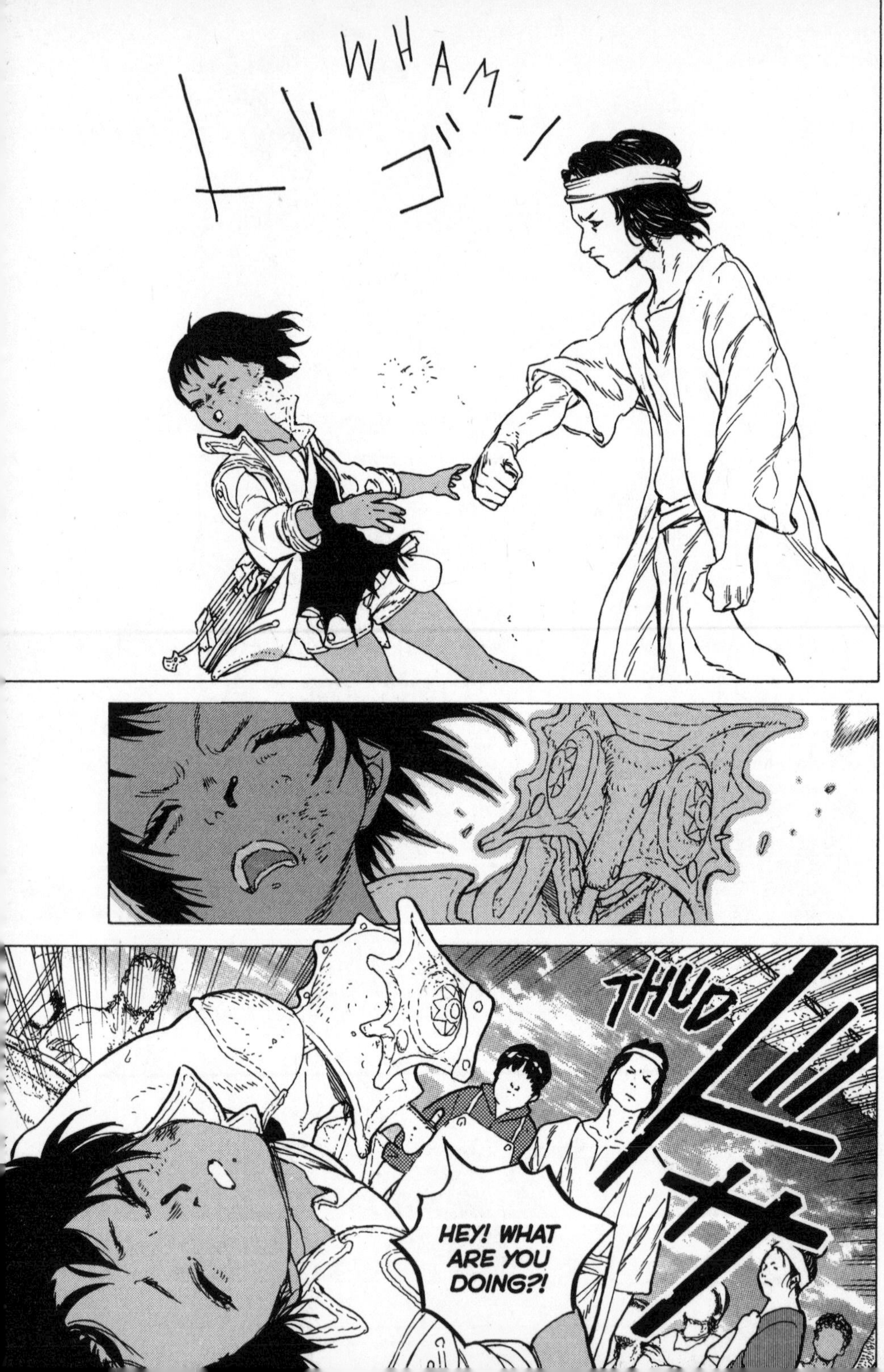
WHAM
THUD
HEY! WHAT ARE YOU DOING?!

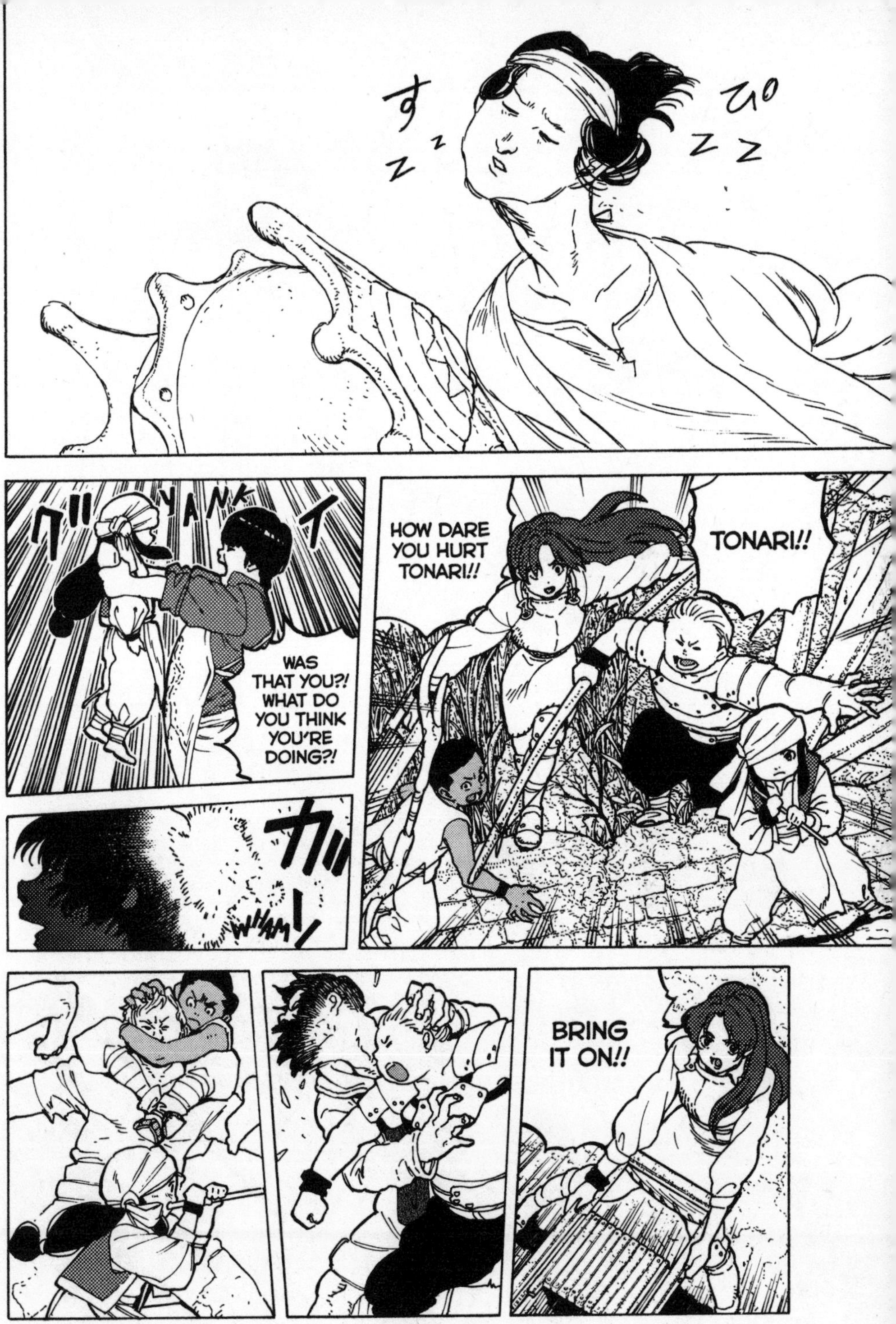
すぴ
ZZZ
ZZ
グイ
YANK
TONARI!!
HOW DARE YOU HURT TONARI!!
WAS THAT YOU?! WHAT DO YOU THINK YOU'RE DOING?!
カッ
WHAM!
BRING IT ON!!

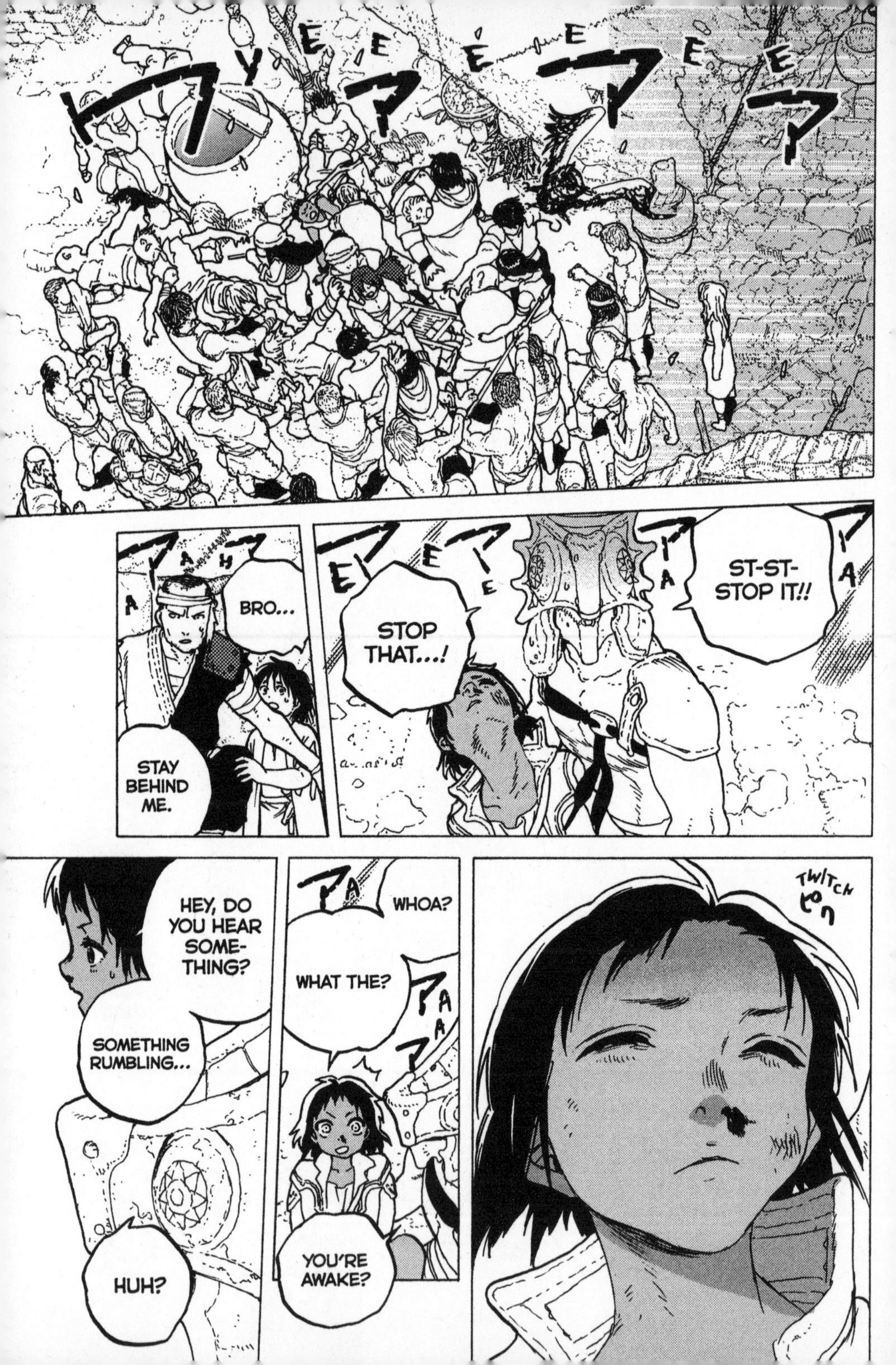
YEEEEEE
ST-ST-STOP IT!!
A
A
STOP THAT...!
E
E
E
AAH
BRO...
STAY BEHIND ME.
TWITCH
WHOA?
A
WHAT THE?
AA
YOU'RE AWAKE?
HEY, DO YOU HEAR SOMETHING?
SOMETHING RUMBLING...
HUH?

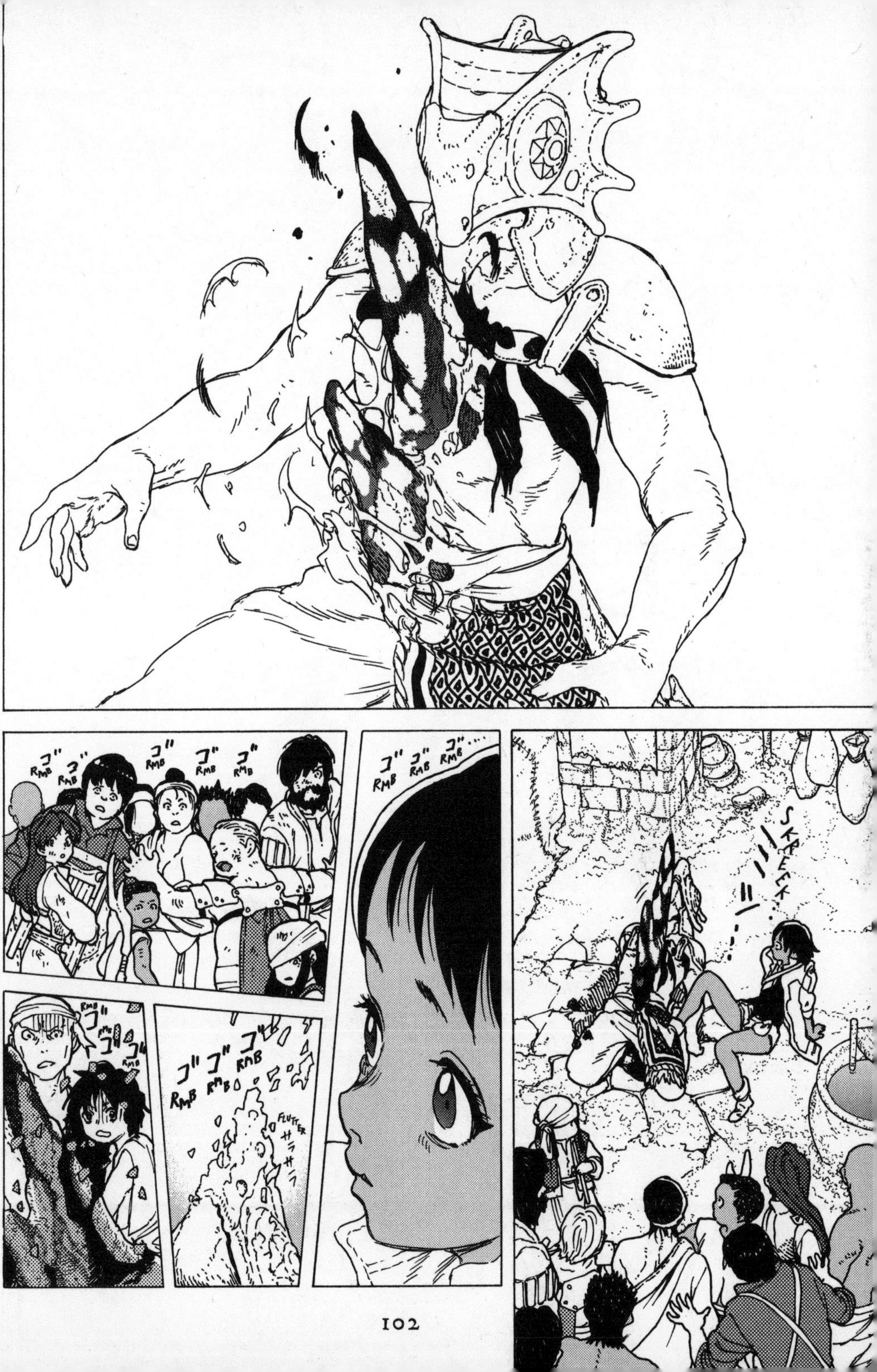
SKREECK...
ジリ...
ゴ" ゴ" ゴ"...
RMB RMB RMB
ゴ" ゴ" ゴ" ゴ" ゴ"
RMB RMB RMB RMB RMB
ゴ" ゴ" ゴ"
RMB RMB RMB
FLUTTER
ヒラヒラ
ゴ" ゴ" ゴ"
RMB RMB RMB

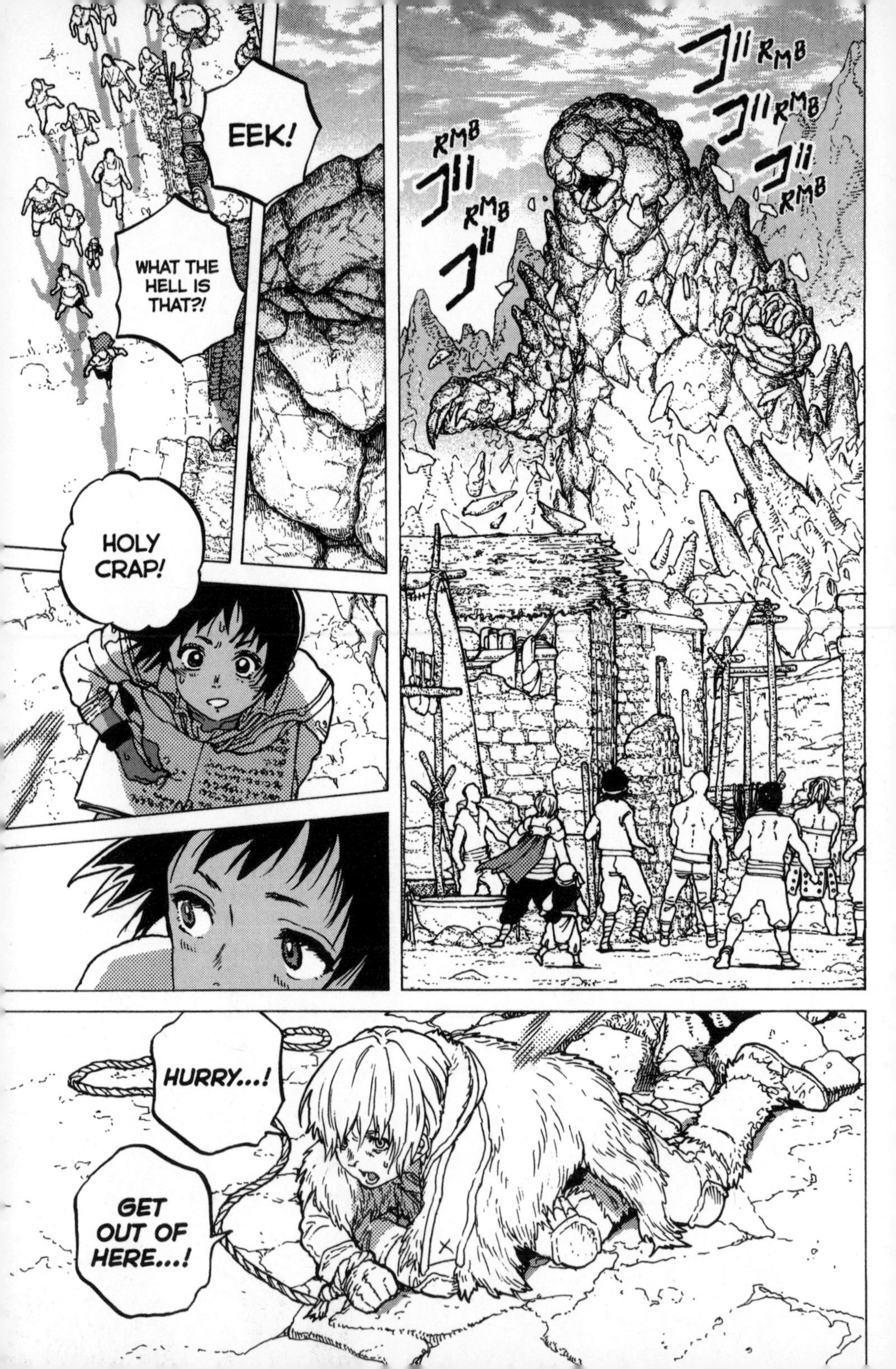
ゴ RMB
ゴ RMB
ゴ RMB
RMB ゴ
RMB ゴ
EEK!
WHAT THE HELL IS THAT?!
HOLY CRAP!
HURRY...!
GET OUT OF HERE...!

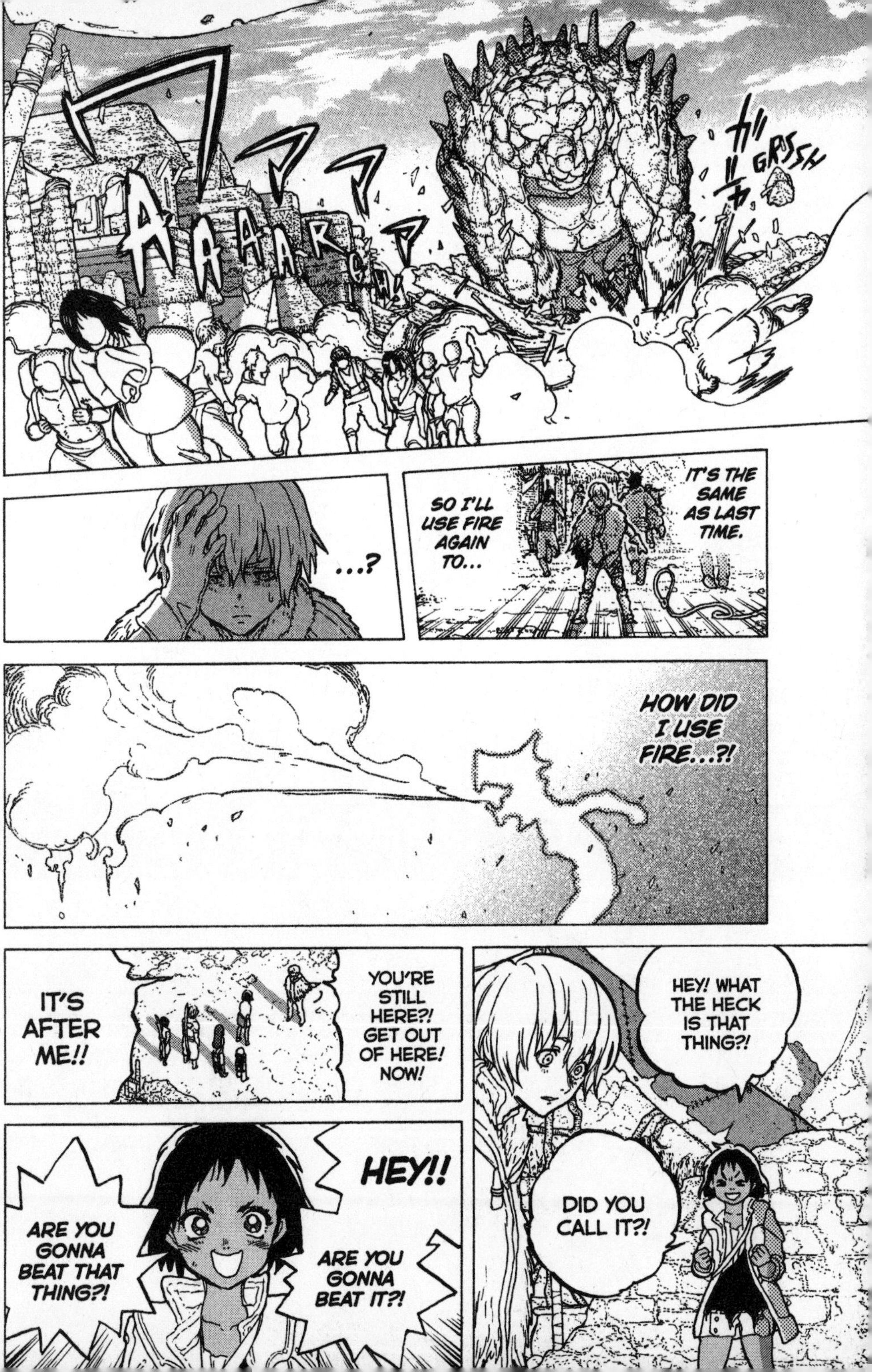
GRSSH
AAAARGH!
IT'S THE SAME AS LAST TIME.
SO I'LL USE FIRE AGAIN TO...
...?
HOW DID I USE FIRE...?!
HEY! WHAT THE HECK IS THAT THING?!
DID YOU CALL IT?!
YOU'RE STILL HERE?! GET OUT OF HERE! NOW!
IT'S AFTER ME!!
HEY!!
ARE YOU GONNA BEAT IT?!
ARE YOU GONNA BEAT THAT THING?!

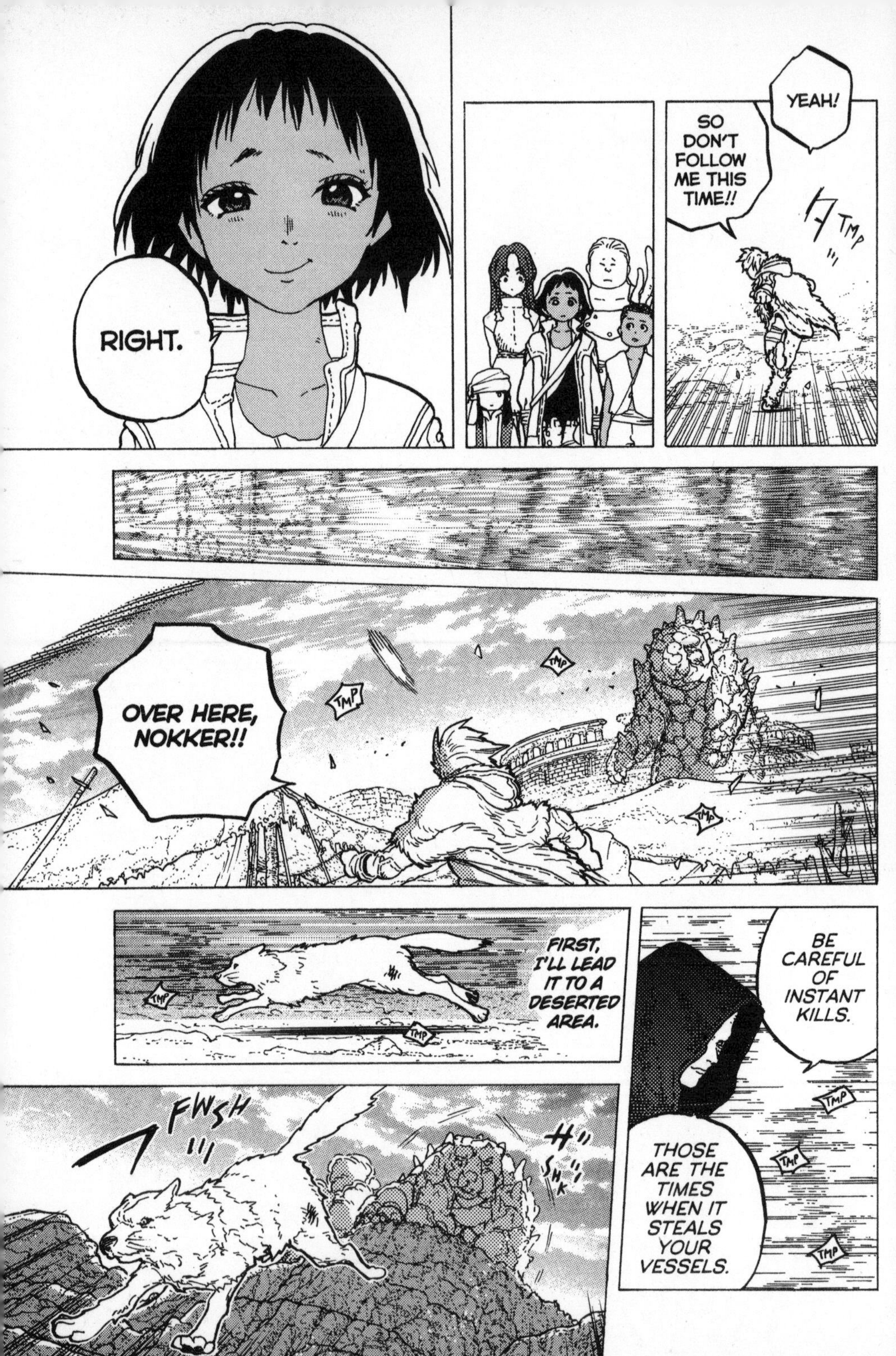
YEAH!
SO DON'T FOLLOW ME THIS TIME!!
TMP
RIGHT.
OVER HERE, NOKKER!!
TMP
TMP
TMP
BE CAREFUL OF INSTANT KILLS.
THOSE ARE THE TIMES WHEN IT STEALS YOUR VESSELS.
TMP
TMP
TMP
FIRST, I'LL LEAD IT TO A DESERTED AREA.
TMP
TMP
FWSH
SHK

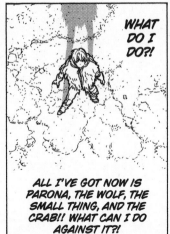

WHAT DO I DO?!

ALL I'VE GOT NOW IS PARONA, THE WOLF, THE SMALL THING, AND THE CRAB!! WHAT CAN I DO AGAINST IT?!

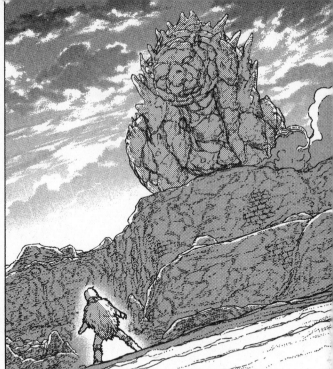

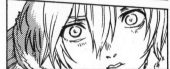

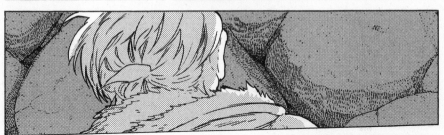

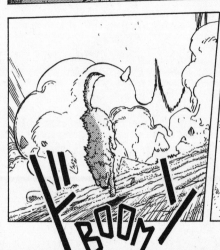

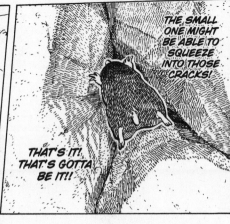

THE SMALL ONE MIGHT BE ABLE TO SQUEEZE INTO THOSE CRACKS!

THAT'S IT! THAT'S GOTTA BE IT!!

BOOM

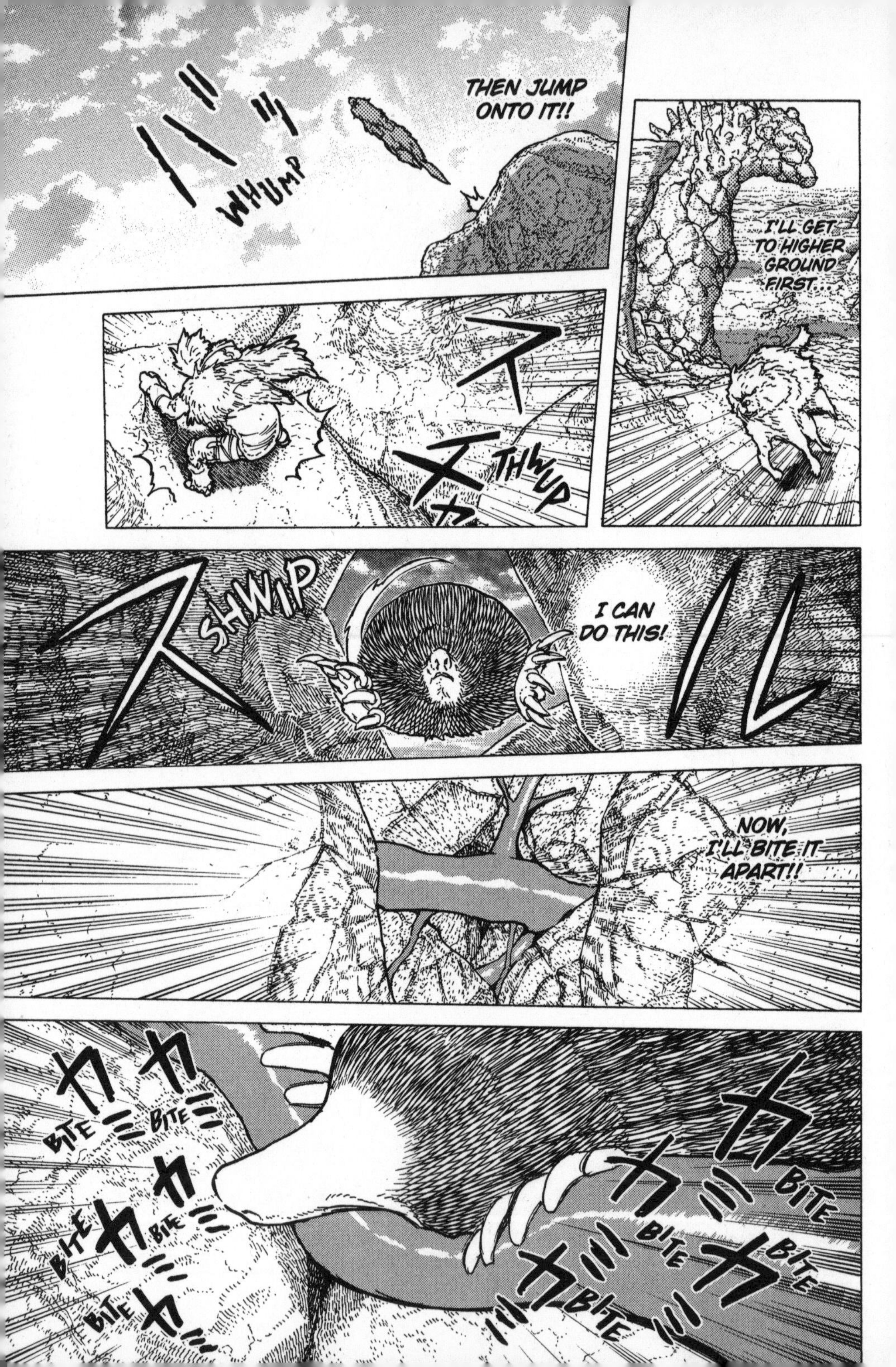
I'LL GET TO HIGHER GROUND FIRST...
THEN JUMP ONTO IT!!
WHUMP
THWUP
SHWIP
I CAN DO THIS!
NOW, I'LL BITE IT APART!!
BITE
BITE
BITE
BITE
BITE
BITE
BITE
BITE
BITE

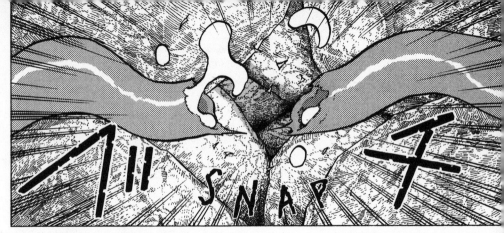

SNAP
CRUNCH CRUNCH
...
BITE BITE BITE BITE
SO I'M GONNA HAVE TO DO THIS THE HARD WAY?
BITE BITE BITE BITE BITE BITE
SHWIP
?!

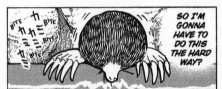

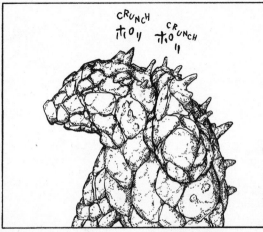

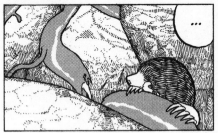

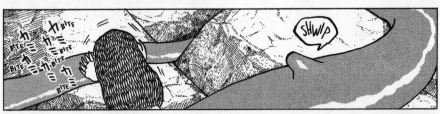

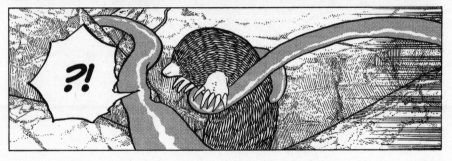

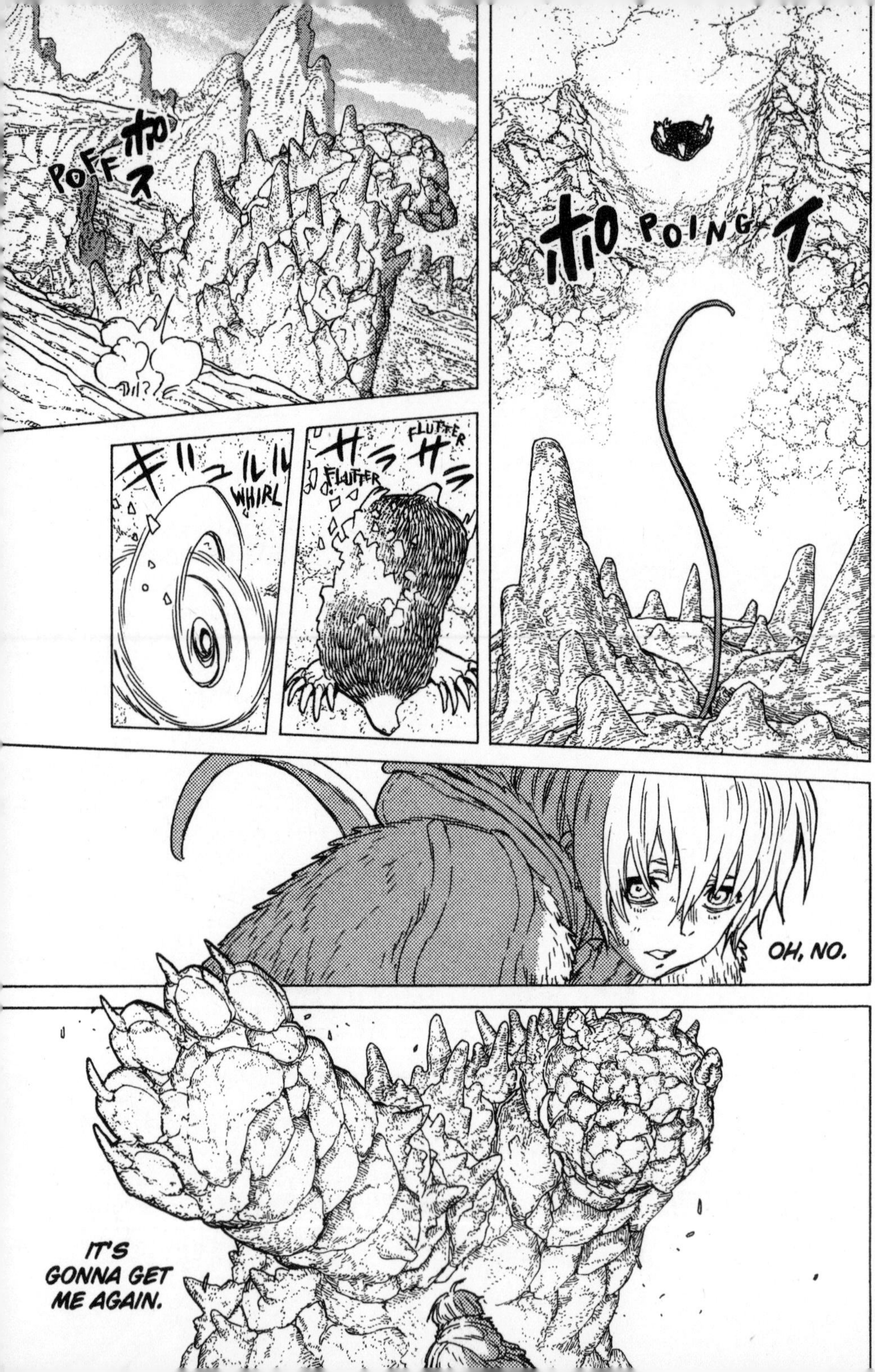

ポイ POING
ポス POFF
サラサラ
FLUTTER
FLUTTER
キリュルル
WHIRL
OH, NO.
IT'S GONNA GET ME AGAIN.

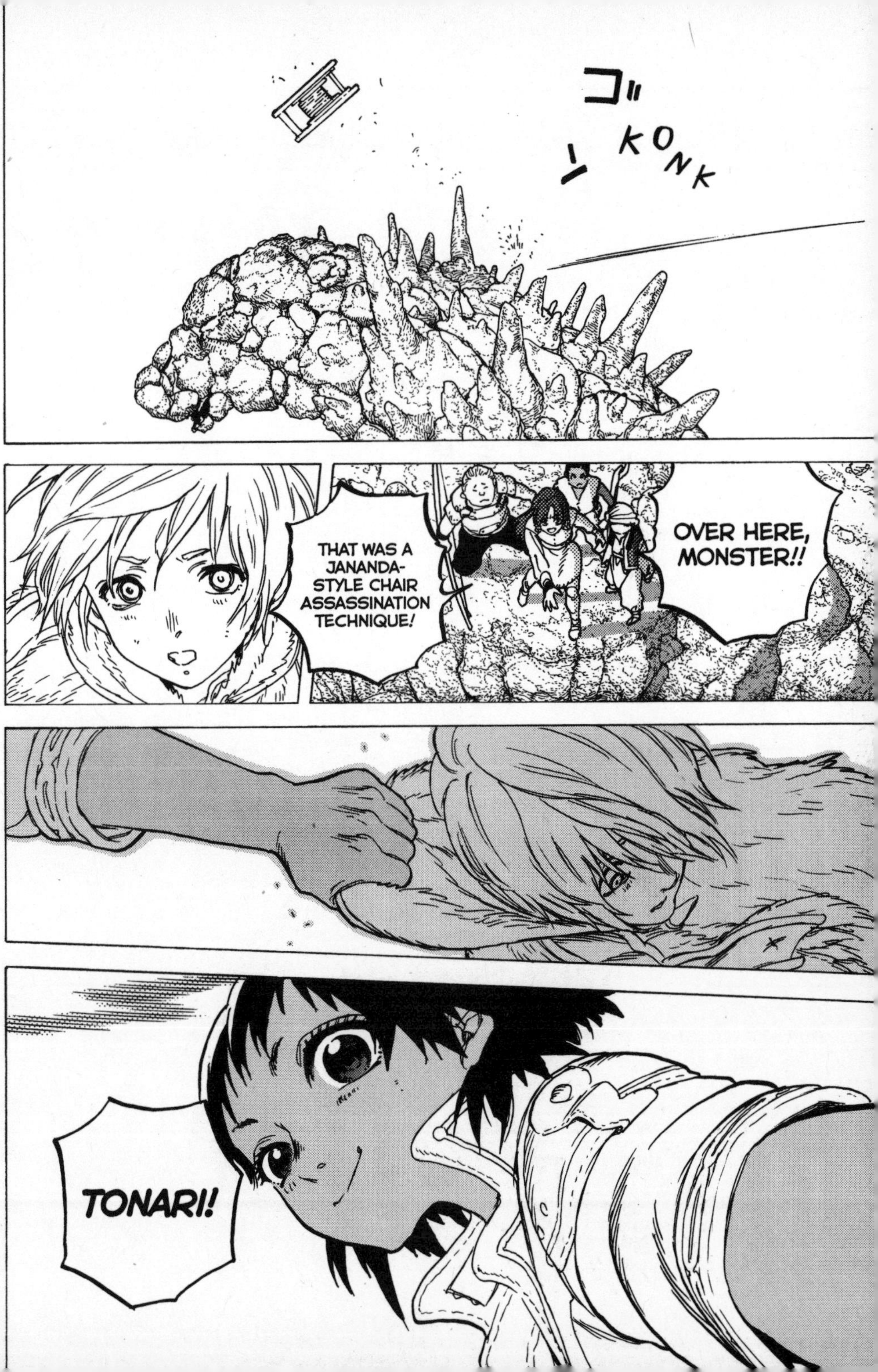
ゴ
KONK
ン
OVER HERE, MONSTER!!
THAT WAS A JANANDA-STYLE CHAIR ASSASSINATION TECHNIQUE!
TONARI!

TO YOUR ETERNITY

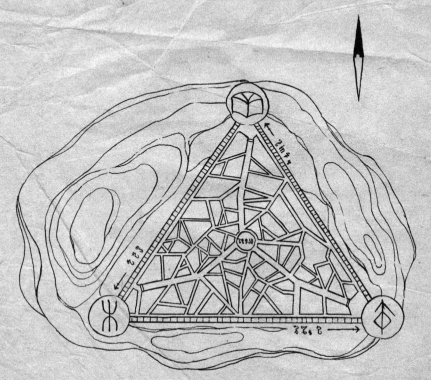

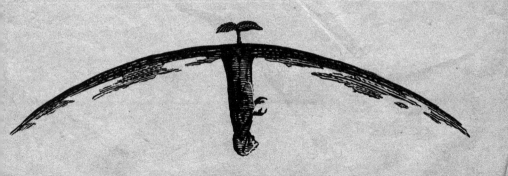

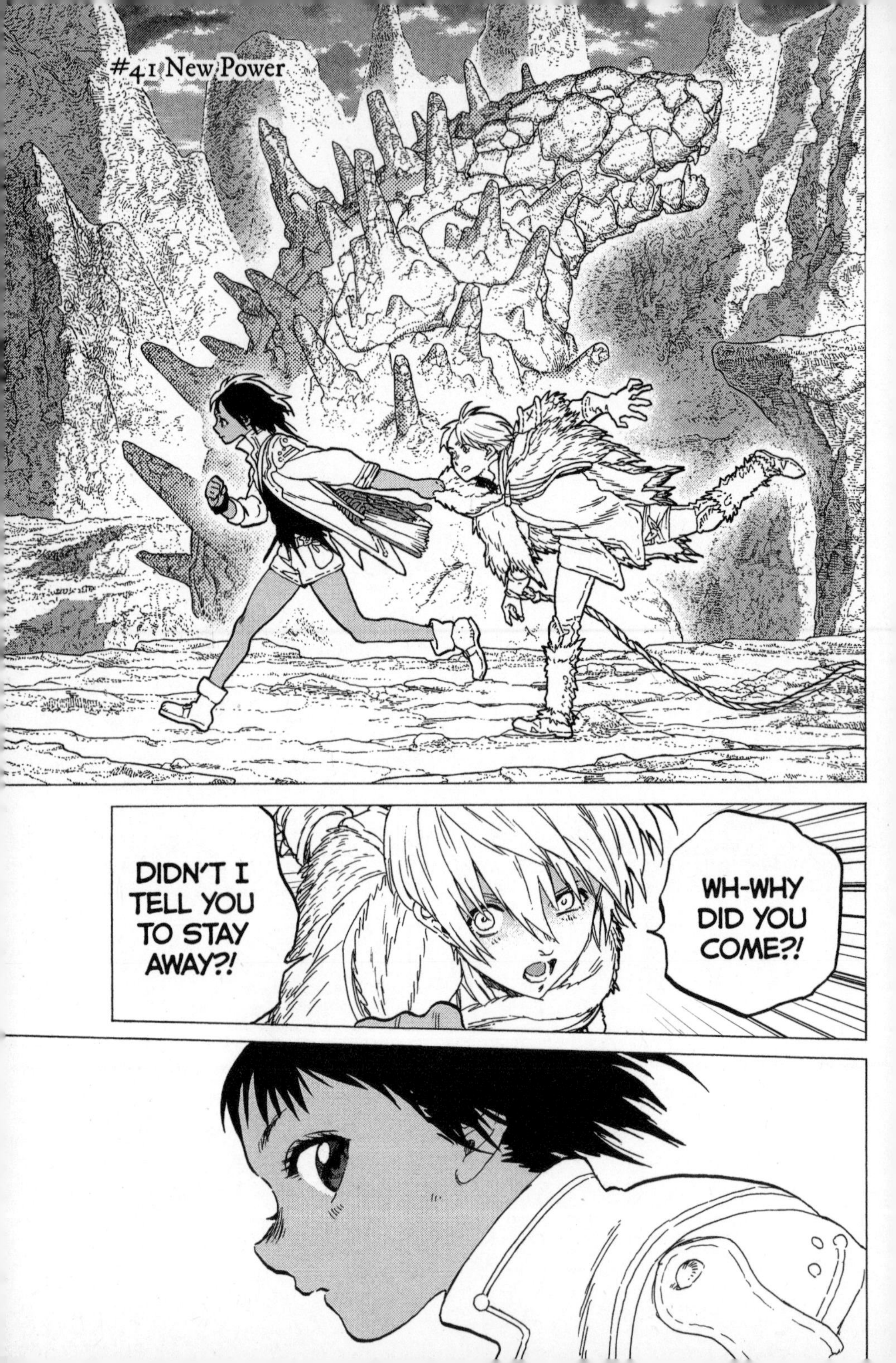
#41 New Power
WH-WHY DID YOU COME?!
DIDN'T I TELL YOU TO STAY AWAY?!

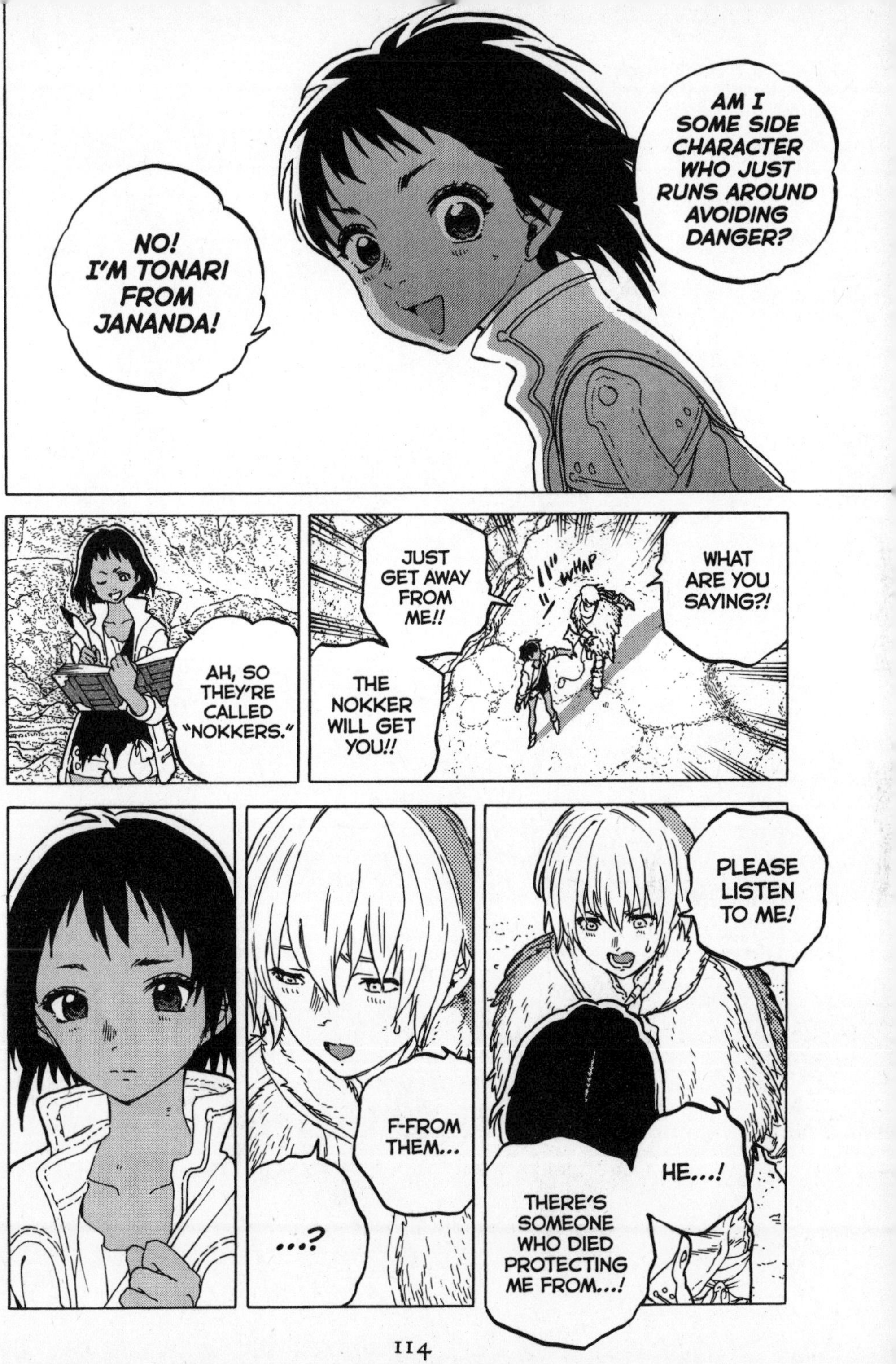
AM I SOME SIDE CHARACTER WHO JUST RUNS AROUND AVOIDING DANGER?
NO! I'M TONARI FROM JANANDA!
WHAT ARE YOU SAYING?!
WHAP
JUST GET AWAY FROM ME!!
THE NOKKER WILL GET YOU!!
AH, SO THEY'RE CALLED "NOKKERS."
PLEASE LISTEN TO ME!
HE...!
THERE'S SOMEONE WHO DIED PROTECTING ME FROM...!
F-FROM THEM...
...?

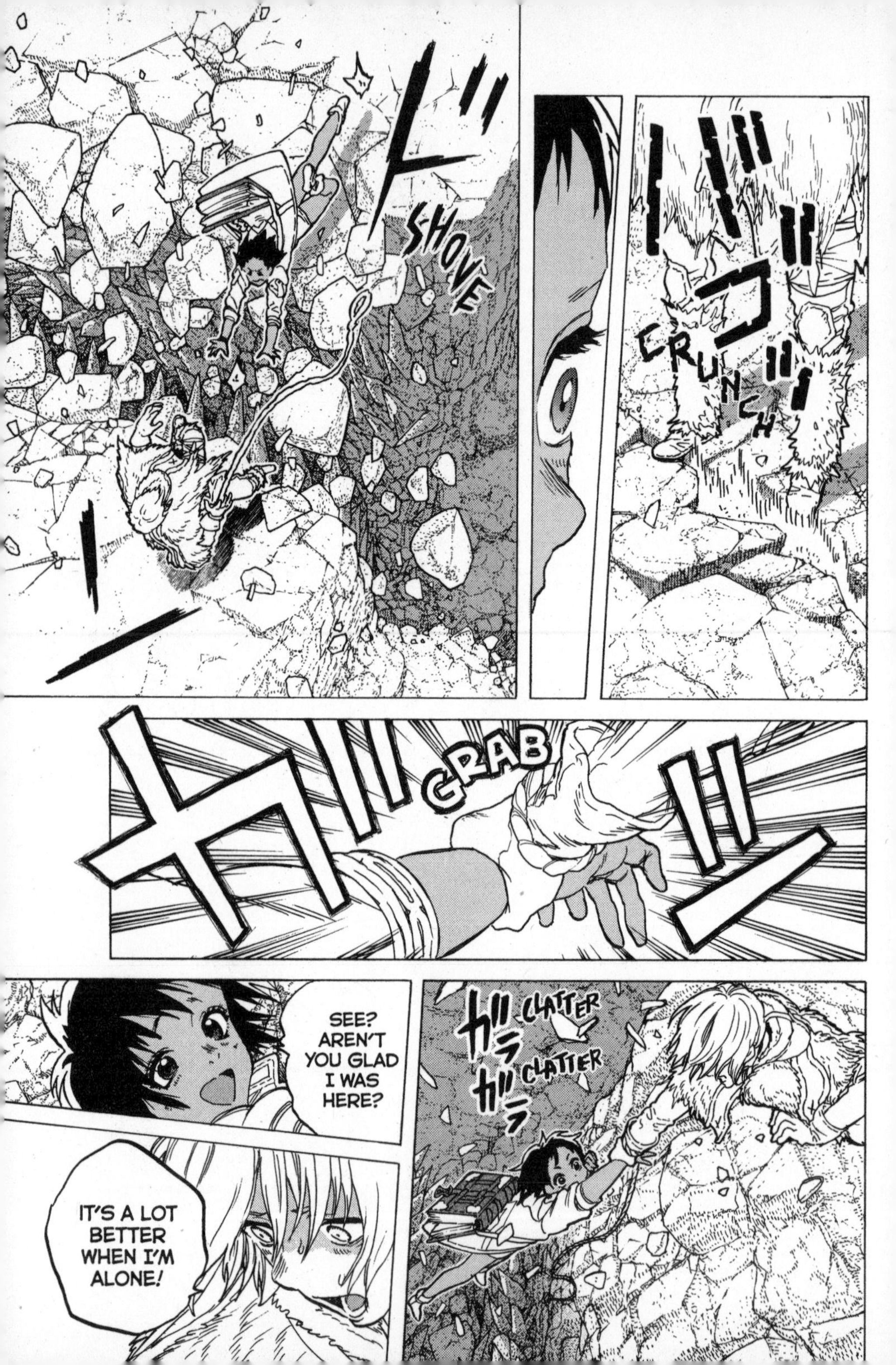
CRUNCH
SHOVE
GRAB
CLATTER
ガラ
CLATTER
ガラ
SEE? AREN'T YOU GLAD I WAS HERE?
IT'S A LOT BETTER WHEN I'M ALONE!

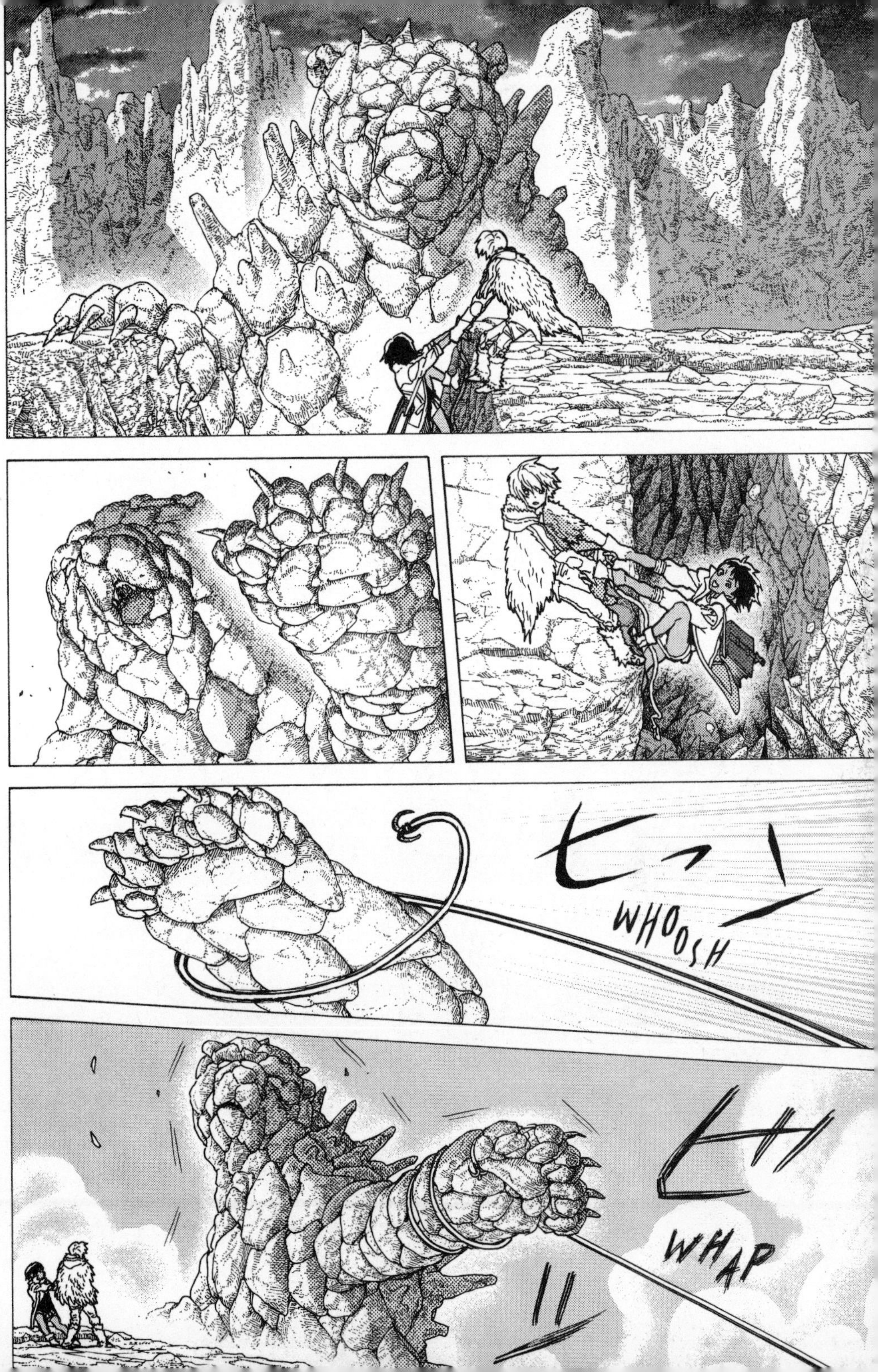
WHOOSH
WHAP

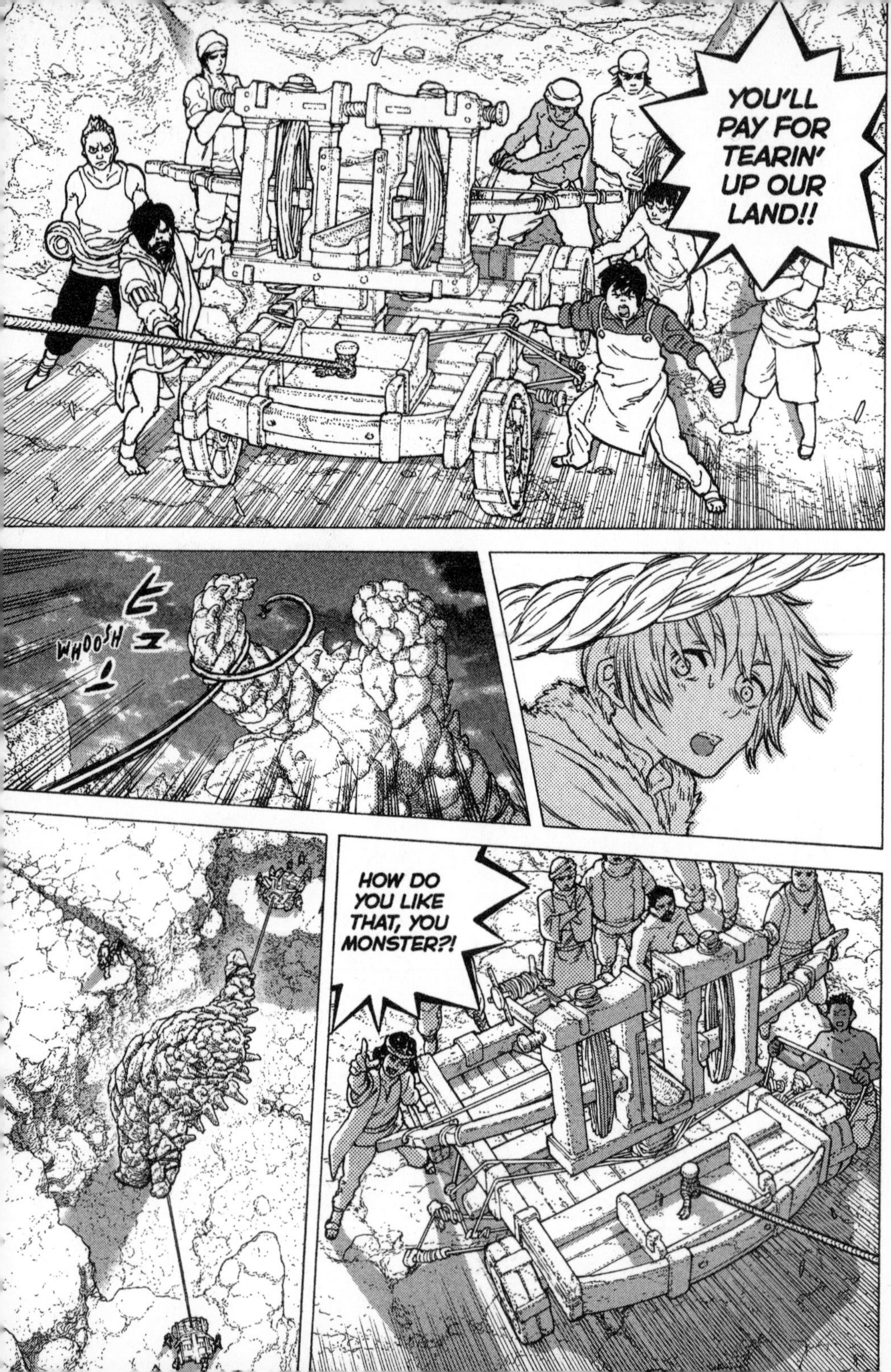
YOU'LL PAY FOR TEARIN' UP OUR LAND!!
WHOOSH
HOW DO YOU LIKE THAT, YOU MONSTER?!

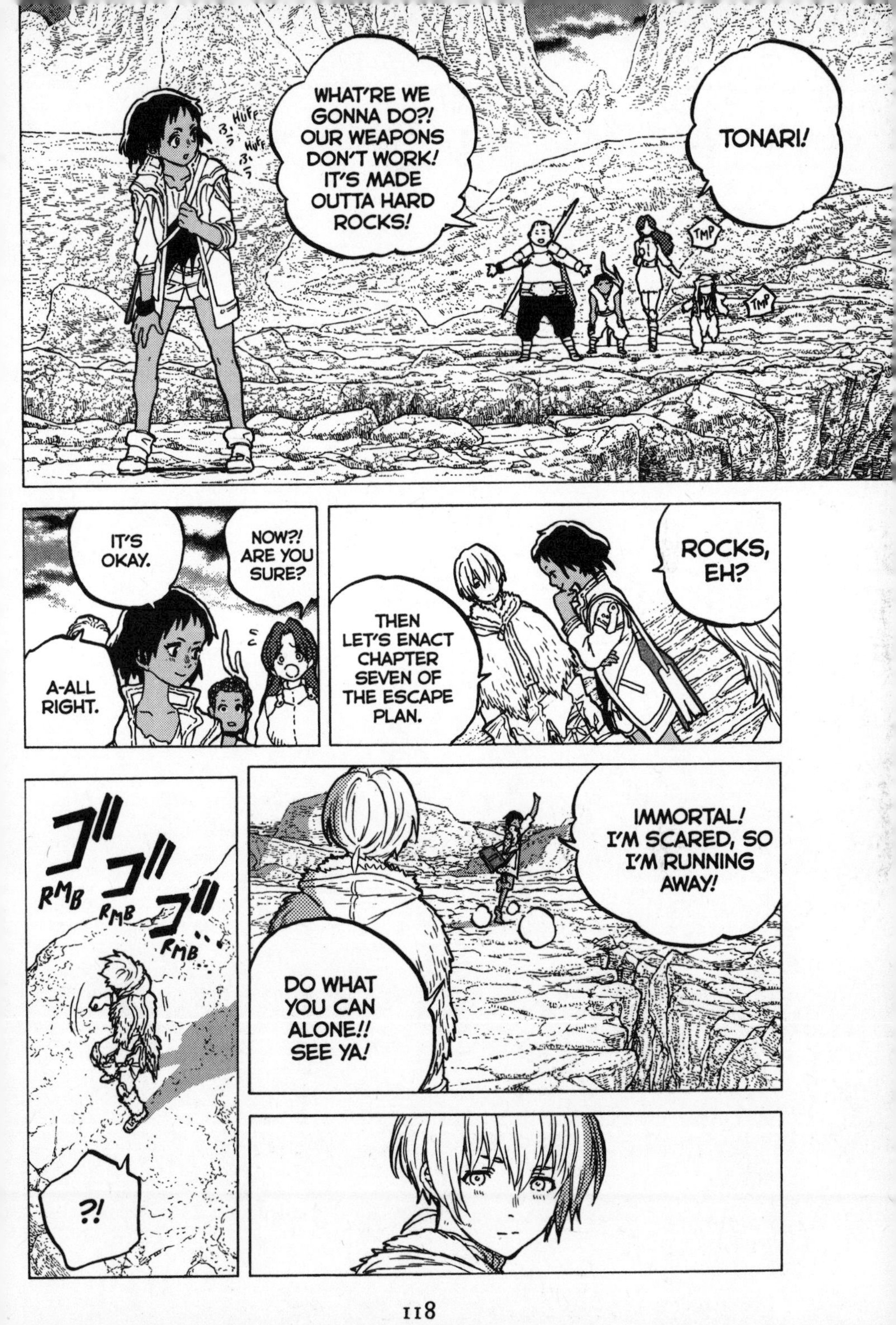
TONARI!
TMP
TMP
WHAT'RE WE GONNA DO?! OUR WEAPONS DON'T WORK! IT'S MADE OUTTA HARD ROCKS!
HUFF
HUFF
ROCKS, EH?
THEN LET'S ENACT CHAPTER SEVEN OF THE ESCAPE PLAN.
NOW?! ARE YOU SURE?
IT'S OKAY.
A-ALL RIGHT.
IMMORTAL! I'M SCARED, SO I'M RUNNING AWAY!
DO WHAT YOU CAN ALONE!! SEE YA!
ゴ RMB
ゴ RMB
ゴ... RMB
?!

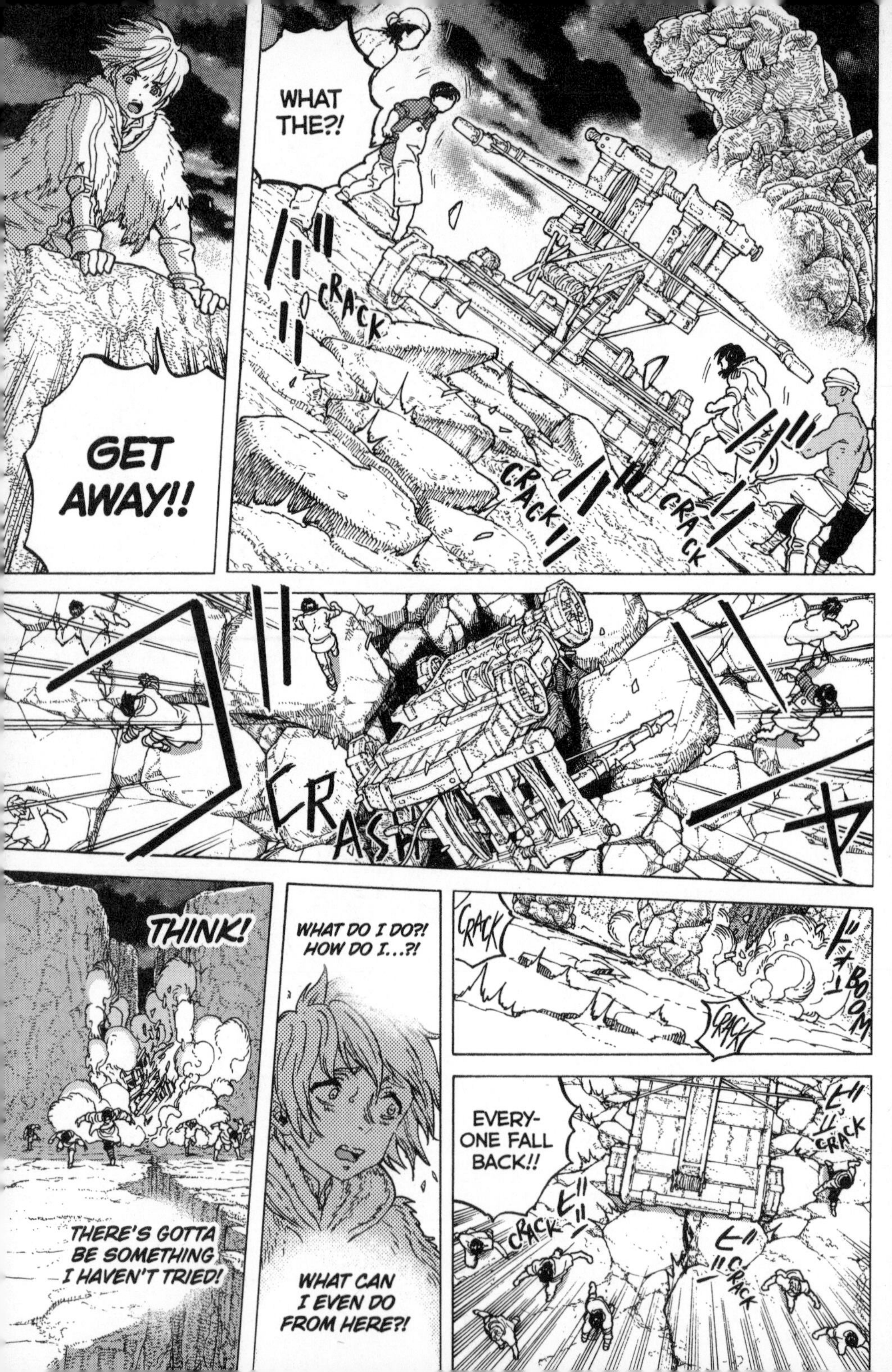
WHAT THE?!
CRACK
CRACK
CRACK
GET AWAY!!
CRASH
CRACK
BOOM
CRACK
EVERY-ONE FALL BACK!!
CRACK
CRACK
CRACK
WHAT DO I DO?! HOW DO I...?!
WHAT CAN I EVEN DO FROM HERE?!
THINK!
THERE'S GOTTA BE SOMETHING I HAVEN'T TRIED!

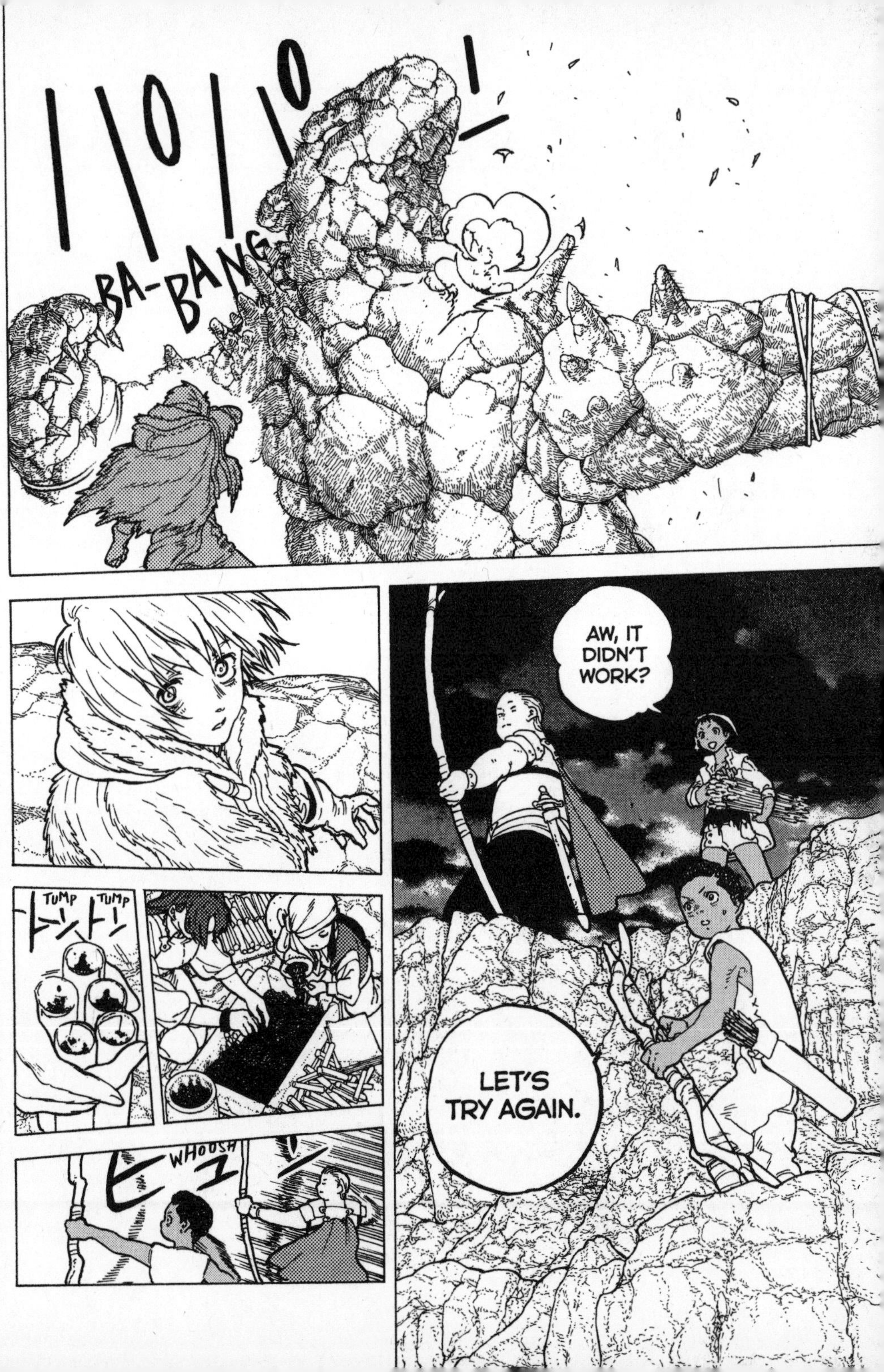
BA-BANG
AW, IT DIDN'T WORK?
LET'S TRY AGAIN.
TUMP TUMP
WHOOSH

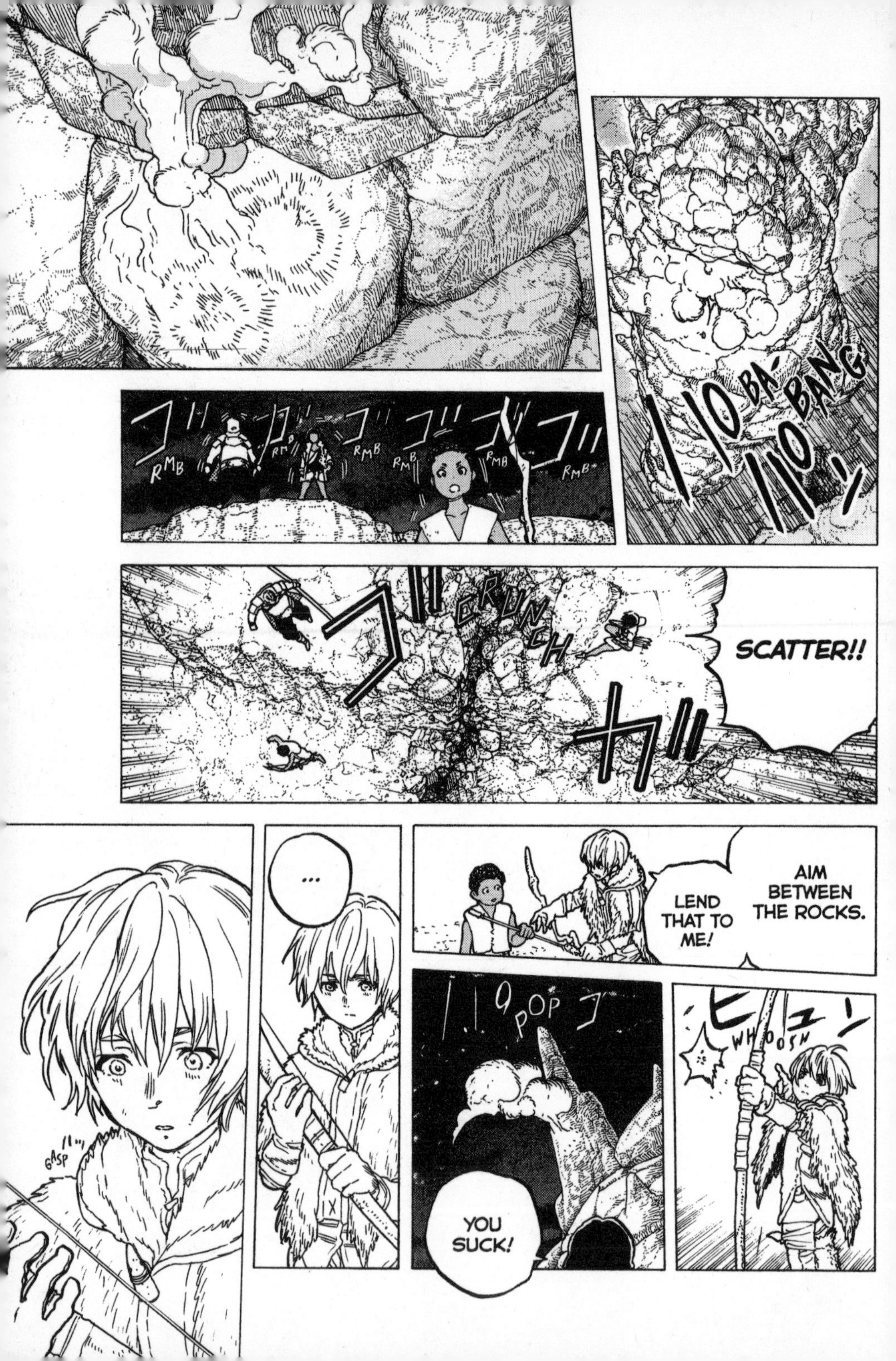
BA-BANG
RMB
RMB
RMB
RMB
RMB
RMB
CRUNCH
SCATTER!!
AIM BETWEEN THE ROCKS.
LEND THAT TO ME!
WHOOSH
POP
YOU SUCK!
...
GASP

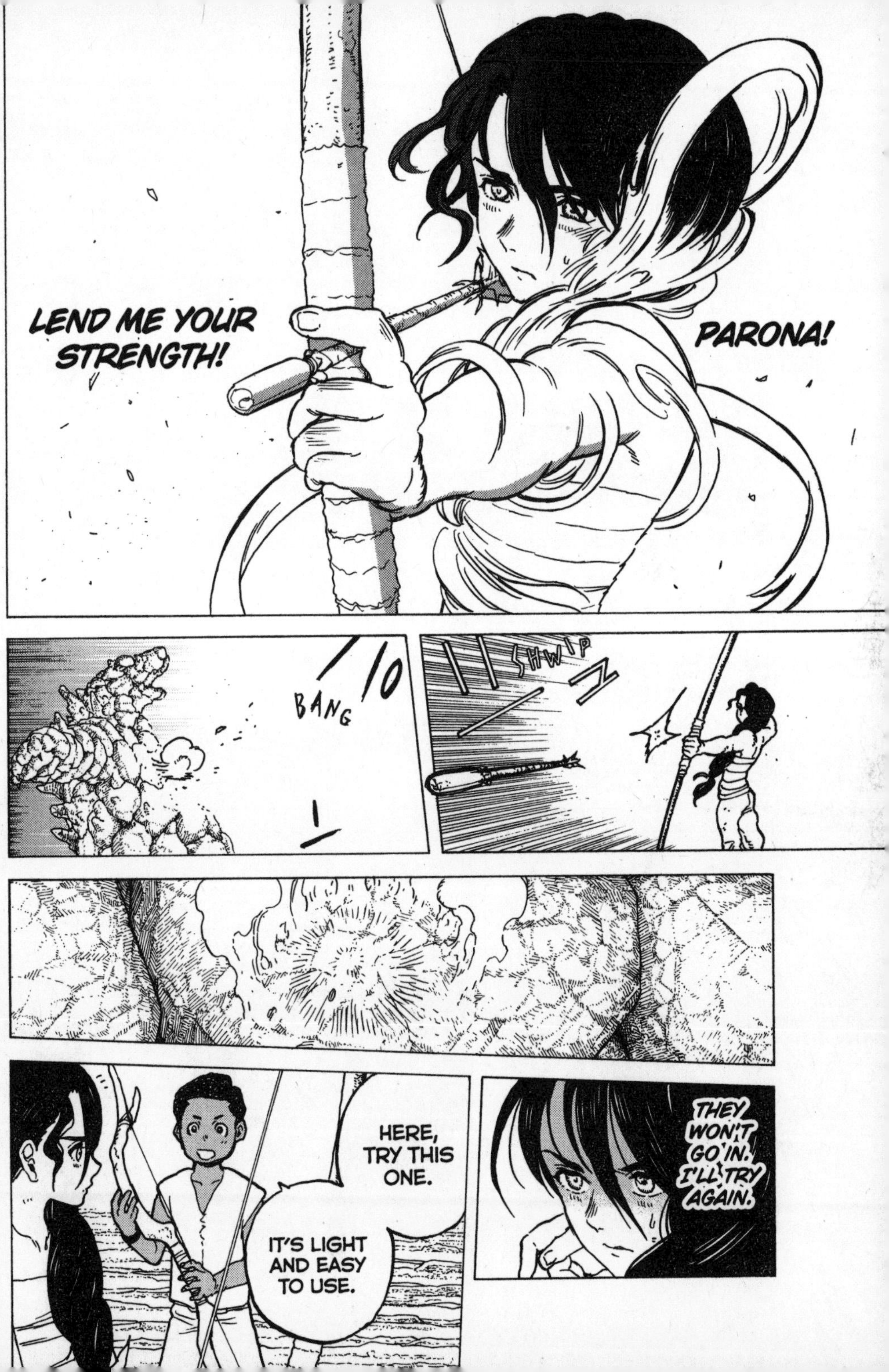
LEND ME YOUR STRENGTH!
PARONA!
SHWIP
BANG
THEY WON'T GO IN. I'LL TRY AGAIN.
HERE, TRY THIS ONE.
IT'S LIGHT AND EASY TO USE.

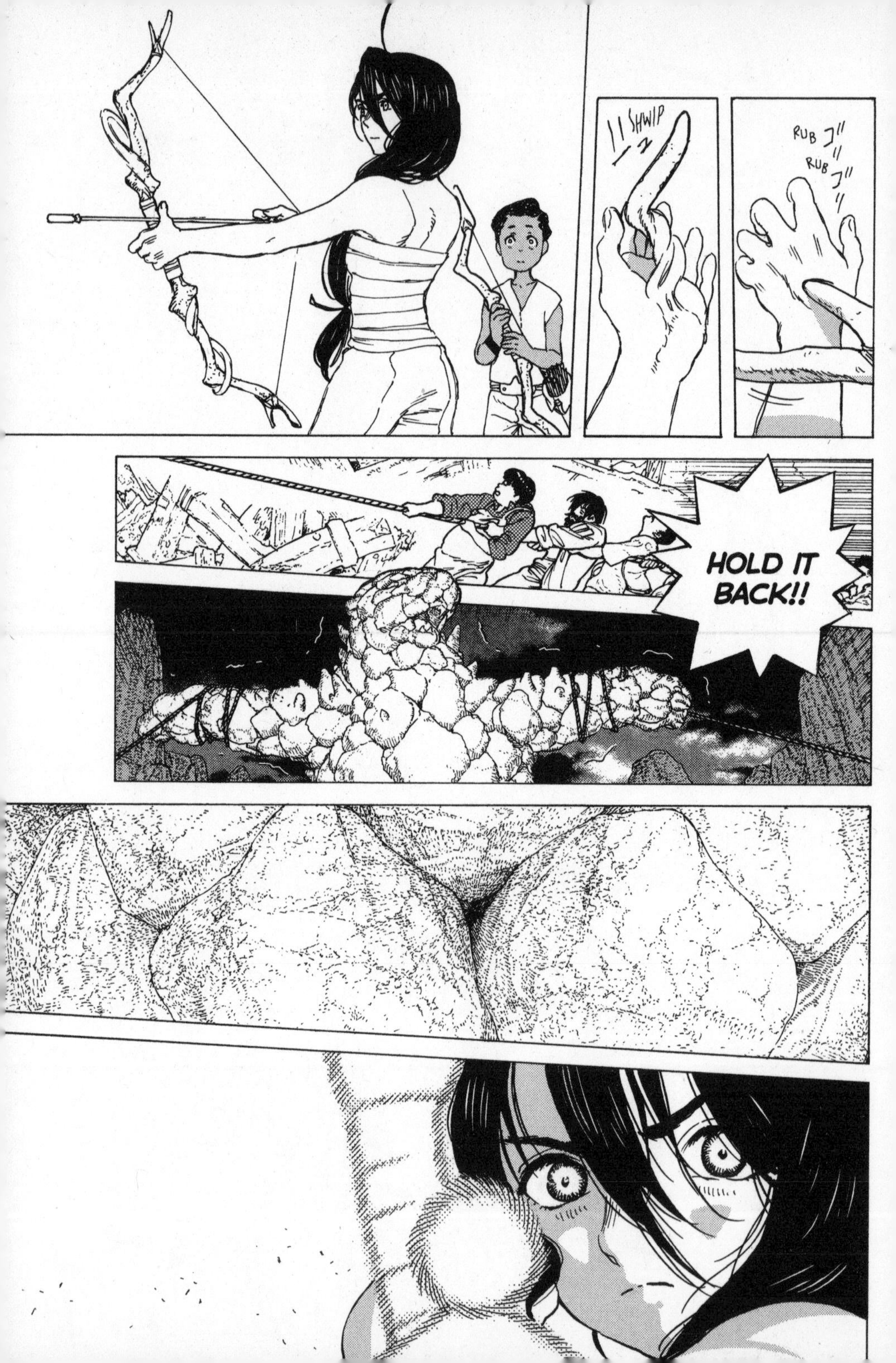
RUB
RUB
SHWIP
HOLD IT BACK!!

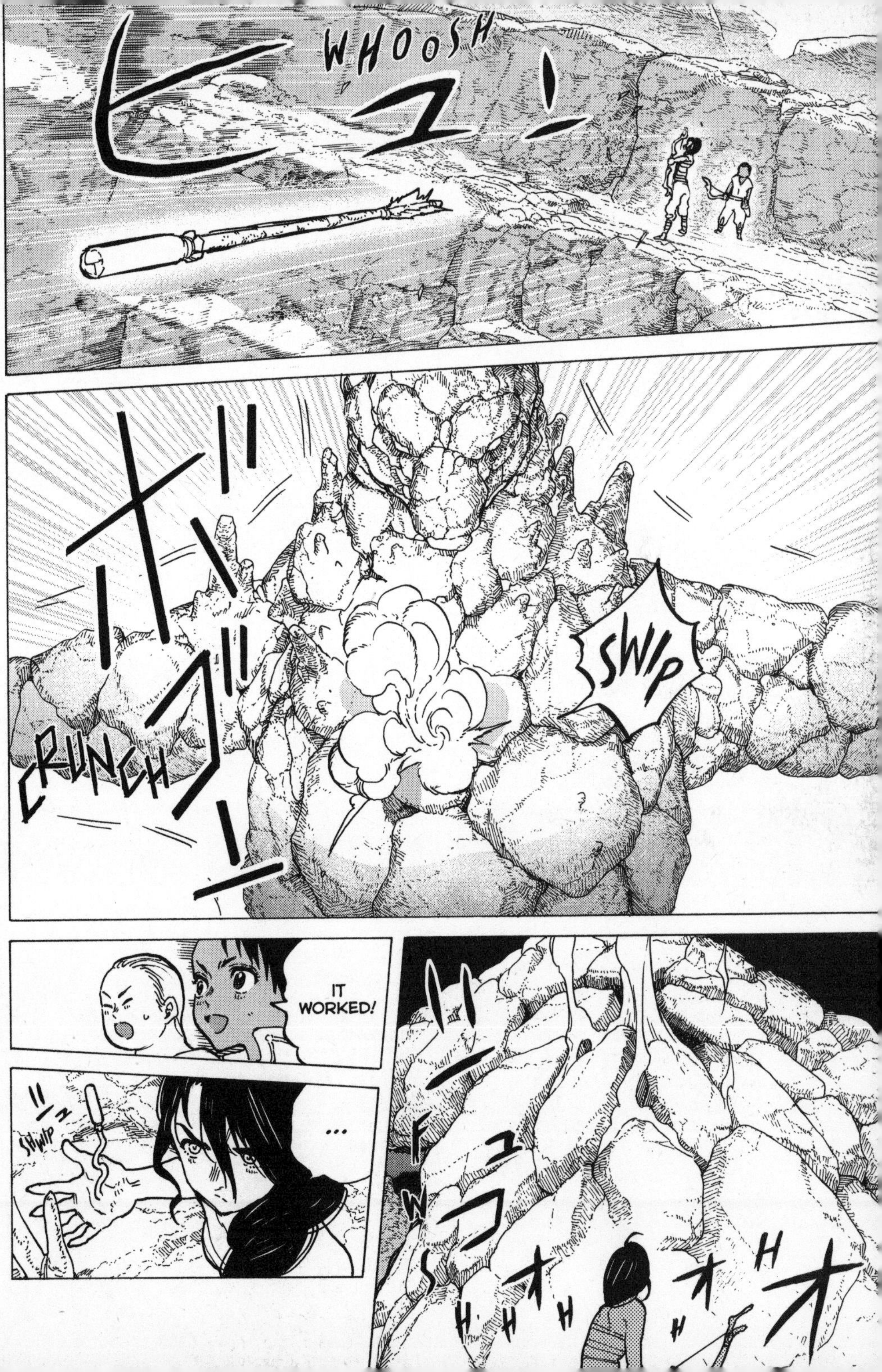
WHOOSH
CRUNCH
SWIP
FWSHHHHH
IT WORKED!
SHWIP
...

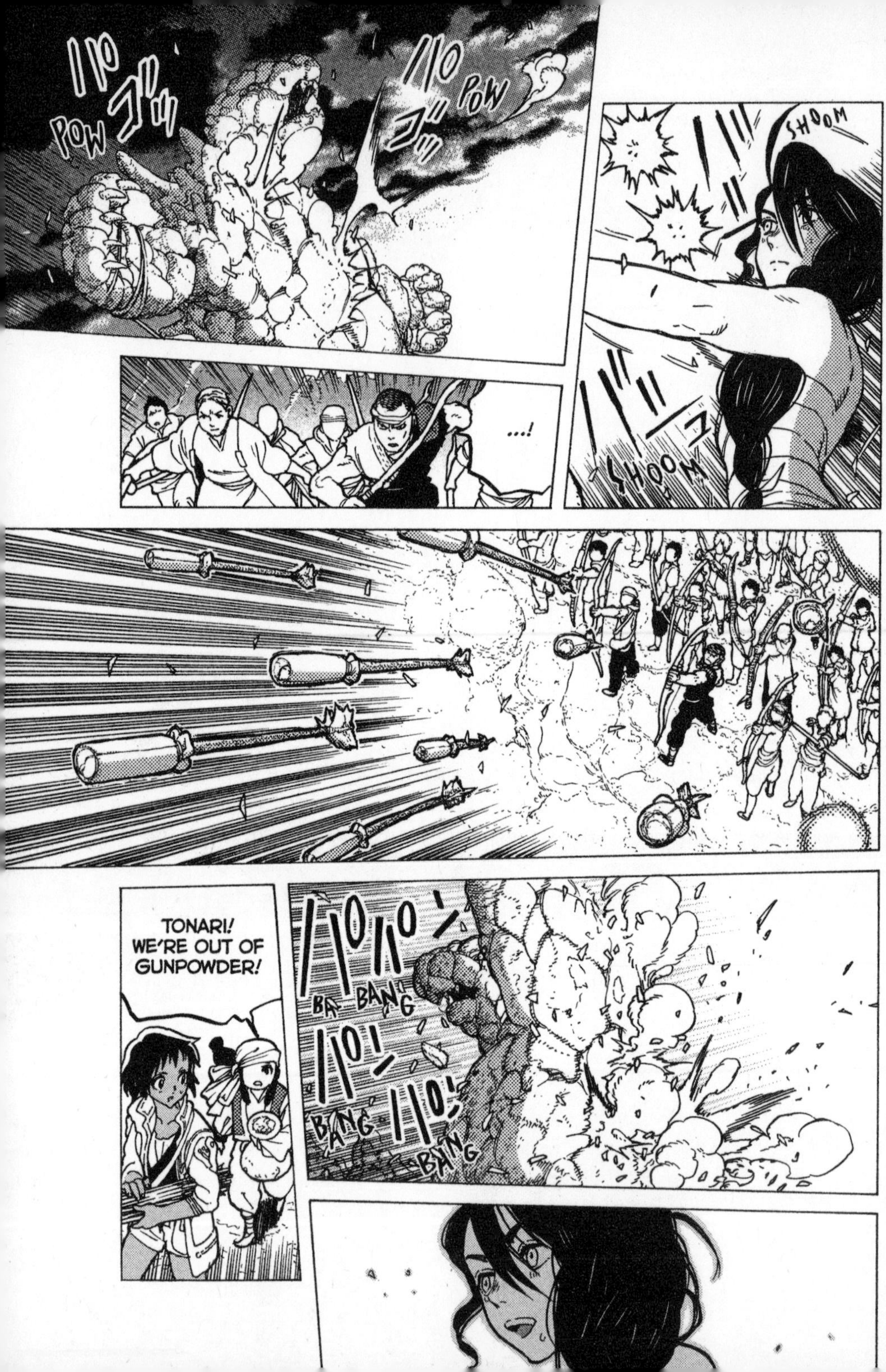
POW
POW
SHOOM
SHOOM
...!
BA BANG
BA BANG
BANG
TONARI! WE'RE OUT OF GUNPOWDER!

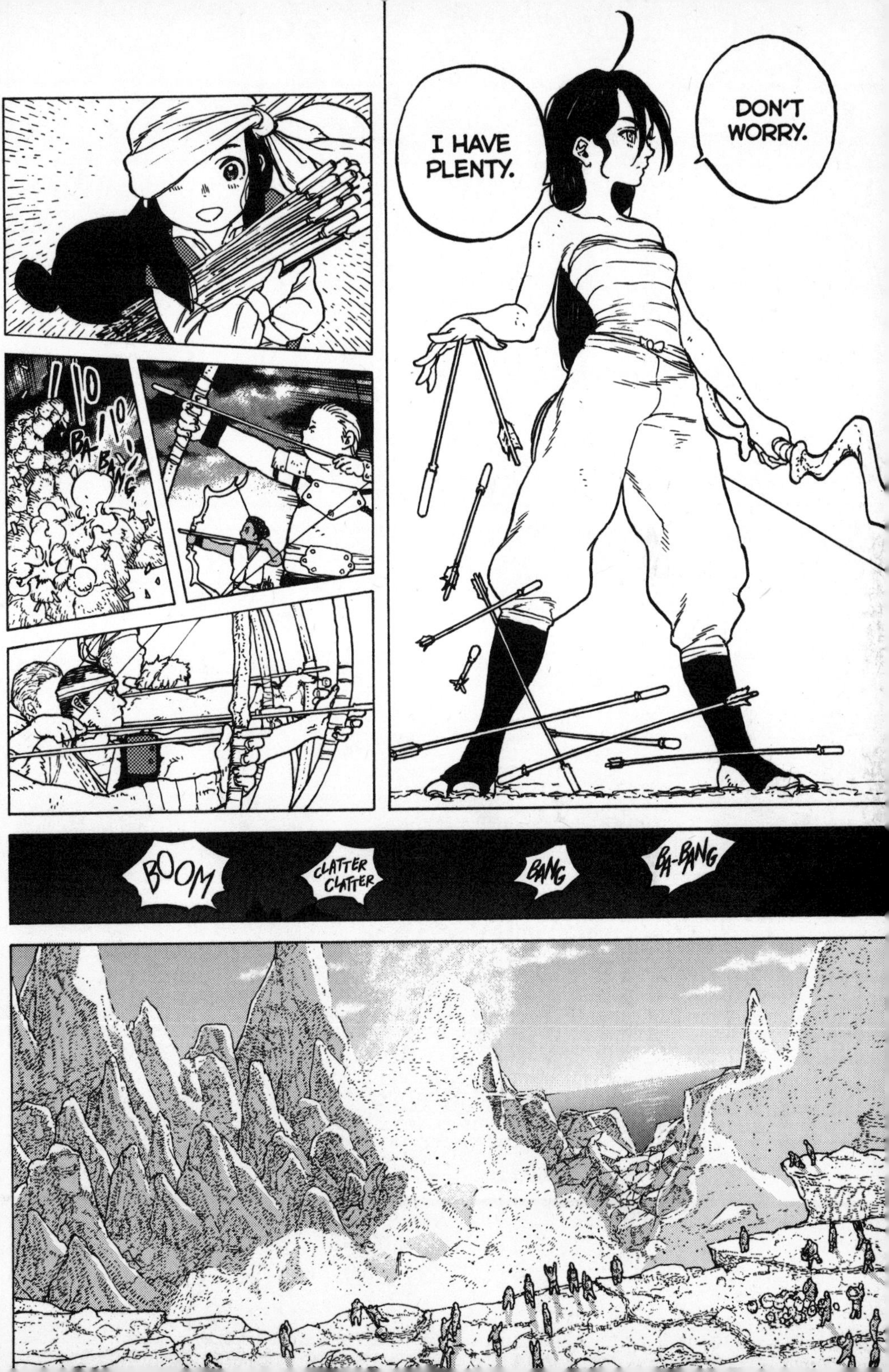
DON'T WORRY.
I HAVE PLENTY.
BA-BANG
BA-BANG
BANG
CLATTER CLATTER
BOOM

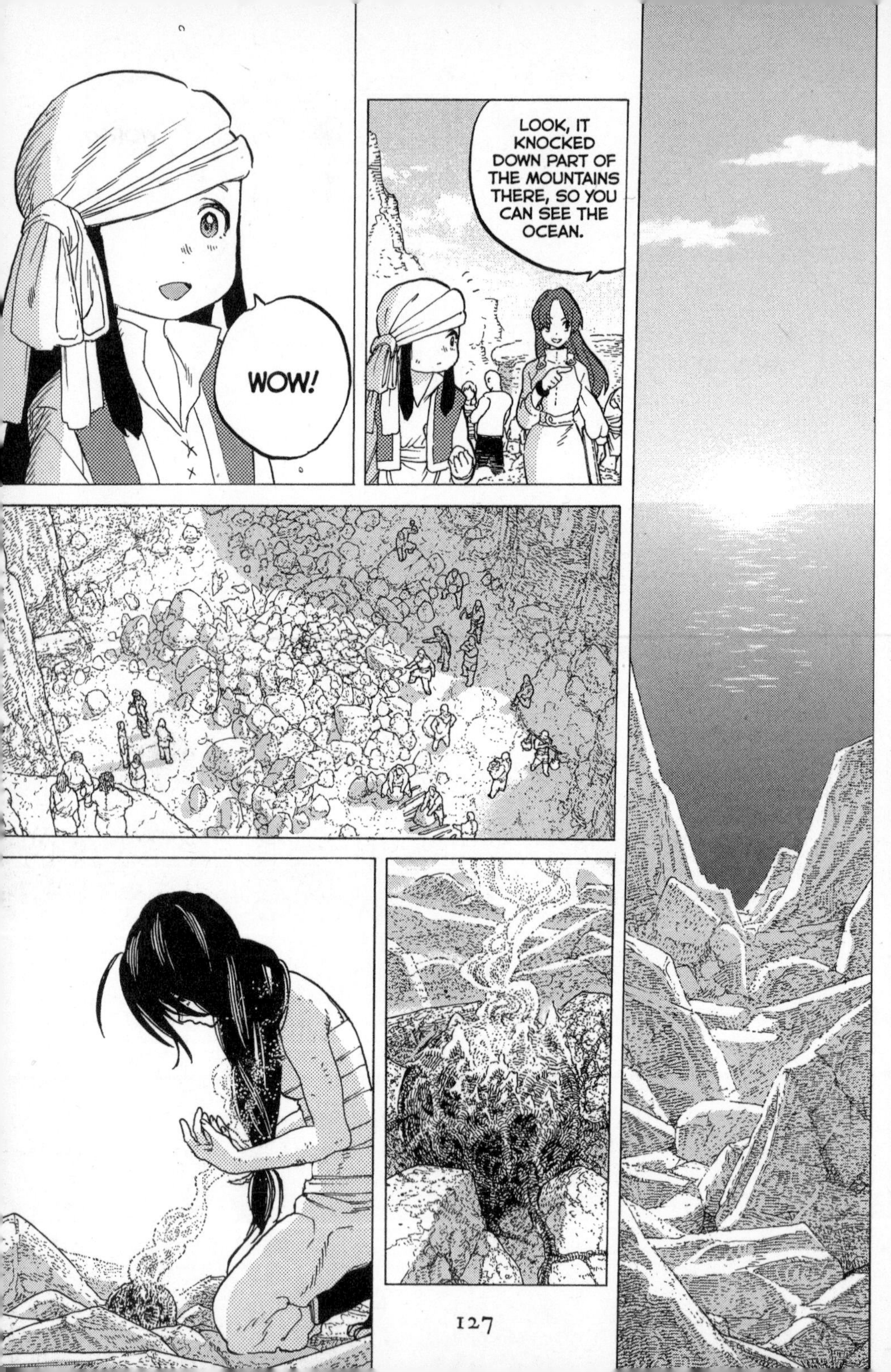
LOOK, IT KNOCKED DOWN PART OF THE MOUNTAINS THERE, SO YOU CAN SEE THE OCEAN.
WOW!

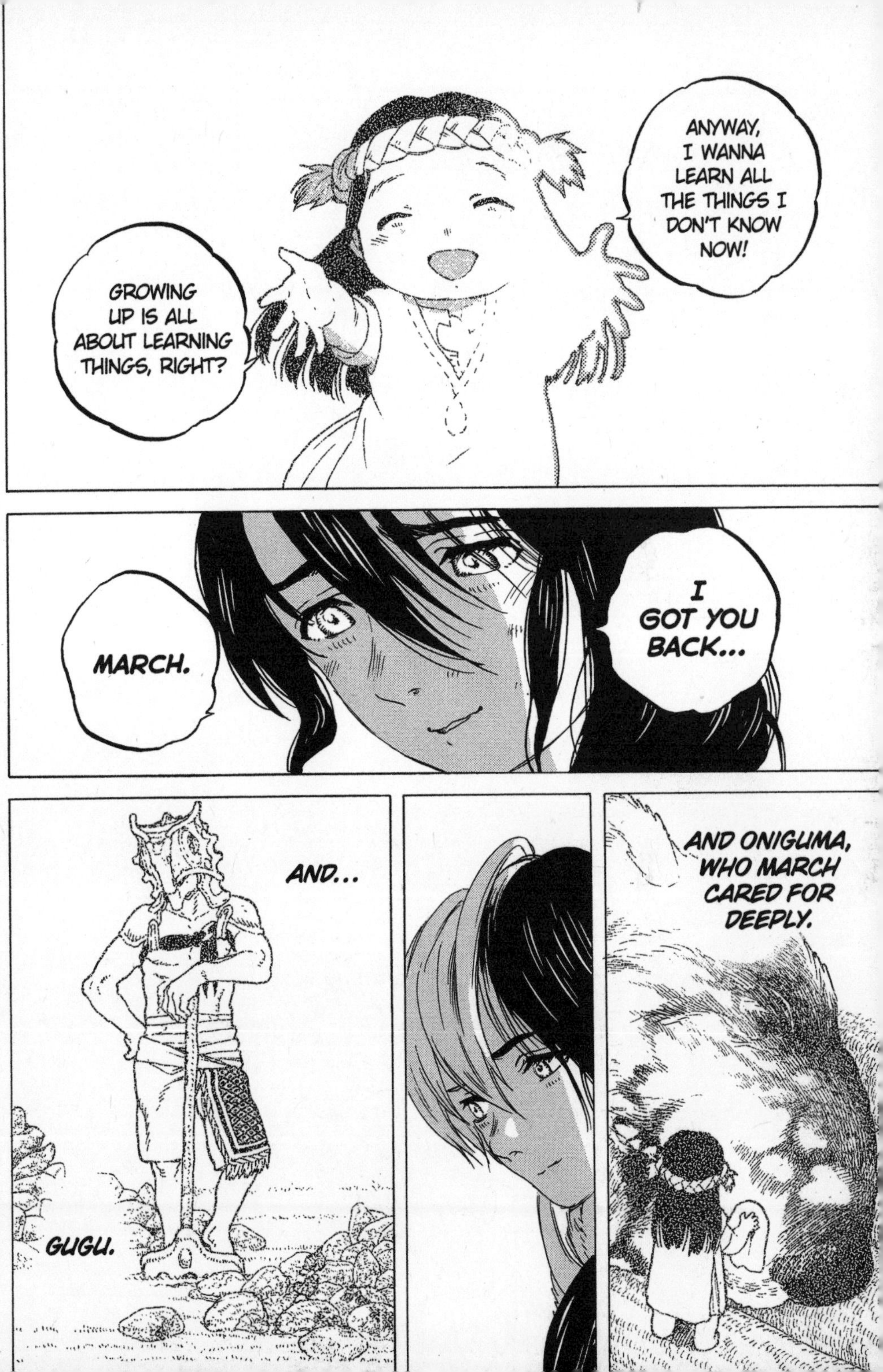
ANYWAY, I WANNA LEARN ALL THE THINGS I DON'T KNOW NOW!
GROWING UP IS ALL ABOUT LEARNING THINGS, RIGHT?
I GOT YOU BACK...
MARCH.
AND ONIGUMA, WHO MARCH CARED FOR DEEPLY.
AND...
GUGU.

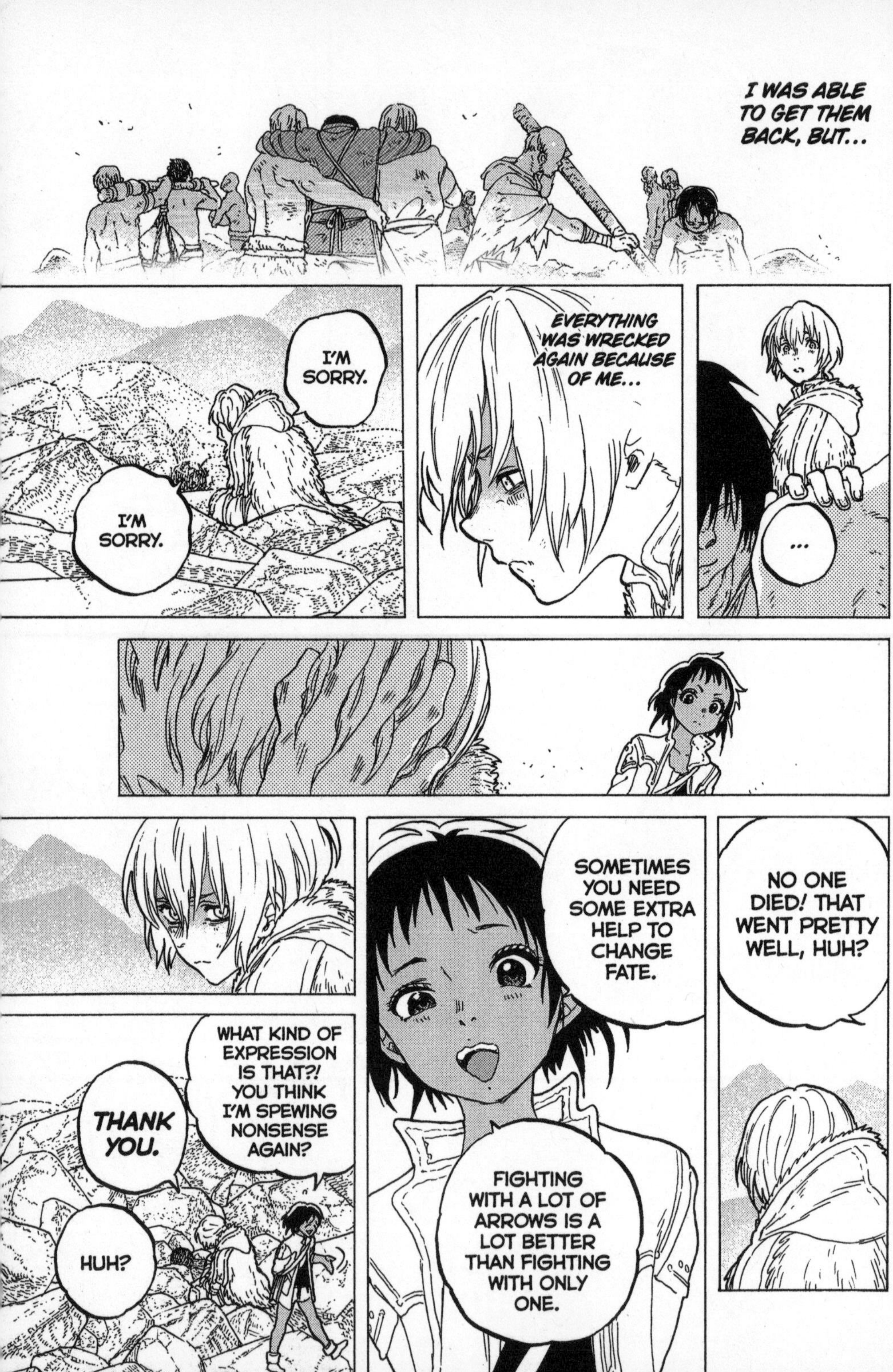
I WAS ABLE TO GET THEM BACK, BUT...
...
EVERYTHING WAS WRECKED AGAIN BECAUSE OF ME...
I'M SORRY.
I'M SORRY.
NO ONE DIED! THAT WENT PRETTY WELL, HUH?
SOMETIMES YOU NEED SOME EXTRA HELP TO CHANGE FATE.
FIGHTING WITH A LOT OF ARROWS IS A LOT BETTER THAN FIGHTING WITH ONLY ONE.
WHAT KIND OF EXPRESSION IS THAT?! YOU THINK I'M SPEWING NONSENSE AGAIN?
THANK YOU.
HUH?

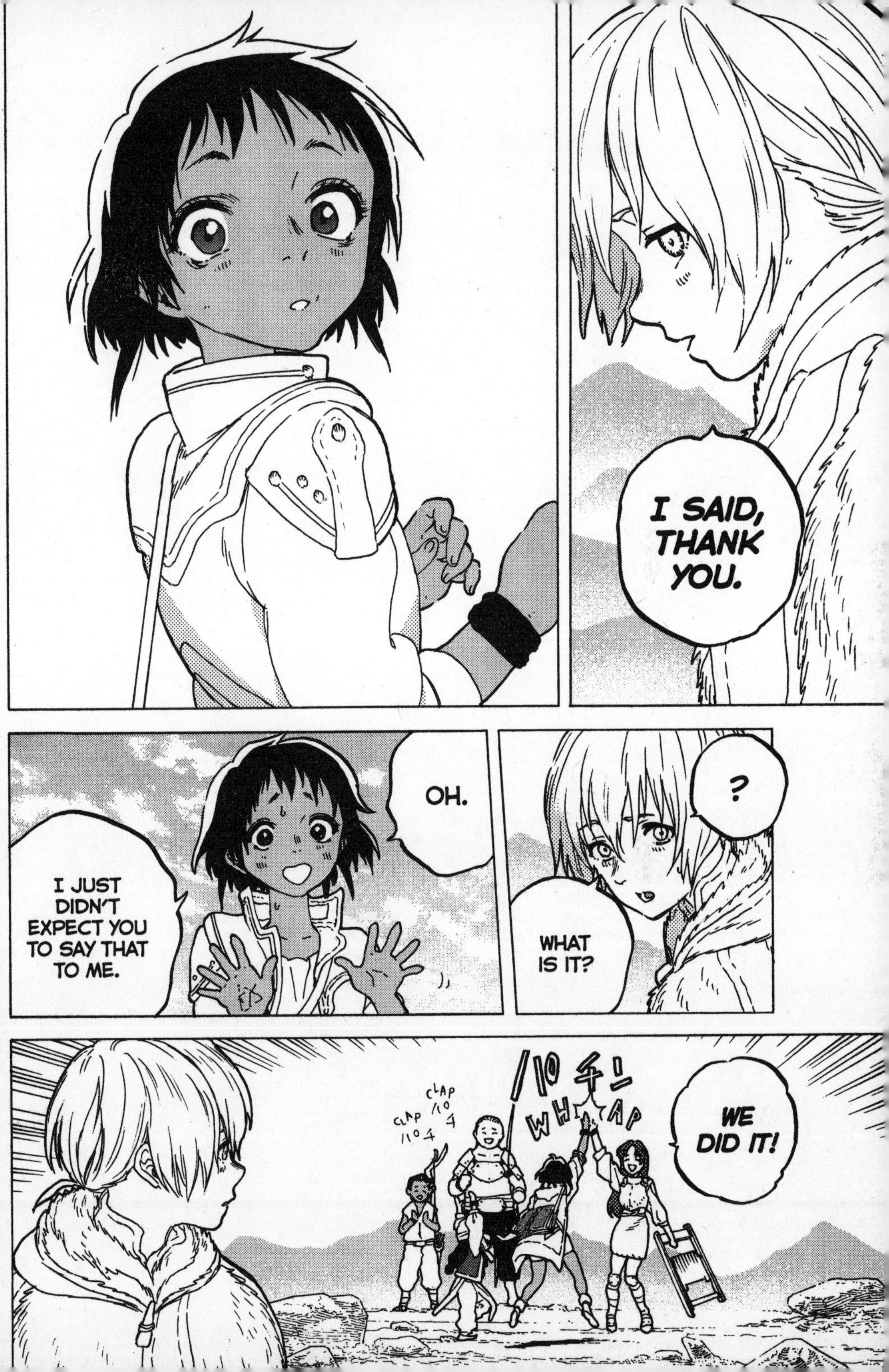
I SAID, THANK YOU.
?
WHAT IS IT?
OH.
I JUST DIDN'T EXPECT YOU TO SAY THAT TO ME.
WE DID IT!
WHAP
CLAP
CLAP

TO YOUR ETERNITY

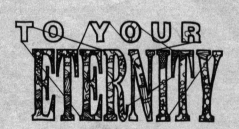

TOP SECRET TONARI'S NEW PLOT

Title: The Prison Diary of Ligard the Pirate
(Working Title)

Chapter 1 The Necessary Preparations
Chapter 2 Acquiring the Materials
Chapter 3 Kitchen Duty
Chapter 4 Sweets for the Captain
Chapter 5 Enacting the Plan
Chapter 6 The Emergency Route
Chapter 7 Blast 'em with Gunpowder!
Chapter 8 Epilogue

134 PAGES

RELEASE PLANNED FOR NEXT SPRING

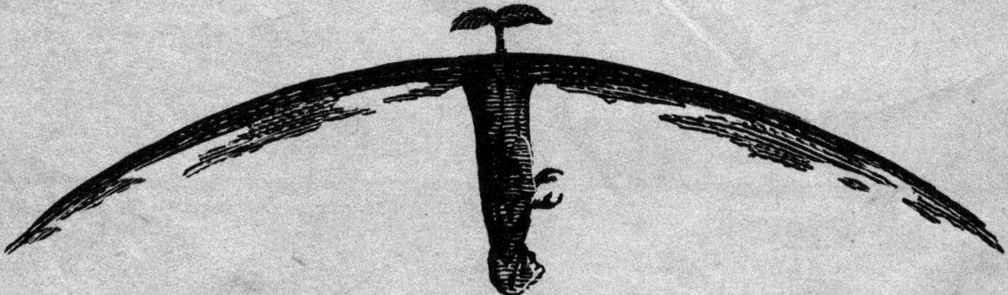

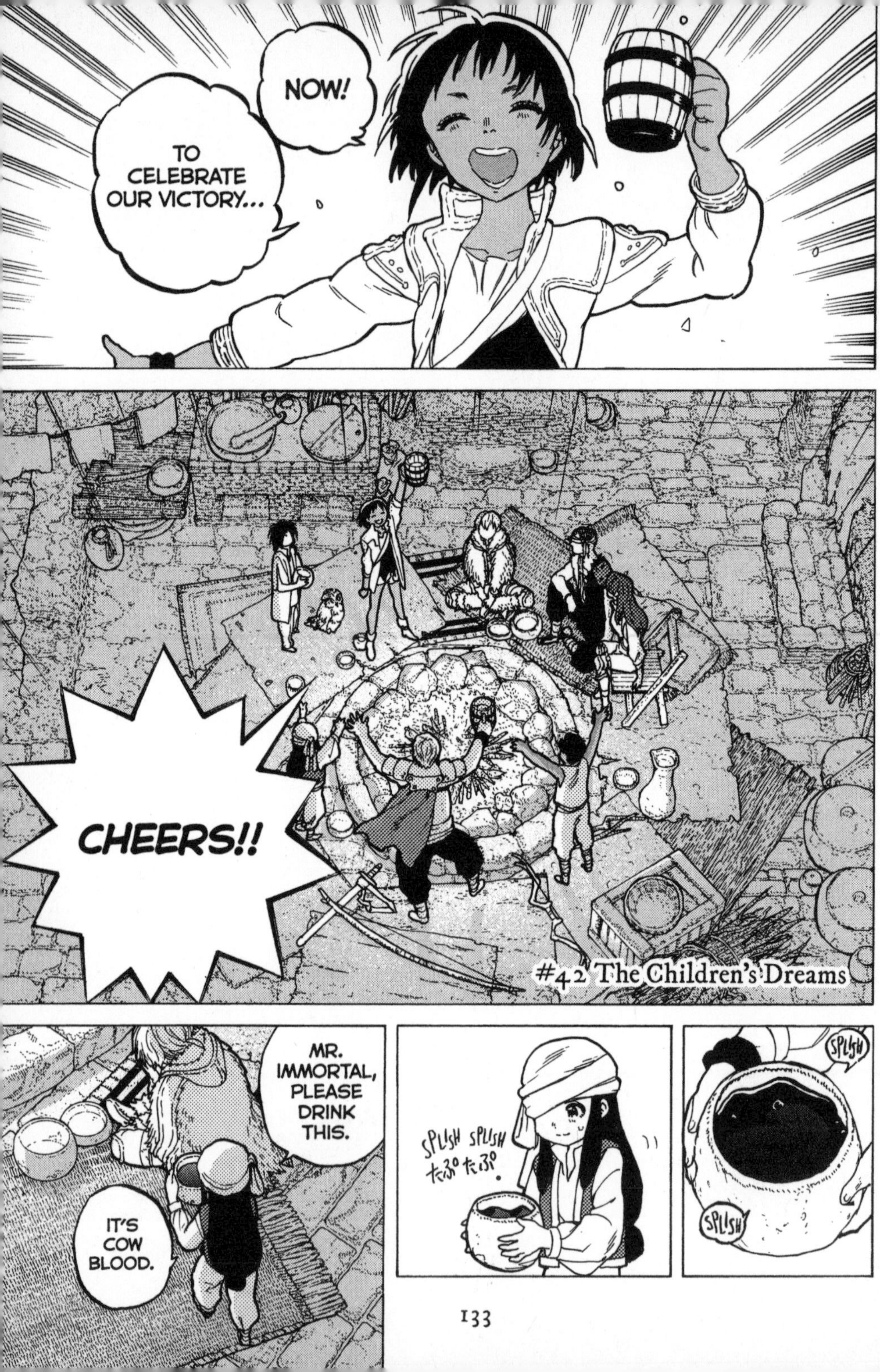
NOW!
TO CELEBRATE OUR VICTORY...
CHEERS!!
#42 The Children's Dreams
SPLISH
SPLISH
SPLISH SPLISH
たぷたぷ
MR. IMMORTAL, PLEASE DRINK THIS.
IT'S COW BLOOD.

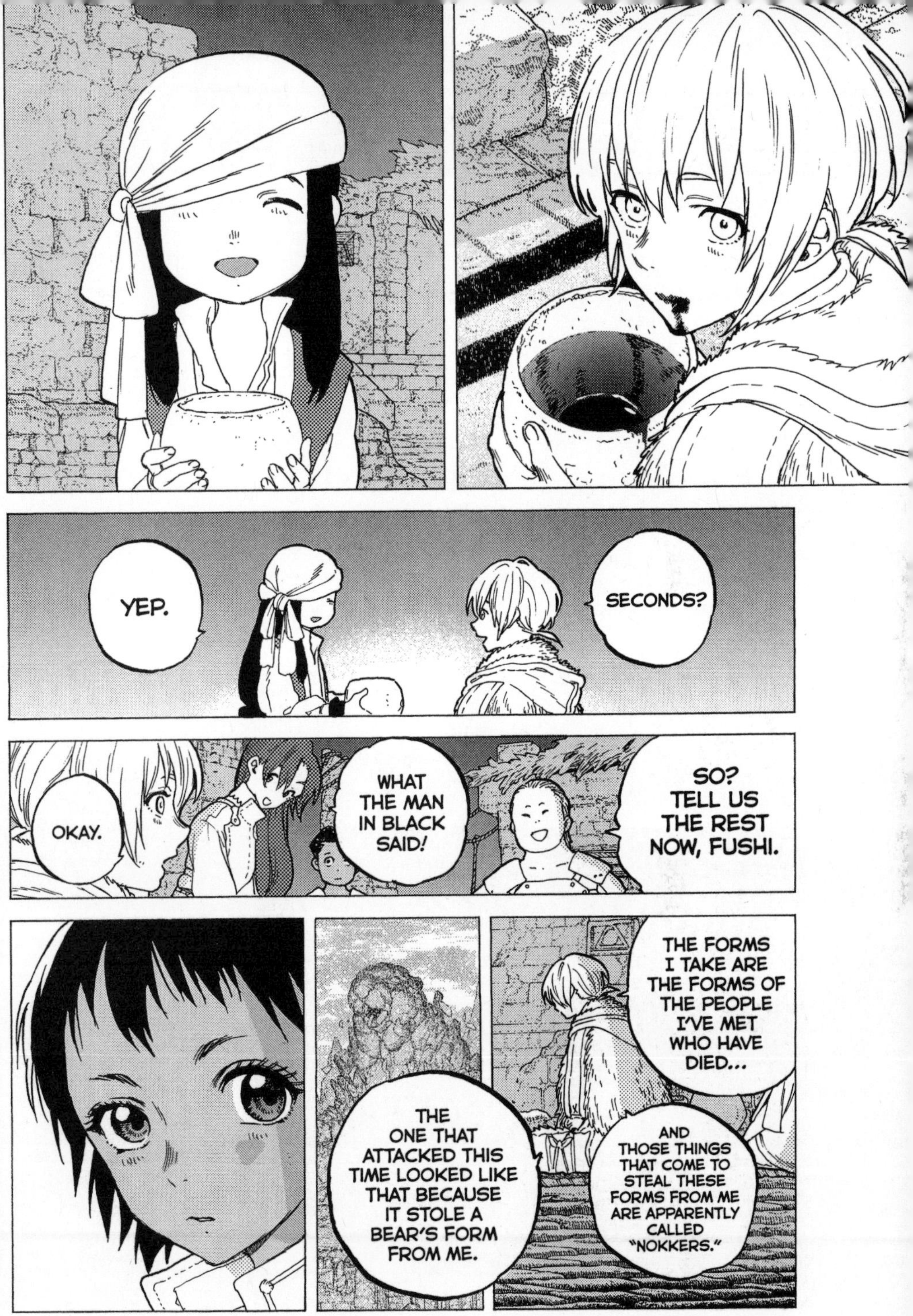
SECONDS?
YEP.
SO? TELL US THE REST NOW, FUSHI.
WHAT THE MAN IN BLACK SAID!
OKAY.
THE FORMS I TAKE ARE THE FORMS OF THE PEOPLE I'VE MET WHO HAVE DIED...
AND THOSE THINGS THAT COME TO STEAL THESE FORMS FROM ME ARE APPARENTLY CALLED "NOKKERS."
THE ONE THAT ATTACKED THIS TIME LOOKED LIKE THAT BECAUSE IT STOLE A BEAR'S FORM FROM ME.

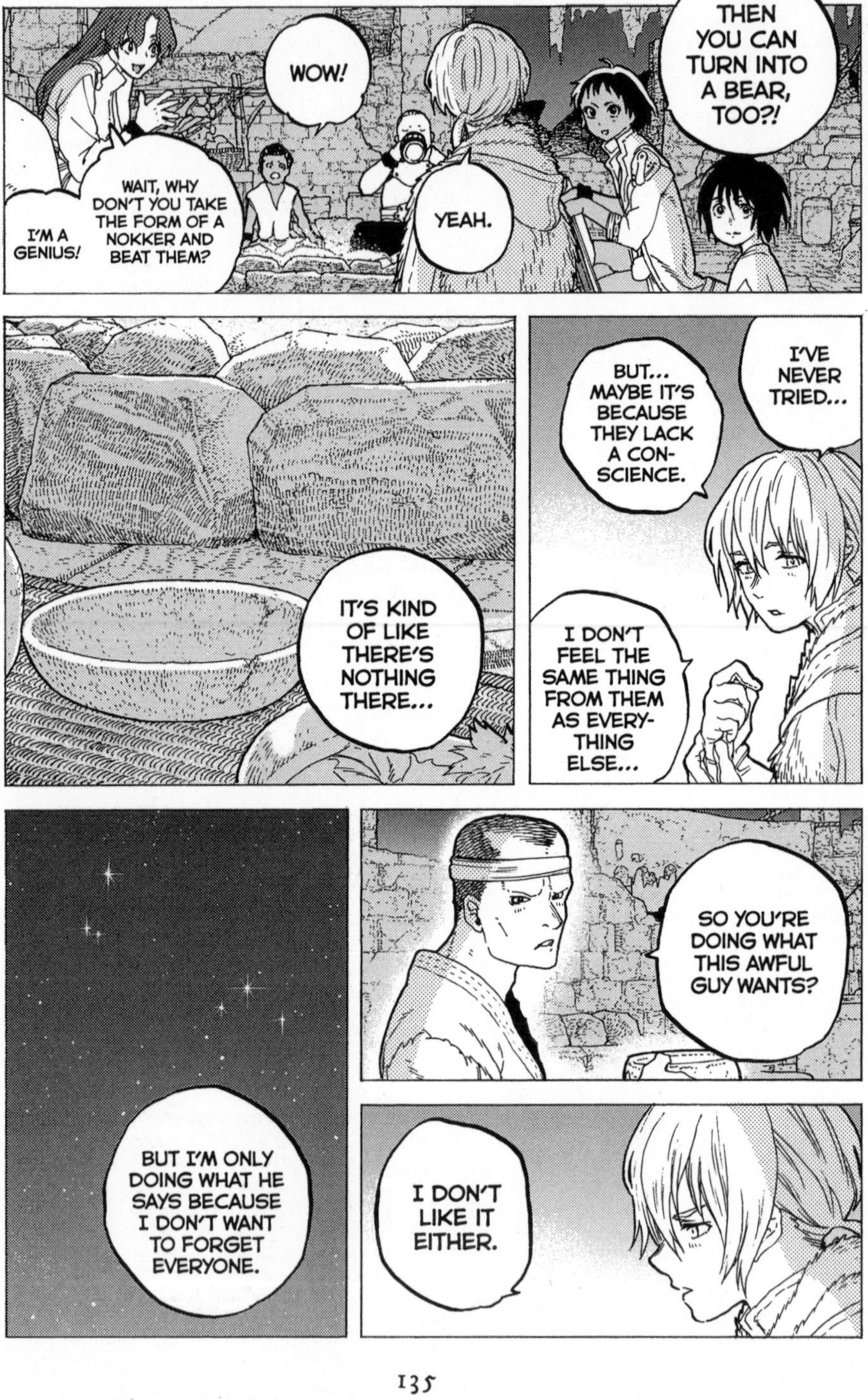
THEN YOU CAN TURN INTO A BEAR, TOO?!
WOW!
YEAH.
WAIT, WHY DON'T YOU TAKE THE FORM OF A NOKKER AND BEAT THEM?
I'M A GENIUS!
I'VE NEVER TRIED...
BUT... MAYBE IT'S BECAUSE THEY LACK A CON-SCIENCE.
I DON'T FEEL THE SAME THING FROM THEM AS EVERY-THING ELSE...
IT'S KIND OF LIKE THERE'S NOTHING THERE...
SO YOU'RE DOING WHAT THIS AWFUL GUY WANTS?
I DON'T LIKE IT EITHER.
BUT I'M ONLY DOING WHAT HE SAYS BECAUSE I DON'T WANT TO FORGET EVERYONE.

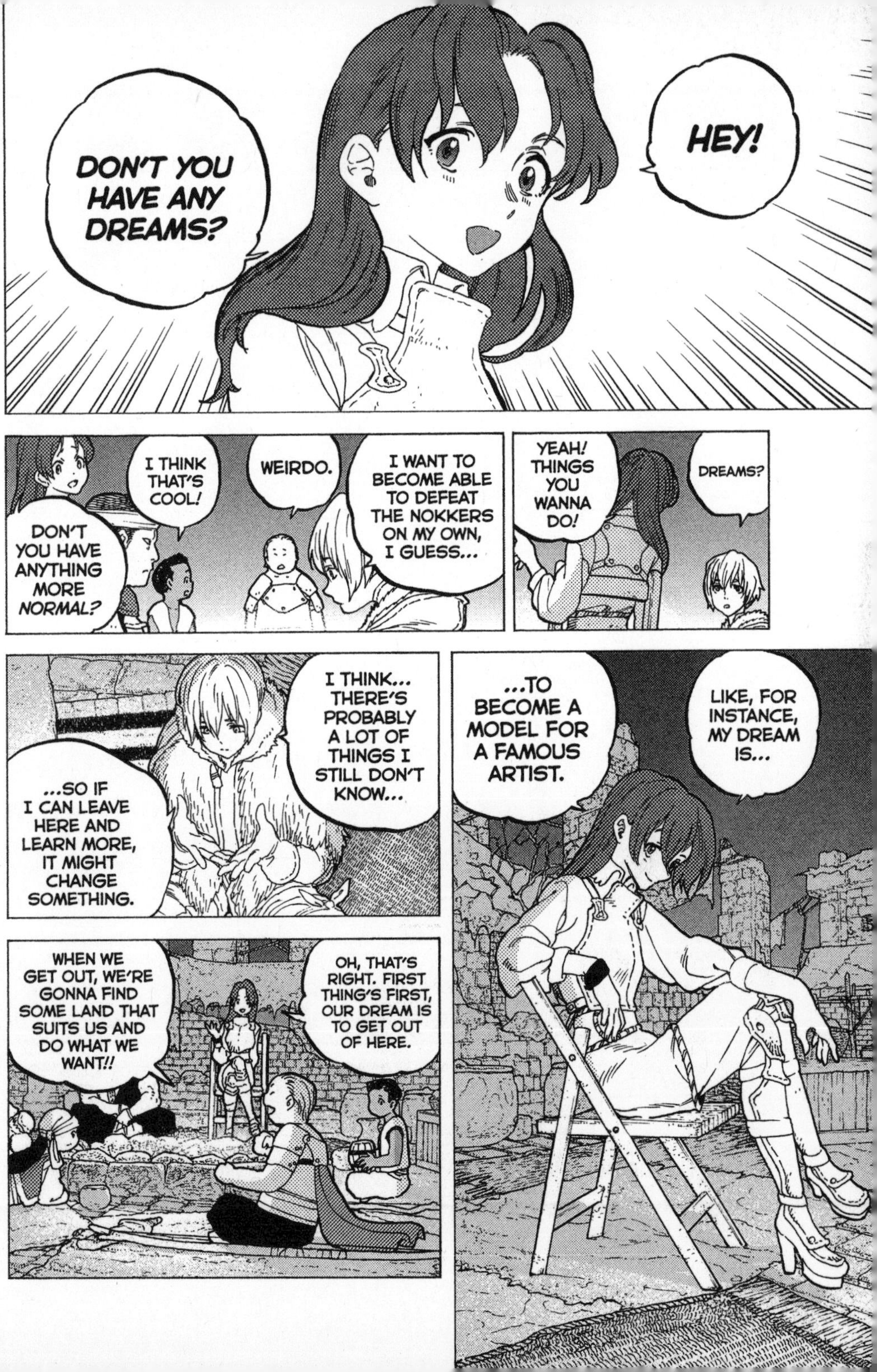
HEY!
DON'T YOU HAVE ANY DREAMS?
DREAMS?
YEAH! THINGS YOU WANNA DO!
I WANT TO BECOME ABLE TO DEFEAT THE NOKKERS ON MY OWN, I GUESS...
WEIRDO.
I THINK THAT'S COOL!
DON'T YOU HAVE ANYTHING MORE NORMAL?
LIKE, FOR INSTANCE, MY DREAM IS...
...TO BECOME A MODEL FOR A FAMOUS ARTIST.
I THINK... THERE'S PROBABLY A LOT OF THINGS I STILL DON'T KNOW...
...SO IF I CAN LEAVE HERE AND LEARN MORE, IT MIGHT CHANGE SOMETHING.
OH, THAT'S RIGHT. FIRST THING'S FIRST, OUR DREAM IS TO GET OUT OF HERE.
WHEN WE GET OUT, WE'RE GONNA FIND SOME LAND THAT SUITS US AND DO WHAT WE WANT!!

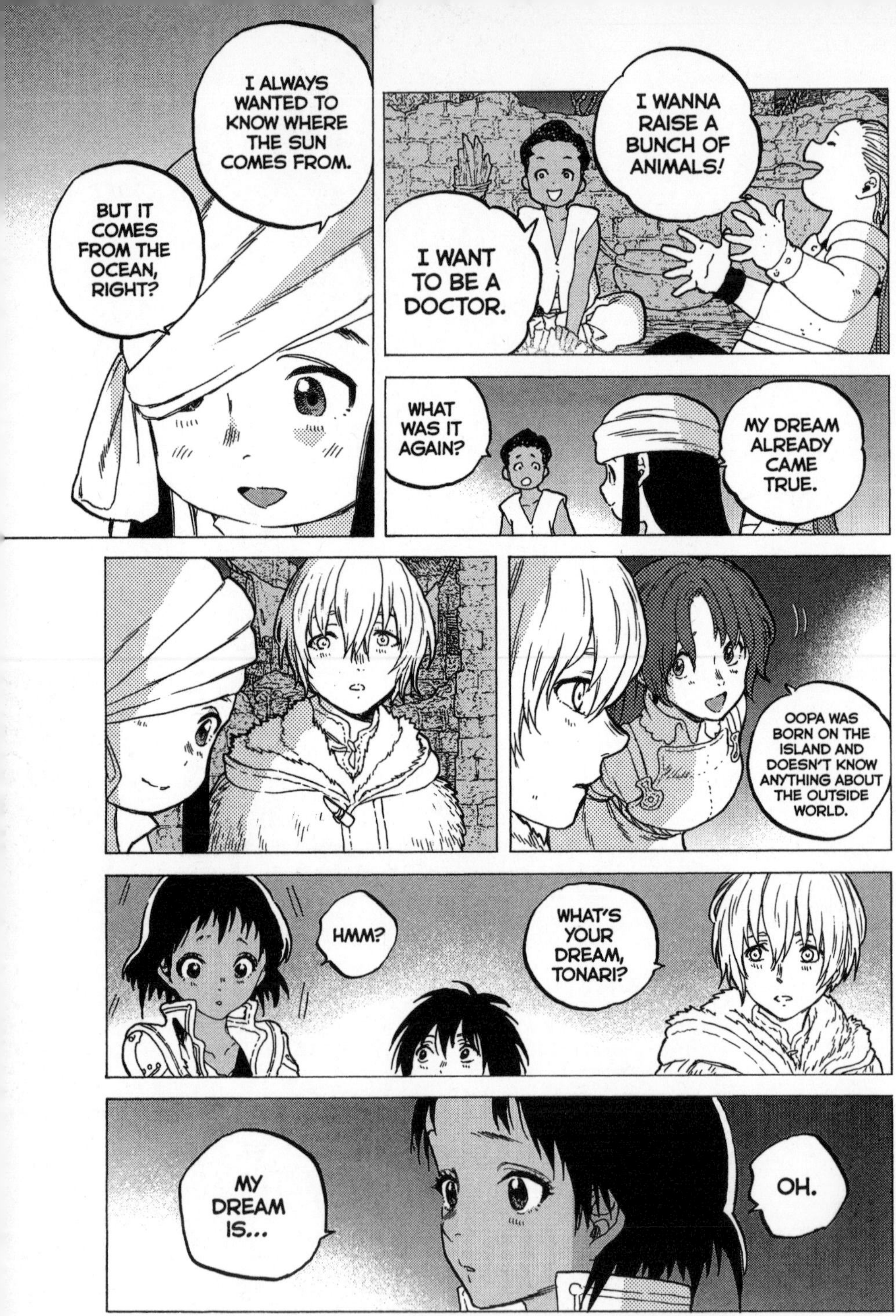
I WANNA RAISE A BUNCH OF ANIMALS!
I WANT TO BE A DOCTOR.
MY DREAM ALREADY CAME TRUE.
WHAT WAS IT AGAIN?
I ALWAYS WANTED TO KNOW WHERE THE SUN COMES FROM.
BUT IT COMES FROM THE OCEAN, RIGHT?
OOPA WAS BORN ON THE ISLAND AND DOESN'T KNOW ANYTHING ABOUT THE OUTSIDE WORLD.
WHAT'S YOUR DREAM, TONARI?
HMM?
OH.
MY DREAM IS...

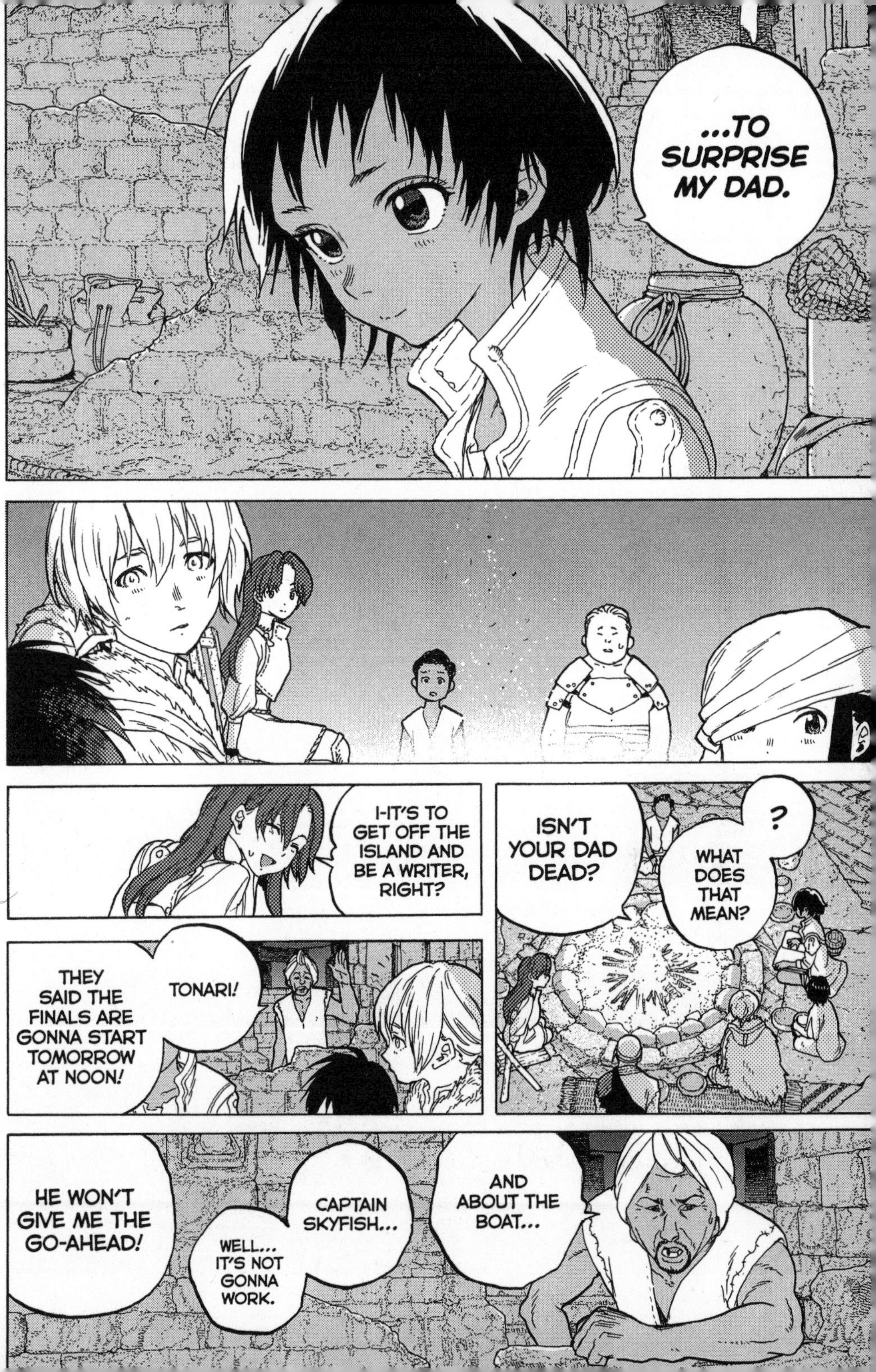
...TO SURPRISE MY DAD.
?
WHAT DOES THAT MEAN?
ISN'T YOUR DAD DEAD?
I-IT'S TO GET OFF THE ISLAND AND BE A WRITER, RIGHT?
TONARI!
THEY SAID THE FINALS ARE GONNA START TOMORROW AT NOON!
AND ABOUT THE BOAT...
CAPTAIN SKYFISH...
WELL... IT'S NOT GONNA WORK.
HE WON'T GIVE ME THE GO-AHEAD!

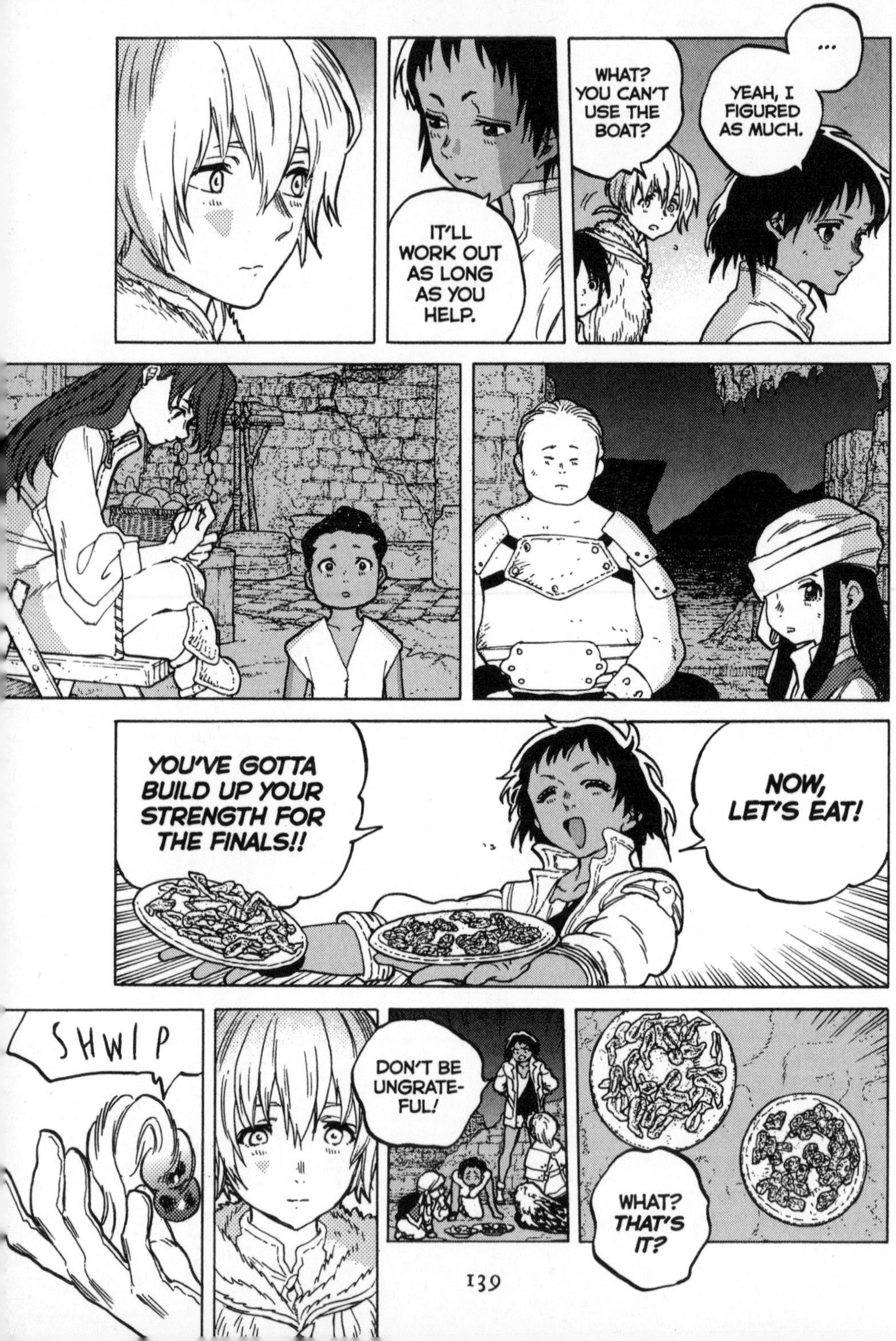
...
YEAH, I FIGURED AS MUCH.
WHAT? YOU CAN'T USE THE BOAT?
IT'LL WORK OUT AS LONG AS YOU HELP.
NOW, LET'S EAT!
YOU'VE GOTTA BUILD UP YOUR STRENGTH FOR THE FINALS!!
WHAT? THAT'S IT?
DON'T BE UNGRATE-FUL!
SHWIP

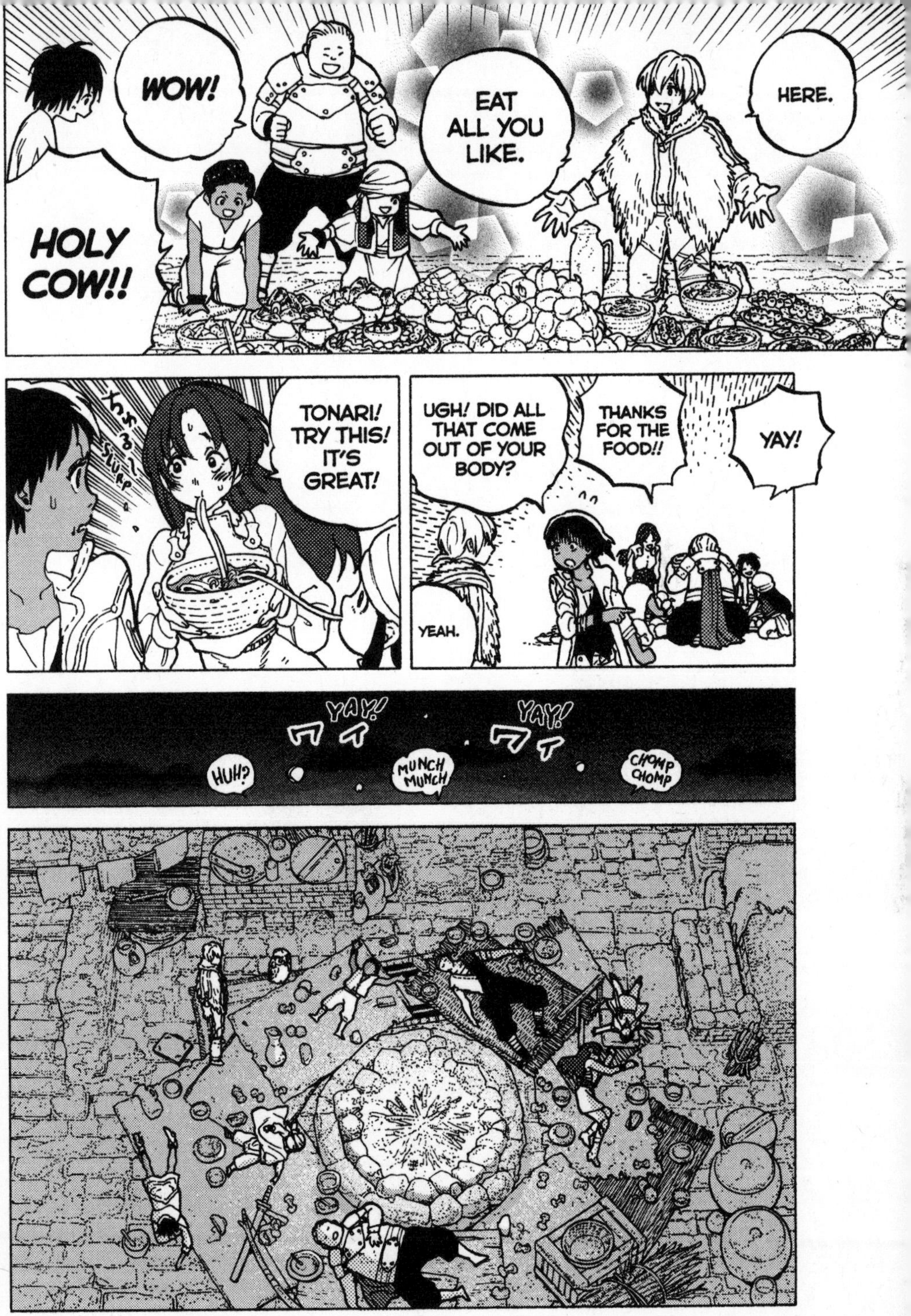
HERE.
EAT ALL YOU LIKE.
WOW!
HOLY COW!!
YAY!
THANKS FOR THE FOOD!!
UGH! DID ALL THAT COME OUT OF YOUR BODY?
YEAH.
TONARI! TRY THIS! IT'S GREAT!
SLURP
CHOMP CHOMP
YAY!
ワイ
MUNCH MUNCH
YAY!
ワイ
HUH?

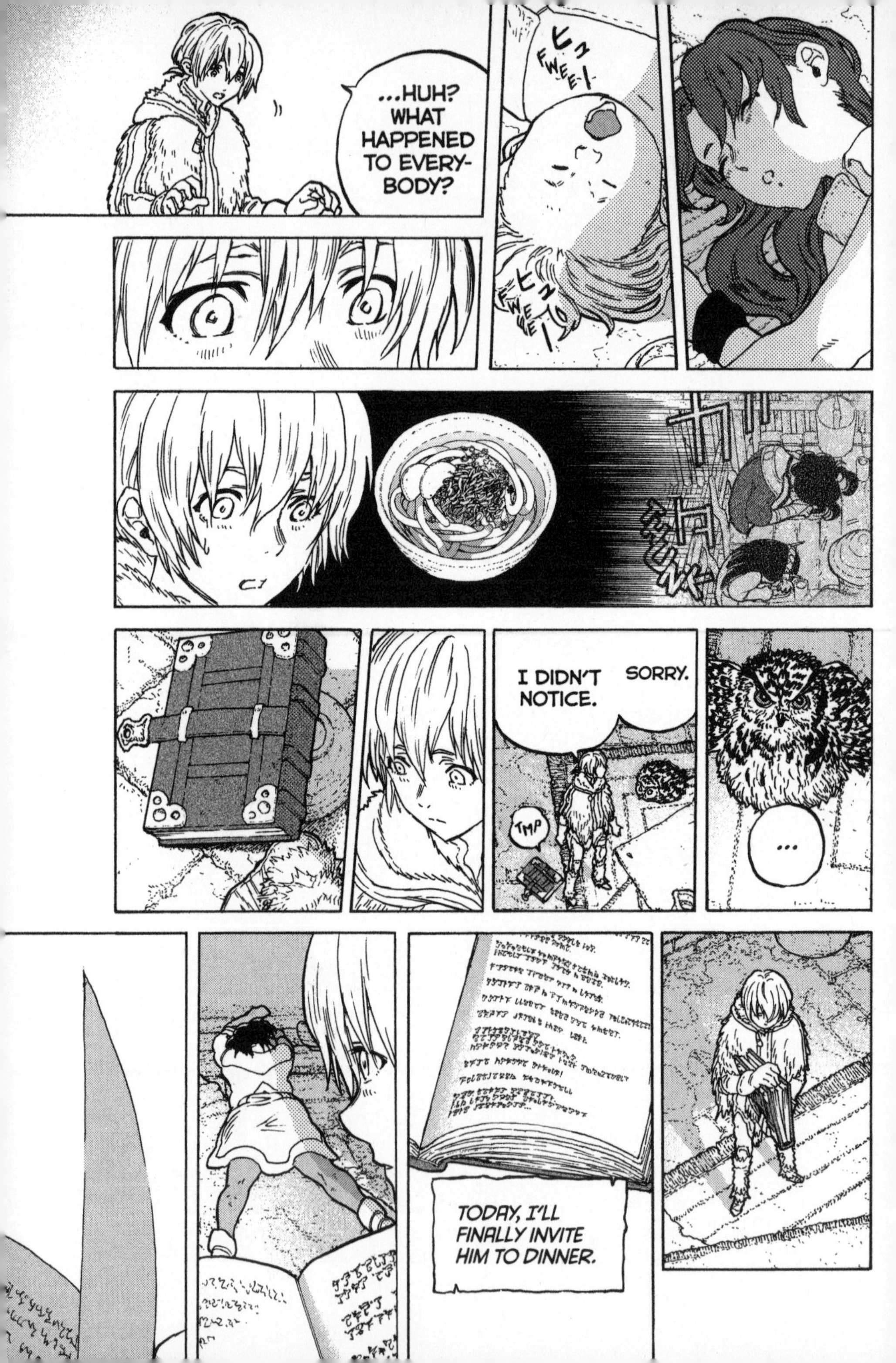

ヒュ
FWEE-
ヒュ
FWEEE-
...HUH? WHAT HAPPENED TO EVERY-BODY?
THUNK
...
SORRY.
I DIDN'T NOTICE.
TMP
TODAY, I'LL FINALLY INVITE HIM TO DINNER.

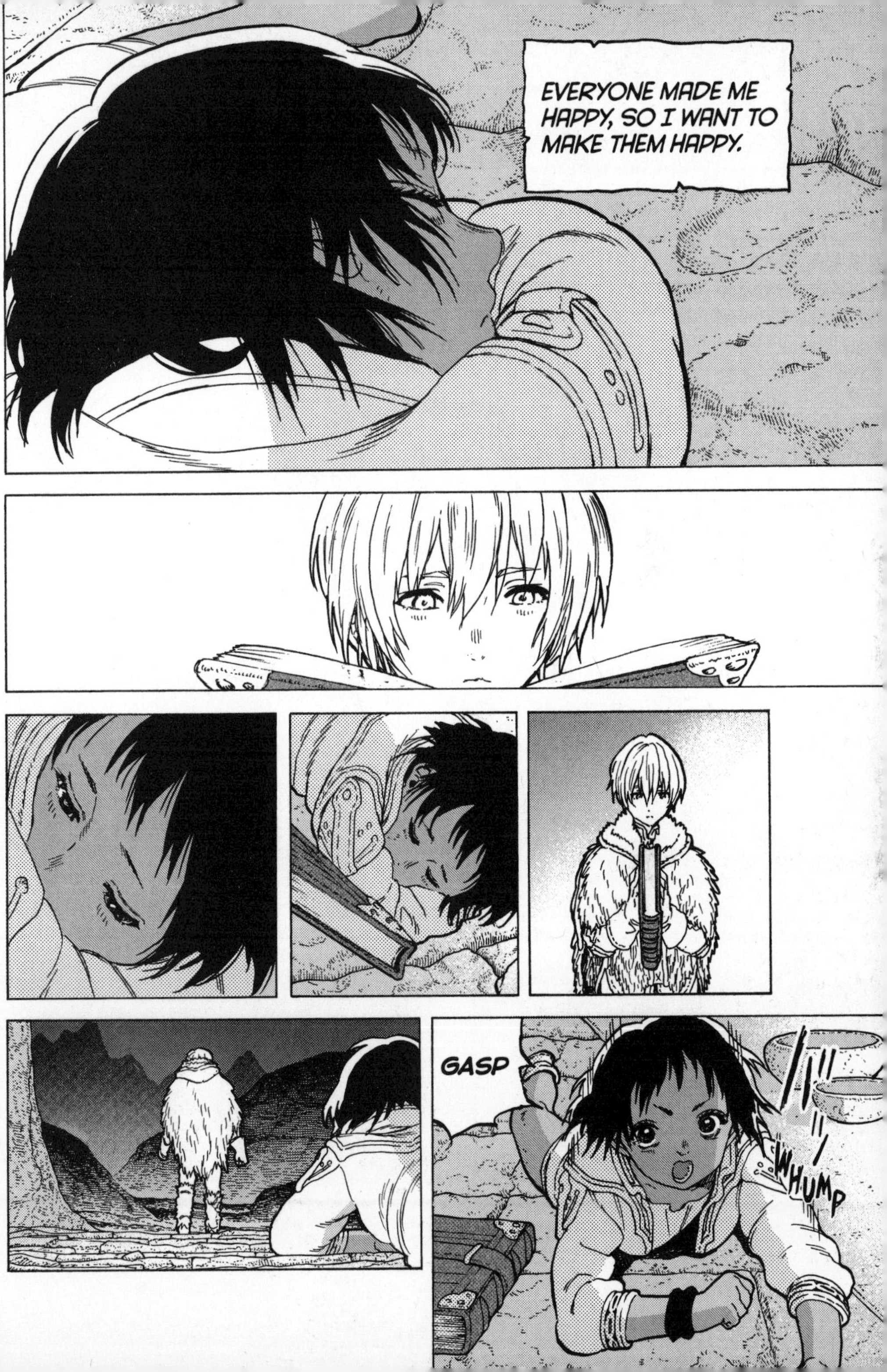
EVERYONE MADE ME HAPPY, SO I WANT TO MAKE THEM HAPPY.
GASP
WHUMP

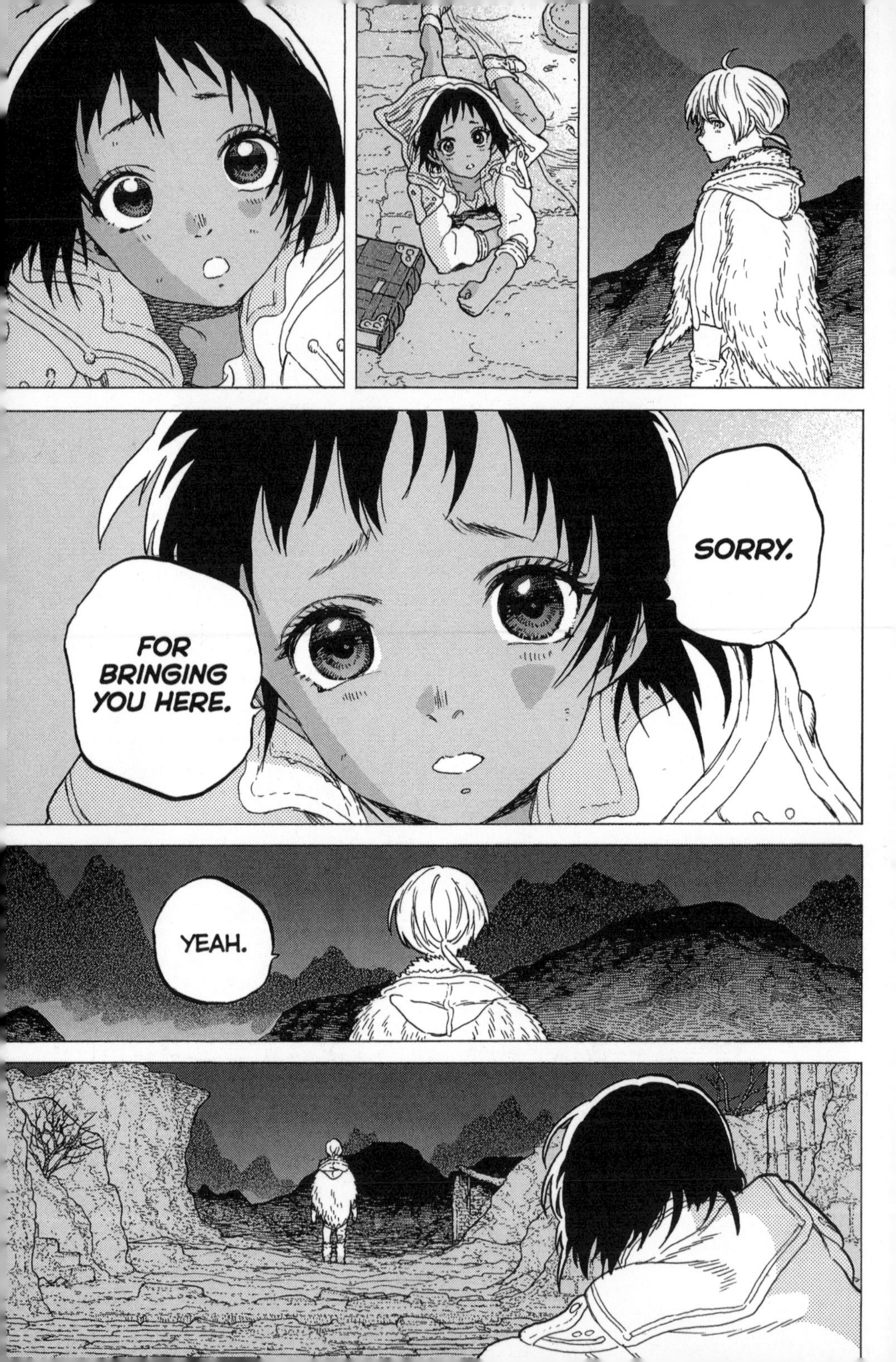
SORRY.
FOR BRINGING YOU HERE.
YEAH.

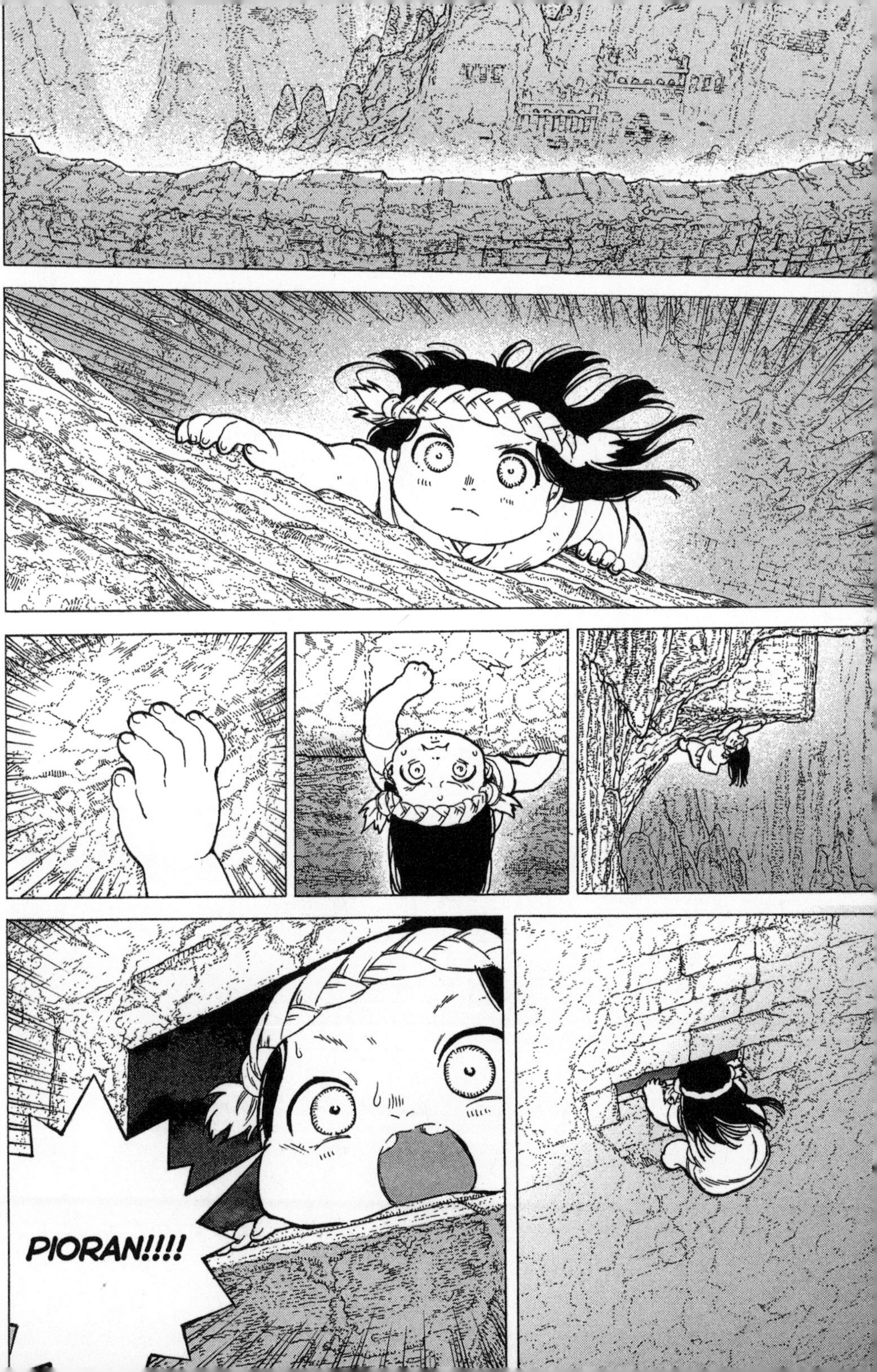
PIORAN!!!!

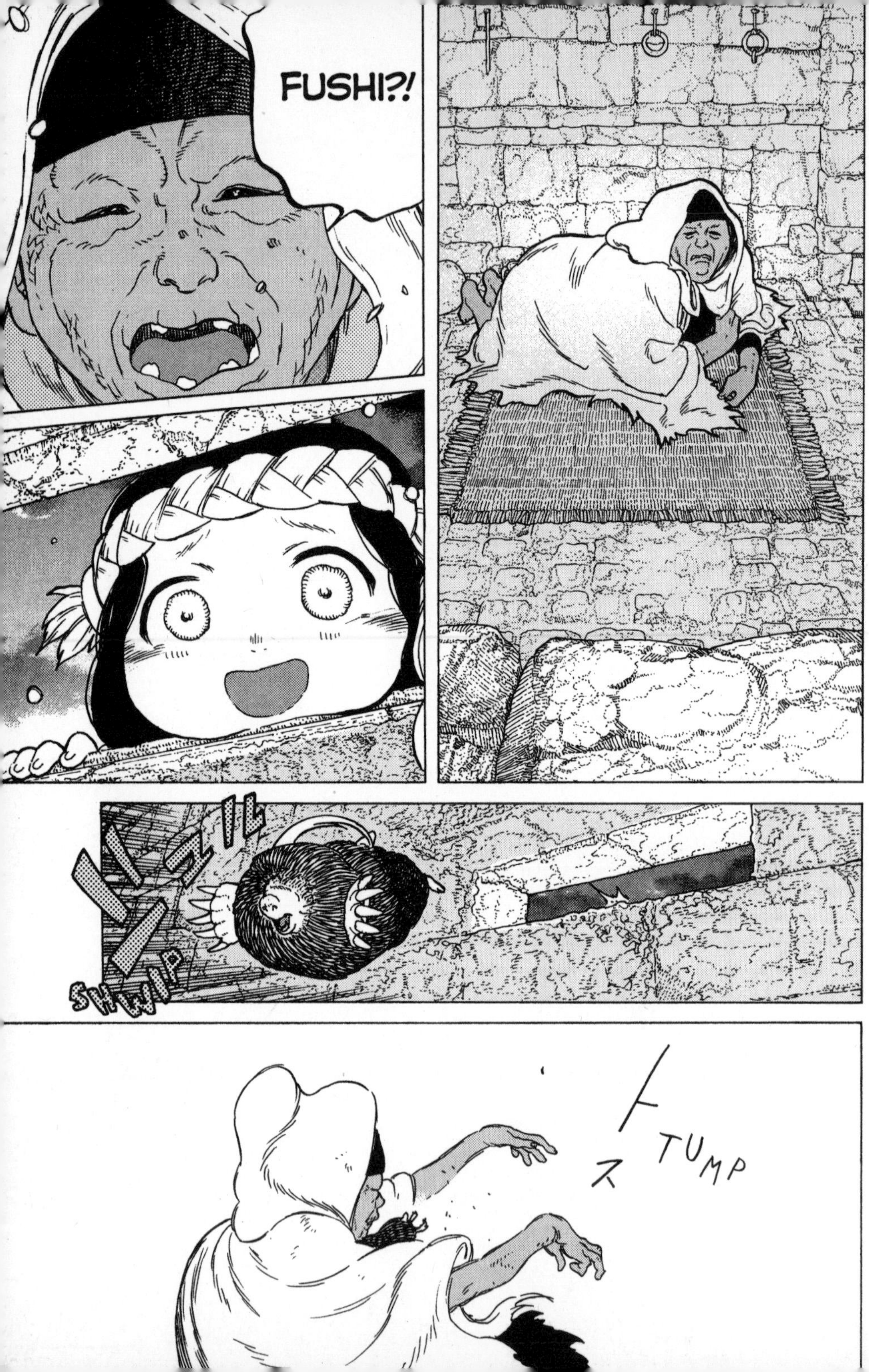
FUSHI?!
SHWIP
TUMP

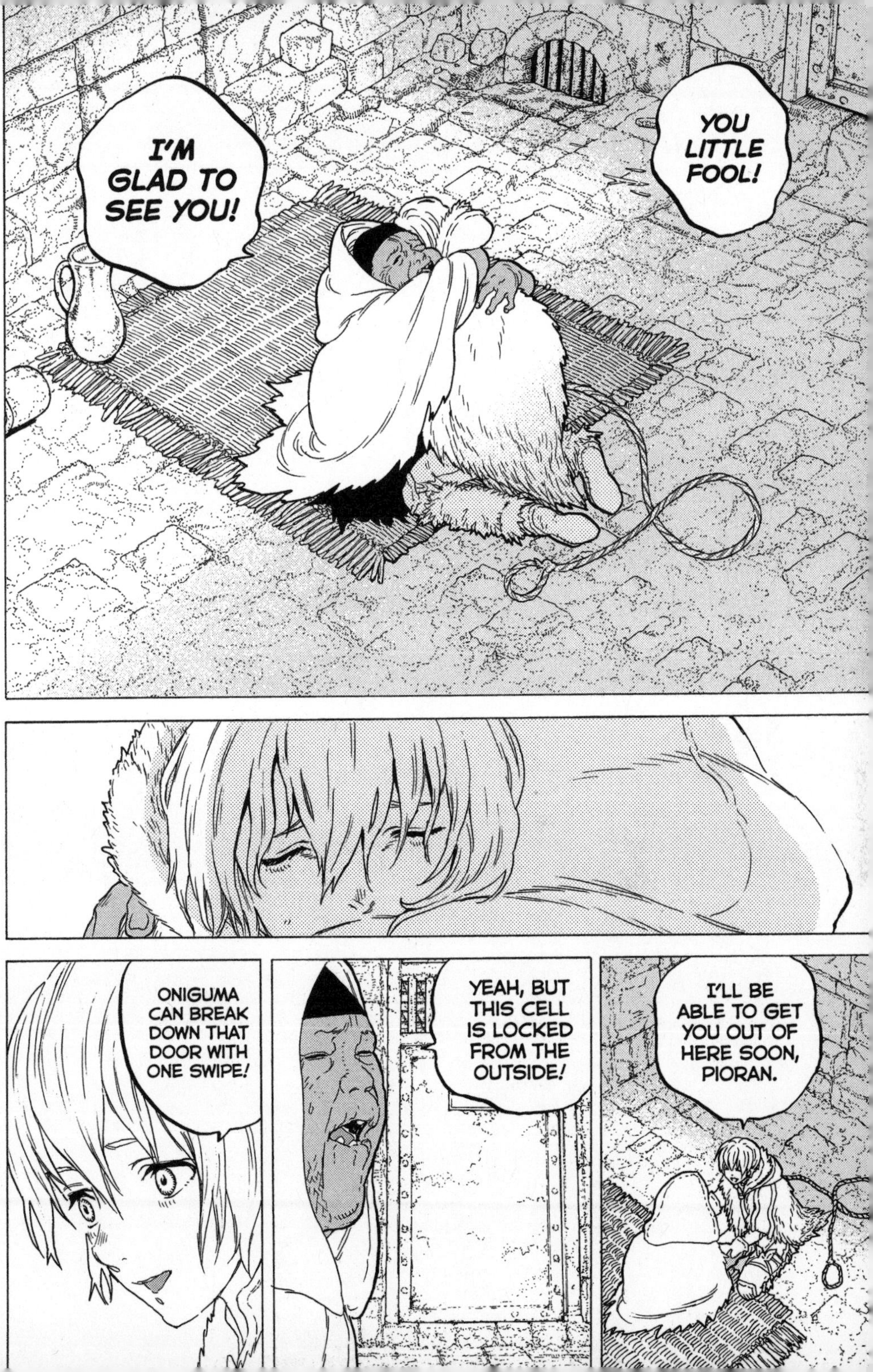
YOU LITTLE FOOL!
I'M GLAD TO SEE YOU!
I'LL BE ABLE TO GET YOU OUT OF HERE SOON, PIORAN.
YEAH, BUT THIS CELL IS LOCKED FROM THE OUTSIDE!
ONIGUMA CAN BREAK DOWN THAT DOOR WITH ONE SWIPE!

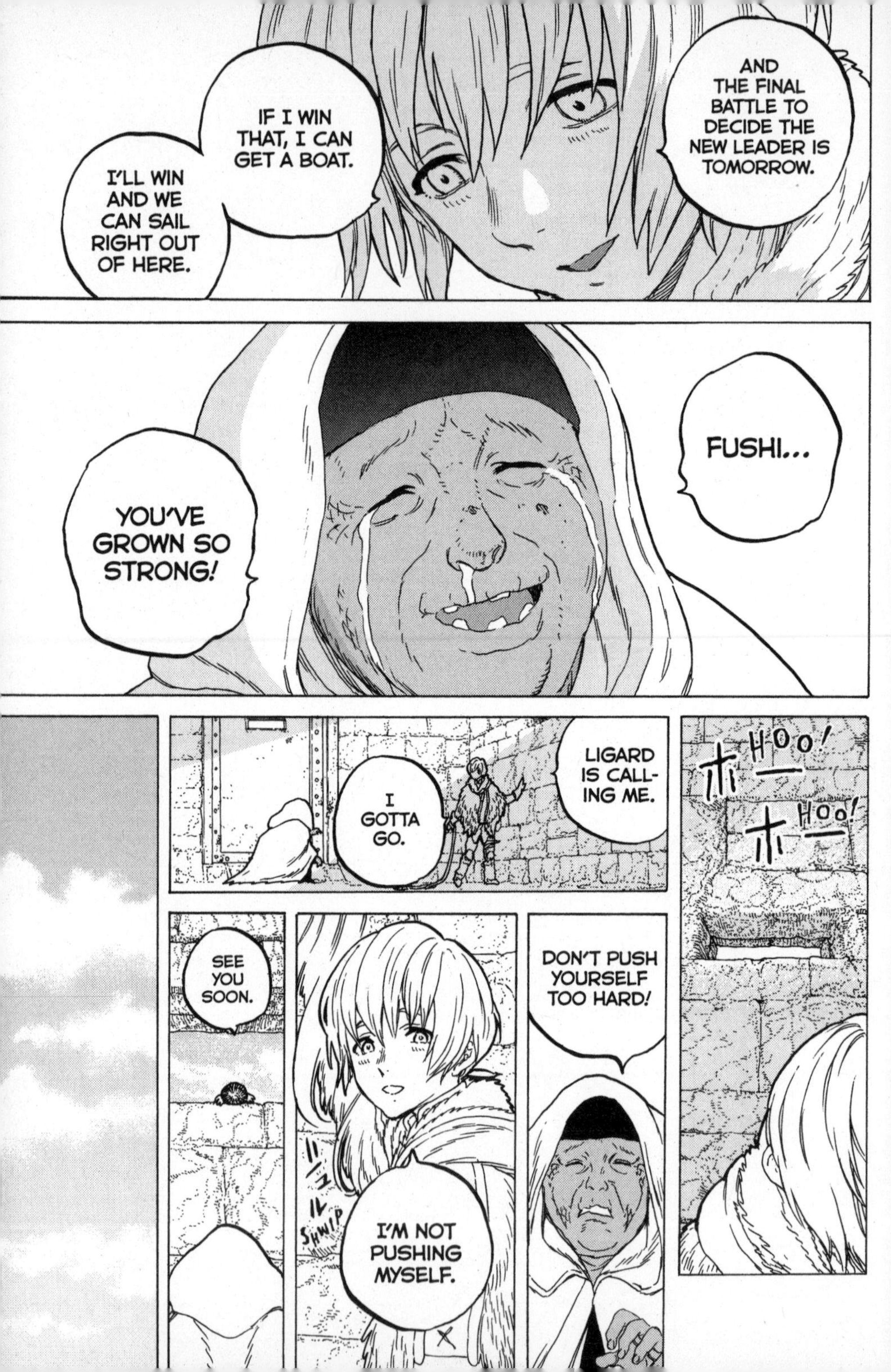
AND THE FINAL BATTLE TO DECIDE THE NEW LEADER IS TOMORROW.
IF I WIN THAT, I CAN GET A BOAT.
I'LL WIN AND WE CAN SAIL RIGHT OUT OF HERE.
FUSHI...
YOU'VE GROWN SO STRONG!
HOO!
HOO!
LIGARD IS CALL-ING ME.
I GOTTA GO.
DON'T PUSH YOURSELF TOO HARD!
I'M NOT PUSHING MYSELF.
SHWIP
SEE YOU SOON.

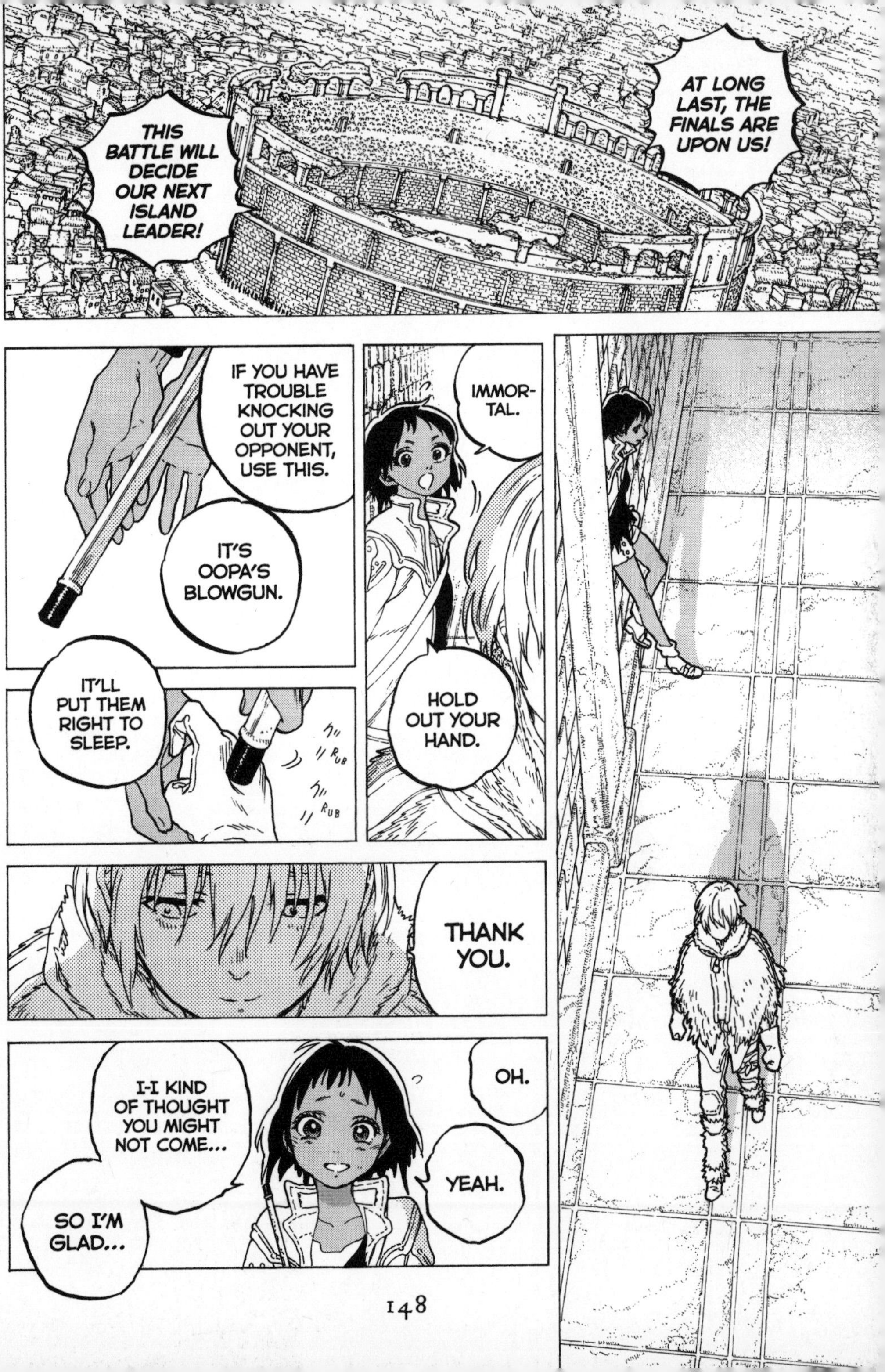
AT LONG LAST, THE FINALS ARE UPON US!
THIS BATTLE WILL DECIDE OUR NEXT ISLAND LEADER!
IMMORTAL.
HOLD OUT YOUR HAND.
IF YOU HAVE TROUBLE KNOCKING OUT YOUR OPPONENT, USE THIS.
IT'S OOPA'S BLOWGUN.
IT'LL PUT THEM RIGHT TO SLEEP.
RUB
RUB
THANK YOU.
OH.
YEAH.
I-I KIND OF THOUGHT YOU MIGHT NOT COME...
SO I'M GLAD...

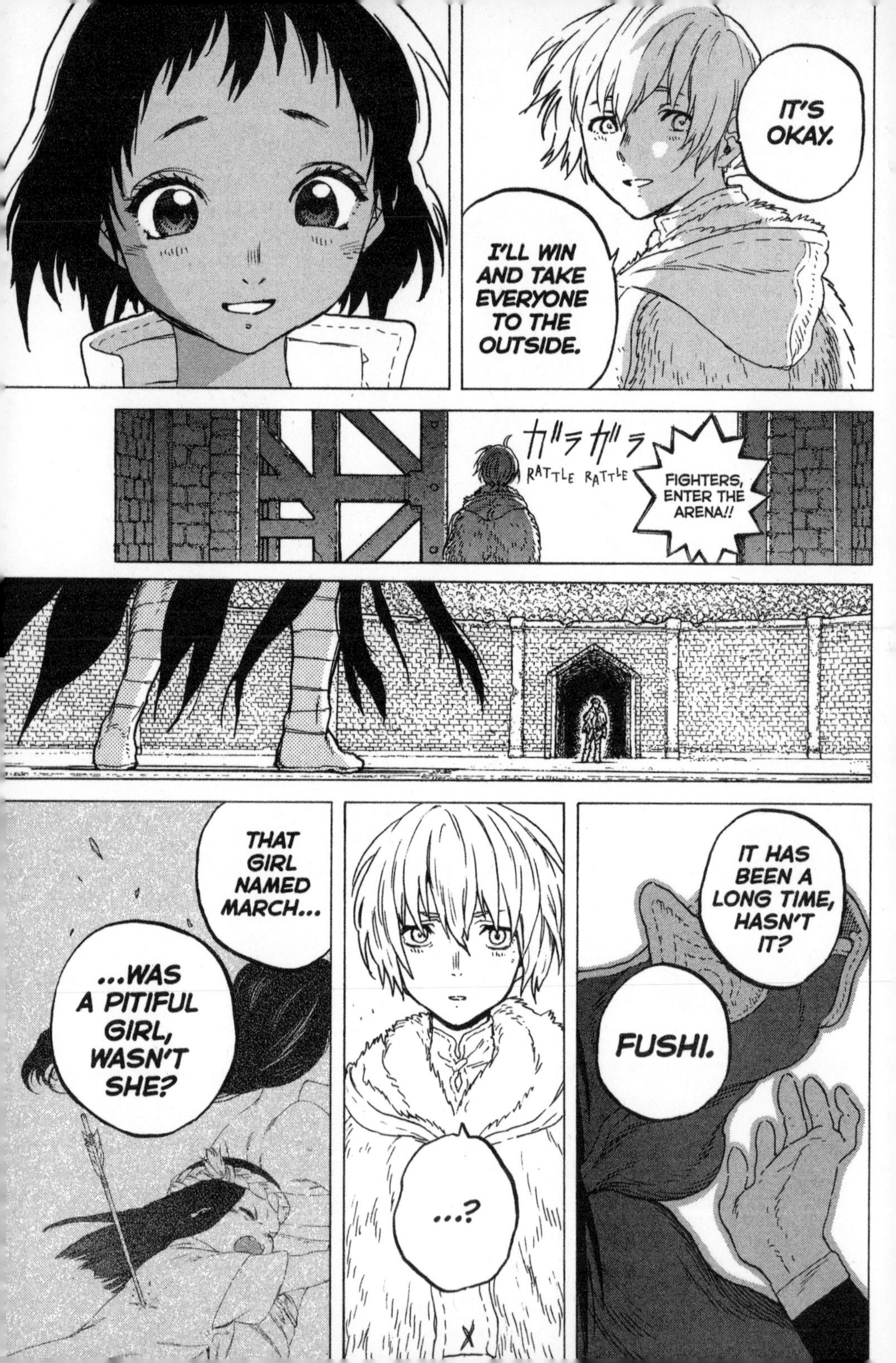
IT'S OKAY.
I'LL WIN AND TAKE EVERYONE TO THE OUTSIDE.
ガラガラ
RATTLE RATTLE
FIGHTERS, ENTER THE ARENA!!
IT HAS BEEN A LONG TIME, HASN'T IT?
FUSHI.
...?
THAT GIRL NAMED MARCH...
...WAS A PITIFUL GIRL, WASN'T SHE?

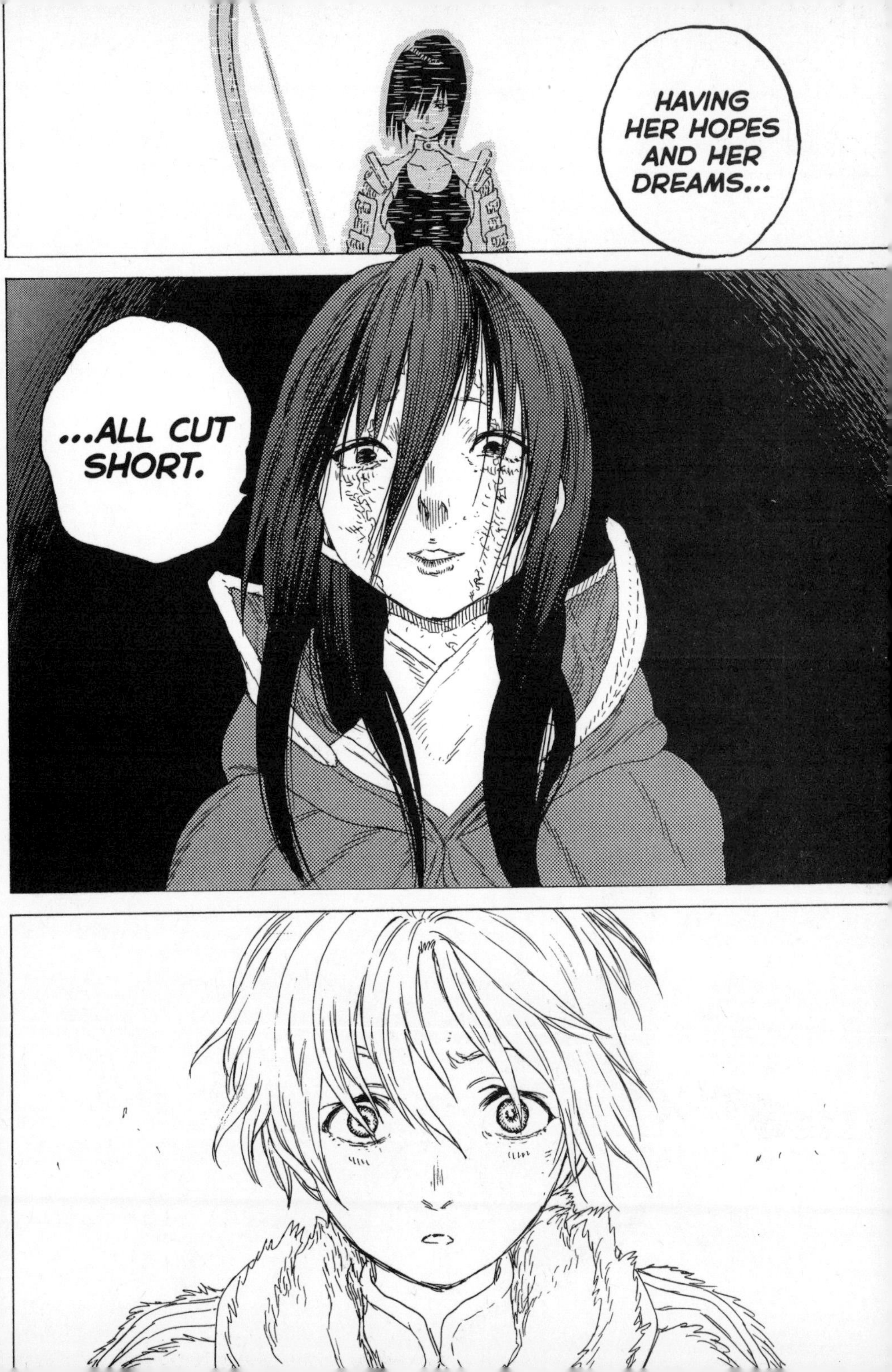
HAVING HER HOPES AND HER DREAMS...
...ALL CUT SHORT.

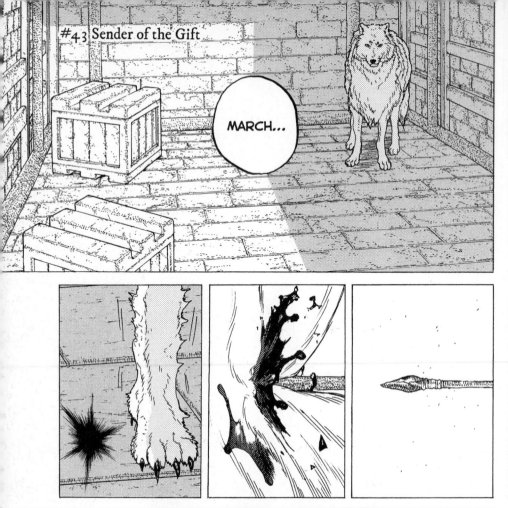

#43 Sender of the Gift

MARCH...

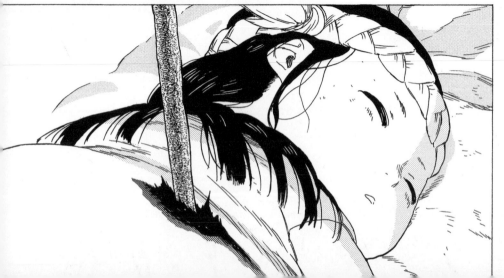

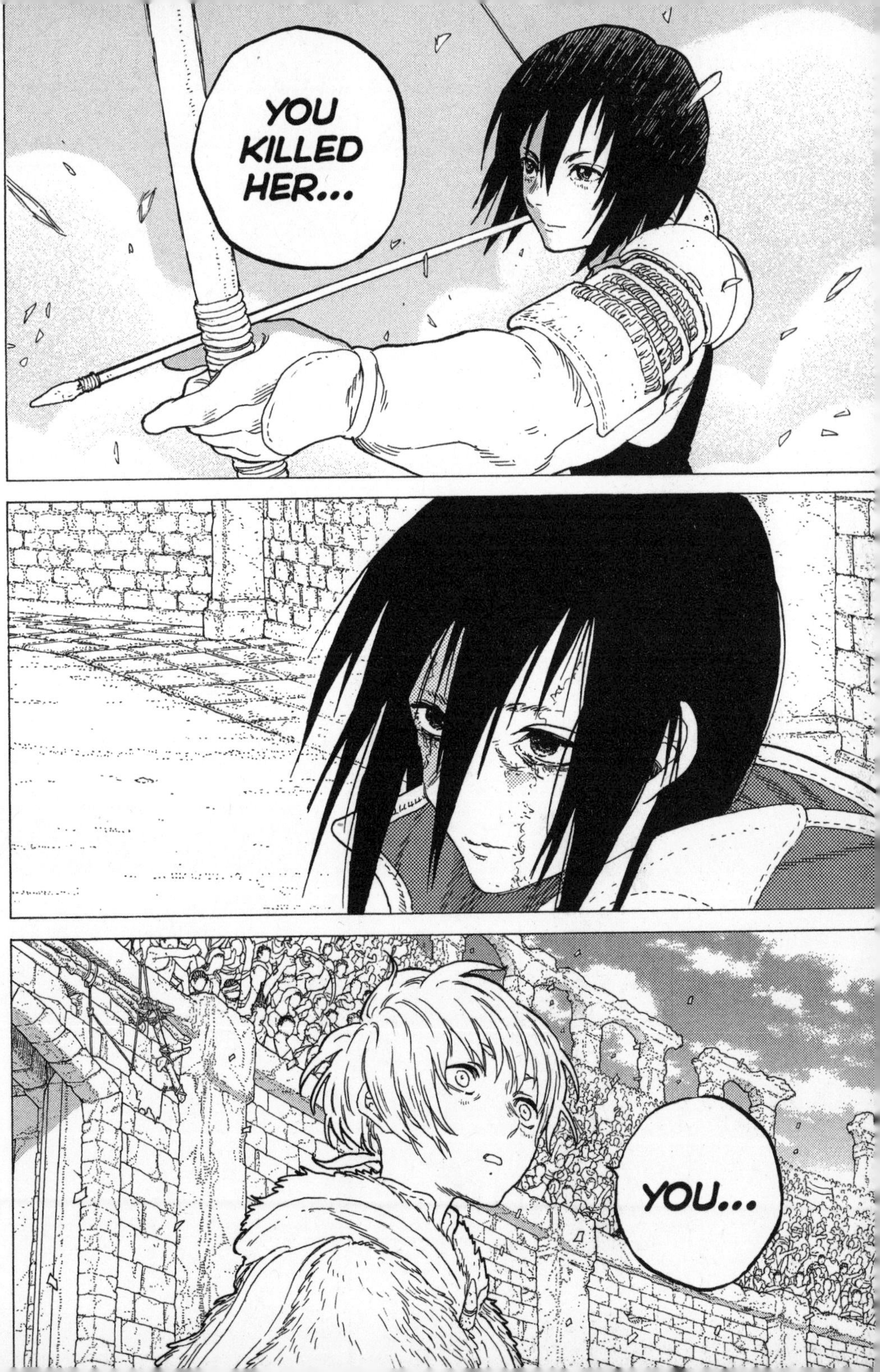
YOU KILLED HER...
YOU...

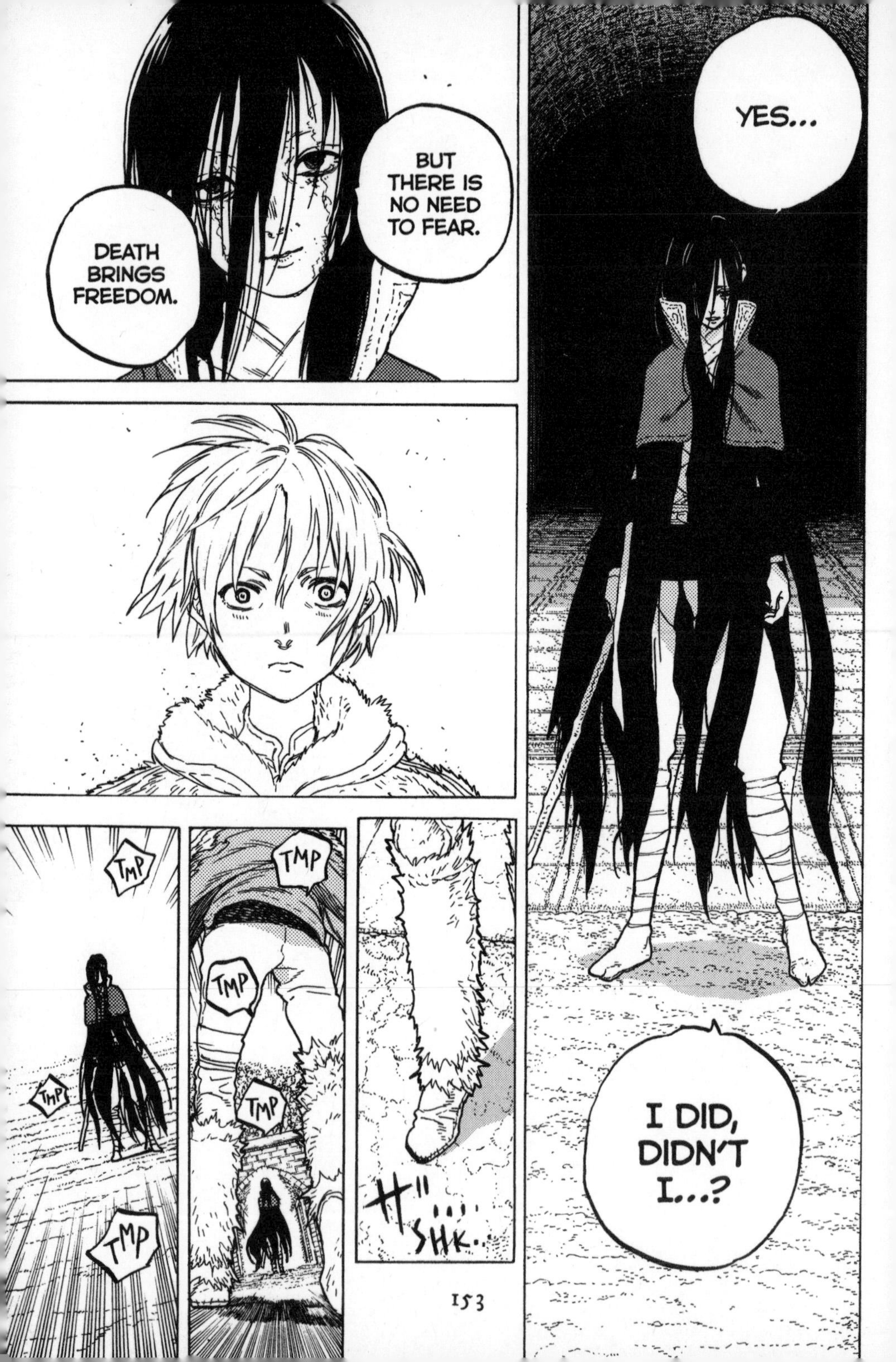
YES...
I DID, DIDN'T I...?
BUT THERE IS NO NEED TO FEAR.
DEATH BRINGS FREEDOM.
SHK..
TMP
TMP
TMP
TMP
TMP
TMP
TMP

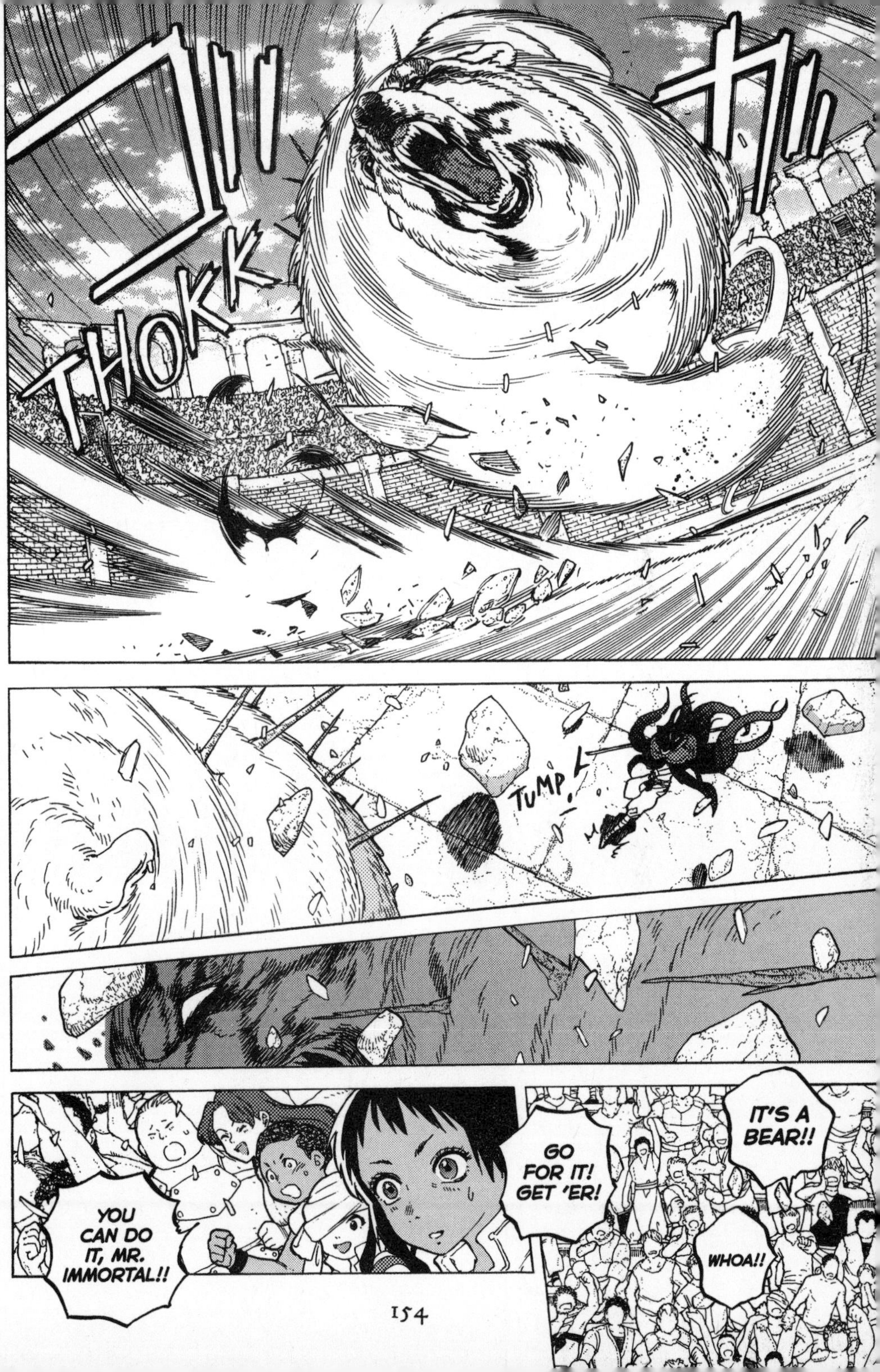
THOKK
TUMP!
IT'S A BEAR!!
GO FOR IT! GET 'ER!
WHOA!!
YOU CAN DO IT, MR. IMMORTAL!!

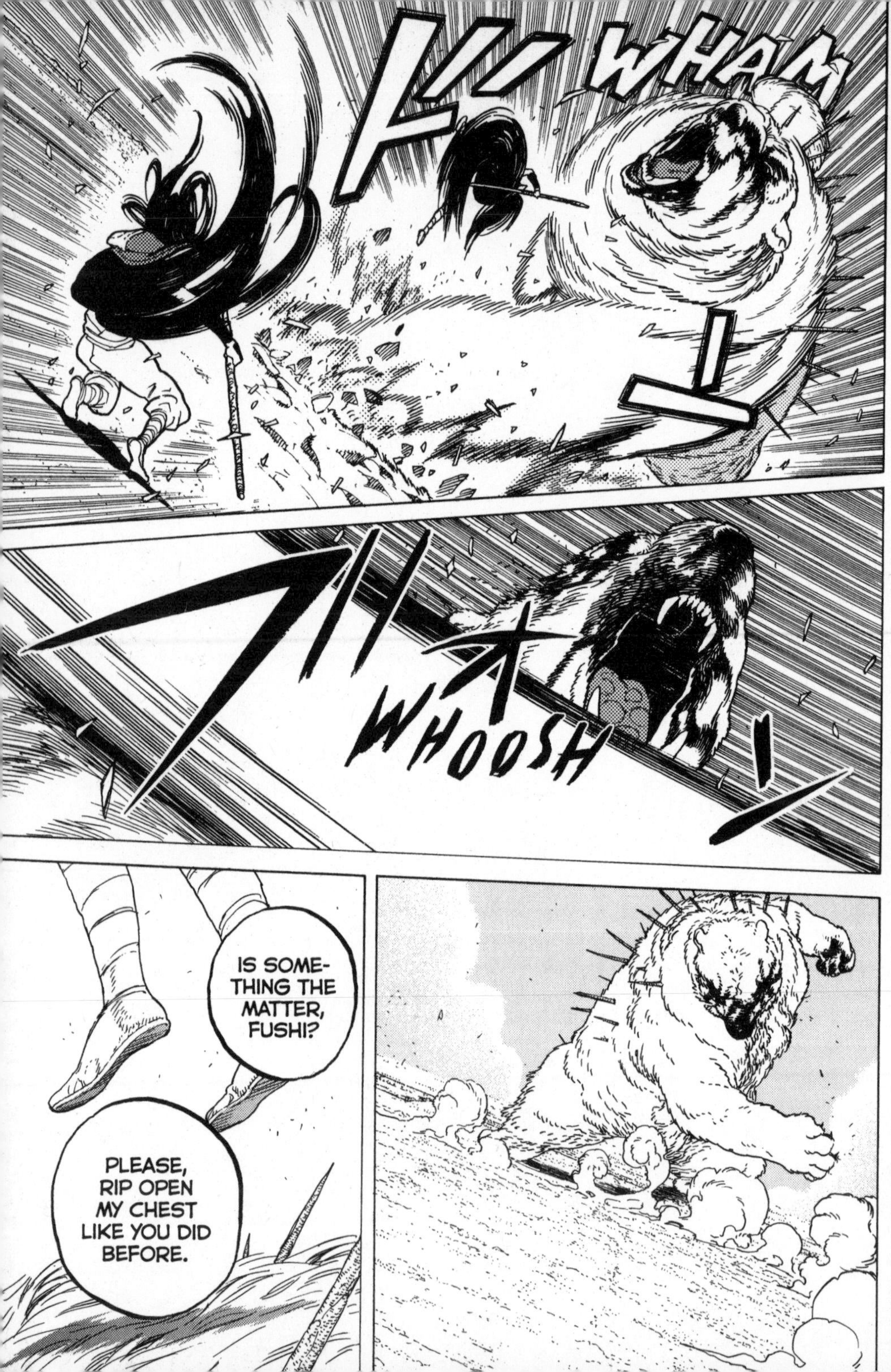
WHAM
WHOOSH
IS SOMETHING THE MATTER, FUSHI?
PLEASE, RIP OPEN MY CHEST LIKE YOU DID BEFORE.

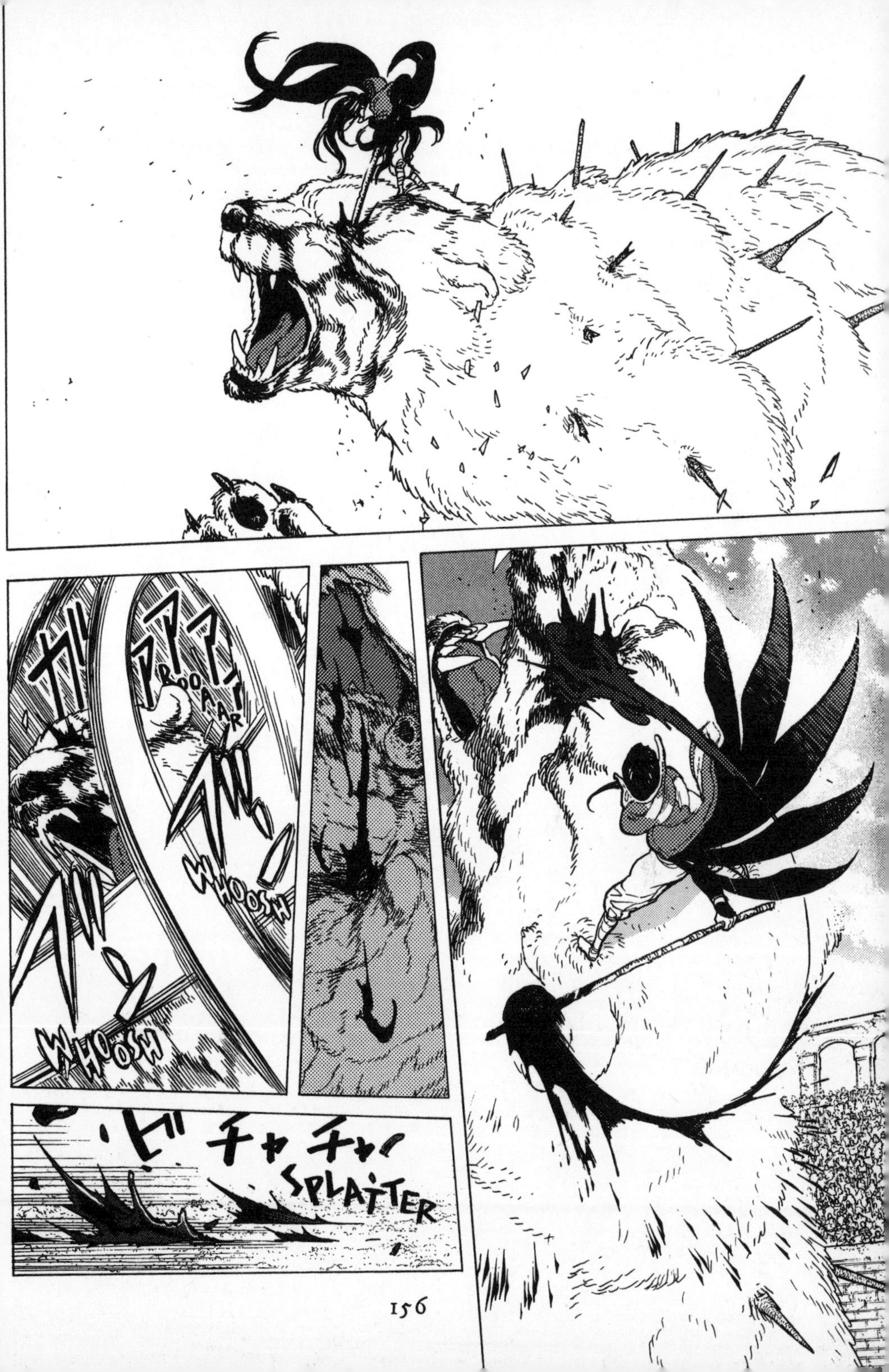
ガアアア
ROOAAR
WHOOSH
WHOOSH
ビチャチャ
SPLATTER

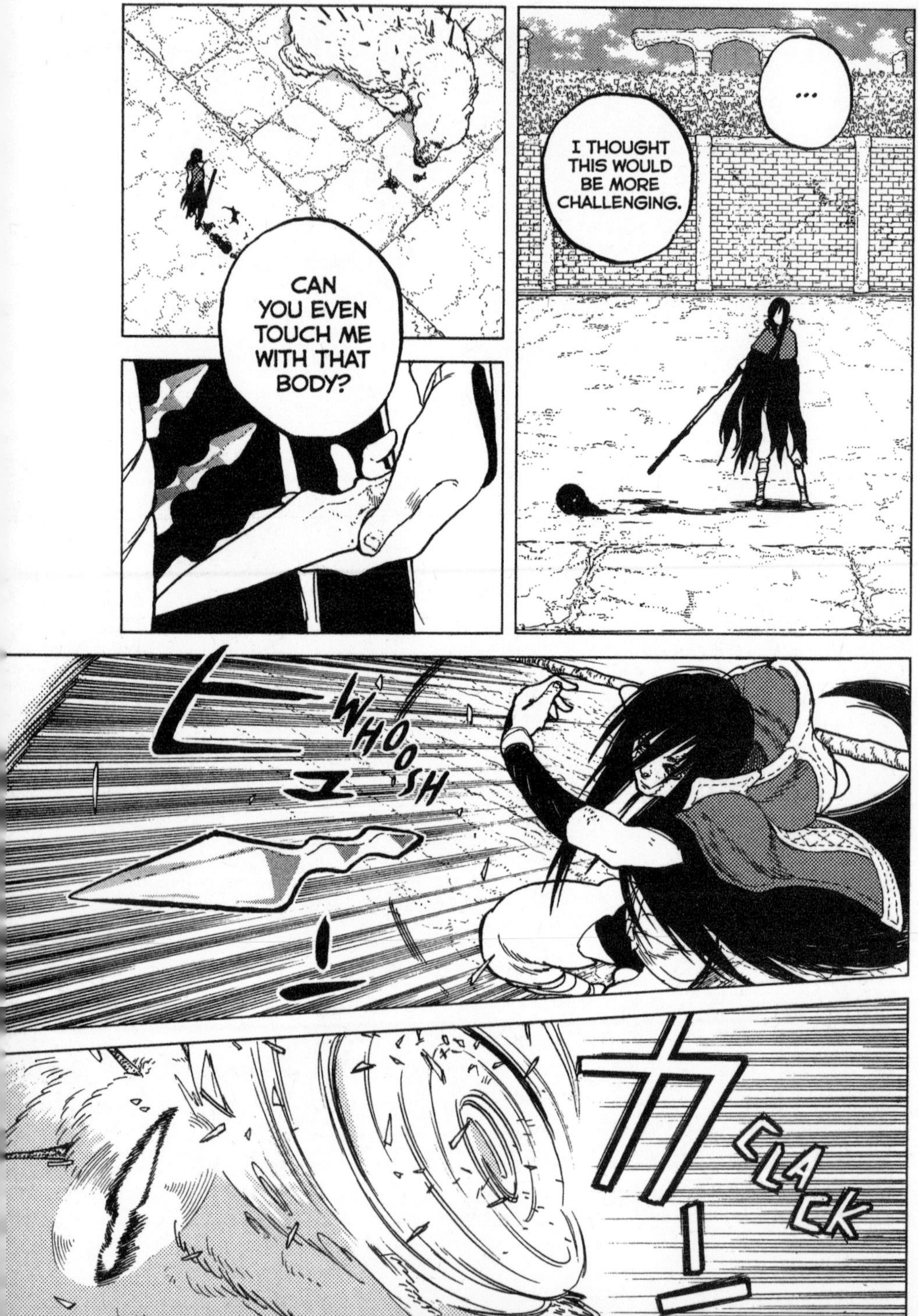
...
I THOUGHT THIS WOULD BE MORE CHALLENGING.
CAN YOU EVEN TOUCH ME WITH THAT BODY?
WHOOSH
CLACK

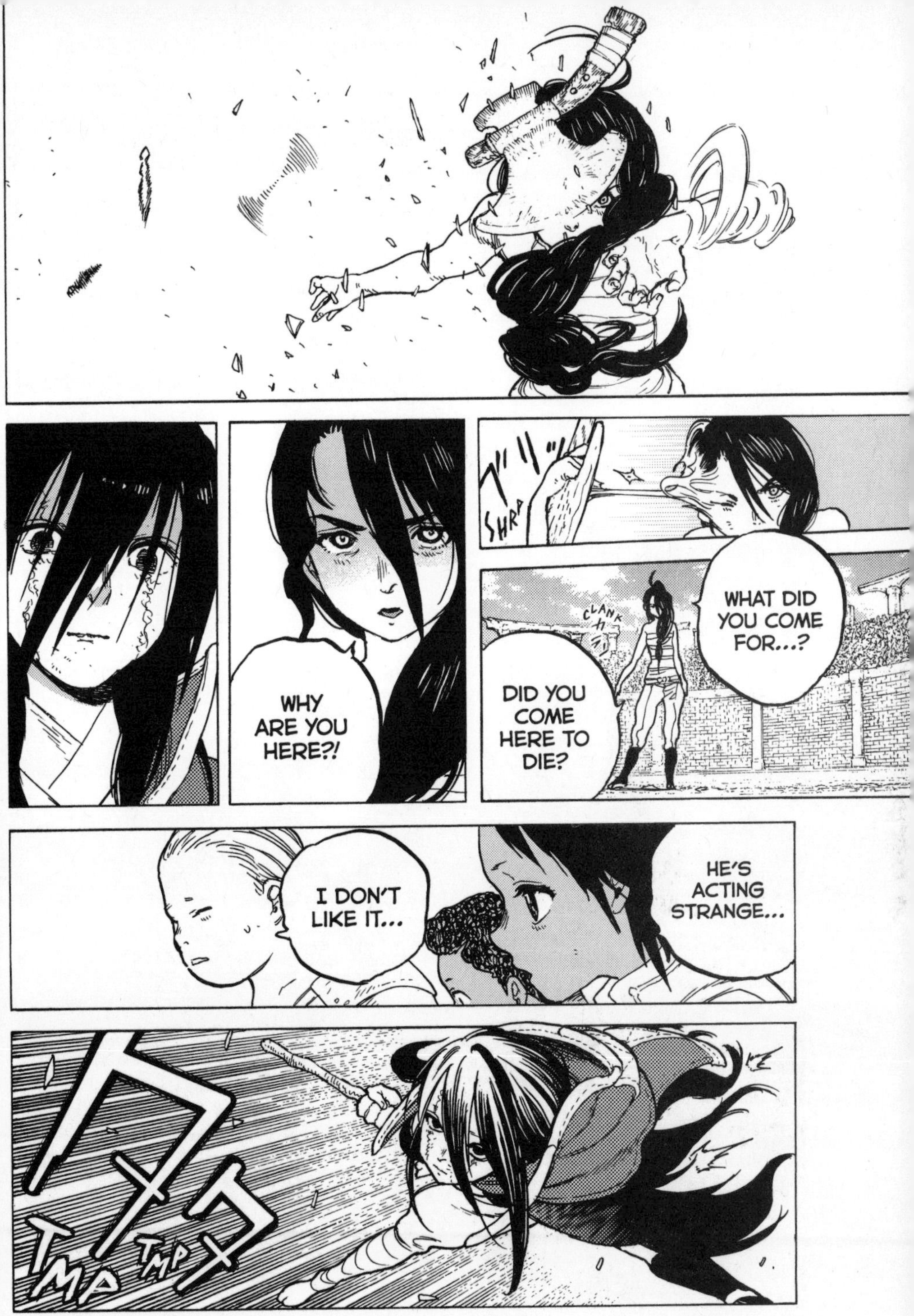
SHRP
WHAT DID YOU COME FOR...?
DID YOU COME HERE TO DIE?
CLANK
WHY ARE YOU HERE?!
HE'S ACTING STRANGE...
I DON'T LIKE IT...
TMP TMP

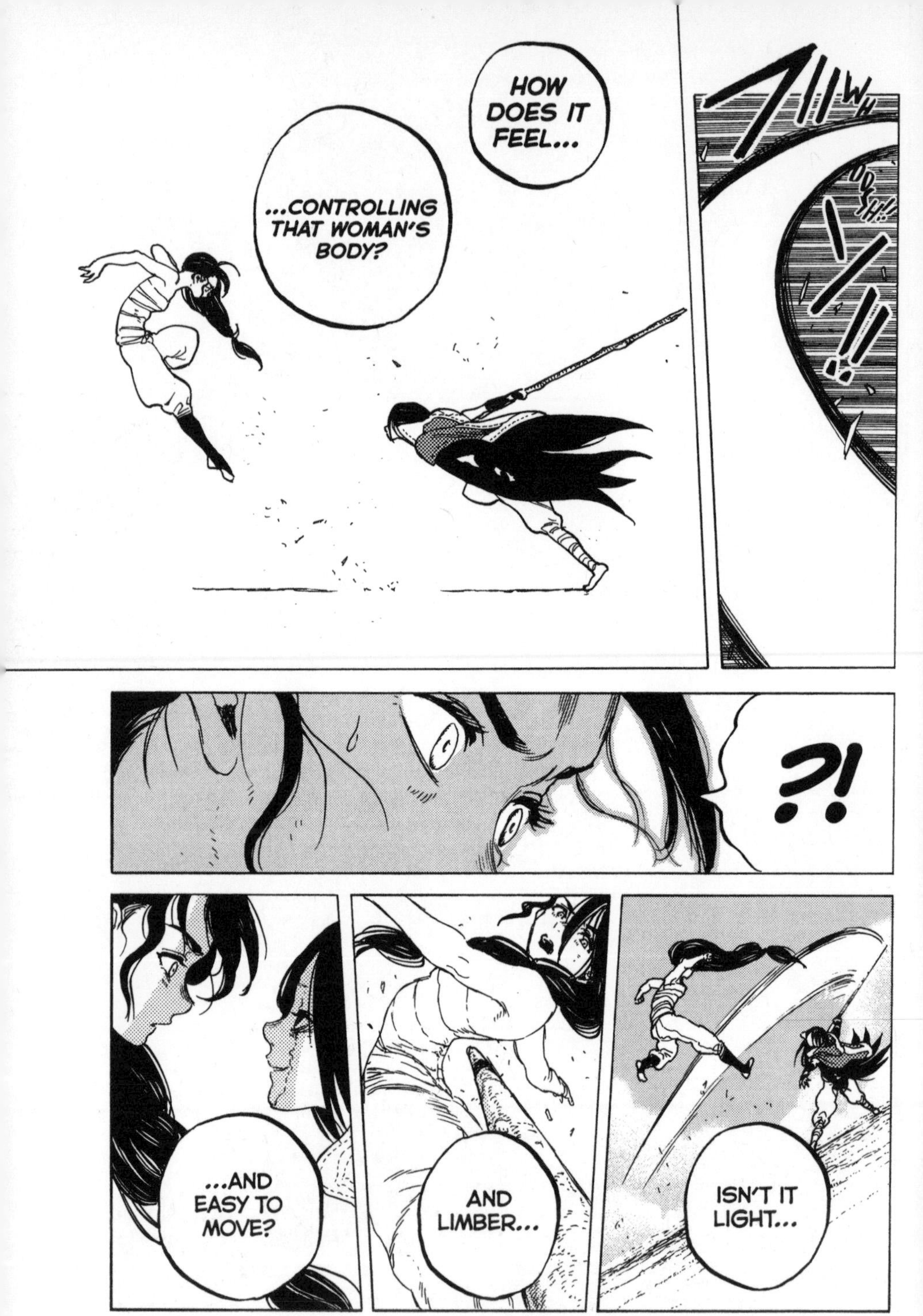
WHOOSH!!
HOW DOES IT FEEL...
...CONTROLLING THAT WOMAN'S BODY?
?!
ISN'T IT LIGHT...
AND LIMBER...
...AND EASY TO MOVE?

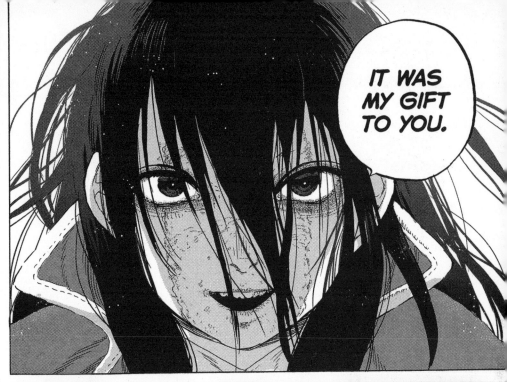

IT WAS MY GIFT TO YOU.

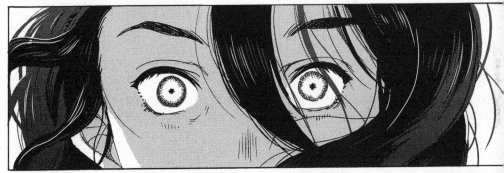

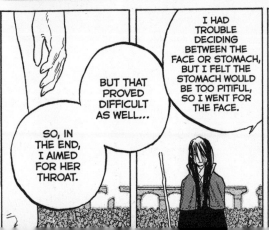

I HAD TROUBLE DECIDING BETWEEN THE FACE OR STOMACH, BUT I FELT THE STOMACH WOULD BE TOO PITIFUL, SO I WENT FOR THE FACE.

BUT THAT PROVED DIFFICULT AS WELL...

SO, IN THE END, I AIMED FOR HER THROAT.

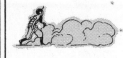

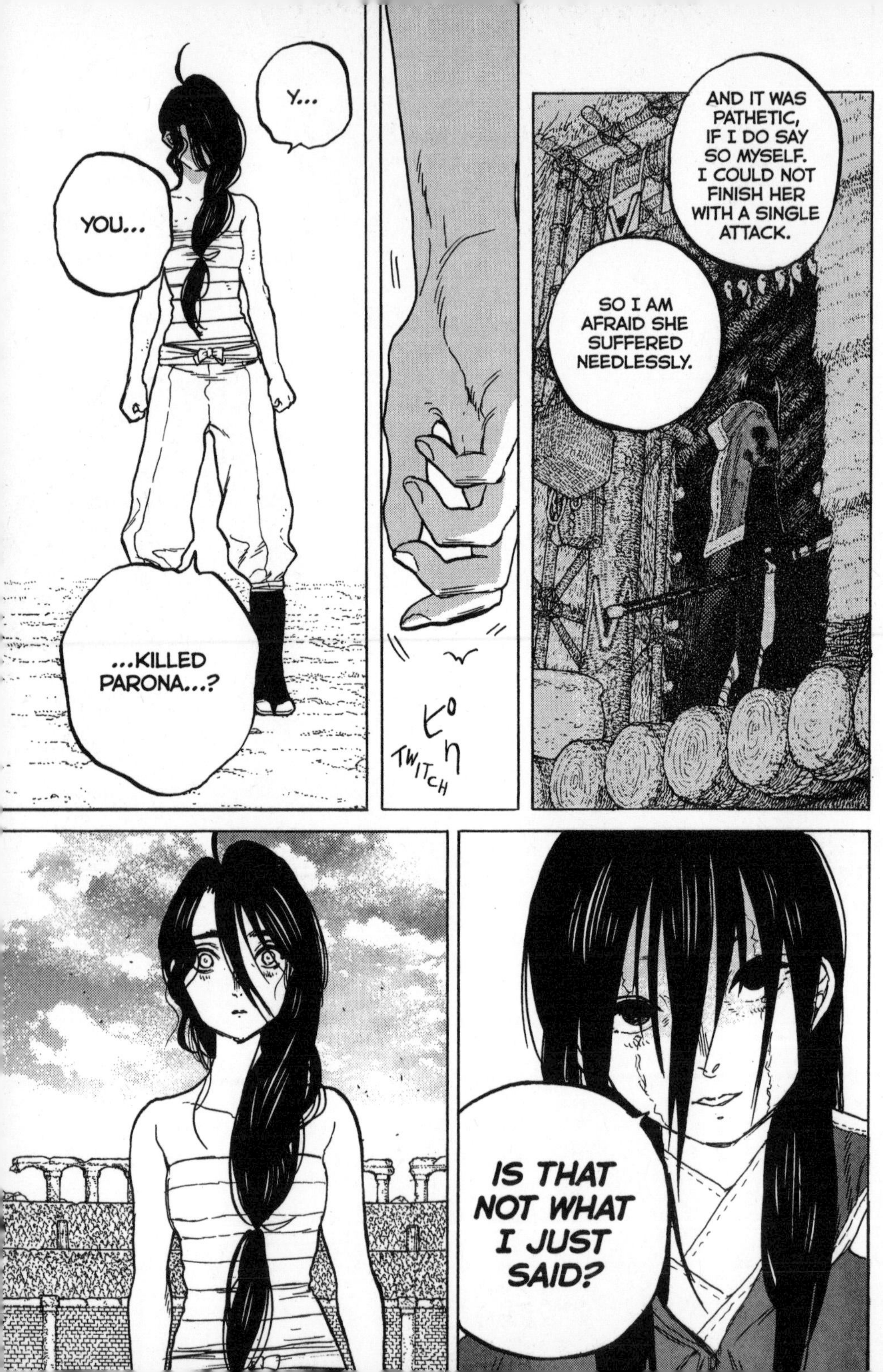
AND IT WAS PATHETIC, IF I DO SAY SO MYSELF. I COULD NOT FINISH HER WITH A SINGLE ATTACK.
SO I AM AFRAID SHE SUFFERED NEEDLESSLY.
ピン
TWITCH
Y...
YOU...
...KILLED PARONA...?
IS THAT NOT WHAT I JUST SAID?

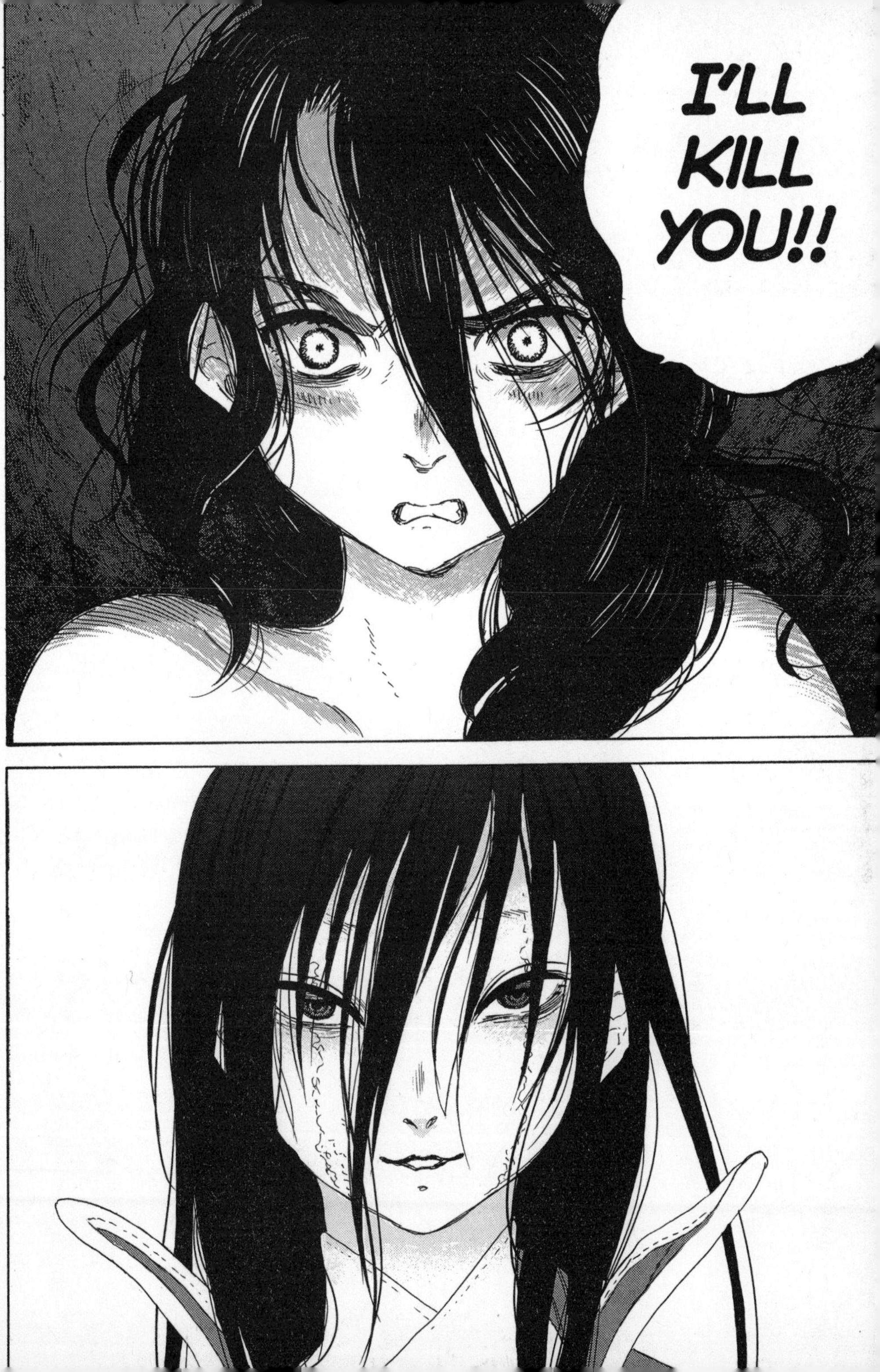
I'LL KILL YOU!!

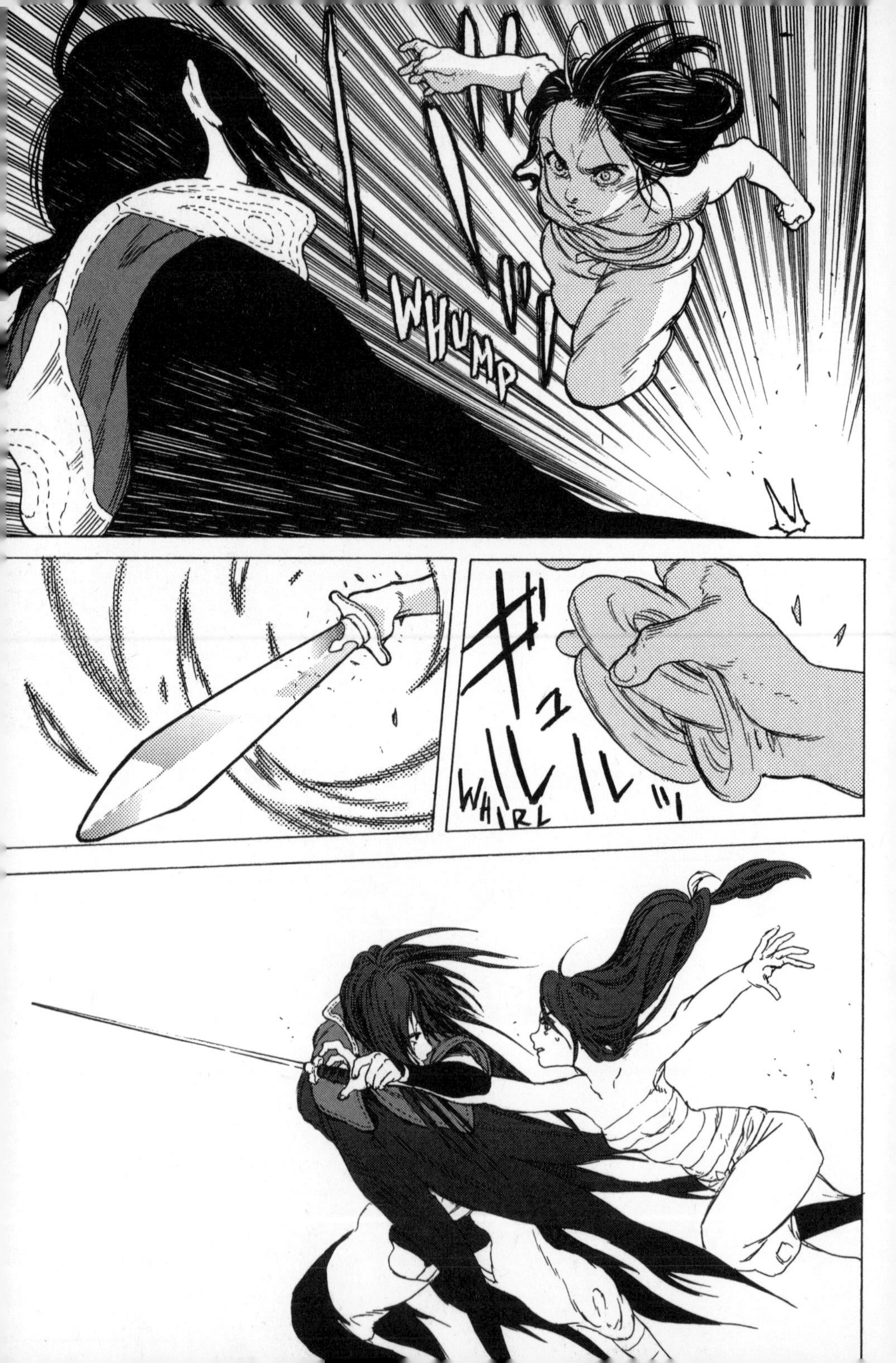
WHUMP
ギュルルッ
WHIRL

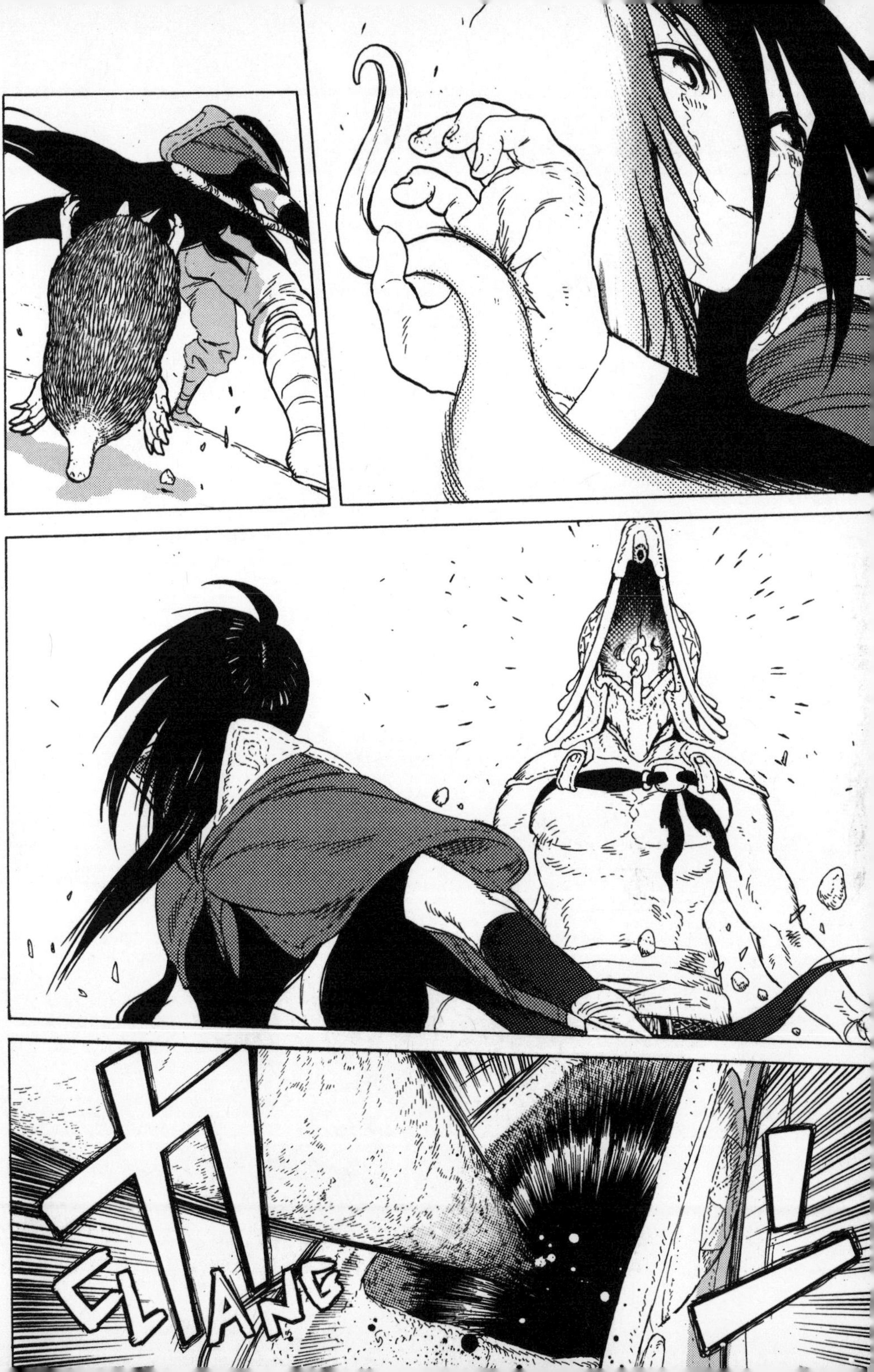
CLANG

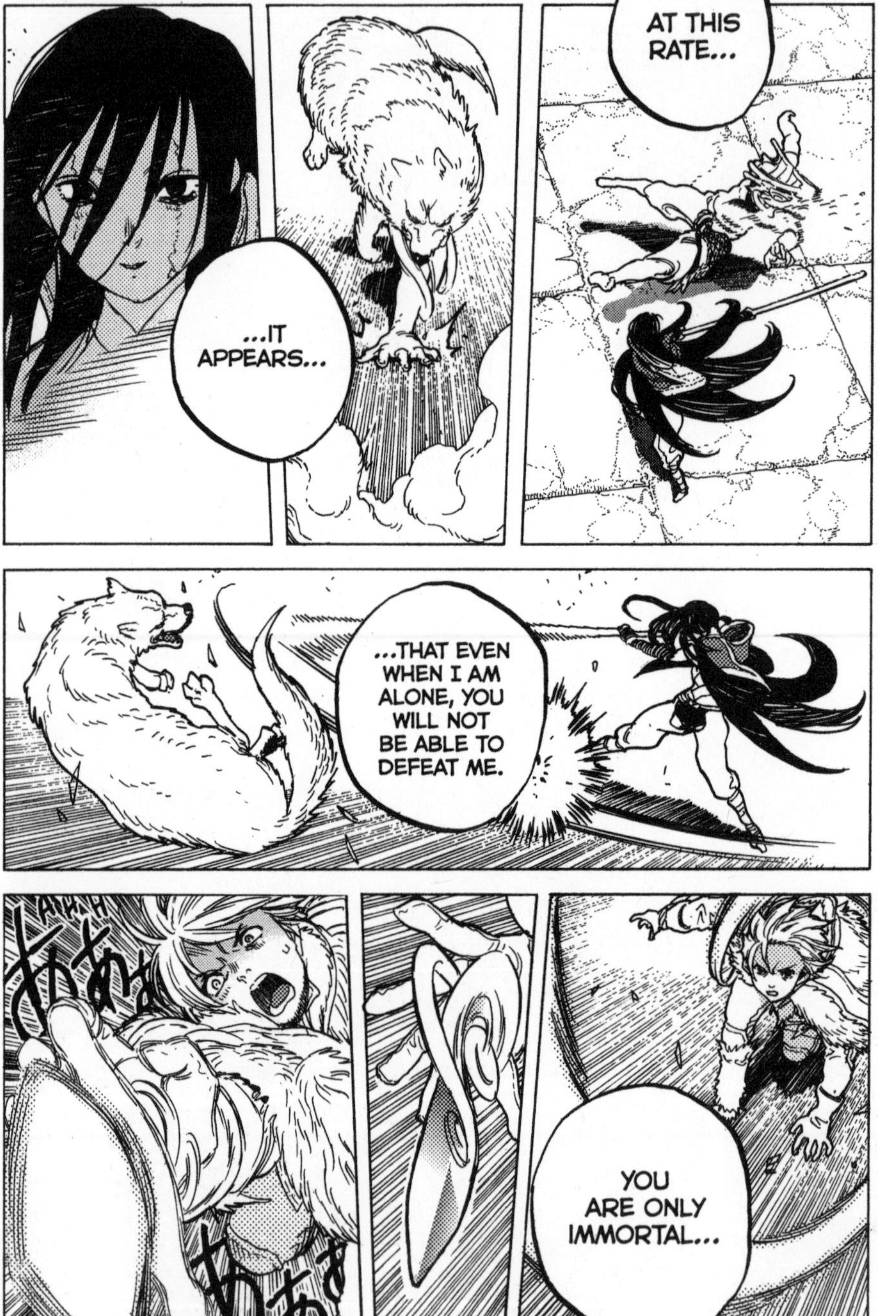
AT THIS RATE...
...IT APPEARS...
...THAT EVEN WHEN I AM ALONE, YOU WILL NOT BE ABLE TO DEFEAT ME.
YOU ARE ONLY IMMORTAL...

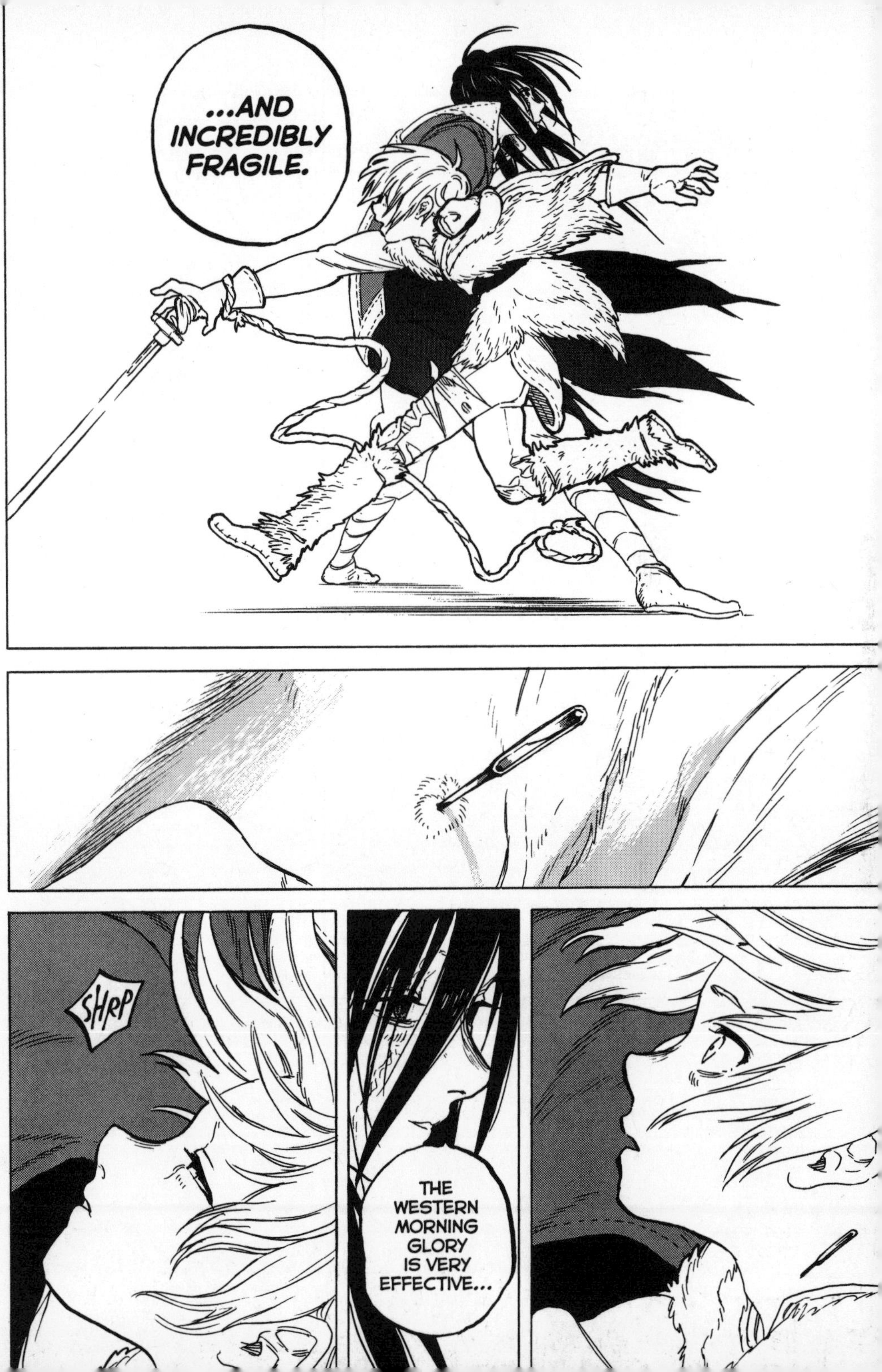
...AND INCREDIBLY FRAGILE.
THE WESTERN MORNING GLORY IS VERY EFFECTIVE...
SHRP

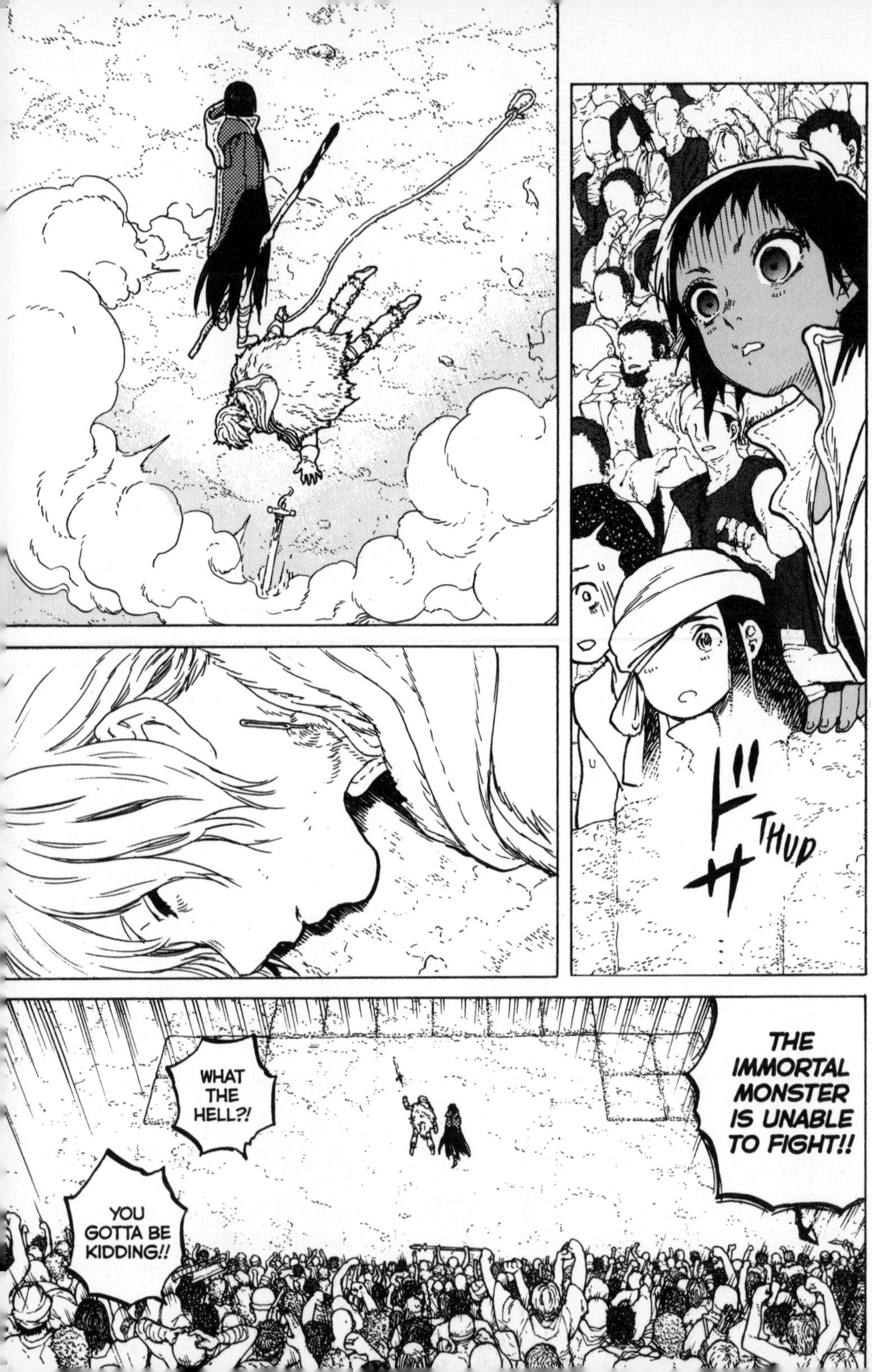
ドッ
THUD
THE IMMORTAL MONSTER IS UNABLE TO FIGHT!!
WHAT THE HELL?!
YOU GOTTA BE KIDDING!!

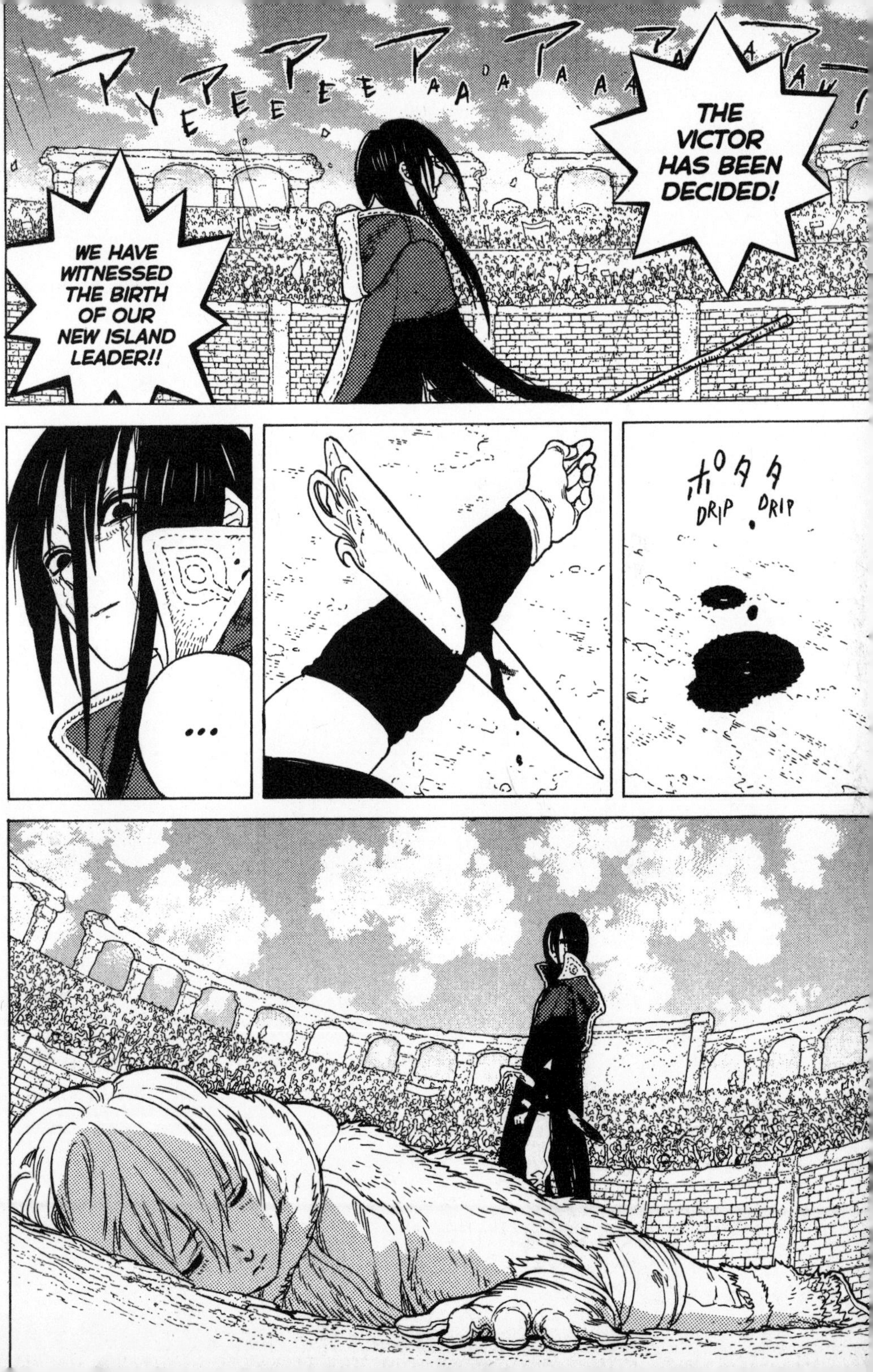
YEEEEEAAAAAAAAAW!
THE VICTOR HAS BEEN DECIDED!
WE HAVE WITNESSED THE BIRTH OF OUR NEW ISLAND LEADER!!
DRIP DRIP
...

TO YOUR ETERNITY

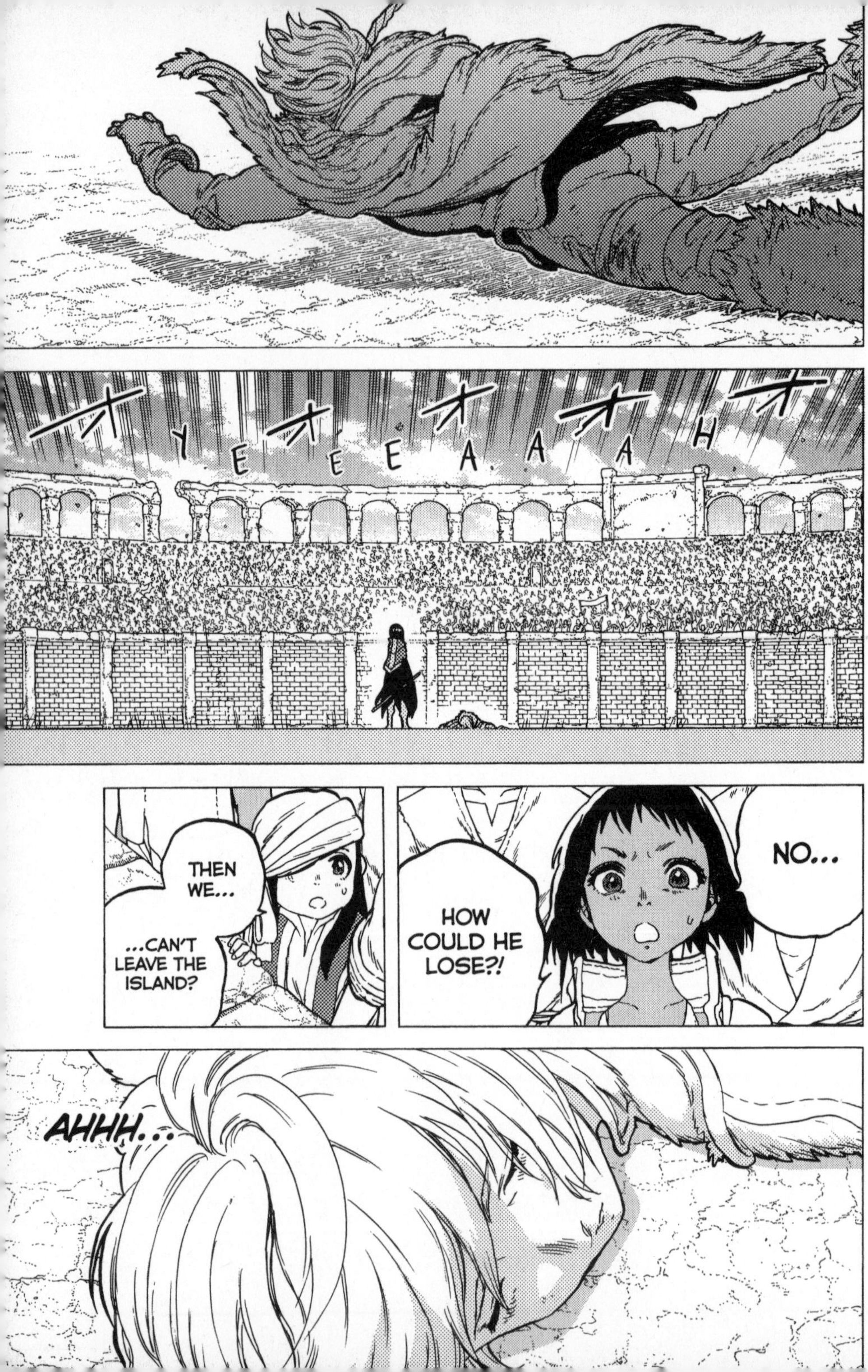
YEEAAAH
NO...
HOW COULD HE LOSE?!
THEN WE...
...CAN'T LEAVE THE ISLAND?
AHHH...

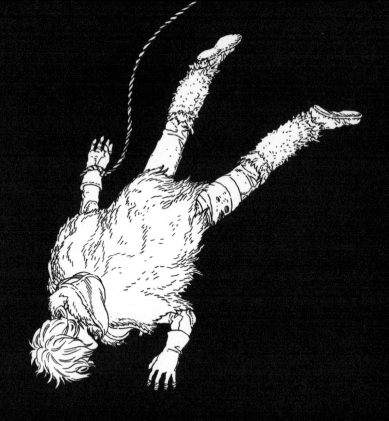

THIS IS THE
WORST...

#44 Pioneer

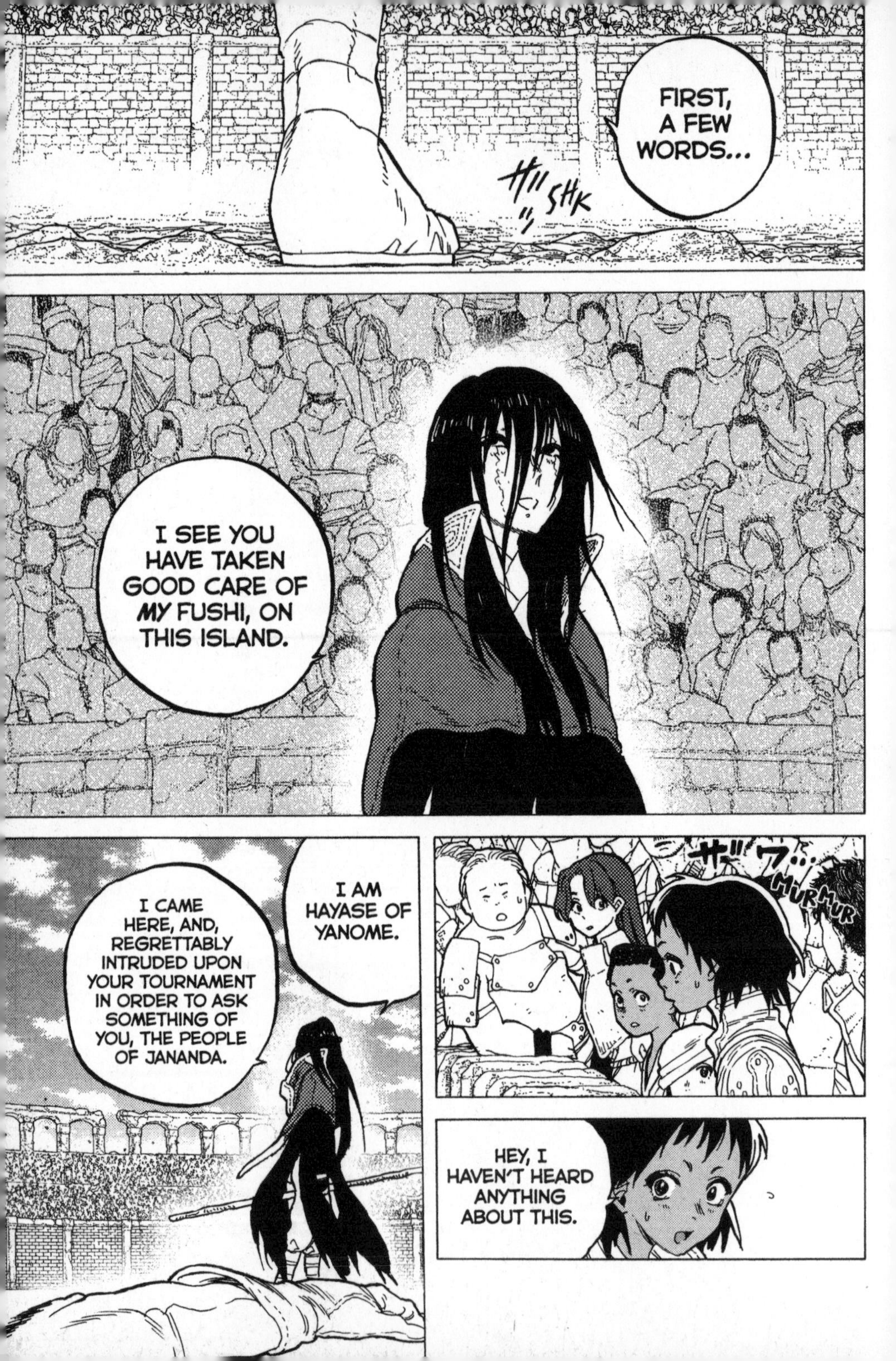
FIRST, A FEW WORDS...
SHK
I SEE YOU HAVE TAKEN GOOD CARE OF *MY* FUSHI, ON THIS ISLAND.
ザワ…
MURMUR
HEY, I HAVEN'T HEARD ANYTHING ABOUT THIS.
I AM HAYASE OF YANOME.
I CAME HERE, AND, REGRETTABLY INTRUDED UPON YOUR TOURNAMENT IN ORDER TO ASK SOMETHING OF YOU, THE PEOPLE OF JANANDA.

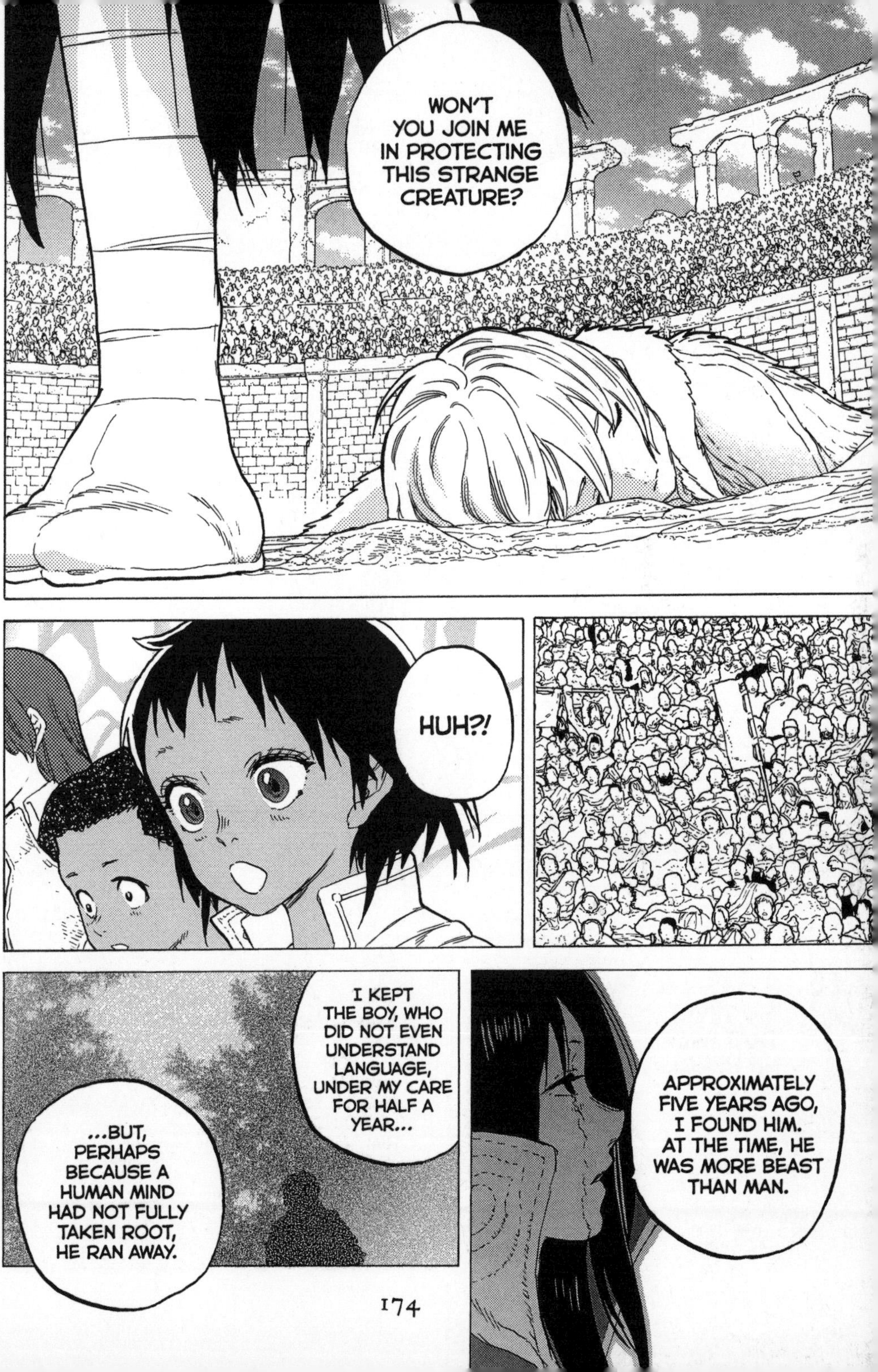
WON'T YOU JOIN ME IN PROTECTING THIS STRANGE CREATURE?
HUH?!
APPROXIMATELY FIVE YEARS AGO, I FOUND HIM. AT THE TIME, HE WAS MORE BEAST THAN MAN.
I KEPT THE BOY, WHO DID NOT EVEN UNDERSTAND LANGUAGE, UNDER MY CARE FOR HALF A YEAR...
...BUT, PERHAPS BECAUSE A HUMAN MIND HAD NOT FULLY TAKEN ROOT, HE RAN AWAY.

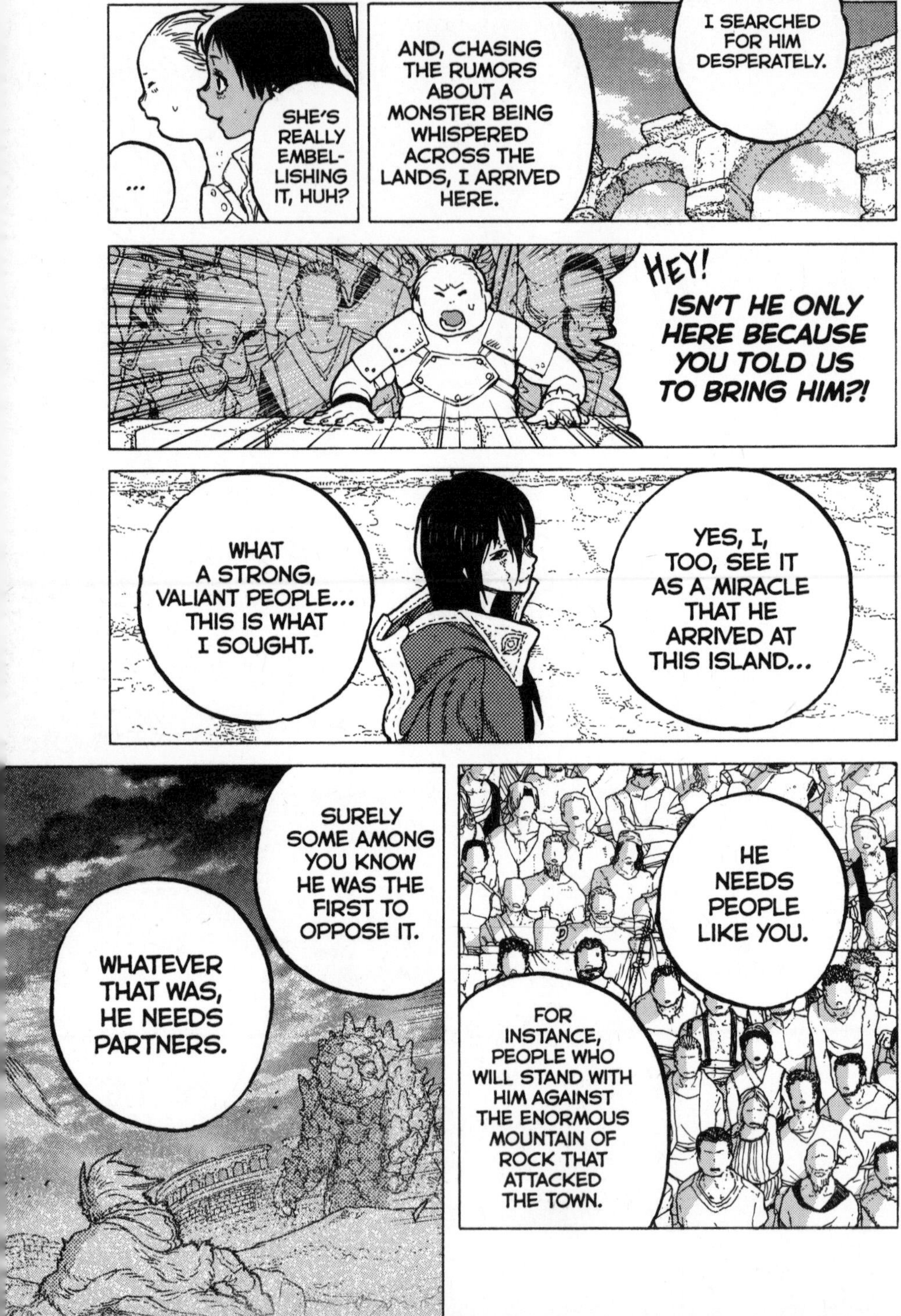
I SEARCHED FOR HIM DESPERATELY.
AND, CHASING THE RUMORS ABOUT A MONSTER BEING WHISPERED ACROSS THE LANDS, I ARRIVED HERE.
SHE'S REALLY EMBEL-LISHING IT, HUH?
...
HEY!
ISN'T HE ONLY HERE BECAUSE YOU TOLD US TO BRING HIM?!
YES, I, TOO, SEE IT AS A MIRACLE THAT HE ARRIVED AT THIS ISLAND...
WHAT A STRONG, VALIANT PEOPLE... THIS IS WHAT I SOUGHT.
HE NEEDS PEOPLE LIKE YOU.
FOR INSTANCE, PEOPLE WHO WILL STAND WITH HIM AGAINST THE ENORMOUS MOUNTAIN OF ROCK THAT ATTACKED THE TOWN.
SURELY SOME AMONG YOU KNOW HE WAS THE FIRST TO OPPOSE IT.
WHATEVER THAT WAS, HE NEEDS PARTNERS.

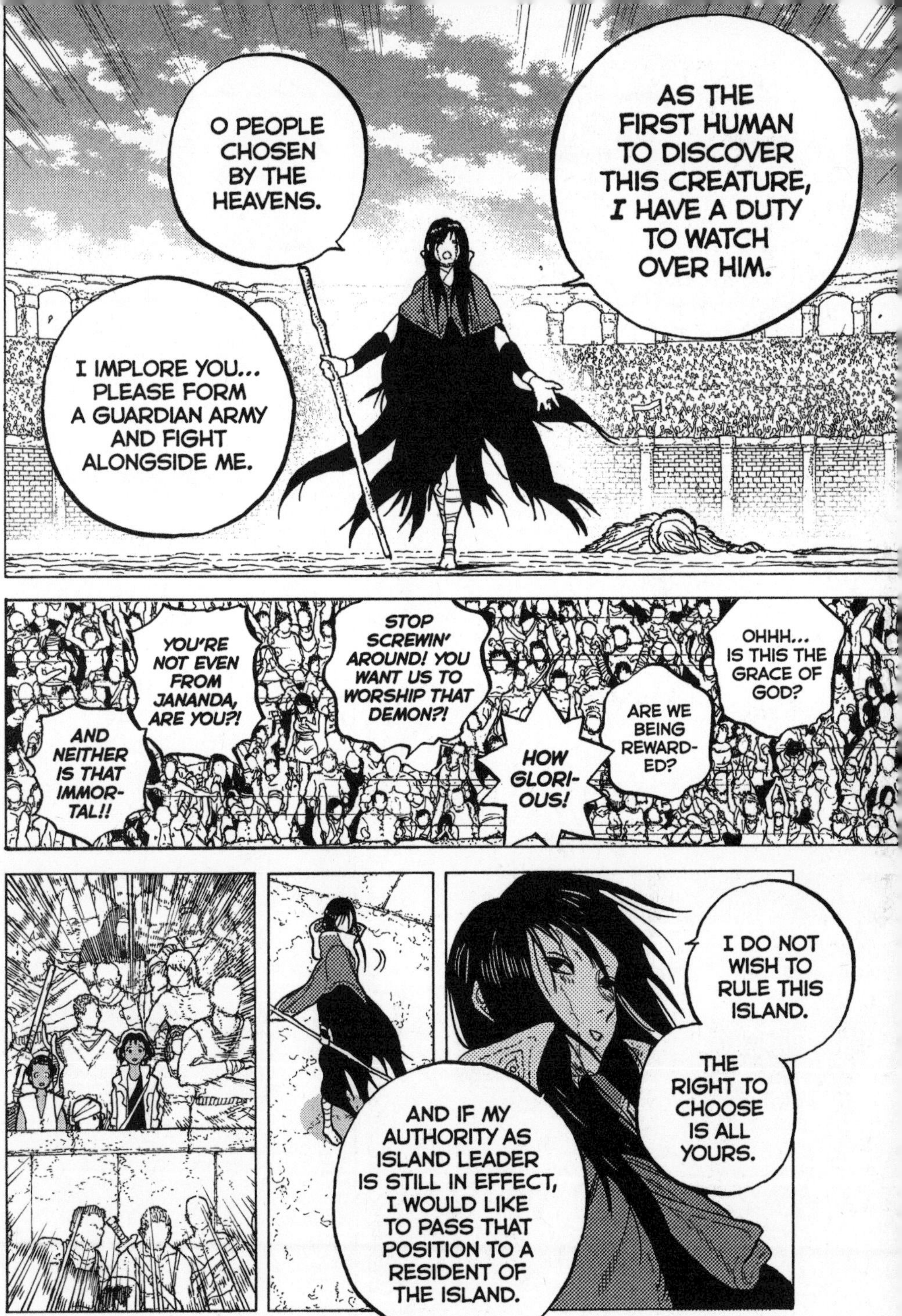
AS THE FIRST HUMAN TO DISCOVER THIS CREATURE, *I* HAVE A DUTY TO WATCH OVER HIM.
O PEOPLE CHOSEN BY THE HEAVENS.
I IMPLORE YOU... PLEASE FORM A GUARDIAN ARMY AND FIGHT ALONGSIDE ME.
OHHH... IS THIS THE GRACE OF GOD?
ARE WE BEING REWARDED?
HOW GLORIOUS!
STOP SCREWIN' AROUND! YOU WANT US TO WORSHIP THAT DEMON?!
YOU'RE NOT EVEN FROM JANANDA, ARE YOU?!
AND NEITHER IS THAT IMMORTAL!!
I DO NOT WISH TO RULE THIS ISLAND.
THE RIGHT TO CHOOSE IS ALL YOURS.
AND IF MY AUTHORITY AS ISLAND LEADER IS STILL IN EFFECT, I WOULD LIKE TO PASS THAT POSITION TO A RESIDENT OF THE ISLAND.

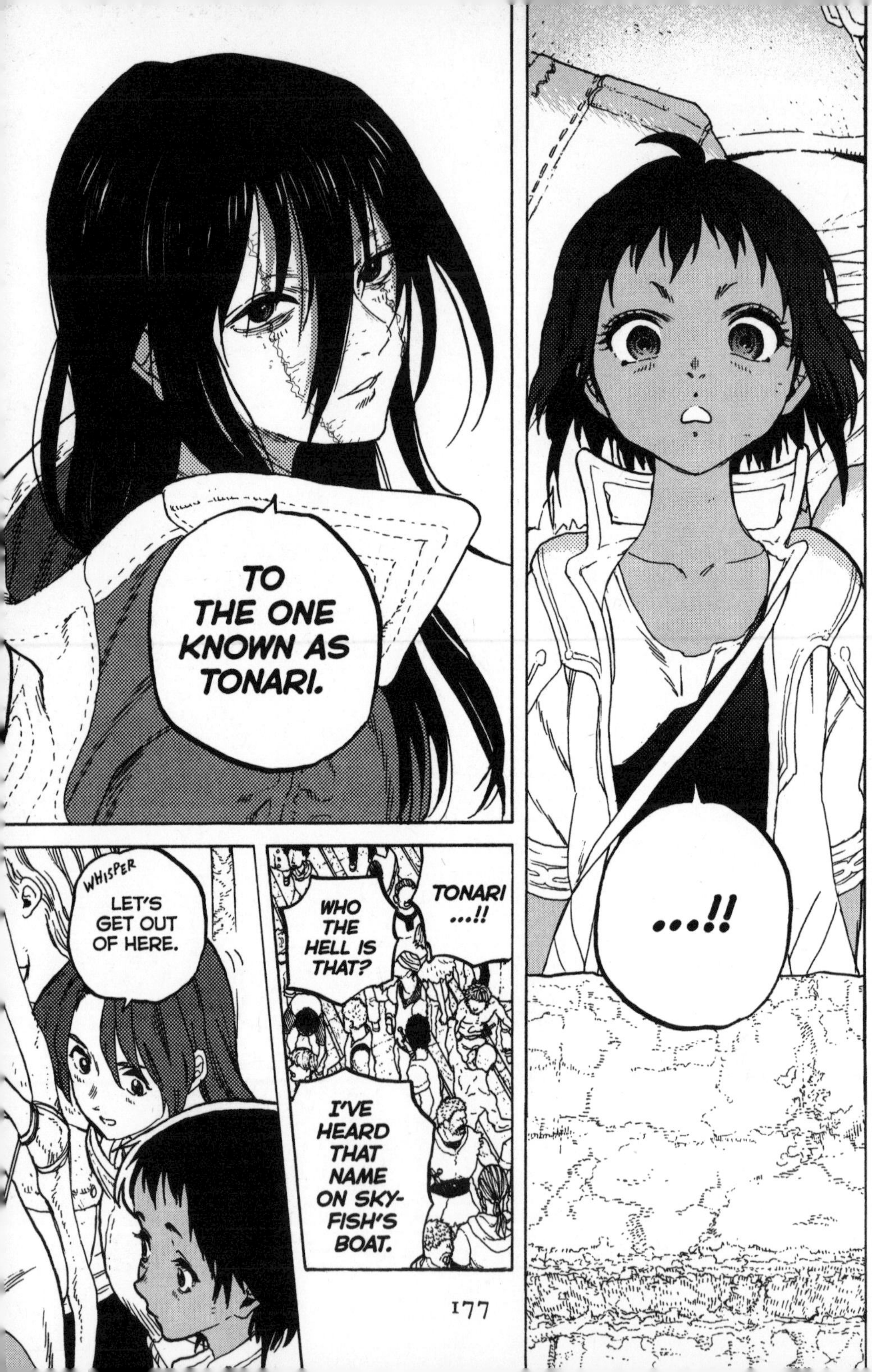
...!!
TO THE ONE KNOWN AS TONARI.
TONARI ...!!
WHO THE HELL IS THAT?
I'VE HEARD THAT NAME ON SKY-FISH'S BOAT.
WHISPER
LET'S GET OUT OF HERE.

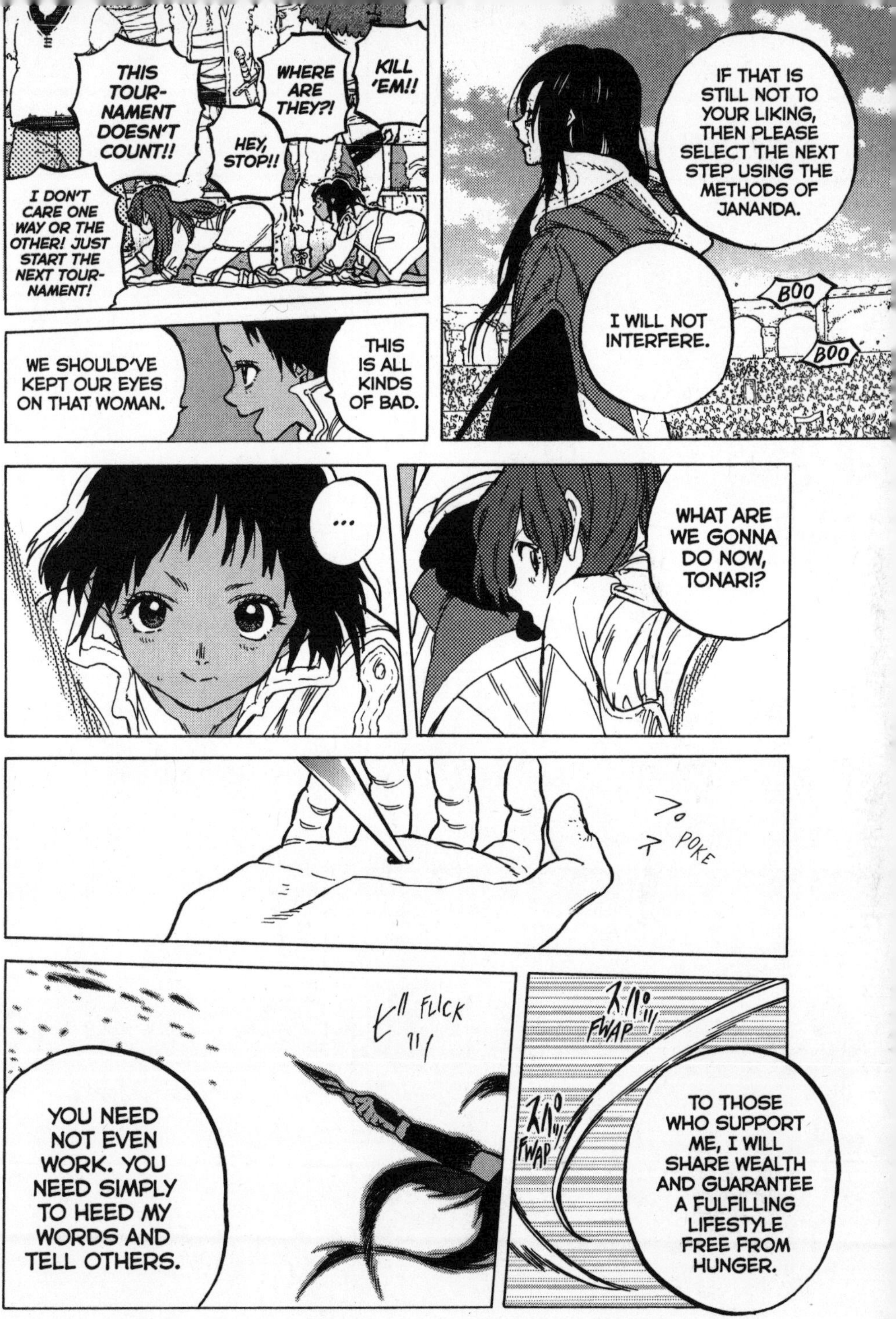
IF THAT IS STILL NOT TO YOUR LIKING, THEN PLEASE SELECT THE NEXT STEP USING THE METHODS OF JANANDA.
I WILL NOT INTERFERE.
BOO
BOO
KILL 'EM!!
WHERE ARE THEY?!
HEY, STOP!!
THIS TOURNAMENT DOESN'T COUNT!!
I DON'T CARE ONE WAY OR THE OTHER! JUST START THE NEXT TOURNAMENT!
THIS IS ALL KINDS OF BAD.
WE SHOULD'VE KEPT OUR EYES ON THAT WOMAN.
WHAT ARE WE GONNA DO NOW, TONARI?
...
POKE
FWAP
FWAP
TO THOSE WHO SUPPORT ME, I WILL SHARE WEALTH AND GUARANTEE A FULFILLING LIFESTYLE FREE FROM HUNGER.
FLICK
YOU NEED NOT EVEN WORK. YOU NEED SIMPLY TO HEED MY WORDS AND TELL OTHERS.

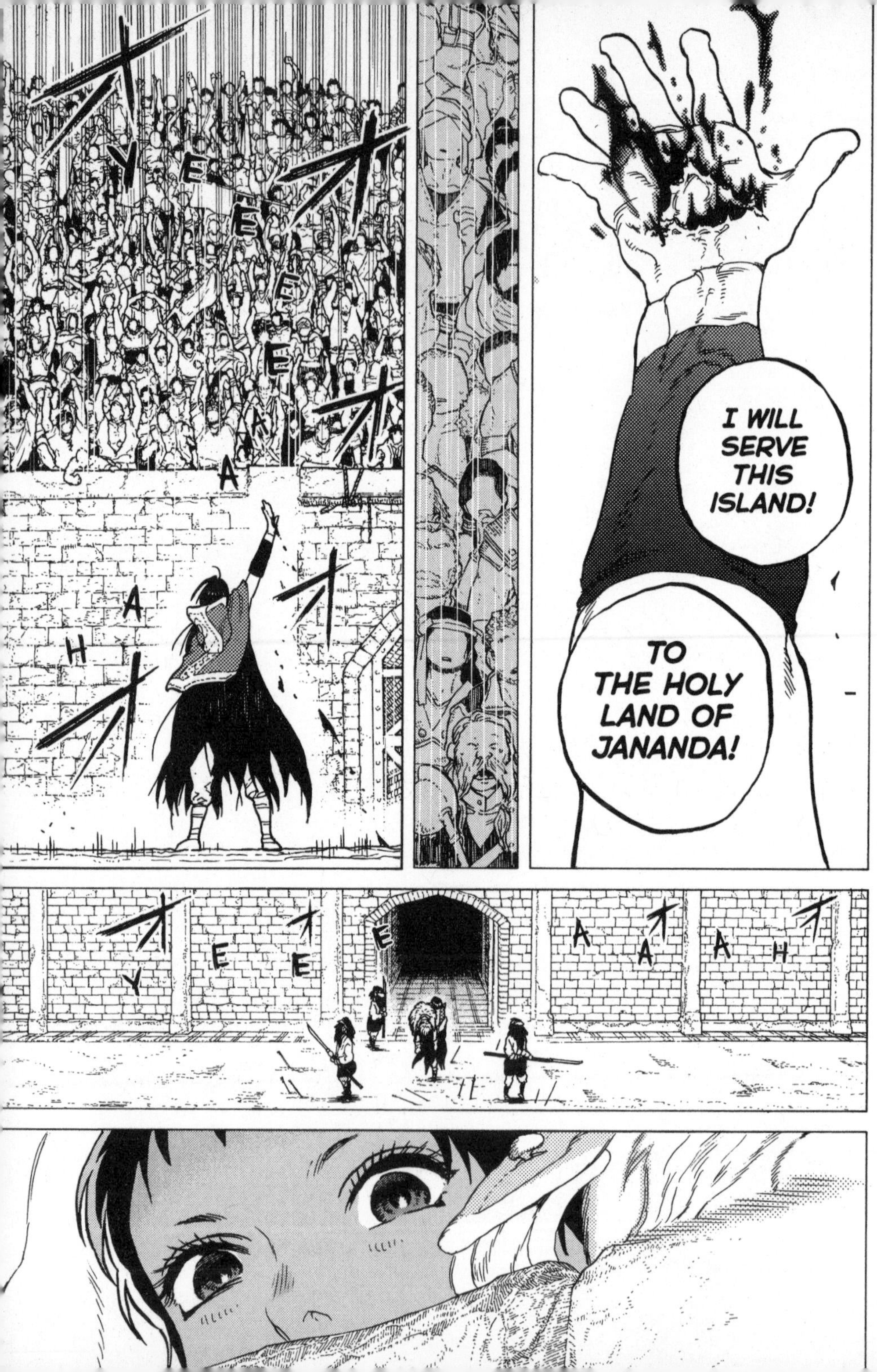
I WILL SERVE THIS ISLAND!
TO THE HOLY LAND OF JANANDA!
YEEEEAAAH
YEEEAAAH

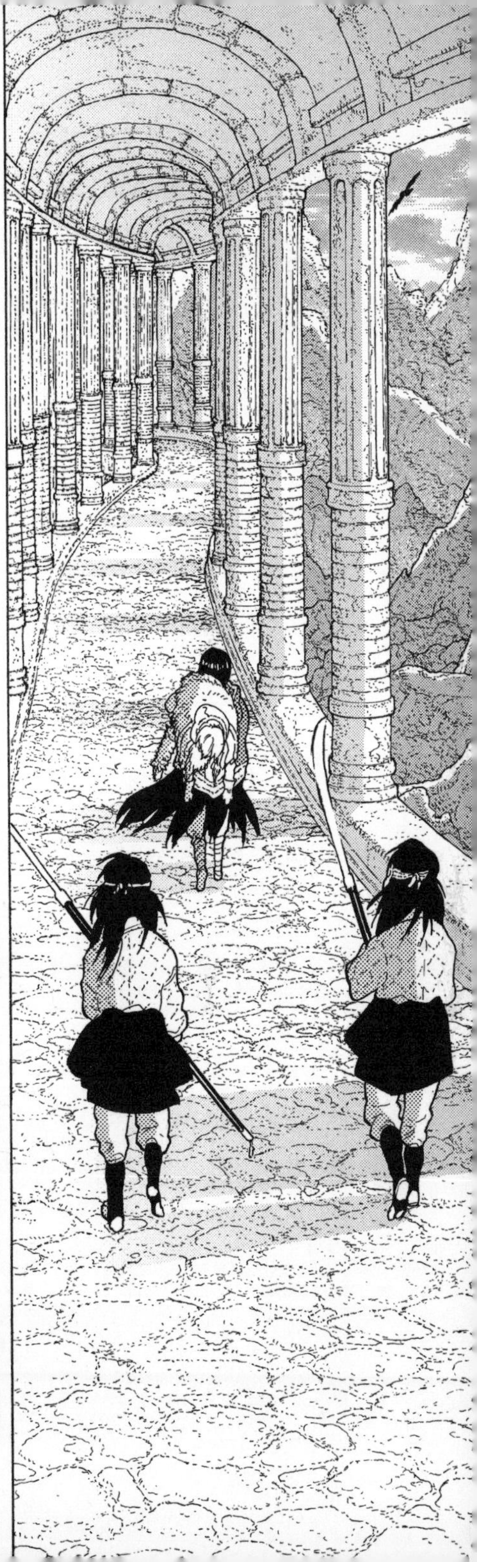
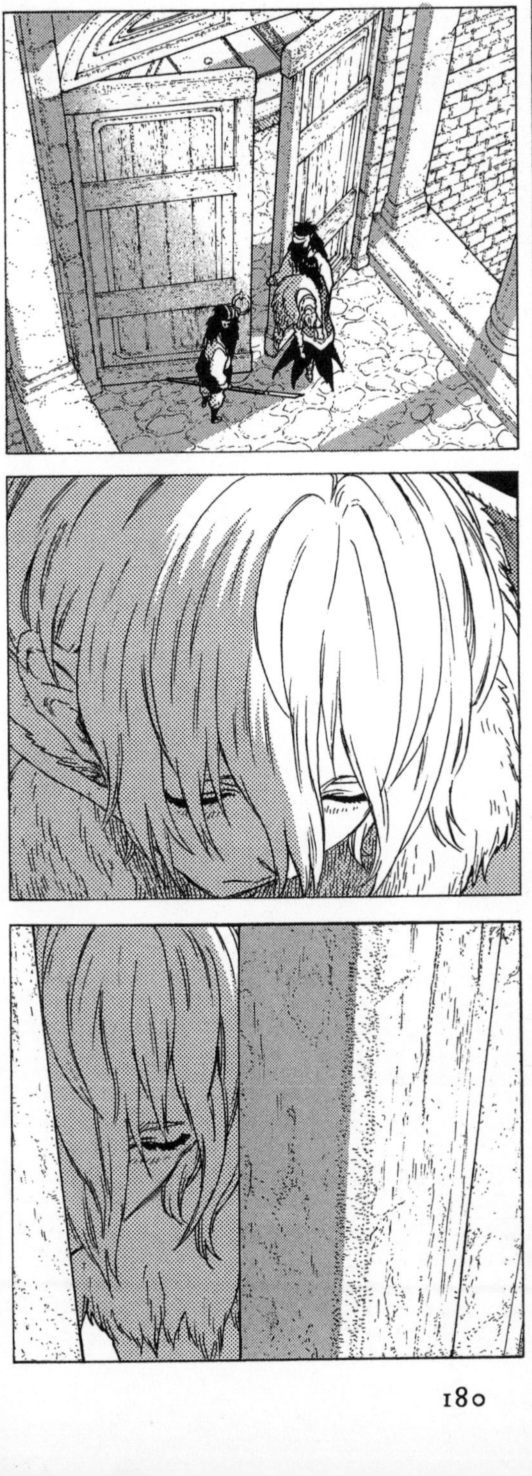

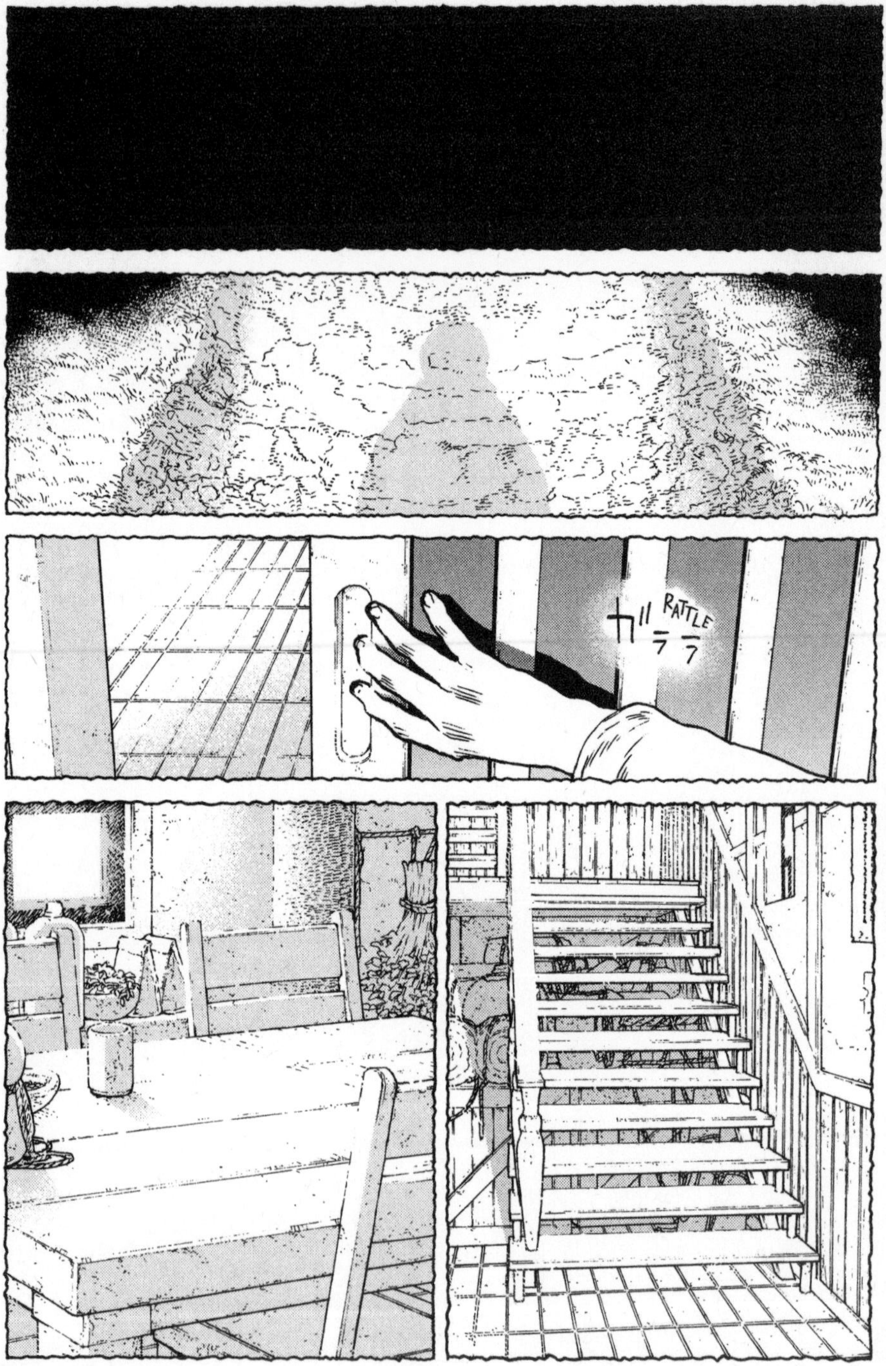
ガララ
RATTLE

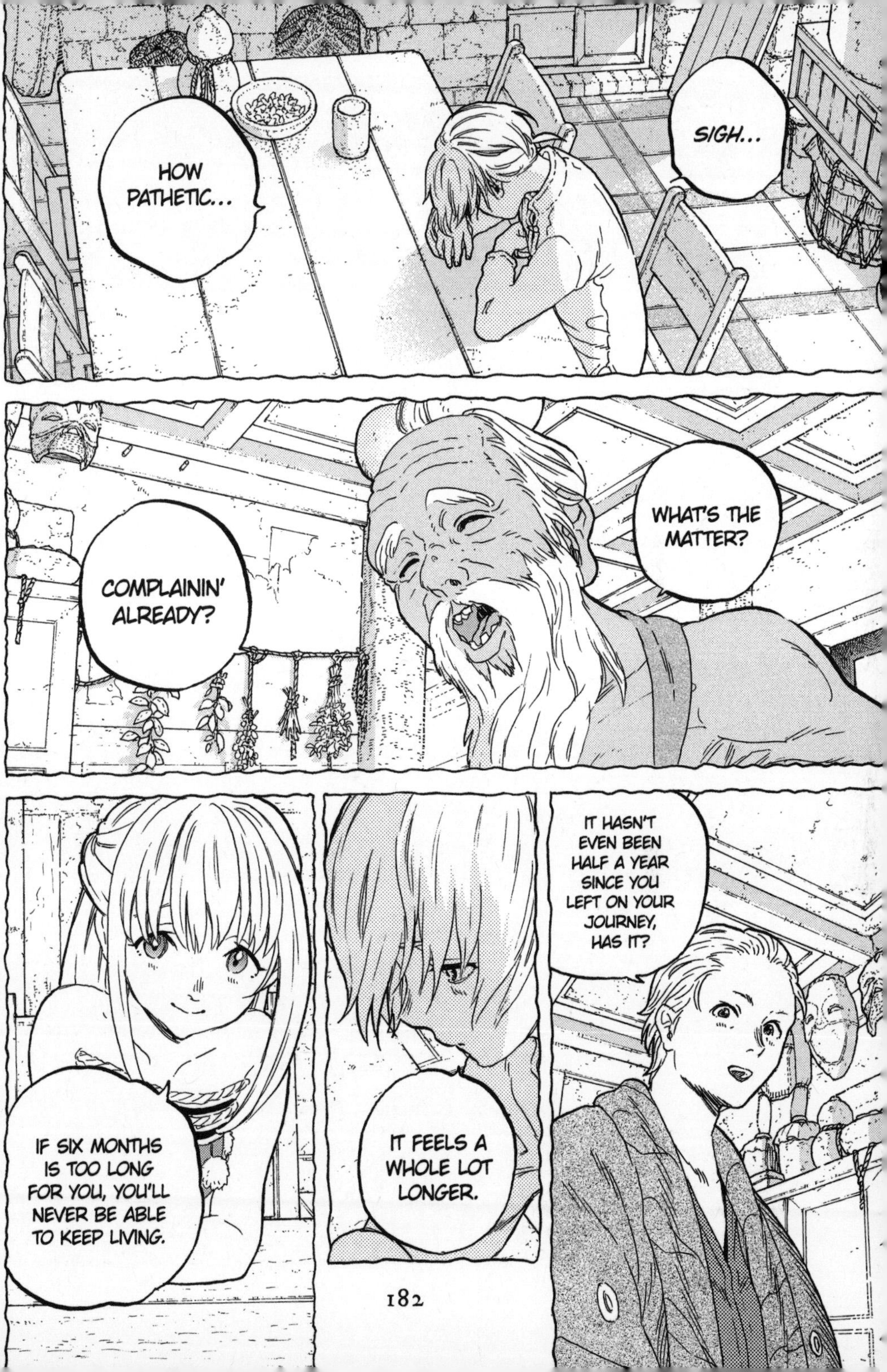
SIGH...
HOW PATHETIC...
WHAT'S THE MATTER?
COMPLAININ' ALREADY?
IT HASN'T EVEN BEEN HALF A YEAR SINCE YOU LEFT ON YOUR JOURNEY, HAS IT?
IT FEELS A WHOLE LOT LONGER.
IF SIX MONTHS IS TOO LONG FOR YOU, YOU'LL NEVER BE ABLE TO KEEP LIVING.

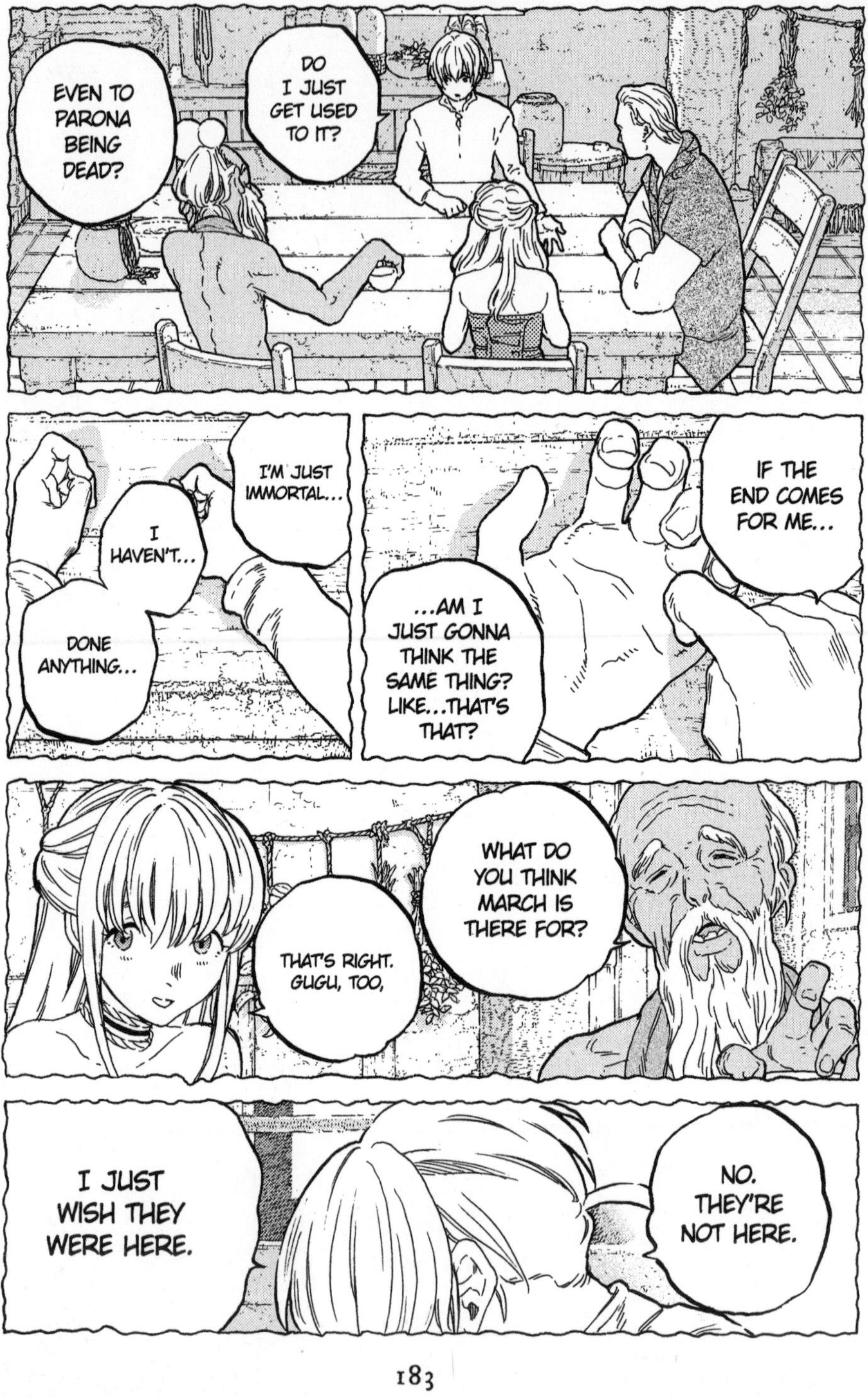
DO I JUST GET USED TO IT?
EVEN TO PARONA BEING DEAD?
IF THE END COMES FOR ME...
...AM I JUST GONNA THINK THE SAME THING? LIKE...THAT'S THAT?
I'M JUST IMMORTAL...
I HAVEN'T...
DONE ANYTHING...
WHAT DO YOU THINK MARCH IS THERE FOR?
THAT'S RIGHT. GUGU, TOO,
NO. THEY'RE NOT HERE.
I JUST WISH THEY WERE HERE.

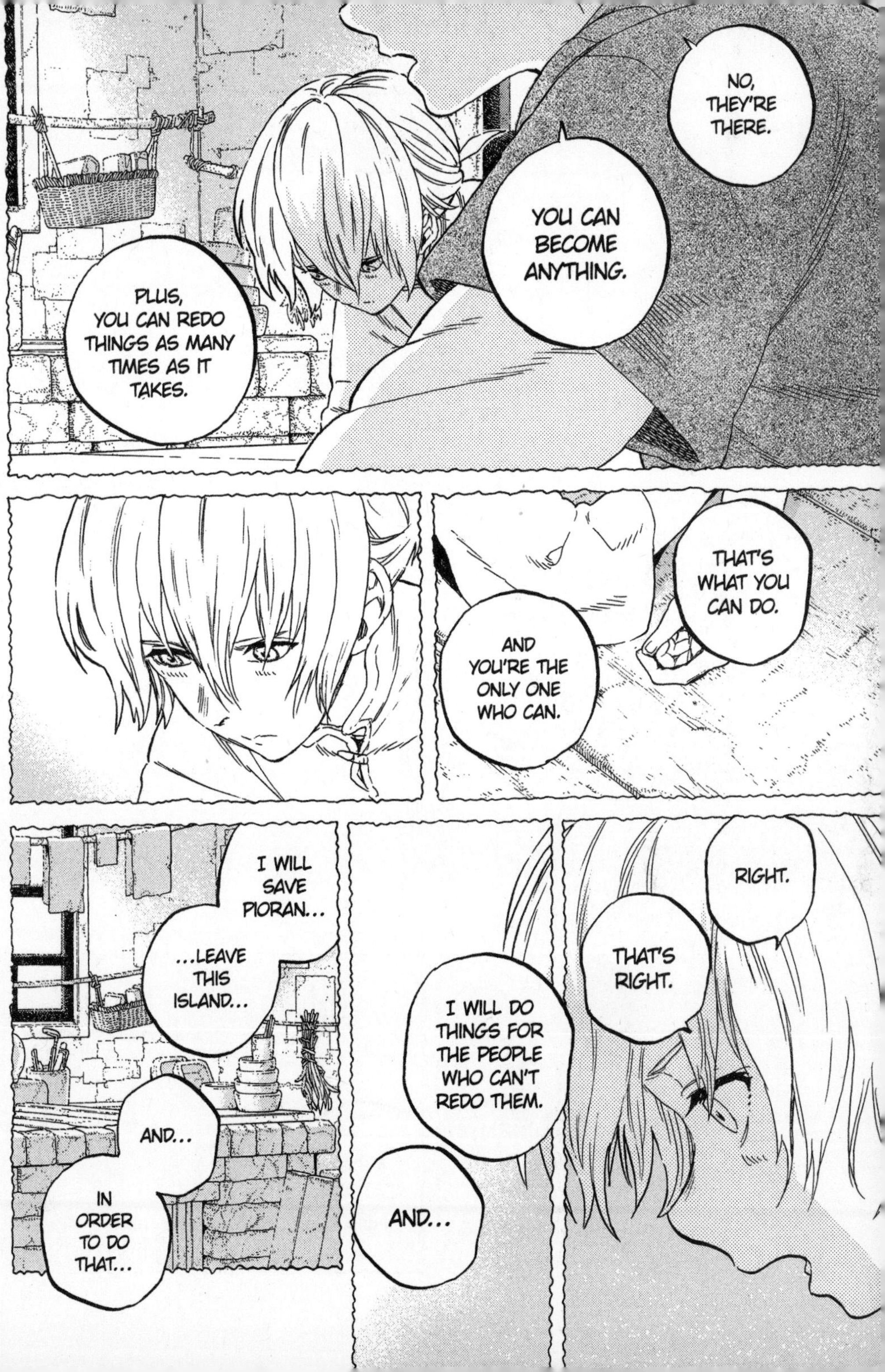
NO, THEY'RE THERE.
YOU CAN BECOME ANYTHING.
PLUS, YOU CAN REDO THINGS AS MANY TIMES AS IT TAKES.
THAT'S WHAT YOU CAN DO.
AND YOU'RE THE ONLY ONE WHO CAN.
RIGHT.
THAT'S RIGHT.
I WILL DO THINGS FOR THE PEOPLE WHO CAN'T REDO THEM.
AND...
I WILL SAVE PIORAN...
...LEAVE THIS ISLAND...
AND...
IN ORDER TO DO THAT...

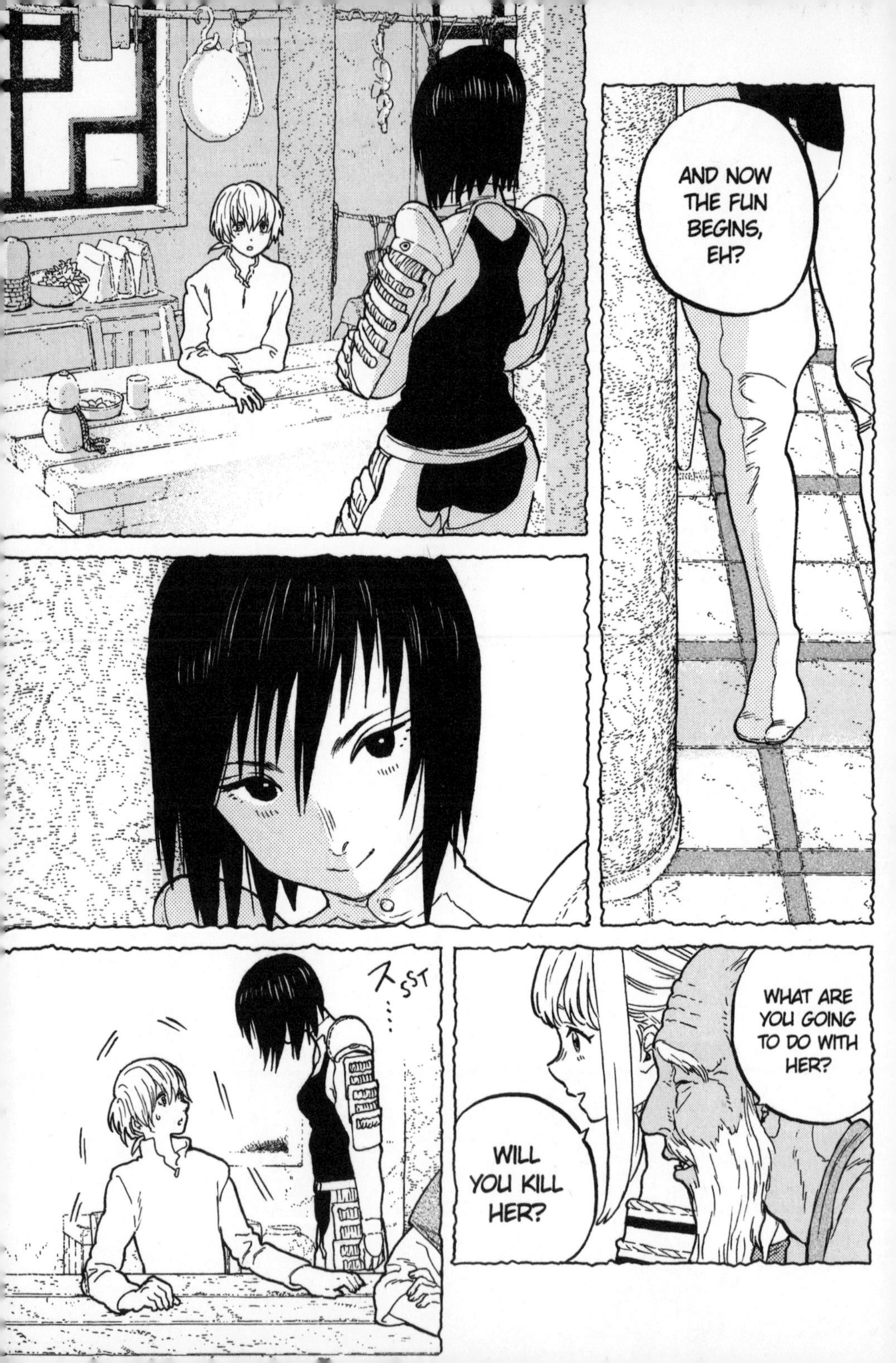
AND NOW THE FUN BEGINS, EH?
WHAT ARE YOU GOING TO DO WITH HER?
WILL YOU KILL HER?
SST

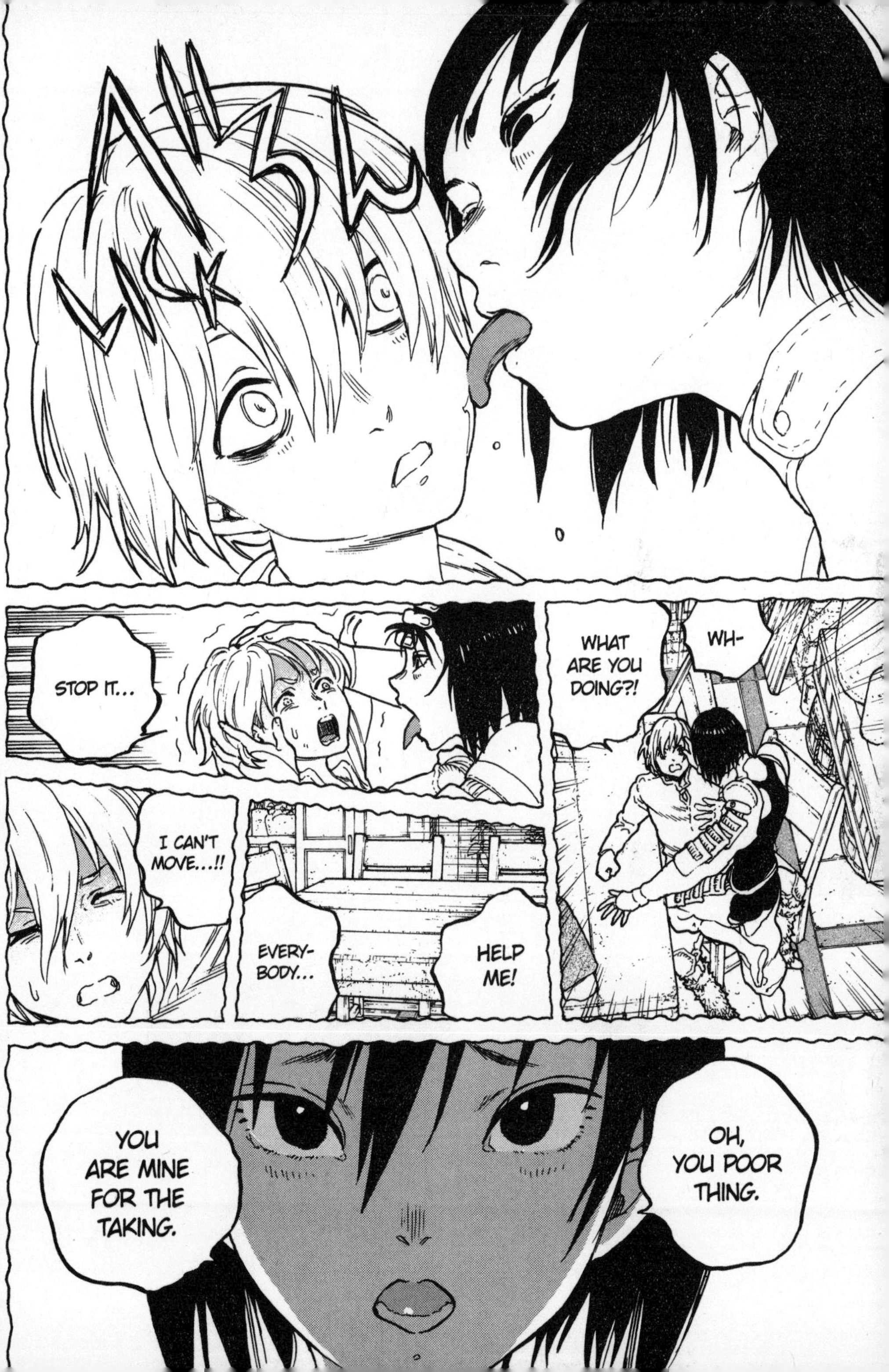
LICK
WH-
WHAT ARE YOU DOING?!
STOP IT...
HELP ME!
EVERY-BODY...
I CAN'T MOVE...!!
OH, YOU POOR THING.
YOU ARE MINE FOR THE TAKING.

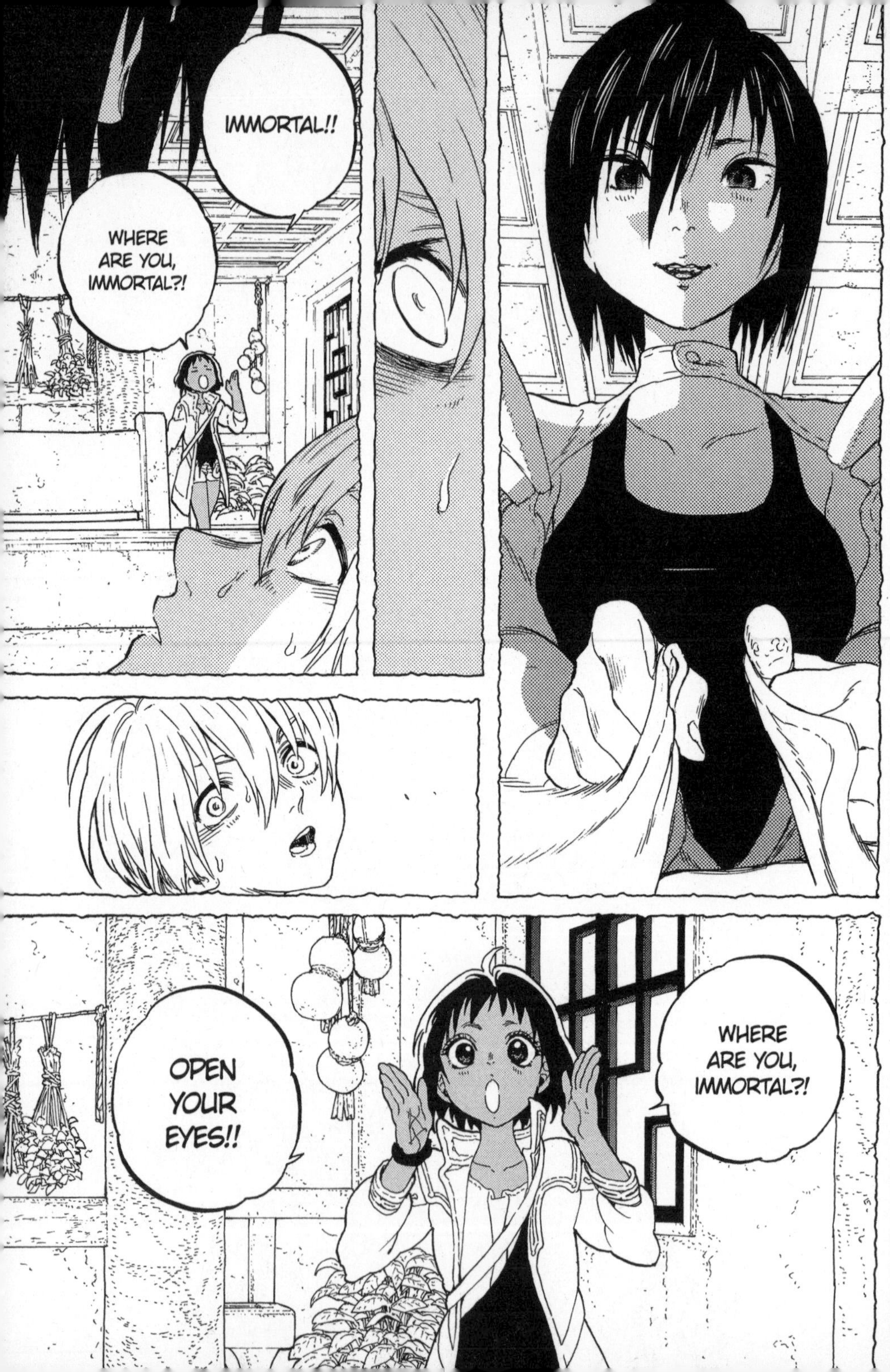
IMMORTAL!!
WHERE ARE YOU, IMMORTAL?!
WHERE ARE YOU, IMMORTAL?!
OPEN YOUR EYES!!

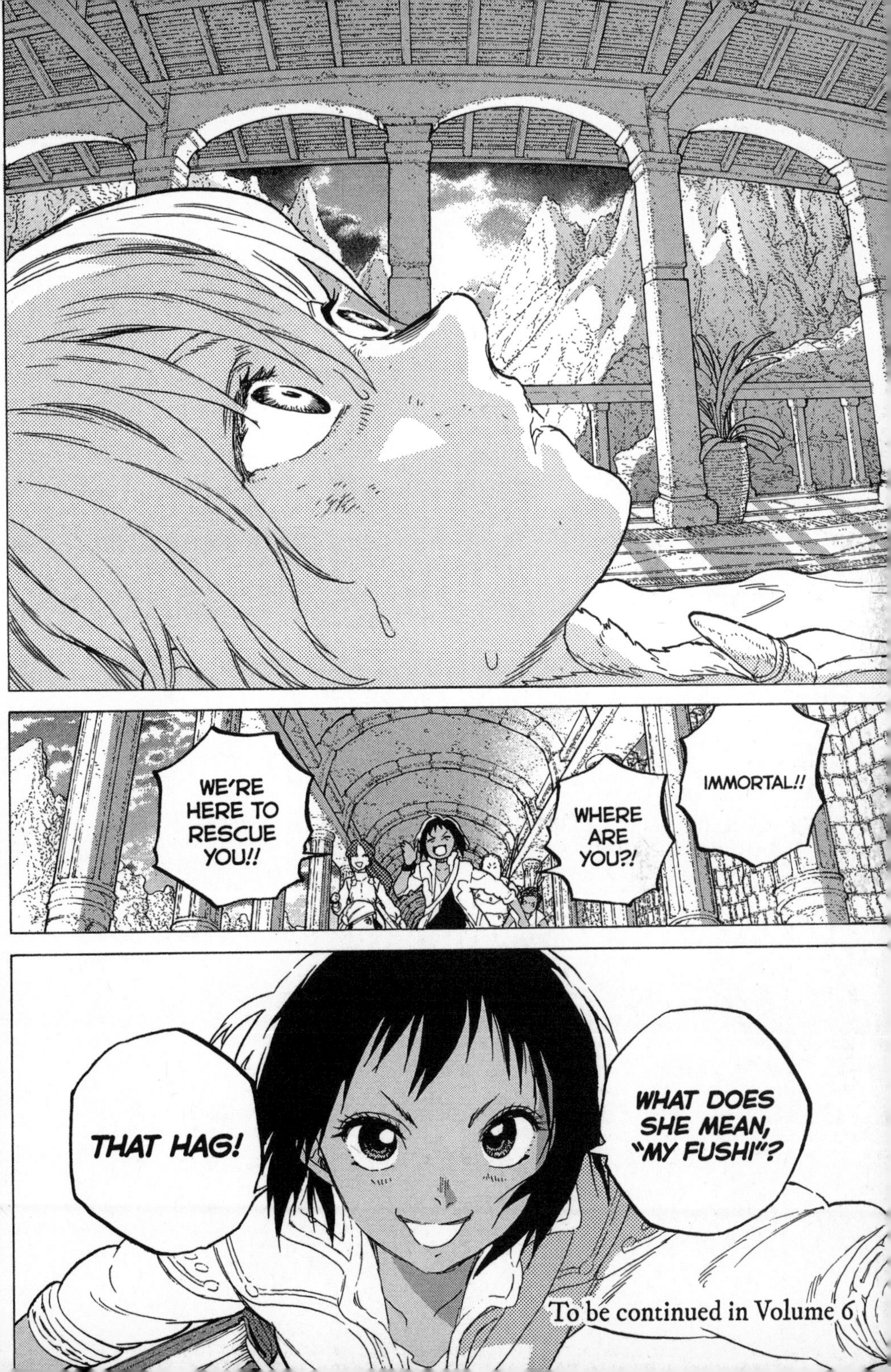
IMMORTAL!!
WHERE ARE YOU?!
WE'RE HERE TO RESCUE YOU!!
WHAT DOES SHE MEAN, "MY FUSHI"?
THAT HAG!
To be continued in Volume 6

TO YOUR

ETERNITY

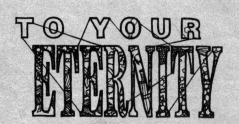

..irreplaceable fragments.

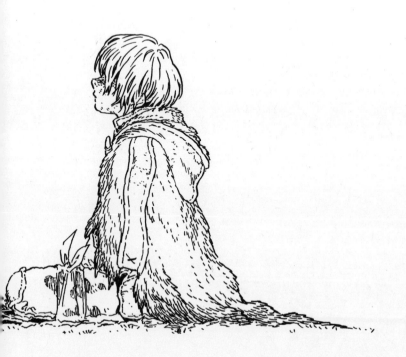

...ITS CONCLUSION IN VOL. 6. ON SALE SUMMER 2018

NEXT VOLUME PREVIEW

He is left now with...

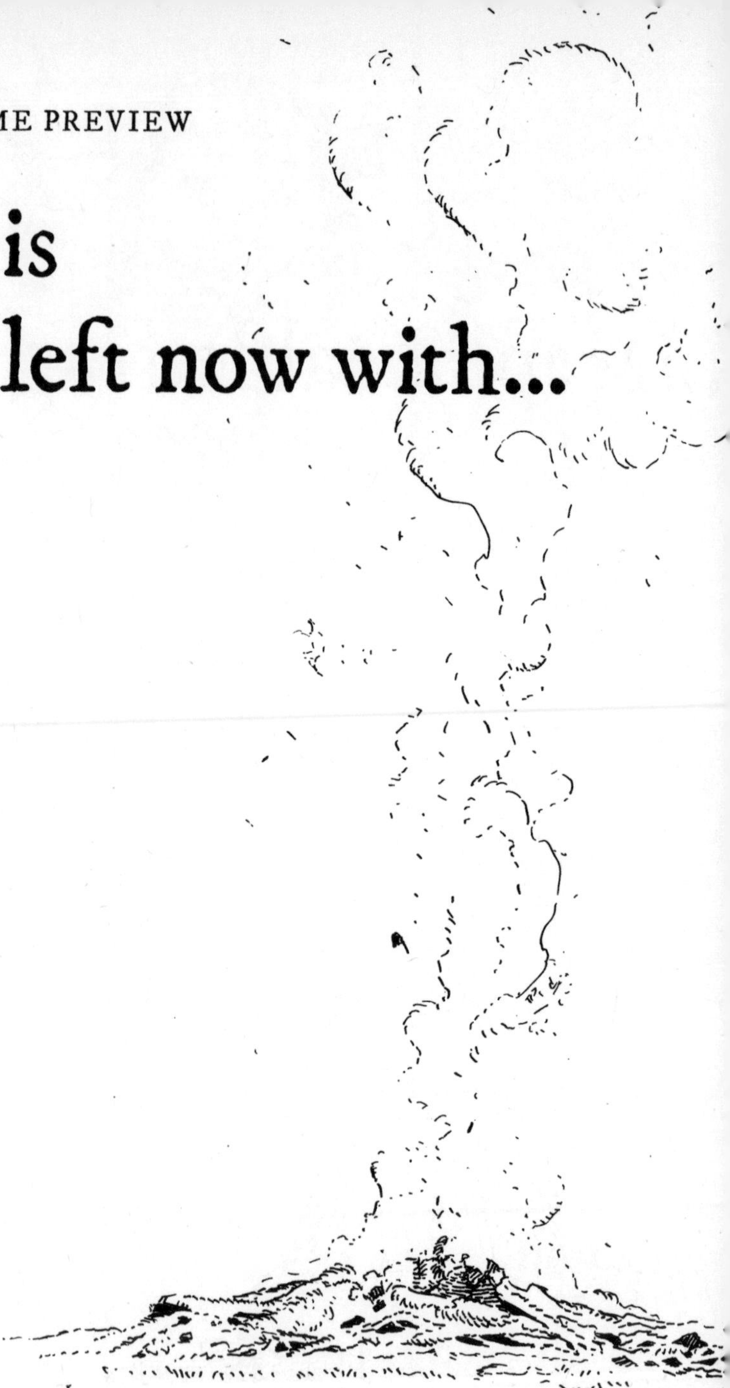

THE PRISON ISLAND JANANDA ARC REACHES...

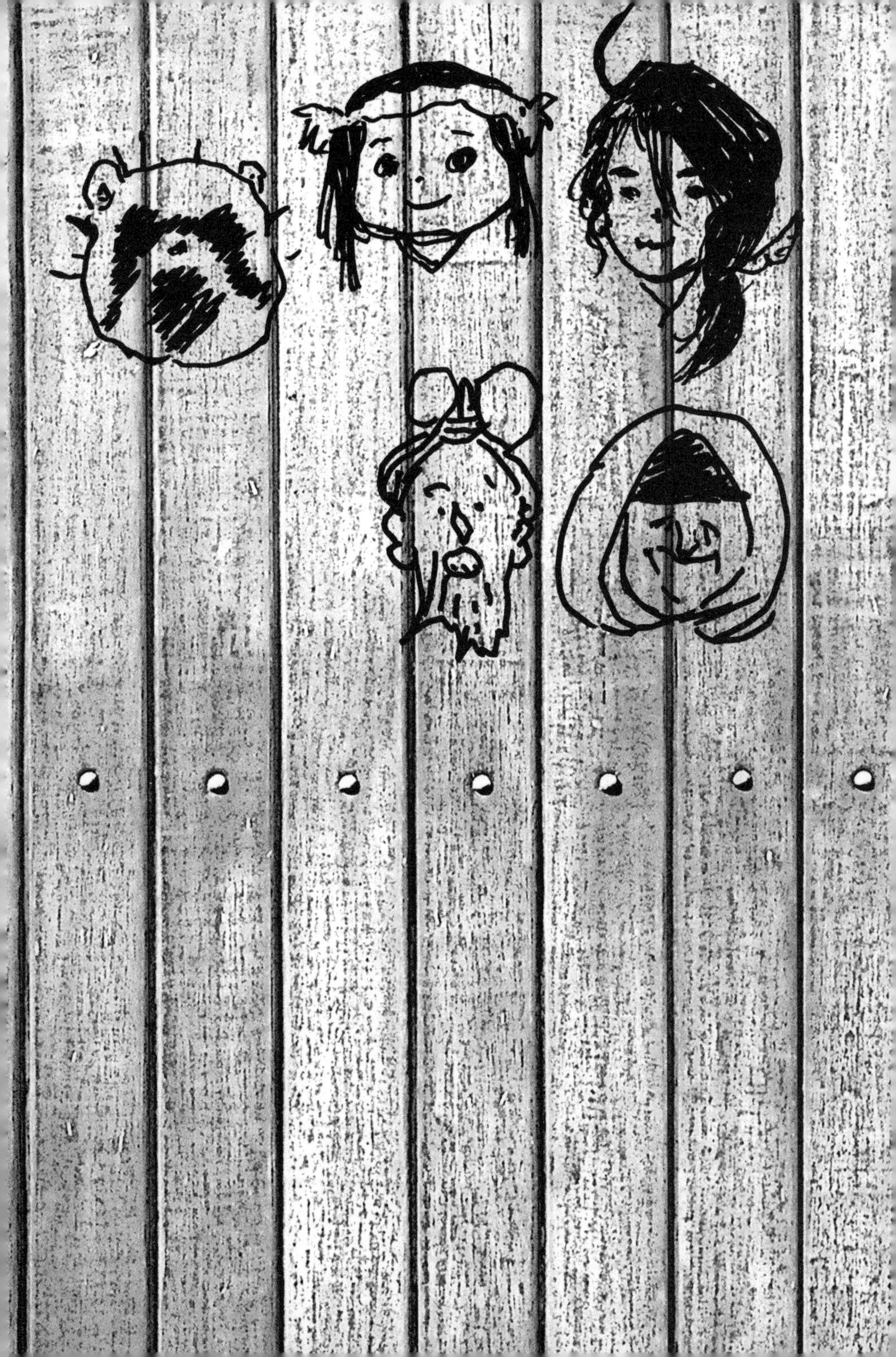

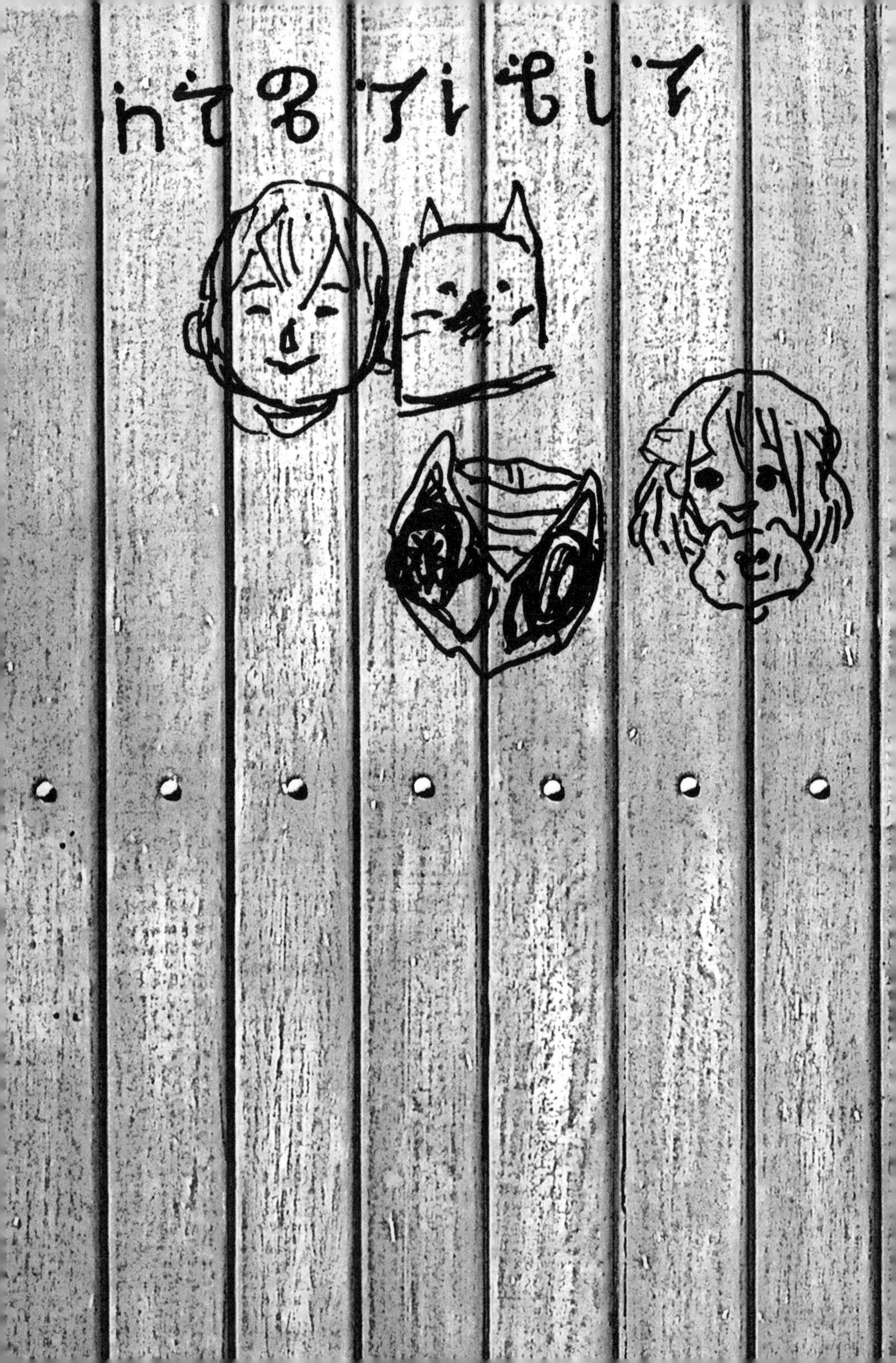

To Your Eternity volume 5 is a work of fiction.
Names, characters, places, and incidents are the products of the author's imagination or are used fictitiously. Any resemblance to actual events, locales, or persons, living or dead, is entirely coincidental.

A Kodansha Comics Trade Paperback Original.

Published in the United States by Kodansha Comics,
an imprint of Kodansha USA Publishing, LLC, New York.

Publication rights for this English edition arranged through Kodansha Ltd., Tokyo.

First published in Japan in 2017 by Kodansha Ltd., Tokyo,
as *Fumetsu no Anata e* volume 5.

Cover Design: Tadashi Hisamochi (hive&co., Ltd.)
Title Logo Design: Shinobu Ohashi

ISBN 978-1-63236-575-0

Printed in the United States of America.

www.kodanshacomics.com

9 8 7 6 5 4 3 2 1

Translation: Steven LeCroy
Lettering: Darren Smith
Editing: Haruko Hashimoto, Alexandra Swanson
Editorial Assistance: YKS Services LLC/SKY Japan, INC.
Kodansha Comics Edition Cover Design: Phil Balsman